ENVIRONMENTAL CONCERN

Personal Attitudes and Behavior Toward Environmental Problems

Edited by
Arvin W. Murch
Wheaton College

MSS Information Corporation
655 Madison Avenue, New York, N.Y. 10021

This is a custom-made book of readings prepared for the courses taught by the editor, as well as for related courses and for college and university libraries. For information about our program, please write to:

MSS INFORMATION CORPORATION
655 Madison Avenue
New York, New York 10021

MSS wishes to express its appreciation to the authors of the articles in the collection for their cooperation in making their work available in this format.

Library of Congress Cataloging in Publication Data

Murch, Arvin, comp.
  Environmental concern.

  CONTENTS: Murch, A.W. Who cares about the environment. — White, L., Jr. The historical roots of our ecological crisis. — Moncrief, L.W. The cultural basis for our environmental crisis. [etc.]
  1. Human ecology — United States — Public opinion — Addresses, essays, lectures. 2. Environmental protection — United States — Public opinion — Addresses, essays, lectures. 3. Human ecology — Canada — Public opinion— Addresses, essays, lectures. 4. Environmental protection — Canada — Public opinion — Addresses, essays, lectures. 5. Public opinion — United States. 6. Public opinion — Canada
I. Title.
GF503.M87 1974   301.15'43'301310973   74-8174
ISBN 0-8422-5169-3
ISBN 0-8422-0410-5 (pbk.)

CONTENTS

PREFACE

This book is unlike most other ecology texts that have appeared in recent months. It does not attempt to "cover the field" with three dozen assorted articles. Nor is it an extended essay on the philosophical and moral implications of our environmental crisis. Rather it is intended to cover a fairly specific and heretofore neglected topic in a reasonably balanced way.

Most recent texts have made some passing reference to the process of decision-making about pollution and related issues, but nearly always they have emphasized the role that social structures, demographic and biological processes play in these problems. To put it another way, they have tended to focus on the objective constraints of environmental concern, without closely examining the nature of that concern and its potential for meaningful change. Yet our current environmental problems are largely caused by man, and man is a conscious being, so that these problems are as much a matter of subjective perceptions, attitudes and beliefs as they are of objective forces. Although personal concern and public opinion is not always a decisive element in social problems of this kind, it is an important element, and one that deserves more adequate attention. This book is designed to meet that need.

More specifically, these readings examine the social and psychological forces that stimulate personal concern for the quality of our environment, and the forces that act to suppress that concern. Ultimately this leads to the question of how that concern gets translated into overt behavior and what forms that behavior may take. There are clear implications in all of this for environmental tactics and policy, and some of these are made explicit (as, for example, in my discussion of the role of the media). Beyond all this lies the fact that broad public support will never be mobilized behind rational environmental policy until public thinking on this issue is better understood. This is the larger goal that this volume is intended to serve.

The book's core is provided by my monograph on the stages and the determinants of environmental concern. My object here is to bring together what has been learned so far about personal concern for the physical environment, and to take off from that basis to provide some fresh insights into this process. Clustered around this is a group of shorter pieces by other authors that amplify and supplement various stages identified in my model. Following this are several pieces devoted to the study of that small segment of the public whose decisions most directly affect the quality of the environment. These studies give some further insight into the factors that shape the thinking and the behavior of these "environmental decision-makers." A third set of readings examines that loose collection of individuals and organizations known as the "environmental movement." Here our focus shifts to the study of environmental concern at the aggregate level. Among other things these studies deal with the "movement's" problems and its prospects for effecting meaningful change.

The appendix contains two sources of information that will be useful to anyone who is interested in this general area of study. The first is an extensive list of references on "environmental psychology," knit together by several pages of introductory remarks. The second is a set of two articles from the *Public Opinion Quarterly* which summarize a large number of polls and surveys of attitudes toward environmental issues.

Given its attempt to define the role of subjective factors in our current ecological crisis, this book may be useful to a variety of environmentally-related courses, both in the social and the physical sciences. Its subject matter and its approach should also fit very well into a more general discussion of current social problems. Finally, since it brings together a great deal of recent information on a particular aspect of our ecological crisis, it should be a useful reference not only to academics, but also to policy-makers and laymen who are interested in this issue.

My sincerest appreciation to the authors who granted me permission to include their articles in this volume.

SECTION I

INTRODUCTION

WHO CARES ABOUT THE ENVIRONMENT?

The Nature and Origins of Environmental Concern

Arvin Murch

Wheaton College

Recently much time, effort and money has been spent to mobilize public concern for environmental issues - witness the television and other media coverage that has culminated in Earth Day ceremonies over the past few years. No doubt these efforts have had some effect, but we still have no clear idea of how well public concern has been mobilized. Who is most apt to be seriously troubled by the growing threat to our environment, and who is most prone to ignore it? Does recognition of these environmental problems necessarily lead to active concern for them, and if not, why? Which social groups are most easily mobilized on this issue? We need to know much more about all of these questions. Beyond that, we need to better understand just how attitudes toward social problems like this emerge.

This is not to say that we have learned nothing at all. In the wake of our renewed national interest in the environment a growing number of studies have examined various aspects of this social problem, including how individuals react to it. Some of this information is cumulative, but more often these studies have been unrelated to each other, or to any broader perspective. It seems time, then, to try to draw together what we now know within the framework of a comprehensive analytical model, one which can help to articulate specific bits of information and make them more meaningful. The following describes one framework that might be useful to the study of environmental concern, and then uses it to bring together some of what we have learned about that concern and its origins.

A MODEL OF PERSONAL CONCERN FOR SOCIAL PROBLEMS

Although opinion polls often portray it as a simple "yes or no" proposition, personal concern for problems like racism, Vietnam and pollution is far more complex than that. Such concern is better viewed as an emergent phenomenon, as something which develops through a series of identifiable stages. This approach is commonly used in the study of social problems, although it is usually applied at the collective level. Fuller and Myer's classic description of a social problem's "natural history," for example, focussed on the reaction of the community as a whole to certain objective situations, beginning with its first awareness of a threat to its central values, through debate and policy determination and finally on to administrative action to solve the problem that it has defined (Fuller and Myers, 1941).

ORIGINAL MANUSCRIPT, 1974.

Instructive as this approach is, it only indirectly describes how <u>individuals</u> react to potentially threatening situations. More direct guidelines are provided by Samuel Stouffer's classic analysis of <u>Communism</u>, <u>Conformity</u> <u>and</u> <u>Civil</u> <u>Liberties</u> (1955). Stouffer's ideas are especially useful in showing how varying degrees of personal concern for domestic problems might be measured and interpreted. Communication theory offers further insight into this process, and particularly a model of information flow recently suggested by McGuire (1968). According to this model, a persuasive message will produce its intended attitudinal or behavioral effect only if it: 1) is actually communicated; 2) is "attended to" (perceived) by the subject; 3) is sufficiently understood; 4) is yielded to; 5) remains yielded to (over some period of time); and 6) affects some gross behavior. One virtue of this model is that it clearly distinguishes the simple perception of some idea or condition from the fuller understanding of its significance, and these stages from the more active commitment involved in yielding to the idea, and finally doing something about it. McGuire also points out that although they are interrelated, each stage may be influenced by different sets of conditions.

Building on these and other insights, it is proposed that subjective reactions to social problems involve the following basic stages: 1) the simple awareness of some objective conditions; 2) the definition of these conditions as a "problem"; 3) beliefs about causes and solutions to the "problem"; 4) personal commitment to solving the "problem"; and 5) problem-solving action. Although this seems to be their most logical order, these stages obviously can vary for given individuals faced with specific issues. Personal commitment, for example, may not only lead to participation in problem solving activities, but may also grow out of that participation. For some, these experiences may also lead to a redefinition of the nature of the problem and its causes. The proposed sequence from awareness to action is somewhat of an ideal model, then, but still one which seems to best represent most real situations.

Describing personal concern this way makes it possible to raise and begin to answer certain important questions, such as how these stages of concern are related to each other - whether they are truly progressive (such that earlier stages act as necessary conditions for later ones) or are patterned in other ways; and how social statuses, roles and beliefs influence each of these stages individually, and condition the association between one stage and another.

The next few paragraphs briefly describe each stage of this general model of concern. Following this general description, the model is applied more specifically to concern for environmental problems. Here, a number of empirical studies of environmental concern will be brought to bear on the questions raised above.

<u>Awareness</u> <u>of</u> <u>Objective</u> <u>Conditions</u>. This might be considered to be a basic pre-condition of all the stages that follow. Logically, we would expect simple awareness of some social or environmental condition to precede concern for it, and eventually action to remedy it. Of course, human behavior isn't always so logical. Real awareness of a problem may sometimes emerge only after the individual has been

caught up in some organized effort to solve it.

Logic also suggests that how one perceives objective conditions is largely determined by the conditions themselves. When objective conditions are unusually good or bad, we might expect those who are most exposed to these conditions to be most conscious of them. Yet this is not always the case either. Sociologists from Marx to the present have repeatedly shown that individuals who are objectively deprived may fail to perceive the true conditions of their existence, and therefore fail to realize and act on their common interests. Exposure to skillful propaganda along with a lack of internal communication and leadership all can inhibit real awareness and understanding of one's objective conditions. By the same token there may be others who are not directly affected by these conditions but who are still very conscious of them, perhaps because their education or other qualities enables them to reach out and understand situations that are beyond their own direct experience. These exceptions should make us wary of assuming that perceptions of the "real" world, including the physical environment, are simply reflections of external conditions.

Definition as a "problem." Even if an individual becomes aware of some objective condition, he may or may not choose to define it as a "problem." Hearing sonic booms shatter the air or observing the pall of smoke and grime hanging over his community., he may simply acquiesce to their presence, perhaps choosing to view them as inevitable companions of progress. Some may even find virtue in these conditions, arguing that "smoke means jobs" or as a Pennsylvania court put it two decades ago (Annals, 1970:80):

> "Ones bread is more important than landscape
> or clear skies. Without smoke, Pittsburgh
> would have remained a very pretty village."

More recently the mayor of an earthquake-ridden California town expressed the same point-of-view over national television. When asked if their frequent earthquakes may actually have done his town some good he thought for a moment and then replied brightly, "Why sure, they've put us on the map!" All of this suggests that if the presence of some objective threat does not fully account for awareness, it accounts even less for feelings of concern. To better understand these reactions we must probe more deeply into the role that social, economic and psychological factors play in shaping them.

Even when some condition has been identified as a "problem," concern for it can vary widely. In fact, it is only by attaching varying degrees of importance to specific problems that we are able to sort them out, and avoid being overwhelmed by the many dilemmas that modern society confronts us with. One way of determining the saliency of some identified problem, then, is to compare the concern for it with that felt for other problems. A related question is the threshold of concern that is necessary to produce personal commitment and eventually problem-solving action.

11

Of course, personal concern can't be understood only in quantitative terms. It must be examined qualitatively as well. In addition to measuring how much concern is felt for a given problem, we must also determine the broader meaning of that concern. This is because the definition of some object as a "problem" always involves certain assumptions and beliefs, and it is not always immediately evident just what they may be.

Beliefs about causes and solutions include three basic sets of ideas: beliefs about the causes of the problem, beliefs about the possibility of solving it, and beliefs about the nature of that solution. Since these beliefs may sometimes help to produce awareness of a problem, while at other times they may be shaped by attempts to remedy it, they are the hardest of all to place within an ordered sequence. Generally, though, it seems best to view them as a kind of link between more latent concern and action.

The individual who has perceived some objective condition, such as a chemically-fouled stream, and has defined that insult as a problem may carry his concern no further, if he sees no way to remedy the situation. At this point, his belief in the possibility of solving the problem that he has identified would seem to be critical. To some extent, this belief will be conditioned by his ideas about the problem's causes. Religious convictions about the "divine order of things" or more materialistic conceptions of "unalterable historical processes" may provide the individual some psychic comfort, but they also tend to short-circuit his interest in finding solutions to the problems that he faces. Similarly, those who feel that problems like pollution are the inevitable products of technological development may consciously abhor them, but still fatalistically accept them as "given." A more humanistic conception of causes and a more active belief in the possibility of finding solutions are likely to be more conducive to problem-solving behavior.

Finally, beliefs about the nature of the solution are also important. Even if one's general views about causation allow him to believe that a given problem can be solved, he still may lack any definite idea of how to go about achieving that solution. Without some more-or-less crystallized plan of action, awareness and optimism are unlikely to produce any significant results, either on an individual or a collective level.

Personal commitment to the solution. Having decided that a problem exists and is solvable by some specific means, the question then becomes whether or not the individual feels that he himself can and should take a hand in that solution. Here again responses can vary. Those who are concerned about a problem and are optimistic about its solution might be led to assume some responsibility for solving it, but they may also be content to slough that responsibility off to other agencies ("let the government do it"). This sense of commitment may partly depend on how much concern is felt for the problem at hand, but it may depend even more on those social and psychological factors that underlie the individual's general participation in society. We need to examine, then, not only thresholds of specific concern, but also the conceptions that the individual has of himself, of his physical and social environments, and of his place in them.

Although one may be intellectually committed to solving a given problem, a more telling question is what costs he is willing to pay for that solution. Commitment becomes most meaningful when the individual is willing to devote some values social, economic or other resource to the effort. It is only at this point that personal concern is likely to take on a significance outside of the individual himself, and become a social reality.

Action. If concern is to become socially meaningful, if it is to have an impact on others and on the problem itself, then eventually it must be expressed in some kind of overt behavior. Problem-solving action, then, is the culminating stage of personal concern viewed as a social process. This action may range from simply discussing the problem with friends to contributing funds to more vigorous forms of demonstration and protest. Problem-solving behavior can be categorized in many different ways. One meaningful distinction is between self-initiated action (such as organizing a new pressure group or spontaneously writing a congressman) and more passive action that is taken in response to other's initiative (such as signing a petition). Generally speaking, we might hypothesize that self-initiated action is likely to stem from a deeper concern, and perhaps a better understanding of the problem than are more pssive responses. The latter may, in fact, reflect a wide variety of motives, as well as the "spur of the moment" impulse to respond to some direct appeal.

This does not mean that deep concern will necessarily produce initiative. We all know how tenuous the connection is between good intentions and action, particularly when it comes to doing something about our more significant and widespread social problems. Normally action is much less common than concern, and when some action is taken, it is more apt to be passive than anything else. This "funnelling down" of concern is partly due to the fact that action is seldom determined simply by a single attitude. Most behavior is governed by the interaction between attitudes toward specific issues and more general definitions of the situation, or as another puts it, between "attitude-toward-object" and "attitude-toward-situation" (Rokeach, 1968: 127-28). Even feelings of deep concern for some problem, then, may be conditioned by beliefs about the appropriate ways and places to express those feelings. Here again we must look beyond the nature of the problem itself to understand what is made of it.

THE SOCIAL CONDITIONS OF ENVIRONMENTAL CONCERN

Despite many gaps, there is now enough information available to begin to map out the process of environmental concern, and to identify some of the factors that shape it. In the past few years a growing number of empirical studies have examined various aspects of this process. Further data is provided by my own recent study of attitudes

13

toward environmental problems in Durham, North Carolina. In the Spring of 1970, questionnaires were distributed to a random sample of some 300 Durham residents, and nearly three-fourths of these were completed and returned. The survey dealt with the issue of environmental damage on several different levels, and aimed at discovering how aware people were of this problem, who or what they felt was responsible for it, and how it might be solved.*

Many of these studies, including the Durham survey, have focussed on concern for environmental problems within the local community. On balance, this seems to be a more meaningful level at which to study personal concern for social problems than either a more global or a more immediate context. The local community (city, town or county) is large enough to display the full range of most social problems, and yet small enough to allow the individual to feel that he can do something about them. The local community also is an important focus of personal identification, and the setting for much of the average individual's social participation. Obviously there are exceptions to this rule. By their very nature some problems (like Vietnam) transcend the local community, while others (like neighborhood residential patterns) fall below that level. Nevertheless most of our current social concerns are probably best seen and studied as community problems. Consequently, we will deal here with concern for community-wide environmental problems, unless otherwise indicated.

We might begin by examining the association between each of the previously defined stages of environmental concern to discover just how cumulative they are. From the responses of the Durham sample, it appears that most of these stages are related as we would expect them to be (Table 1). For example, those who define environmental problems as serious are far more willing to pay certain costs to solve them than are people who feel that these problems are minor.

The overall pattern of correlations in Table 1. suggests that environmental concern tends to be a cumulative process, i.e. that earlier stages, such as the simple awareness of environmental conditions, are pre-conditions of later, more active stages of concern. Guttman scaling analysis shows, however, that there is only a moderate tendency in this direction. When the replies given at three stages of concern are arranged into a Guttman scale, 62 per cent of the cases fall into cumulative response patterns.** Although this

---

* Preliminary results of this study were published in the Spring, 1971 issue of The Public Opinion Quarterly. (Murch, 1971)

** In order, these stages are "awareness of environmental conditions," "definition as a problem," and "willingness to pay specified costs for a solution." The number of cases falling into cumulative patterns drops to 44 per cent when "beliefs about solutions" are added to the model.

14

is a fairly high figure, it does fall below the standard for a unidimensional scale and indicates that environmental concern does not
always develop in a simple and logical way from the lower to the
higher levels identified here. This suggests that higher levels of
environmental concern may be heavily conditioned by certain social,
cultural and psychological factors. The following analysis will
attempt to identify some of these factors and describe their effects.

Table 1. ASSOCIATION BETWEEN STAGES OF ENVIRONMENTAL
          CONCERN AMONG RESIDENTS OF DURHAM, NORTH CAROLINA

(Note: Figures indicate correlation between positive responses at
        each stage of concern, as measured by Gamma.)

	AWARENESS OF CONDITIONS	DEFINITION AS A PROBLEM	BELIEF IN SOLUTION	COMMITMENT TO SOLUTION
DEFINITION AS A PROBLEM	.40			
BELIEF IN SOLUTION	.63	.48		
COMMITMENT TO SOLUTION	.05	.36	.64	
WILLINGNESS TO PAY COSTS	.04	.36	.47	.48

15

Awareness of environmental conditions is just as complex as the
awareness of other conditions of life. Simply being exposed to
some unusual environmental condition does not necessarily mean
that the individual will be aware of it, or if he is, that he will
perceive it accurately. Even acute environmental conditions may
not be fully perceived, as is shown by a recent study of public
reactions to "sonic booms." (Borsky, 1965). When residents living
near a major metropolitan airport were surveyed, 81 per cent reported that they had heard these blasts from time to time. Although
a sizeable majority, this still left nearly one-fifth who reported
that they did not hear the noise, even though they lived well within
the range of these "obvious" disturbances.

The more we examine such behavior, the more we realize how
great our capacity to see what we want to see, and to ignore, or
deny, unpleasant realities. This is clearly illustrated by the
apparent indifference of many San Francisco residents to the well
publicized threat of earthquake damage in their Bay Area. Despite
the fact that the San Andreas Fault passes within a few miles of
downtown San Francisco, and that many experts speak of the day when
(and not if) the next great tremor will occur, local developers
have continued to erect hotels, skyscrapers, schools and suburbs
with little regard for the threat of future shocks, and nearly a
thousand people settle on or near the fault line each day. Over
the past decade, in fact, San Francisco has been one of the fastest
growing metropolitan areas in the nation.

Despite the growing attention that has been given to California's
precarious bedrock, it is possible that some may be ignorant of this
condition, while others may be confused by the conflicting opinions
of some experts on the subject. Yet the reasons for such massive
denial seem to go deeper than this. In a postscript to their
chilling account of the great San Francisco earthquake and fire,
Thomas and Witts report that today some San Franciscans deny that
the earthquake of 1906 ever happened (1971:288). They prefer to
believe that their city was destroyed by fire alone. That is a
threat that they can comprehend, and more importantly, that they
can live with.

If even these serious and unmistakable conditions can be ignored
or distorted, then the perception of less obvious conditions must
be even more problematic. Rather than being merely a reflection
of external "reality," individual prerceptions of the environment
must be treated as a variable which is strongly influenced by social
and psychological factors. Unfortunately we still do not know much
about how environmental awareness develops, partly because awareness
usually has not been clearly distinguished from concern. Some past
studies have probed for the individual's awareness of air "pollution"
and other environmental "problems," ignoring the fact that these
pejorative terms call not only for perceptions but evaluations as
well. So far this methodological problem has limited the collection
of relevant data on awareness itself.

Still, we can be certain of some things. Cultural values undoubtedly help to shape the way that we view the natural environment, just as they shape other ways of viewing reality. It appears that within our own society certain Judeo-Christian beliefs have combined with an obsession with material progress to produce a tendency to view nature as an object, as something to be manipulated to man's profit (Campbell and Wade, 1972:337-45; Glacken, 1971; Spoehr, 1973; White, 1967). Some would even characterize our present system of beliefs about man's relationship with the natural world as a "Vandal ideology" (Paradise, 1971). While that may be extreme, it is probably true that we all share some predisposition to exploit the natural environment, or at least to overlook its present exploitation.

Formal education also is likely to have something to do with how one views his social and natural surroundings. In fact the basic function of education, at least at the higher levels, is precisely to expand the individual's understanding of reality - to enlarge his perceptual field, and to improve his ability to examine objects within the field accurately. General participation in the social and cultural life of the community may also have the same effect. What remains to be shown is just how education and other social factors interact to shape perceptions of the physical environment. Exploratory work by Hendee et al (1969) suggests, for example, that highly educated persons and those in upper-middle class occupations are most likely to regard nature as something to be appreciated in its own right, and not to be altered. Whether or not this means that education and upward mobility provide an effective antidote to the exploitive bias of our general culture remains to be seen.

Defining environmental problems. To define some social or natural condition as a "problem" is to invest a certain amount of concern in it. For some this investment may be slight, while for others it may be heavy enough to provoke considerable thought and anxiety. Although we still do not know exactly where the significant thresholds or "breaking points" of this anxiety are located, a fairly high level of concern seems necessary to move most people to become personally committed to a problem and willing to do something to solve it. A good case in point is the recent meat boycott. Although the American consumer has been dismayed by the steady inflation of food prices for several years, it took the dramatic price increases of the first quarter of 1973 to raise this concern above the "threshold" and generate widespread consumer reaction. Even though the resultant flurry of meat counter boycotts, pickets and angry rhetoric may have achieved few substantial gains, it did at least serve to show industry leaders and elected officials that there is a limit to how much the public will tolerate in silence.

There is growing evidence that a large segment of the American public has come to share something approaching this kind of concern for environmental problems as well. In Durham, 62 per cent of those who were questioned expressed their belief that pollution is at least a moderate problem in their community, and 13 per cent

thought that it was a serious one. Other studies report similar
findings. In 1967 over three quarters of a sample of Minnesota
residents described the pollution of their state's rivers and lakes
as a serious problem (Erskine, 1973: 122). More recently in
Alabama 65 per cent of those replying to a statewide survey reported that they were at least moderately concerned, and 35 per cent
were "much concerned" about the quality of their community's air
and water (Johnson, 1971:16). Elsewhere it appears that a large
majority of the public may share some general concern for environmental conditions, while as much as half of the community may be
seriously disturbed by certain forms of pollution (Erksine, 1972:
121-125).

Probing into the meaning of this concern, it becomes evident
that "pollution" has a diffuse meaning for most people. Among
Durham residents the term "pollution" was associated with a broad
spectrum of specific problems ranging from littering and trash
dumping (mentioned by 60 per cent) to air pollution from smoke-
stacks and automobiles (40 per cent), threatened parklands (33 per
cent), water pollution (28 per cent), the wastage of natural resources and noise pollution (both about 20 per cent). The term
"pollution" then appears to be a popular shorthand for the broader
concept of "environmental damage," and concern for pollution en-
compasses concern for a fairly wide range of environmental conditions.

As with other problems, pollution generates concern to the
extent that it is seen as a threat to things that the individual
values deeply. In the case of pollution, this might include the
environment itself. The theme of preserving the environment for
its own sake was prominent in the earlier conservation movement
in this country, and it persists in the debate over ecological issues
today. Yet for most people concern over environmental deterioration seems to be based on other grounds, and particularly on its
perceived threat to health. Several studies report that health
is the single most important basis of environmental concern, and
that it may be so far as much as 90 percent of those who identify
pollution as a problem (Crowe, 1968:155; DeGroot, 1967:680; Smith
et al., 1964:420). It appears that overall health ranks for above
economic, aesthetic and other bases of environmental concern, and
that this is especially true where pollution is most severe (Johnson,
1971:19, 55).

This does not mean that health is the only significant reason
for alarm. Obviously, the kind of values that are threatened may
vary with the kind of pollution that is present. Water pollution,
for example, may be seen as a particular threat to recreation,
particularly by older and wealthier persons who are most apt to use
water resources for this purpose (Frederickson and Magnas, 1968).
In sum, this scattered evidence suggests that concern over current
damage to the environment itself may be confined to a small (and
select?) segment of our population. For the majority of people,
concern for environmental damage is likely to develop as it is
seen to involve some more immediate threat to health, property or
personal well-being.

Whatever its basis, the general level of concern for any issue is unlikely to remain stable for very long, simply because the conditions surrounding it are subject to change. New crises may stimulate increased interest for a time, or other issues may emerge to draw that interest away. In Durham, for example, concern for environmental issues varied noticeably between the late Spring and Summer of 1970. Originally, 55 per cent ranked "pollution" among this country's four greatest social problems, but in a follow-up study only two months later this figure had dropped to 38 per cent. While this might suggest that environmental concern is a fleeting thing, it may also reflect a normal amount of attrition after the peak of interest reached around Earth Day (April 22), 1970. Although general levels of concern may fluctuate in response to specific events like this, the larger trend seems to be toward a steadily increasing level of environmental consciousness on the part of the American public. National surveys report that moderate to serious concern for local pollution has risen steadily from 28 per cent in 1965 to 69 per cent by 1970. In 1971, a Harris poll found that 41 per cent of those questioned considered pollution control to be one of the top problems confronting the Congress, second only to the state of the economy as a salient issue (Erskine, 1972:121, 125).

Turning from description to explanation, many studies have documented the obvious fact that concern for air and water pollution, excessive noise and similar environmental damage increases as these problems become more severe, and as the individual is more directly affected by them. A related fact is that urban residents, who generally are most exposed to these hazards, are most likely to define them as problems (DeGroot, 1967; Johnson, 1971). Yet, important as they are, objective condtions do not entirely account for environmental concern. Some residents living near an obvious environmental hazard may fail to define it as a problem while others, more removed from these conditions, may be very troubled by them. Van Arsdol, for example, has found that there is no simple association between actual environmental hazards and the perception of these hazards; instead, this relationship is heavily conditioned by socio-economic status, race and neighborhood satisfaction (1964). These social factors also played an independent role in shaping environmental concern in Durham. There, expressed concern varied by occupation, education, community involvement and other personal characteristics, regardless of the actual level of pollution that was present.

Just how do these various social factors help to shape environmental concern? One clue is provided by the pattern of concern itself. Overall, Durham residents were more inclined to consider pollution to be a significant problem as the reference moved away from their own immediate surroundings. Only 31 per cent of them considered pollution to be a significant (moderate to serious) problem in their own neighborhood, compared with 62 per cent who saw it as such in Durham, 68 percent in North Carolina as a whole, and 83 per cent in the United States.

One reason for this pattern may be that our present concern for environmental pollution has been heavily influenced by the mass media, and these media have commonly focussed on the broader aspects of the problem. This was clearly true for Durham residents, who reported that the media, and particularly television and magazines, were their most important source of information about the environment. Local newspapers came next, while personal sources such as friends and neighbors provided the least amount of environmental information.

The broader focus of television and of magazines like Saturday Review, Life and others, is understandable. More surprising is the fact that local newspapers also tend to concentrate on national rather than local environmental problems. During the spring of 1970, over a third of all the copy devoted by Durham papers to this subject dealt with national problems, and half of it focused on either the national or the global level. Less than ten per cent dealt with environmental problems within the Durham community. It would seem, then, that the media up and down the line have helped to produce the tendency to view pollution as a general problem, largely external to one's own community.

Another reason may be more psychological. The fact that while Durhamites reported significant pollution less often in the community than in the nation, they reported it far less often yet in their own neighborhoods suggests a basic reluctance to acknowledge serious defects in one's own immediate surroundings. In finding that people tend to judge air pollution in their neighborhood as less serious than that in the community as a whole, DeGroot suggests that just this sort of "denial system" may be at work. As he puts it (1967:680):

> The respondents were quite ready to admit that
> air pollution was bad for the whole community,
> probably because they felt all people in their
> city were equally exposed. But to say that
> their neighborhood was very bad, while the city
> as a whole was perhaps not so poor, appears to
> demand a great deal. It would demand the re-
> spondent to make a decision about whether air
> pollution was sufficient cause for him to move
> out of the neighborhood and uproot his friend-
> ships and usual patterns of life. In addition
> he would have to recognize that the health of
> his family would be impaired if he stayed.

There may also be a more pragmatic reason for this apparent "denial" of immediate environmental problems. Crowe (1968:155) has found that on the local level, environmental issues compete at a disadvantage with other, more immediate concerns. In Buffalo, for example, unemployment, delinquency and communicable disease all were ranked above air pollution as a serious community problem (DeGroot, 1967: 245). St. Louis residents have expressed similar priorities (Schusky, 1966:75), while those in Syracuse assigned water pollution a "middle-level" importance, following education and police protection for suburban residents, and these plus employment and housing conditions for city residents (Frederickson and Magnas, 1968:883-84). In Durham, those who ranked drug addiction and crime high on their list of social problems were relatively unlikely to define local environmental conditions as "serious." On the other hand, those who were less preoccupied with these immediate dangers were more apt to express serious concern for the state of their environment.

In sum, a variety of factors ranging from institutional pressures to psychological mechanisms all help to erode personal concern for environmental conditions at the local level. Yet this may be true only for those who feel no real attachment to the local community. It has been argued that residents who are strongly attached to their community will be more concerned over its pollution than will those who are less attached, simply because that pollution detracts from an environment which they value. And, in fact, at least one study has found that residents who express the most satisfaction with their neighborhood are most apt to recognize its environmental hazards (Van Arsdol, 1964:151-53. But the evidence here is mixed, and some actually suggest that the more attached one is to his locality, the less he is apt to acknowledge serious defects in it (Crowe, 1968:156; Medalia, 1964:158). In Durham, residents with some economic investment in the community (such as owning a home) and those who found it a desirable place to live were, if anything, least inclined to report that their town had a significant pollution problem. Perhaps these more established residents had become so habituated to the defects in their local environment that they no longer even perceived them, or though perceiving them, they preferred to deny the fact to others, and even to themselves.

All of this reasoning is based on the assumption that environmental concern is somehow dependent upon community attachment, or the lack of it. Of course, this relationship may run the other way as well - that is, awareness of local environmental hazards may sometimes produce dissatisfaction and detachment from the community. There is some evidence, for example, that those who recognize local air quality problems are most apt to report dissatisfaction with their neighborhood, and to want to move away from it (Butler, 1972: 7,9). The pattern found in Durham and elsewhere then may not be so much a case of attached residents ignoring local conditions as of environmentally aware residents becoming estranged from the community.

Finally, it is possible that homeowners and more satisfied residents fail to perceive much pollution in the community as a whole simply because they themselves live in more desirable areas of town. Available measures of air pollution indicate, however, that this was not the case in Durham, where more attached residents were no more likely to live in unpolluted areas than were less

21

attached residents.* When the air pollution of residential areas
is held constant, more attached residents still tend to understate
the community's environmental problems, although they are more
likely to do so in areas of lower pollution. This suggests that
where pollution is serious and unmistakable, everyone is more-or-
less obliged to acknowledge the fact. But where the immediate
environment is less obviously threatened, personal factors, such as
attachment to the community, become operative to influence how one
perceives threats to his environment.

While it still isn't clear just how close community attachment
is related to concern for environmental problems, there is little
doubt that such concern is greatest among those in the higher socioeconomic strata, including the better-educated, the better-employed,
and whites. Practically all of the available evidence points in
this direction. In Durham concern also increased with education,
but it was less related to occupational status and race. Setting
aside these other dimensions of class position for the moment, let
us examine the role of education a bit more closely. By broadening
the individual's outlook and increasing his reasoning powers, higher
education itself may tend to make one more concerned with community
problems like pollution. But it may also be that the better educated are more concerned because they are more exposed to channels of
information about the environment, including the mass media. As
Table 2 shows, Durham residents' concern for environmental issues
directly increased with their exposure to news programs, and particularly with exposure to reports about the environment. When this
kind of media contact is taken into account, it explains much of the
difference observed between the better- and the lesser-educated.

This is consistent with the fact that environmental concern was
greatest among those who participated most in the political, social
and cultural life of the Durham community. Residents who frequently
discussed current affairs, were well read and who belonged to one or
more local organizations usually were more concerned with local
environmental problems than were less involved citizens. Such involvement undoubtably increases awareness of existing community
problems, and so provides at least a basis for concern. Since the
more actively involved residents are largely from middle and upper
class backgrounds, their concern may be heightened by the contrast
between the conditions that their social involvement reveals to
them, and their own relatively pleasant surroundings. If this is the

---

* Measures of the annual dustfall in various sections of Durham
were used to estimate the level of air pollution found in each of
the residential areas sampled. Fifty-eight per cent of both satisfied
and dissatisfied residents were found to live in relatively high
dustfall areas. The proportion of longer-term residents and homeowners living in such areas was even higher.

Table 2. CONCERN WITH LOCAL ENVIRONMENTAL PROBLEMS
BY SELECTED SOCIAL CHARACTERISTICS OF DURHAM RESIDENTS

Social characteristics	Percent who consider local problems to be moderate to serious	Total cases
Education		
Attended college	66	(84)
High school graduate	71	(42)
Some high school or less	53	(54)
Occupational level		
Upper white collar	66	(49)
Lower white collar	67	(52)
Blue collar	64	(42)
Occupational situs		
Commerce	66	(42)
Manufacturing & Industry	43	(23)
Other (arts, education, health, etc.)	70	(58)
Race		
White	60	(132)
Black	74	(56)
Sex		
Men	66	(76)
Women	63	(115)
Home ownership		
Rent or other	67	(79)
Own home	62	(113)
Opinion of Durham		
Undesirable place to live	73	(15)
Indifferent	64	(22)
Desirable place to live	63	(161)

Social characteristics	Per cent	Total cases
Discussion of current affairs		
Daily	71	(90)
Occasionally	62	(63)
Rarely or never	56	(33)
Organizational memberships		
Three or more	68	(21)
One or two	66	(103)
None	47	(60)
Vote in 1968		
Voted	61	(183)
Did not vote	52	(22)
Exposure to news programs-		
High	73	(31)
Low	62	(160)
Exposure to environ. reports		
High	68	(103)
Low	43	(81)
Number of magazines read		
Three or more	70	(99)
One or two	56	(45)
None	47	(35)

case, then active residents from poorer backgrounds should be less apt to experience this contrast, and as a result less shocked by the conditions they discover. This interpretation is supported by the fact that socially active Durham residents from lower class backgrounds generally expressed less serious concern about their community's environmental problems then did active middle- and upper-class residents. Here we see how standards for evaluating environmental quality that emerge from personal background and experience may interact with other social variables to affect concern.

There is no consistent evidence that the tendency to regard "pollution" as a serious problem varies much either by sex or by age. Contrary to popular belief the young often are no more ecologically conscious than either middle or older age groups (Borsky, 1965; McEvoy, 1972; Van Arsdol et al., 1964). Environmental attitudes vary more predictably by occupational situs. Businessmen are less apt to express concern about current threats to the environment than are professionals, government officials or other white-collar groups (Buttel and Flinn, 1973; Dillman and Christenson, 1972). This appears to be as true of small businessmen as it is of more prominent business leaders (Constantini and Hanf, 1972). Although they clearly are in a position to recognize the dangers of pollution and resource wastage, members of the business community no doubt view the demand for environmental reform as a threat to their economic interests. Truly effective environmental reform not only will be costly, but may also require extensive governmental regulation and perhaps even a basic reorientation of our whole productive system. To many businessmen, the remedies that loom on the horizon may be a far greater cause for concern than the "disease" of pollution itself.

Many questions about the social origins of environmental concern remain to be answered, but it is possible to draw some conclusions from the evidence at hand. The larger pattern that emerges here indicates that simple explanations such as "self interest" or exposure to offending conditions do not adequately account for concern. Often those who live in the most polluted areas are no more concerned, and in fact they may be less concerned about pollution than others. Generally speaking, concern for environmental problems is greatest among those who are best able to control their own surroundings, who are most involved in the life of the community, and who are in the best position to influence the decisions that shape it. The irony is that it is just these individuals who are most apt to have made or acceded to the decisions that created these problems in the first place. For this and other reasons, those who are most apt to become environmentally conscious may also experience the greatest feelings of ambivalence, particularly toward local environmental problems. This ambivalence may eventually discourage many from expressing their concern more actively.

Beliefs about causes and solutions to environmental problems, though relatively unexplored, appear to be another key factor in the development of more active concern. In general terms, when people are asked to identify the causes of environmental damage they often point to industry and to vehicles (such as autos, trucks and buses). More personalized sources of damage usually rank much lower on their list of responsible agents (Johnson, 1971:20: Schusky, 1966:73). In Durham, industry was also commonly blamed (by 26 per cent) but only 8 per cent attributed environmental damage simply to machines such as the automobile. Many more (40 per cent) saw this problem in human, and even personal terms, blaming themselves, "man," "everybody," or "greed." Government was held responsible by one out of ten respondents, but practically no one felt that government leaders should take the blame for the deterioration of their environment. No clear picture emerges from these findings, although the Durham results suggest that people may be less inclined to shrug off their responsibility for pollution than is commonly assumed.

When asked whether they believed that a solution to environmental problems could be found, most Durham residents replied optimistically. Nearly three fourths (73 per cent) believed that these problems could be significantly reduced, if not solved completely. Although 19 per cent either expressed no opinion or failed to answer the question, no one denied the possibility of some measure of relief from pollution and wastage. Almost identical beliefs appear in another community survey, where 79 per cent said that air pollution could be either reduced or eliminated, 14 per cent had no opinion, and only four per cent felt that no reduction in air contamination was possible (Medalia, 1964:159).

Turning to what that solution might be, however, nearly half of Durham's respondents said that they couldn't decide, or they skipped the question. Some sort of government or personal action was most often mentioned by the rest although these ideas were usually vague. When asked more directly whether they, as individuals, could help to eliminate damage to the environment, this uncertainty appeared again. Forty per cent of the respondents said that they could do something to help, but 44 per cent again couldn't decide or remained silent. Even those who believed that they could do something as individuals often didn't have a clear idea of what that might be. Those who did suggest courses of action most often limited them to changing personal or family behavior. Others mentioned the possibility of becoming involved in citizens' action groups. Very few saw ways in which they could directly affect governmental or corporation policy. All of this may be discouraging to those who pin their hopes for change on a well-informed and highly-motivated citizenry, but it is as much as we can expect from the general lack of public guidance and the imbalanced way in which the media have stressed the "ecological crisis" but not its solutions.

As expected, beliefs about the causes and the solutions of Durham's problems were related. Those who reported that the community's environmental problems were caused by industry, machines or some other impersonal agency were less able to see how these problems might be solved than were those who accounted for pollution in more humanistic terms (Table 3). One reason may be that people who account for problems like pollution in humanistic terms tend to believe that they and others can exert some control over their environment. This underlying sense of human mastery over nature may

25

Table 3. BELIEF IN THE SOLUTION OF DURHAM'S ENVIRONMENTAL
PROBLEMS ACCORDING TO BELIEFS ABOUT THEIR CAUSES

BELIEVE THESE PROBLEMS CAN BE SOLVED:	AGENCY RESPONSIBLE FOR THESE PROBLEMS IS:		
	Human only	Human & non-human	Non-human only
Agree	89%	76%	50%
Disagree or don't know	11%	24%	50%
Total	100%	100%	100%
(cases)	(38)	(17)	(86)

also lead them to see solutions to problems where others, less confident of their control, do not. Such confidence may be further
reinforced by positive views about the future. Polak (1961) has
identified two basic dimensions of these "images of the future."
On the one hand, individuals may hold either positive or negative
images of man's ability to intervene and direct the future, while
on the other hand they may see the future itself as either pro-
gressing or deteriorating. Polak argues that positive images of
the future are necessary to the continued growth and vitality of a
society, because to some extent, beliefs about the future tend to
become realized in the future which actually emerges. Similarly,
positive future images may help to produce the kind of secular and
confident frame of mind that sees both causes and solutions to
social problems like pollution within man's grasp. In Durham, at
least, these feelings of mastery over the present and the future
were strongly associated with the ability to imagine some solution
to local environmental problems.

This underlying positivism is largely the property of the more
advantaged, and for good reason. Those who possess real economic,
political or social power, and who have an intellectual grasp of
things are understandably better able to see how man can control
events than are the more dispossessed. Moreover, the belief in
progress and in human mastery are both embedded in the whole tradition of Enlightenment thought (Mau, 1968:66, 76), to which the
upper classes are particularly exposed by their education and their
larger cultural participation. It is not surprising, then, that the
ability to conceive of some solution to environmental problems and
to develop specific ideas about those solutions increases with
education, occupation and other forms of class position. While those
at the top of the social ladder may or may not be more rational or
more morally conscious than others, they clearly are better endowed
with a way of looking at reality that helps them to move on from
problem-recognition to problem-solving.

Personal commitment to solving environmental problems is the point
where general feelings of concern becomes internalized and liable

26

to produce some overt expression. We may refer to this commitment as "personal" or "active" concern. One of the most meaningful ways to guage his commitment to a solution is to ask what the individual is willing to pay for it in terms of time, money or some other valued resource. By all reports, most citizens in this country are willing to pay at least some minimal costs to help solve environmental problems, and many are willing to make a more substantial investment in these efforts. As early as 1964 two thirds of a sample of St. Louis residents said that they would pay a small (five dollar) tax increase to support air pollution control programs (Schusky 1966:74). More recently, 32 per cent of a national survey went so far as to say that they would pay an additional hundred dollars annually to clean up air and water pollution. Other polls report that half or more of the electorate generally supports proposals to increase federal spending on pollution programs, or at least to cut this spending least (Erskine, 1972:126-35). Although most of these findings can't be compared over time, the few that can suggest that this sentiment is growing. Harris reports that those who were willing to pay fifteen dollars a year more in taxes to control air pollution rose steadily from 44 per cent in 1967 to 59 per cent in 1971 (Erskine, 1972:32). Needless to say these figures should be interpreted cautiously, since they all refer to only one kind of "cost." As some have argued, it may be that pollution control policies which raise money costs are more popular with the public than those which change growth rates or basic life styles (Winham, 1972:400), at least up to a certain level of expense. Furthermore, even the least expensive proposals are not supported by everyone. So again we must ask why do some display this level of concern while others do not?

Everything else being equal, those who define pollution as a significant local problem, as a threat to their health and well-being, should be most actively concerned about it and willing to commit their resources to solve it. And at least in Durham this was generally the case. Those who recognized significant environmental problems in Durham were more inclined than others to feel personally involved, to admit that they could and should do something to help eliminate those problems. The more concerned were also more willing to pay their tax dollars and to make other social and economic sacrifices to improve the environment. (Table 4). Unfortunately, this ready explanation takes us only so far. Many who recognized local environmental problems still seemed to feel little or no personal commitment to help solve them. To understand how this can happen, we must refer again to the individual's more deep-seated beliefs and particularly to his images of human mastery and the future.

It has long been recognized that deprivation alone is not enough to move men to deep concern. Even the most deprived individual may not recognize his deprivation, and if he does he may not necessarily feel that he can or should do anything about it. What is also essential is that he believes that the conditions which degrade his life are not inevitable, and that they can be eliminated through conscious human effort. Underlying this belief is the hope that the

TABLE 4. VARIOUS MEASURES OF PERSONAL CONCERN BY DEFINITION OF
ENVIRONMENTAL PROBLEMS IN DURHAM

| | Opinion of environmental pollution in Durham: | | | |
Percent who are:	Serious problem	Moderate problem	Minor problem	No opinion
Personally willing to help solve environmental problems	56	48	39	4
Sees specific ways to help solve environmental problems	68	41	43	4
Willing to pay tax money on environmental solutions	56	47	25	30
Willing to base vote on environmental issues	52	29	22	21
Willing to exclude polluting industry from community	44	32	29	21
Total number of cases	(25)	(102)	(48)	(23)

future can be altered, and that individuals like himself can play a part in shaping it. Given these beliefs, objective deprivations take on a different and more personal meaning, and a kind of tension is created between reality and expectations which can lead to organized action and even to revolutionary change. This positive syndrome helps to determine how individuals react to conditions not only in their social environment but in their physical environment as well. Among Durham residents personal commitment to solving environmental problems was highest among men, the better educated, those in upper-class occupations and whites - all groups which are able to exercize a relatively high degree of control over their lives and surround-ings (Table 5). This pattern is matched by similar findings in Alabama (Johnson, 1971), Pennsylvania (Crowe, 1968), Los Angeles (Van Arsdol, 1964), Buffalo (DeGroot, 1967), St. Louis (Schusky, 1966), Oklahoma City (Borsky, 1964), Syracuse (Frederickson and Magnas, 1968) and elsewhere (Medalia, 1964; Dillman and Christenson, 1972).

What is important is that these socio-economic groups not only are able to exercize greater objective control over their surround-ings, but that they believe more in this ability than do less-priviledged groups. Among Durham residents, men were more convinced of their control over the environment and the future than were women, as were whites more than blacks, and the better-educated and upper-classes more than less favored groups. As shown earlier, this outlook also is related to how causes and solutions are per-ceived. Those who are most confident of their mastery over their present surroundings and the future are most likely to believe that environmental problems are the work of human agencies and that these problems can be solved. Taken together, this whole syndrome of positive attitudes provides an important link between the simple recognition of environmental problems and active commitment to solve them.

Among the more privileged members of the community, then, the recognition of environmental problems often leads on to more active concern not only because these residents are in a position to do something about such problems, but also because they believe that they can do something, and they believe that what they do can sig-nificantly affect future developments. By contrast, disbelief in their ability to control their surroundings and skepticism about future progress dampens active concern for environmental problems among the less priviledged, even when they recognize that these problems exist.

Active concern for environmental problems seems also to be part of a more general pattern of involvement in community affairs. As Table 5 shows, those who were most exposed to the media and who were most interested and engaged in the political, social and cultural life of the community also expressed the greatest commitment to solving its environmental problems. This commitment might be due to the fact that more involved citizens tend to come from the higher socioeconomic strata, and for that reason they have a greater economic stake in community affairs and, as has been shown, a more positive view of their role as agents of change.

29

TABLE 5.   TWO MEASURES OF ACTIVE ENVIRONMENTAL CONCERN BY SELECTED
SOCIAL CHARACTERISTICS OF DURHAM RESIDENTS

	Percent who are:		
Social characteristics	Personally willing to help solve environmental problems	Willing to pay tax money for environmental solutions	Total cases
Education			
Attended college	58	46	(84)
High school graduate	45	45	(42)
Some high school or less	20	38	(54)
Occupational level			
Upper white collar	61	46	(49)
Lower white collar	44	44	(52)
Blue collar	38	40	(42)
Occupational situs			
Commerce	28	40	(42)
Manufacturing & Industry	39	30	(23)
Other (arts, education, health, etc.)	62	46	(58)
Race			
White	46	46	(132)
Black	33	33	(56)
Sex			
Men	52	44	(76)
Women	36	40	(115)
Home ownership			
Rent or other	43	46	(79)
Own home	41	37	(113)
Length of residence			
Less than three years	0	53	(15)
Three to five years	41	41	(17)
Over five years	39	38	(169)
Discussion of current affairs			
Daily	60	46	(90)
Occasionally	31	39	(63)
Seldom or never	21	36	(33)

(continued)

TABLE 5.   TWO MEASURES OF ACTIVE ENVIRONMENTAL CONCERN BY SELECTED
           SOCIAL CHARACTERISTICS OF DURHAM RESIDENTS (continued)

Percent who are:

Social char- acteristics	Personally willing to help solve environmental problems	Willing to pay tax money for environmental solutions	Total cases
Organizational memberships			
Three or more	61	33	(21)
One or two	46	46	(103)
None	30	36	(60)
Vote in 1968 elections			
Voted	42	39	(183)
Did not vote	22	40	(22)
Exposure to new programs			
High	51	51	(31)
Low	46	41	(160)
Exposure to environmental reports			
High	60	48	(103)
Low	22	34	(81)
Number of magazines read			
Three or more	55	45	(99)
One or two	42	44	(45)
None	14	28	(35)

Yet there may be something about participation itself which further stimulates active concern. Participation in one area of community life (such as voluntary associations) tends to be associated with participation in other areas (such as voting and discussing current affairs), which suggests that a general inclination and ability to participate, a kind of "participation syndrome," may underlie each of these specific activities, including active concern for environmental problems (see also Hausknecht, 1962). Data from the Durham study indicate that socio-economic status does not account for this effect. When SES is controlled for, active concern for the environment remains associated with general community involvement at each class level. To some extent, then, general social participation itself may make persons more inclined to commit themselves to the solution of environmental problems.

From all of this we might conclude that privileged social status, and the things that are associated with it, consistently leads to personal concern for recognized environmental problems. Yet when we look at socioeconomic status more closely, we see that its effects are more complex. Offsetting their other tendencies is the fact that higher-status residents are most apt to have some economic investment in their community (such as owning a home) and to be especially tied to it in other ways as well. Rather than stimulating active environmental concern this kind of community attachment actually dampens it, just as it seems to produce a reluctance to recognize these problems in the first place.

Table 5 shows, for example, that homeowners and long-term residents generally express less personal concern for local environmental problems than do renters and newcomers to the Durham community. Again it appears that strong ties to a given area may produce a tendency to deny its physical defects, at least when those defects are not overwhelming. Paralleling this is the fact that persons who are especially committed to some program are least likely to react to its negative consequences. In Oklahoma City, for example, it was found that residents who were convinced that the SST project is "necessary for our country to have" were far less inclined to complain to the FAA about sonic booms than were residents who were skeptical of this project (Borsky, 1965:26ff.). When environmental deterioration reaches the point where it can no longer be ignored, however, community commitment may have just the opposite effect; rather than dampening concern, it may stimulate active concern for these conditions. Here again we need to know more about the interaction between different levels of community commitment and actual pollution.

Despite the fact that they have been directed more to publicizing the existence of environmental problems than to illuminating their solutions, the media have had some effect on how those solutions are viewed. Durham residents were more willing to commit themselves to environmental solutions as their exposure to the media increased, and this was especially true for exposure to reports about environmental issues. This effect isn't fully accounted for by social class, although it is stronger among the better-educated and more affluent. The "message" here may be that the media have been most effective in activating those who are inclined to be personally concerned about the environment in the first place. What they have reported so far seems to have had less effect on the deprived and the apathetic. In fact, by stressing the enormity of our present ecological crisis, the media actually may be doing more to dampen their concern than to stimulate it.

Nor are the mass media alone at fault. Scientific and professional literature also has been prone to this "doomsday" approach, as is seen in this passage from The Environmental Journal (1972):

> The threat of impending doom is so pervasive,
> so serious, that there are loud cries of alarm
> from many quarters. Explosive and still-
> uncontrolled population growth is threatening
> catastrophe. The desecration of the earth
> threatens to poison or smother us even before
> we breed ourselves into extinction.

The author's own deep concern is evident here, and that much is commendable. But such alarms, if they are unrelieved by more positive messages, may be so numbing that they help to insure the catastrophe that they describe.

In sum, personal commitment to solving environmental problems is perhaps more widespread than is commonly thought, but it is certainly not universal. To some extent it depends upon the recognition of those problems, and on how their causes and solutions are perceived. Social background also has a bearing on this commitment, but in a rather complex way. Active environmental concern among middle and upper-class residents is stimulated by their positivist outlook on the present and the future, by their general pattern of social participation and by their exposure to mass communicated information. It is dampened by the fact that their economic or psychological investment in the community may lead them at times to deny its defects. The media also have played a rather ambivalent role to date, especially at this level of concern.

Environmental action involves some behavioral commitment to solving environmental problems as distinguished from the kinds of psychological commitment discussed above. Although these two levels are obviously related, they are still separated by the sometimes wide gulf that exists between intentions and behavior. Many things may intervene to short-circuit that connection and this is as true of environmental concern as it is of concern for other major social problems.

At the broadest level, recent shifts in consumer behavior indicate that there may be a growing desire to begin to do something about our current environmental problems. In the past few years American consumers have come to accept (if not demand) such non-polluting products as lead-free gasoline, bio-degradable detergents and returnable containers. From time to time clean-up campaigns, petitions and demonstrations also have been able to mobilize segments of the community behind the cause of ecology. Yet, despite all of this it is clear that not everyone is actively involved in "saving the environment," or is involved to the same degree. Who then, are the more active, and what has prompted them to action?

The most obvious answer is that the most active are those who are most aroused to the dangers of pollution - those who have been touched by it in some way, or who for other reasons are deeply concerned about it. However true this is, it cannot be said that action automatically flows from concern, even when that concern is deeply felt. Those who actively confront some problem are usually far fewer than those who are affected by it. Despite the clear and present nuisance of sonic booms to most Oklahoma City residents, for example, it has been found that only a small fraction of those who "felt like complaining" actually bothered to register their concern with F.A.A. officials (Borsky, 1965:14). Most of these complainers, incidentally, were prompted to action by their concern over property damage. This wide gap between recognizing environmental problems and doing something about them is not uncommon (DeGroot et al, 1966: 247; O'Riordan, 1971). Furthermore it appears that people may be as unwilling to retreat from such problems as they are reluctant to take more positive forms of action. A recent national survey shows that people who recognize serious air pollution problems in their neighborhood may be more inclined to move away than less concerned residents, but that such dissatisfaction has practically no effect at all on actual mobility behavior (Butler et al, 1972).

It would be easy to attribute this disengagement to common "laziness" and let it go at that. Unfortunately this simple explanation fails to tell us why some are "lazy" while others are not. It also might be pointed out that action usually costs something - either in time, effort or money, and people are naturally reluctant to pay this price. Yet we have already seen that many individuals are willing to assume at least some of these costs in order to salvage the environment. As before, then, to better understand environmental action we must probe more deeply into its social and psychological conditions.

We might start by recalling that behavior of any kind is determined both by attitudes toward a given object (such as pollution) and by perceptions of the particular situation at hand. The critical question is just how these attitudes and perceptions interact with each other. "Thus, attitude(s) may provide a baseline factor for decision-making about action toward the relevant issue or object. Against this base-line the individual raises other considerations, such as the views held by his reference groups, considering in particular, possible sanctions for acting one way or another; then he makes his action decision." (Adcock and DeFleur, 1972:724-25). A concerned businessman might speak out against abuses to the environment among his close friends, for example, but refrain from such criticism among his colleagues. Similarly, during a time when ecological issues are openly debated people generally may be more willing to discuss and act on their concern then when these issues are less publicly acceptable. Although much more needs to be learned here, generally it is safe to assume that under "normal" conditions most people will confine themselves to more passive forms of environmental action in order to minimize both objective costs and the risk of public censure. Furthermore, their inclination to act may vary more with their perception of the situation (or "climate of opinion") than with the amount of their concern for the environment itself.

Knowledge about possible courses of action may be an equally important factor. Ignorance about what they can do to help preserve the environment undoubtedly keeps many from taking more positive action. "Ignorance" is really an unfair term, since it appears that external forces like the media may be as responsible for this inaction as are personal shortcomings. This is not to deny that more internal factors may also be at work. It has been suggested that positive action on environmental issues may be linked to the individual's basic sex identification, for example. According to one report men who are strong in male characteristics are most likely to take action when they are told that the problem can be solved, while men with a more female identification are inclined to act when the problem seems to be unsolvable (White, 1966:123). The significance of basic personality traits like these clearly needs to be investigated more fully.

Finally action can be hindered by the same factors that erode personal concern for and even awareness of pollution. Objective powerlessness, coupled with negative self and future images, isolation from community involvement and media "overkill" all may help to destroy any intention to act on environmental issues, even when they are recognized as serious problems. Butler suggests, for example, that the perception of environmental hazards seldom leads to actual residential mobility because "...those most affected are the poor, the minorities, and the aged, and they are the population segments least able to actualize desires and plans to move" (Butler et al, 1972:11). We might add that they are the population segments least able to visualize effective solutions to their problems in the first place, and most inclined to be apathetic about improving their surroundings and re-shaping their future.

Because of its focus on personal concern, this discussion has dealt only with individual action on environmental issues. Beyond this lies the question of how these individual behaviors become organized into group activities, and how all of this ultimately affects environmental policy. It also would be useful to identify key environmental decision-makers in public and private life, and to examine their own particular dispositions toward the environment. All of these questions deserve more detailed attention. Hopefully, the ideas that are presented here will provide a useful background for discussing these topics.

CONCLUSION

We have learned a great deal in recent years about the nature of our ecological crisis, about the "killing" of Lake Erie and the pollution of our other waterways, about the noxious elements that we have poured into our atmosphere, about the relentless erosion of our parklands, prairies and our urban landscape. Yet all of this illuminates only one side of the question, for we also need to know how we as individuals and as citizens react to these problems. Fortunately there is enough evidence available to begin to understand that reaction, and to speculate on what role the public might play in dealing with these problems in the future.

First of all it is clear that concern for the environment, like concern for any social issue, cannot be described as a simple "yes or no" proposition. Rather it is a process which contains several distinct stages, although each of these stages are only loosely related to the others. Feelings of concern for a given condition cannot be confidently predicted from the fact that it exists and is recognized, any more than problem-solving action necessarily follows from even the deepest sense of concern.

Secondly, what we have learned forces us to question some common assumptions about the causes of this concern. Some, for example, would argue that concern is simply a function of proximity. According to this theory, those who are close to the problem or whose interests are directly threatened by it will be concerned about it, while those who are less touched by the problem will be less concerned. But things aren't that simple, since many who are directly confronted by traffic noise, smog, polluted streams and the like don't even perceive these conditions, much less become alarmed by them. In fact, once an individual has committed himself to a given locale there may be good reasons for him to want to deny even its most evident flaws, both to himself and to others.

Unfortunately there is no other equally simple explanation for environmental concern. Each level of concern may be shaped by a variety of social and psychological factors, sometimes tugging the individual in opposite directions at the same time. Some of these factors may be more important at certain stages than at others. Basic cultural values seem to heavily influence how one perceives his surroundings to begin with, including whether he feels in harmony with nature or at odds with it, and whether he is inclined to preserve or exploit his natural environment. Given the exploitative tendencies embedded within some of our own cultural values it may be an ironic fact that those who are most socialized into the mainstream of American culture are most disposed to ruin the American landscape, or at least to be blind to that destruction. It remains to be seen whether other aspects of our culture, including its ability to produce problem-solving technology, sufficiently balance off these negative strains.

36

Socioeconomic status probably goes farther than anything else
to explain how and why people take an interest in preserving their
environment, but it also may have diverse effects. Despite the
fact that various forms of pollution and the cost of wasted resources often weighs most heavily on the deprived, that very deprivation may numb their concern for these problems. In fact it is the
more priviledged strata who are most alert to community problems
all along the line. This is because they not only possess greater
resources, but also because they are better endowed with a frame of
reference, including a firm belief in human mastery over the environment and the future, which allows them to move on from problem-
recognition to problem-solving.

Yet other aspects of priviledged status dampen this tendency.
There is some evidence that environmental concern and personal
"investment" in the community may be mutually corrosive, and this
investment, along with other competing economic interests, is most
common among the middle and upper classes. The upper class frame
of reference may also contain important contradictions. It is
quite possible, for example, that their belief in human mastery
tends to encourage an exploitative attitude toward nature. The irony
here is that the perspectives which are necessary to produce a
solution-seeking frame of mind may be bound up with the very attitudes
that have helped to create the problem in the first place.

No wonder that vigorous concern for the environment is so uncommon, particularly at the local level. Those who are physically
close to environmental problems often are most apathetic about the
possibility of improvement, while those who are more distant from
these threats may be more mobilizeable, but at the same time more
apt to have an investment in the conditions that create these problems. The net result is a feeling of ambiguity at both ends of the
class scale. Undoubtably, this kind of ambiguity has given astute
political and business interests the latitude to do just about what
they please in most cases. It also casts a pall on current proposals
to provide legislation that would enable private citizens to bring
suit against major air and water pollutors. Even if this legal
machinery were established, it is highly questionable that the general public would be willing to pick it up and make effective use
of it at this time.

It would be encouraging to report that the media have helped
to overcome this impasse by raising the public's environmental
consciousness, but this is only partly true at best. Certainly
media reports have publicized the ecological crisis in general terms
and so have contributed to a climate of interest that may sometimes encourage most positive action. But beyond that our newspapers, magazines and broadcast media have given a mixed performance.
Their tendency to focus on abuses at the broader level may tend to
obscure very real local problems and contribute to the general
inclination to de-emphasize or ignore those problems. Moreover
it often seems as if broadcasters are operating on the belief that
by simply publicizing environmental damage they will move people
to get behind efforts to remedy it. In fact, over-saturation by

37

this kind of publicity may actually have the opposite effect. Both willingness to acknowledge problems and more active concern for them may be dampened if these problems are or <u>seem</u> to be too severe. We might refer to this narrow line between informing and discouraging as the "apathy threshold." Because some individuals are more inclined toward apathy than others this threshold may vary, but it certainly must exist in every mind, and should be better recognized in future media policy.

It may be unfair to conclude that whatever the media have contributed to the situation they have also taken away from it, but certainly they can do more than they have to mobilize public concern for environmental quality. There should, for example, be a more systematic investigation of problems <u>within</u> the community, and this is a job for the local press in particular. A good example is the <u>Sunday Globe</u> series which has spotlighted the Boston area's "Polluter of the Week." Efforts like this should help to swing citizens' attention back within the community and create a better balance between immediate and general concern. Descriptions of the threat itself also need to be balanced by more thorough examinations of just how the average citizen might be able to participate in effective solutions. Finally, all of those who communicate with the general public can become more skilled in shaping the definition of "pollution" by using the evidence at their disposal to draw explicit connections between environmental damage and threats to health, property and other common concerns. Here environmentalists might follow the lead of the oil and electric industry spokesmen who have charged that current environmental regulations are partly responsible for rising consumer energy prices, and should be suspended for the duration of the "energy crisis."

Having said all this we must finally recognize that media campaigns alone cannot mobilize lasting public concern for the environment, because that concern involves some very basic patterns of thought and behavior. We are only beginning to understand how reactions to social problems like pollution are rooted in fundamental orientations toward the future, society and even the self. (Klausner, 1971:57-62). These orientations remain largely untouched by education in the narrow sense of disseminating information and propaganda, although they are more significantly shaped by that deeper kind of education which molds personality and broad life perspectives. In the final analysis this deeper experience can be extended only by overcoming all of those deprivations in schooling, employment, housing and other areas of social life which act to limit personal development and to thwart personal initiative. Here we encounter one final irony. Although it appears that the various stages of concern for the environment (and perhaps other social problems) are only loosely interrelated, we are reminded that these problems <u>themselves</u> are very closely related. This is not to say that the damage to our environment will be remedied only when all of our other social ills are solved, or that everything must be solved at once. It only means that major domestic problems cannot be approached piecemeal, that their intimate connections need to be much more closely examined than they have been so far, and that the time to do so is now.

References

Adcock, Alan C. and Melvin L. DeFleur
1972   "A configurational approach to contingent consistency
            in the attitude-behavior relationship." American
            Sociological Review 37:714-26.

Annals of the American Academy of Political and Social Science
1970   Society and its Physical Environment (May).

Borsky, Paul N.
1965   Community Reactions to Sonic Booms: Oklahoma City Area,
            N.O.R.C. Report no. 101 (January).

Butler, Edgar W., Ronald J. McAllister and Edward J. Kaiser
1972   "Air pollution and metropolitan population redistribution."
            Monograph.

Buttel, Frederick H. and William L. Flinn
1973   The Structure of Support for the Environmental Movement:
            1968-1970. Monograph.

Campbell, Rex R. and Jerry L. Wade
1972   Society and Environment: The Coming Collision. Boston:
            Allyn and Bacon.

Constantini, Edmond and Kenneth Hanf
1972   "Environmental concern and Lake Tahoe; A study of elite
            perceptions, backgrounds and attitudes." Environment and
            Behavior 4 (June):209-42.

Crowe, M. Jay
1968   "Toward a 'definitional model' of public perceptions
            of air pollution." J. Air Pollution Control Administra-
            tion (March):154-57.

DeGroot, Ido
1966   "People and air pollution: A study of attitudes in
            Buffalo, N.Y." J. Air Pollution Control Administration
            16 (May):245-47.

1967   "Trends in public attitudes toward air pollution." J. Air
            Pollution Control Administration 17 (October):679-81.

Dillman, Don A. and James A. Christenson
1972   "The public value for pollution control." Pp. 237-56
            in William R. Burch, Noel H. Cheek, Jr. and Lee Taylor,
            Social Behavior, Natural Resources and the Environment.
            New York: Harper and Row.

Erskine, Hazel
1972a   "The polls: pollution and its costs."
            Public Opinion Quarterly 36 (Spring):120-35.

1972b   "The polls: pollution and industry."
            Public Opinion Quarterly 36 (Summer):263-80.

Frederickson, H. George and Howard Magnas
1968   "Comparing attitudes toward water pollution in Syracuse."
            Water Resources Research 4 (October):877-89.

Fuller, Richard C. and Richard R. Myers
1941   "The natural history of a social problem." American
            Sociological Review 6:24-31.

Glacken, Clarence J.
1971   "Man against nature: An outmoded concept." Pp. 16-27
            in Esther Penchef, ed., Four Horsemen: Pollution,
            Poverty, Famine, Violence. San Francisco: Canfield Press.

Hausknecht, Murray
1962   The Joiners. New York: Bedminster.

Hendee, John C., Richard P. Gale and Joseph Harry
1969   "Conservation, politics and democracy." J. Soil and
            Water Conservation 24 (November/December):212-15.

Johnson, Gerald W.
1971   "The Alabama environment: A survey analysis." Pp. 10-93
            in Fred M. Hudson, ed., Environmental Quality: A Survey
            of Costs, Benefits, Citizens' Attitudes. Report to the
            Second Annual Alabama Environmental Conference (October).

Klausner, Samuel Z.
1971   On Man in His Environment. San Francisco: Jossey-Bass.

Mau, James A.
1968   Social Change and Images of the Future: A Study of the
            Pursuit of Progress in Jamaica, Cambridge, Mass.:
            Schenkman.

McEvoy, James III
1972   "The American concern with environment." Pp. 214-36
            in William R. Burch, Noel H. Cheek, Jr. and Lee Taylor,
            Social Behavior, Natural Resources and the Environment.
            New York: Harper and Row.

McGuire, William J.
1968   "Personality and attitude change: An information-
            processing theory." Pp. 171-96 in Anthony G. Greenwald,
            Timothy C. Brock and Thomas M. Ostrom, Psychological
            Foundations of Attitudes. New York: Academic Press.

Means, Richard L.
1972   "Public opinion and planned changes in social behavior:
            The ecological crisis." Pp. 203-13 in William R. Burch,
            Jr., Neil H. Cheek, Jr. and Lee Taylor, Social Behavior,
            Natural Resources and the Environment. New York: Har-
            per and Row.

Medalia, Nahum Z.
1965   "Air pollution as a socio-environmental health problem:
            A survey report." J. Health and Human Behavior 7
            (Winter):154-65.

Murch, Arvin W.
1971   "Public concern for environmental pollution." Public
          Opinion Quarterly 35 (Spring): 100-106.

O'Riordan, Timothy
1971   "Public opinion and environmental quality: a reappraisal."
          Environment and Behavior 3 (June):191-214.

Paradise, Scott
1971   "The vandal ideology." The Nation 209 (December 29):
          729-32.

Polak, Frederick L.
1961   The Image of the Future: Enlightening the Past, Orient-
          ing the Present, Forecasting the Future. New York:
          Oceana.

Rokeach, Milton
1968   Beliefs, Attitudes and Values: San Francisco: Jossey-
          Bass.

Schusky, Jane
1966   "Public awareness and concern with air pollution in the
          St. Louis metropolitan area." J. Air Pollution Control
          Administration 16 (February):72-76.

Smith, Walter S., Jean J. Schueneman and Louis D. Zeidberg
1964   "Public reaction to air pollution in Nashville, Tennessee."
          J. Air Pollution Control Administration 14 (October):
          418-23.

Spoehr, Alexander
1973   "Cultural differences in the interpretation of natural
          resources," Pp. 195-207 in Michael Micklin, ed.,
          Population, Environment and Social Organization: Current
          Issues in Human Ecology. Hinsdale, Ill.: Dryder Press.

Stouffer, Samuel A.
1955   Communism, Conformity and Civil Liberties. New York:
          Doubleday.

Thomas, Gordon and Max Morgan Witts
1971   The San Francisco Earthquake. New York: Stein and Day.

Tognacci, Louis N. et al.
1972   "Environmental quality: How universal is public conern?"
          Environment and Behavior 4 (March):73-86.

Van Arsdol, Maurice D., Jr., Georges Sabaugh and Francesca Alexander
1965   "Reality and the perception of environmental hazards."
          J. Health and Human Behavior 5 (Winter):144-53.

White, Gilbert F.
    1966   "Formation and role of public attitudes," Pp. 105-27
                in Henry Jarrett, ed., Environmental Quality in a
                Growing Economy. Baltimore: Johns Hopkins Press.

Winham, Gilbert
                "Attitudes on pollution and growth in Hamilton."
                Canadian Journal of Political Science 3 (September):
                389-401.

SECTION II

THE NATURE OF ENVIRONMENTAL CONCERN

PREFACE TO SECTION II

THE NATURE OF ENVIRONMENTAL CONCERN

It should be clear by now that concern for the environment
and its problems can't be adequately accounted for by "self interest"
or by other equally simplistic explanations. Although narrowly-
defined self-interest may sometimes motivate concern, or the lack
of it, more often it does not. Self-interest becomes an even less
meaningful explanation when we consider that in a broader sense, it
is in everyone's interest to preserve their environment. If all
this is true, then we have much to learn about the nature of environmental concern. The following articles help to do just that.

The selections by White and Moncrief explore the deeper roots
of our current attitudes toward the physical environment. Their
common assumption is that these attitudes are part of a larger
mentality which may characterize not only Americans but Western
man in general, and their common interest is in explaining how
that mentality has come about. Winham goes on to remind us of the
complexity of attitudes toward environmental damage, and indicates
how broad environmental concerns are linked to more substantive
economic attitudes. He also points out some implications for future
environmental policy. Shifting from the individual to the aggregate
level. Downs suggests that environmental concern, like all other
public issues, tends to pass through a series of stages culminating

in a kind of "prolonged limbo." This raises the question of whether
public attention is likely to remain focused on this issue long
enough to produce sufficient political pressure to cause effective
change. Downs suggests that the environmental issue has some pe-
culiar strengths which just might give it the kind of staying power
that it needs, but he also warns that we should not "underestimate
the American public's capacity to become bored."

O'Riordan places public opinion on this issue within the whole
framework of decision-making on environmental quality, a process
which involves not only the general public but also threatened and
unthreatened interest groups, politicians and public agencies. He
comments on ways to evaluate public opinion, to identify its role
and to better incorporate it into the larger decision-making process.
Not all publics, of course, are equally significant to this process.
Dunlop, Gale and Rutherford identify the environmental attitudes
and concerns of the critical sub-population of college youth. This
particular public is likely to play an increasingly important role
in future decisions on environmental quality. Our final selection
briefly examines the prospects for a change in environmental attitudes
from what Heberlein calls an "economic to a moral orientation." His
argument is very speculative at times, but still one that is well
worth considering. Heberlein suggests that the same technology
that has contributed to our current environmental crisis has also

helped to "create the necessary conditions for a change in public attitudes" toward environmental abuse. This in turn raises several larger questions. In fact does our social system tend to be self-regulating as Heberlein suggest, and even if it does, is that natural tendancy working fast enough to avoid ecological disaster?

The Historical Roots of Our Ecologic Crisis

Lynn White, Jr.

A conversation with Aldous Huxley not infrequently put one at the receiving end of an unforgettable monologue. About a year before his lamented death he was discoursing on a favorite topic: Man's unnatural treatment of nature and its sad results. To illustrate his point he told how, during the previous summer, he had returned to a little valley in England where he had spent many happy months as a child. Once it had been composed of delightful grassy glades; now it was becoming overgrown with unsightly brush because the rabbits that formerly kept such growth under control had largely succumbed to a disease, myxomatosis, that was deliberately introduced by the local farmers to reduce the rabbits' destruction of crops. Being something of a Philistine, I could be silent no longer, even in the interests of great rhetoric. I interrupted to point out that the rabbit itself had been brought as a domestic animal to England in 1176, presumably to improve the protein diet of the peasantry.

All forms of life modify their contexts. The most spectacular and benign instance is doubtless the coral polyp. By serving its own ends, it has created a vast undersea world favorable to thousands of other kinds of animals and plants. Ever since man became a numerous species he has affected his environment notably. The hypothesis that his fire-drive method of hunting created the world's great grasslands and helped to exterminate the monster mammals of the Pleistocene from much of the globe is plausible, if not proved. For 6 millennia at least, the banks of the lower Nile have been a human artifact rather than the swampy African jungle which nature, apart from man, would have made it. The Aswan Dam, flooding 5000 square miles, is only the latest stage in a long process. In many regions terracing or irrigation, overgrazing, the cutting of forests by Romans to build ships to fight Carthaginians or by Crusaders to solve the logistics problems of their expeditions, have profoundly changed some ecologies. Observation that the French landscape falls into two basic types, the open fields of the north and the *bocage* of the south and west, inspired Marc Bloch to undertake his classic study of medieval agricultural methods. Quite unintentionally, changes in human ways often affect nonhuman nature. It has been noted, for example, that the advent of the automobile eliminated huge flocks of sparrows that once fed on the horse manure littering every street.

The history of ecologic change is still so rudimentary that we know little about what really happened, or what the results were. The extinction of the European aurochs as late as 1627 would seem to have been a simple case of overenthusiastic hunting. On more intricate matters it often is impossible

SCIENCE, March 10, 1967, Vol. 155, No. 3767, pp. 1203-1207.

to find solid information. For a thousand years or more the Frisians and Hollanders have been pushing back the North Sea, and the process is culminating in our own time in the reclamation of the Zuider Zee. What, if any, species of animals, birds, fish, shore life, or plants have died out in the process? In their epic combat with Neptune have the Netherlanders overlooked ecological values in such a way that the quality of human life in the Netherlands has suffered? I cannot discover that the questions have ever been asked, much less answered.

People, then, have often been a dynamic element in their own environment, but in the present state of historical scholarship we usually do not know exactly when, where, or with what effects man-induced changes came. As we enter the last third of the 20th century, however, concern for the problem of ecologic backlash is mounting feverishly. Natural science, conceived as the effort to understand the nature of things, had flourished in several eras and among several peoples. Similarly there had been an age-old accumulation of technological skills, sometimes growing rapidly, sometimes slowly. But it was not until about four generations ago that Western Europe and North America arranged a marriage between science and technology, a union of the theoretical and the empirical approaches to our natural environment. The emergence in widespread practice of the Baconian creed that scientific knowledge means technological power over nature can scarcely be dated before about 1850, save in the chemical industries, where it is anticipated in the 18th century. Its acceptance as a normal pattern of action may mark the greatest event in human history since the invention of agriculture, and perhaps in nonhuman terrestrial history as well.

Almost at once the new situation forced the crystallization of the novel concept of ecology; indeed, the word *ecology* first appeared in the English language in 1873. Today, less than a century later, the impact of our race upon the environment has so increased in force that it has changed in essence. When the first cannons were fired, in the early 14th century, they affected ecology by sending workers scrambling to the forests and mountains for more potash, sulfur, iron ore, and charcoal, with some resulting erosion and deforestation. Hydrogen bombs are of a different order: a war fought with them might alter the genetics of all life on this planet. By 1285 London had a smog problem arising from the burning of soft coal, but our present combustion of fossil fuels threatens to change the chemistry of the globe's atmosphere as a whole, with consequences which we are only beginning to guess. With the population explosion, the carcinoma of planless urbanism, the now geological deposits of sewage and garbage, surely no creature other than man has ever managed to foul its nest in such short order.

There are many calls to action, but specific proposals, however worthy as individual items, seem too partial, palliative, negative: ban the bomb, tear down the billboards, give the Hindus contraceptives and tell them to eat their sacred cows. The simplest solution to any suspect change is, of course, to stop it, or, better yet, to revert to a romanticized past: make those ugly gasoline stations look like Anne Hathaway's cottage or (in the Far West) like ghost-town saloons. The "wilderness area" mentality invariably advocates deep-freezing an ecology, whether San Gimignano or the High Sierra, as it was before the first Kleenex was dropped. But neither atavism nor prettification will cope with the ecologic crisis of our time.

What shall we do? No one yet knows. Unless we think about fundamentals, our specific measures may produce new backlashes more serious than those they are designed to remedy.

As a beginning we should try to clarify our thinking by looking, in some historical depth, at the presuppositions that underlie modern technology and science. Science was traditionally aristocratic, speculative, intellectual in intent; technology was lower-class, empirical, action-oriented. The quite sudden fusion of these two, towards the middle of the 19th century, is surely related to the slightly prior and contemporary democratic revolutions which, by reducing social barriers, tended to assert a functional unity of brain and hand. Our ecologic crisis is the product of an emerging, ·entirely novel, democratic culture. The issue is whether a democratized world can survive its own implications. Presumably we cannot unless we rethink our axioms.

The Western Traditions of Technology and Science

One thing is so certain that it seems stupid to verbalize it: both modern technology and modern science are distinctively *Occidental*. Our technology has absorbed elements from all over the world, notably from China; yet everywhere today, whether in Japan or in Nigeria, successful technology is Western. Our science is the heir to all the sciences of the past, especially perhaps to the work of the great Islamic scientists of the Middle Ages, who so often outdid the ancient Greeks in skill and perspicacity: al-Rāzi in medicine, for example; or ibn-al-Haytham in optics; or Omar Khayyám in mathematics. Indeed, not a few works of such geniuses seem to have vanished in the original Arabic and to survive only in medieval Latin translations that helped to lay the foundations for later Western developments. Today, around the globe, all significant science is Western in style and method, whatever the pigmentation or language of the scientists.

A second pair of facts is less well recognized because they result from quite recent historical scholarship. The leadership of the West, both in technology and in science, is far older than the so-called Scientific Revolution of the 17th century or the so-called Industrial Revolution of the 18th century. These terms are in fact outmoded and obscure the true nature of what they try to describe—significant stages in two long and separate developments. By· A.D. 1000 at the latest —and perhaps, feebly, as much as 200 years earlier—the West began to apply water power to industrial processes other than milling grain. This was followed in the late 12th century by the harnessing of wind power. From simple beginnings, but with remarkable consistency of style, the West rapidly expanded its skills in the development of power machinery, labor-saving devices, and automation. Those who doubt should contemplate that most monumental achievement in the history of automation: the weight-driven mechanical clock, which appeared in two forms in the early 14th century. Not in craftsmanship but in basic technological capacity, the Latin West of the later Middle Ages far outstripped its elaborate, sophisticated, and esthetically magnificent sister cultures, Byzantium and Islam. In 1444 a great Greek ecclesiastic, Bessarion, who had gone to Italy, wrote a letter to a prince in Greece. He is amazed by the superiority of Western ships, arms, textiles, glass. But above all he is astonished by the spectacle of waterwheels sawing timbers and pumping the bellows of blast furnaces. Clearly, he had seen nothing of the sort in the Near East.

By the end of the 15th century the technological superiority of Europe was such that its small, mutually hostile nations could spill out over all the rest of the world, conquering, looting, and colonizing. The symbol of this technological superiority is the fact that Portugal, one of the weakest states of the Occident, was able to become, and to remain for a century, mistress of the East Indies. And we must remember that the technology of Vasco da Gama and Albuquerque was built by pure empiricism, drawing remarkably little support or inspiration from science.

In the present-day vernacular understanding, modern science is supposed to have begun in 1543, when both Copernicus and Vesalius published their great works. It is no derogation of their accomplishments, however, to point out that such structures as the *Fabrica* and the *De revolutionibus* do not appear overnight. The distinctive Western tradition of science, in fact, began in the late 11th century with a massive movement of translation of Arabic and Greek scientific works into Latin. A few notable books—Theophrastus, for example—escaped the West's avid new appetite for science, but within less than 200 years effectively the entire corpus of Greek and Muslim science was available in Latin,

and was being eagerly read and criticized in the new European universities. Out of criticism arose new observation, speculation, and increasing distrust of ancient authorities. By the late 13th century Europe had seized global scientific leadership from the faltering hands of Islam. It would be as absurd to deny the profound originality of Newton, Galileo, or Copernicus as to deny that of the 14th century scholastic scientists like Buridan or Oresme on whose work they built. Before the 11th century, science scarcely existed in the Latin West, even in Roman times. From the 11th century onward, the scientific sector of Occidental culture has increased in a steady crescendo.

Since both our technological and our scientific movements got their start, acquired their character, and achieved world dominance in the Middle Ages, it would seem that we cannot understand their nature or their present impact upon ecology without examining fundamental medieval assumptions and developments.

Medieval View of Man and Nature

Until recently, agriculture has been the chief occupation even in "advanced" societies; hence, any change in methods of tillage has much importance. Early plows, drawn by two oxen, did not normally turn the sod but merely scratched it. Thus, crossplowing was needed and fields tended to be squarish. In the fairly light soils and semiarid climates of the Near East and Mediterranean, this worked well. But such a plow was inappropriate to the wet climate and often sticky soils of northern Europe. By the latter part of the 7th century after Christ, however, following obscure beginnings, certain northern peasants were using an entirely new kind of plow, equipped with a vertical knife to cut the line of the furrow, a horizontal share to slice under the sod, and a moldboard to turn it over. The friction of this plow with the soil was so great that it normally required not two but eight oxen. It attacked the land with such violence that cross-plowing was not needed, and fields tended to be shaped in long strips.

In the days of the scratch-plow, fields were distributed generally in units capable of supporting a single family. Subsistence farming was the presupposition. But no peasant owned eight oxen: to use the new and more efficient plow, peasants pooled their oxen to form large plow-teams, originally receiving (it would appear) plowed strips in proportion to their contribution. Thus, distribution of land was based no longer on the needs of a family but, rather, on the capacity of a power machine to till the earth. Man's relation to the soil was profoundly changed. Formerly man had been part of nature; now he was the exploiter of nature. Nowhere else in the world did farmers develop any analogous agricultural implement. Is it coincidence that modern technology, with its ruthlessness toward nature, has so largely been produced by descendants of these peasants of northern Europe?

This same exploitive attitude appears slightly before A.D. 830 in Western illustrated calendars. In older calendars the months were shown as passive personifications. The new Frankish calendars, which set the style for the Middle Ages, are very different: they show men coercing the world around them—plowing, harvesting, chopping trees, butchering pigs. Man and nature are two things, and man is master.

These novelties seem to be in harmony with larger intellectual patterns. What people do about their ecology depends on what they think about themselves in relation to things around them. Human ecology is deeply conditioned by beliefs about our nature and destiny—that is, by religion. To Western eyes this is very evident in, say, India or Ceylon. It is equally true of ourselves and of our medieval ancestors.

The victory of Christianity over paganism was the greatest psychic revolution in the history of our culture. It has become fashionable today to say that, for better or worse, we live in "the post-Christian age." Certainly the forms of our thinking and language have largely ceased to be Christian, but to my eye the substance often remains amazingly akin to that of the past. Our daily habits of action, for example, are dominated by an implicit faith in perpetual progress which was unknown either to Greco-Roman antiquity or to the Orient. It is rooted in, and is indefensible apart from, Judeo-Christian teleology. The fact that Communists share it merely helps to show what can be demonstrated on many other grounds: that Marxism, like Islam, is a Judeo-Christian heresy. We continue today to live, as we have lived for about 1700 years, very largely in a context of Christian axioms.

What did Christianity tell people about their relations with the environment?

While many of the world's mythologies provide stories of creation, Greco-Roman mythology was singularly incoherent in this respect. Like Aristotle, the intellectuals of the ancient West denied that the visible world had had a beginning. Indeed, the idea of a beginning was impossible in the framework of their cyclical notion of time. In sharp contrast, Christianity inherited from Judaism not only a concept of time as nonrepetitive and linear but also a striking story of creation. By gradual stages a loving and all-powerful God had created light and darkness, the heavenly bodies, the earth and all its plants, animals, birds, and fishes. Finally, God had created Adam and, as an afterthought, Eve to keep man from being lonely. Man named all the animals, thus establishing his dominance over them. God planned all of this explicitly for man's benefit and rule: no item in the physical creation had any purpose save to serve man's purposes. And, although man's body is made of clay, he is not simply part of nature: he is made in God's image.

Especially in its Western form, Christianity is the most anthropocentric religion the world has seen. As early as the 2nd century both Tertullian and Saint Irenaeus of Lyons were insisting that when God shaped Adam he was foreshadowing the image of the incarnate Christ, the Second Adam. Man shares, in great measure, God's transcendence of nature. Christianity, in absolute contrast to ancient paganism and Asia's religions (except, perhaps, Zoroastrianism), not only established a dualism of man and nature but also insisted that it is God's will that man exploit nature for his proper ends.

At the level of the common people this worked out in an interesting way. In Antiquity every tree, every spring, every stream, every hill had its own *genius loci,* its guardian spirit. These spirits were accessible to men, but were very unlike men; centaurs, fauns, and mermaids show their ambivalence. Before one cut a tree, mined a mountain, or dammed a brook, it was important to placate the spirit in charge of that particular situation, and to keep it placated. By destroying pagan animism, Christianity made it possible to exploit nature in a mood of indifference to the feelings of natural objects.

It is often said that for animism the Church substituted the cult of saints. True; but the cult of saints is functionally quite different from animism. The saint is not *in* natural objects; he may have special shrines, but his citizenship is in heaven. Moreover, a saint is entirely a man; he can be approached in human terms. In addition to saints, Christianity of course also had angels and demons inherited from Judaism and perhaps, at one remove, from Zoroastrianism. But these were all as mobile as the saints themselves. The spirits *in* natural objects, which formerly had protected nature from man, evaporated. Man's effective monopoly on spirit in this world was confirmed, and the old inhibitions to the exploitation of nature crumbled.

When one speaks in such sweeping terms, a note of caution is in order. Christianity is a complex faith, and its consequences differ in differing contexts. What I have said may well apply to the medieval West, where in fact technology made spectacular advances. But the Greek East, a highly civilized realm of equal Christian devotion, seems to have produced no marked technological innovation after the late 7th century, when Greek fire was invented. The key to the contrast may perhaps be found in a difference in the tonality of piety and thought which students of comparative theology find between the Greek and the Latin Churches. The Greeks believed that sin was intellectual blindness, and that salvation was found in illumination, orthodoxy—that is, clear thinking. The Latins, on the other hand, felt that sin was moral evil, and that salvation was to be found in right conduct. Eastern theology has been intellectualist. Western theology has been voluntarist. The Greek saint contemplates; the Western saint acts. The implications of Christianity for the conquest of nature would emerge more easily in the Western atmosphere.

The Christian dogma of creation, which is found in the first clause of all the Creeds, has another meaning for our comprehension of today's ecologic crisis. By revelation, God had given man the Bible, the Book of Scripture. But since God had made nature, nature also must reveal the divine mentality. The religious study of nature for the better understanding of God was known as natural theology. In the early Church, and always in the Greek East, nature was conceived primarily as a symbolic system through which God speaks to men: the ant is a sermon to sluggards; rising flames are the symbol of the soul's aspiration. This view of nature was essentially artistic rather than scientific. While Byzantium preserved and copied great numbers of ancient Greek scientific texts, science as we conceive it could scarcely flourish in such an ambience.

However, in the Latin West by the early 13th century natural theology was following a very different bent. It was ceasing to be the decoding of the physical symbols of God's communication with man and was becoming the effort to understand God's mind by discovering how his creation operates. The rainbow was no longer simply a symbol of hope first sent to Noah after the Deluge: Robert Grosseteste, Friar Roger Bacon, and Theodoric of Freiberg produced startlingly sophisticated work on the optics of the rainbow, but they did it as a venture in religious understanding. From the 13th century onward, up to and including Leibnitz and Newton, every major scientist, in effect, explained his motivations in religious terms. Indeed, if Galileo had not been so expert an amateur theologian he would have got into far less trouble: the professionals resented his intrusion. And Newton seems to have regarded himself more as a theologian than as a scientist. It was not until the late 18th century that the hypothesis of God became unnecessary to many scientists.

It is often hard for the historian to judge, when men explain why they are doing what they want to do, whether they are offering real reasons or merely culturally acceptable reasons. The consistency with which scientists during the long formative centuries of Western science said that the task and the reward of the scientist was "to think God's thoughts after him" leads one to believe that this was their real motivation. If so, then modern Western science was cast in a matrix of Christian theology. The dynamism of religious devotion, shaped by the Judeo-Christian dogma of creation, gave it impetus.

An Alternative Christian View

We would seem to be headed toward conclusions unpalatable to many Christians. Since both *science* and *technology* are blessed words in our contemporary vocabulary, some may be happy at the notions, first, that, viewed historically, modern science is an extrapolation of natural theology and, second, that modern technology is at least partly to be explained as an Occidental, voluntarist realization of the

Christian dogma of man's transcendence of, and rightful mastery over, nature. But, as we now recognize, somewhat over a century ago science and technology—hitherto quite separate activities—joined to give mankind powers which, to judge by many of the ecologic effects, are out of control. If so, Christianity bears a huge burden of guilt.

I personally doubt that disastrous ecologic backlash can be avoided simply by applying to our problems more science and more technology. Our science and technology have grown out of Christian attitudes toward man's relation to nature which are almost universally held not only by Christians and neo-Christians but also by those who fondly regard themselves as post-Christians. Despite Copernicus, all the cosmos rotates around our little globe. Despite Darwin, we are *not*, in our hearts, part of the natural process. We are superior to nature, contemptuous of it, willing to use it for our slightest whim. The newly elected Governor of California, like myself a churchman but less troubled than I, spoke for the Christian tradition when he said (as is alleged), "when you've seen one redwood tree, you've seen them all." To a Christian a tree can be no more than a physical fact. The whole concept of the sacred grove is alien to Christianity and to the ethos of the West. For nearly 2 millennia Christian missionaries have been chopping down sacred groves, which are idolatrous because they assume spirit in nature.

What we do about ecology depends on our ideas of the man-nature relationship. More science and more technology are not going to get us out of the present ecologic crisis until we find a new religion, or rethink our old one. The beatniks, who are the basic revolutionaries of our time, show a sound instinct in their affinity for Zen Buddhism, which conceives of the man-nature relationship as very nearly the mirror image of the Christian view. Zen, however, is as deeply conditioned by Asian history as Christianity is by the experience of the West, and I am dubious of its viability among us.

Possibly we should ponder the greatest radical in Christian history since Christ: Saint Francis of Assisi. The prime miracle of Saint Francis is the fact that he did not end at the stake, as many of his left-wing followers did. He was so clearly heretical that a General of the Franciscan Order, Saint Bonaventura, a great and perceptive Christian, tried to suppress the early accounts of Franciscanism. The key to an understanding of Francis is his belief in the virtue of humility—not merely for the individual but for man as a species. Francis tried to depose man from his monarchy over creation and set up a democracy of all God's creatures. With him the ant is no longer simply a homily for the lazy, flames a sign of the thrust of the soul toward union with God; now they are Brother Ant and Sister Fire, praising the Creator in their own ways as Brother Man does in his.

Later commentators have said that Francis preached to the birds as a rebuke to men who would not listen. The records do not read so: he urged the little birds to praise God, and in spiritual ecstasy they flapped their wings and chirped rejoicing. Legends of saints, especially the Irish saints, had long told of their dealings with animals but always, I believe, to show their human dominance over creatures. With Francis it is different. The land around Gubbio in the Apennines was being ravaged by a fierce wolf. Saint

Francis, says the legend, talked to the wolf and persuaded him of the error of his ways. The wolf repented, died in the odor of sanctity, and was buried in consecrated ground.

What Sir Steven Ruciman calls "the Franciscan doctrine of the animal soul" was quickly stamped out. Quite possibly it was in part inspired, consciously or unconsciously, by the belief in reincarnation held by the Cathar heretics who at that time teemed in Italy and southern France, and who presumably had got it originally from India. It is significant that at just the same moment, about 1200, traces of metempsychosis are found also in western Judaism, in the Provençal *Cabbala*. But Francis held neither to transmigration of souls nor to pantheism. His view of nature and of man rested on a unique sort of pan-psychism of all things animate and inanimate, designed for the glorification of their transcendent Creator, who, in the ultimate gesture of cosmic humility, assumed flesh, lay helpless in a manger, and hung dying on a scaffold.

I am not suggesting that many contemporary Americans who are concerned about our ecologic crisis will be either able or willing to counsel with wolves or exhort birds. However, the present increasing disruption of the global environment is the product of a dynamic technology and science which were originating in the Western medieval world against which Saint Francis was rebelling in so original a way. Their growth cannot be understood historically apart from distinctive attitudes toward nature which are deeply grounded in Christian dogma. The fact that most people do not think of these attitudes as Christian is irrelevant. No new set of basic values has been accepted in our society to displace those of Christianity. Hence we shall continue to have a worsening ecologic crisis until we reject the Christian axiom that nature has no reason for existence save to serve man.

The greatest spiritual revolutionary in Western history, Saint Francis, proposed what he thought was an alternative Christian view of nature and man's relation to it: he tried to substitute the idea of the equality of all creatures, including man, for the idea of man's limitless rule of creation. He failed. Both our present science and our present technology are so tinctured with orthodox Christian arrogance toward nature that no solution for our ecologic crisis can be expected from them alone. Since the roots of our trouble are so largely religious, the remedy must also be essentially religious, whether we call it that or not. We must rethink and refeel our nature and destiny. The profoundly religious, but heretical, sense of the primitive Franciscans for the spiritual autonomy of all parts of nature may point a direction. I propose Francis as a patron saint for ecologists.

The Cultural Basis for Our Environmental Crisis

Lewis W. Moncrief

One hundred years ago at almost any location in the United States, potable water was no farther away than the closest brook or stream. Today there are hardly any streams in the United States, except in a few high mountainous reaches, that can safely satisfy human thirst without chemical treatment. An oft-mentioned satisfaction in the lives of urbanites in an earlier era was a leisurely stroll in late afternoon to get a breath of fresh air in a neighborhood park or along a quiet street. Today in many of our major metropolitan areas it is difficult to find a quiet, peaceful place to take a leisurely stroll and sometimes impossible to get a breath of fresh air. These contrasts point up the dramatic changes that have occurred in the quality of our environment.

It is not my intent in this article, however, to document the existence of an environmental crisis but rather to discuss the cultural basis for such a crisis. Particular attention will be given to the institutional structures as expressions of our culture.

Social Organization

In her book entitled *Social Institutions* (1), J. O. Hertzler classified all social institutions into nine functional categories: (i) economic and industrial, (ii) matrimonial and domestic, (iii) political, (iv) religious, (v) ethical, (vi) educational, (vii) communications, (viii) esthetic, and (ix) health. Institutions exist to carry on each of these functions in all cultures, regardless of their location or relative complexity. Thus, it is not surprising that one of the analytical criteria used by anthropologists in the study of various cultures is the comparison and contrast of the various social institutions as to form and relative importance (2).

A number of attempts have been made to explain attitudes and behavior that are commonly associated with one institutional function as the result of influence from a presumably independent institutional factor. The classic example of such an analysis is *The Protestant Ethic and the Spirit of Capitalism* by Max Weber (3). In this significant work Weber attributes much of the economic and industrial growth in Western Europe and North America to capitalism, which, he argued, was an economic form that developed as a result of the religious teachings of Calvin, particularly spiritual determinism.

Social scientists have been particularly active in attempting to assess the influence of religious teaching and prac-

SCIENCE, October, 1970, Vol. 170, pp. 508-512.

tice and of economic motivation on other institutional forms and behavior and on each other. In this connection, L. White (4) suggested that the exploitative attitude that has prompted much of the environmental crisis in Western Europe and North America is a result of the teachings of the Judeo-Christian tradition, which conceives of man as superior to all other creation and of everything else as created for his use and enjoyment. He goes on to contend that the only way to reduce the ecologic crisis which we are now facing is to "reject the Christian axiom that nature has no reason for existence save to serve man." As with other ideas that appear to be new and novel, Professor White's observations have begun to be widely circulated and accepted in scholarly circles, as witness the article by religious writer E. B. Fiske in the *New York Times* earlier this year (5). In this article, note is taken of the fact that several prominent theologians and theological groups have accepted this basic premise that Judeo-Christian doctrine regarding man's relation to the rest of creation is at the root of the West's environmental crisis. I would suggest that the wide acceptance of such a simplistic explanation is at this point based more on fad than on fact.

Certainly, no fault can be found with White's statement that "Human ecology is deeply conditioned by beliefs about our nature and destiny—that is, by religion." However, to argue that it is the primary conditioner of human behavior toward the environment is much more than the data that he cites to support this proposition will bear. For example, White himself notes very early in his article that there is evidence for the idea that man has been dramatically altering his environment since antiquity. If this be true, and there is evidence

that it is, then this mediates against the idea that the Judeo-Christian religion uniquely predisposes cultures within which it thrives to exploit their natural resources with indiscretion. White's own examples weaken his argument considerably. He points out that human intervention in the periodic flooding of the Nile River basin and the fire-drive method of hunting by prehistoric man have both probably wrought significant "unnatural" changes in man's environment. The absence of Judeo-Christian influence in these cases is obvious.

It seems tenable to affirm that the role played by religion in man-to-man and man-to-environment relationships is one of establishing a very broad system of allowable beliefs and behavior and of articulating and invoking a system of social and spiritual rewards for those who conform and of negative sanctions for individuals or groups who approach or cross the pale of the religiously unacceptable. In other words, it defines the ball park in which the game is played, and, by the very nature of the park, some types of games cannot be played. However, the kind of game that ultimately evolves is not itself defined by the ball park. For example, where animism is practiced, it is not likely that the believers will indiscriminately destroy objects of nature because such activity would incur the danger of spiritual and social sanctions. However, the fact that another culture does not associate spiritual beings with natural objects does not mean that such a culture will invariably ruthlessly exploit its resources. It simply means that there are fewer social and psychological constraints against such action.

In the remainder of this article, I present an alternative set of hypotheses based on cultural variables which, it seems to me, are more plausible and more defensible as an explanation of the environmental crisis that is now confronting us.

No culture has been able to completely screen out the egocentric tendencies of human beings. There also exists in all cultures a status hierarchy of positions and values, with certain groups partially or totally excluded from access to these normatively desirable goals. Historically, the differences in most cultures between the "rich" and the "poor" have been great. The many very poor have often produced the wealth for the few who controlled the means of production. There may have been no alternative where scarcity of supply and unsatiated demand were economic reality. Still, the desire for a "better life" is universal; that is, the desire for higher status positions and the achievement of culturally defined desirable goals is common to all societies.

The Experience in the Western World

In the West two significant revolutions that occurred in the 18th and 19th centuries completely redirected its political, social, and economic destiny (6). These two types of revolutions were unique to the West until very recently. The French revolution marked the beginnings of widespread democratization. In specific terms, this revolution involved a redistribution of the means of production and a reallocation of the natural and human resources that are an integral part of the production process. In effect new channels of social mobility were created, which theoretically made more wealth accessible to more people. Even though the revolution was partially perpetrated in the guise of overthrowing the control of presumably Christian institutions

and of destroying the influence of God over the minds of men, still it would be superficial to argue that Christianity did not influence this revolution. After all, biblical teaching is one of the strongest of all pronouncements concerning human dignity and individual worth.

At about the same time but over a more extended period, another kind of revolution was taking place, primarily in England. As White points out very well, this phenomenon, which began with a number of technological innovations, eventually consummated a marriage with natural science and began to take on the character that it has retained until today (7). With this revolution the productive capacity of each worker was amplified by several times his potential prior to the revolution. It also became feasible to produce goods that were not previously producible on a commercial scale.

Later, with the integration of the democratic and the technological ideals, the increased wealth began to be distributed more equitably among the population. In addition, as the capital to land ratio increased in the production process and the demand grew for labor to work in the factories, large populations from the agrarian hinterlands began to concentrate in the emerging industrial cities. The stage was set for the development of the conditions that now exist in the Western world.

With growing affluence for an increasingly large segment of the population, there generally develops an increased demand for goods and services. The usual by-product of this affluence is waste from both the production and consumption processes. The disposal of that waste is further complicated by the high concentration of heavy waste producers in urban areas. Under these conditions the maxim that "Dilution is the solution to pollution" does not withstand the test of time, because the volume of such wastes is greater than the system can absorb and purify through natural means. With increasing population, increasing production, increasing urban concentrations, and increasing real median incomes for well over a hundred years, it is not surprising that our environment has taken a terrible beating in absorbing our filth and refuse.

The American Situation

The North American colonies of England and France were quick to pick up the technical and social innovations that were taking place in their motherlands. Thus, it is not surprising that the inclination to develop an industrial and manufacturing base is observable rather early in the colonies. A strong trend toward democratization also evidenced itself very early in the struggle for nationhood. In fact, Thistlewaite notes the significance of the concept of democracy as embodied in French thought to the framers of constitutional government in the colonies (8, pp. 33–34, 60).

From the time of the dissolution of the Roman Empire, resource ownership in the Western world was vested primarily with the monarchy or the Roman Catholic Church, which in turn bestowed control of the land resources on vassals who pledged fealty to the sovereign. Very slowly the concept of private ownership developed during the Middle Ages in Europe, until it finally developed into the fee simple concept.

In America, however, national policy from the outset was designed to convey ownership of the land and other natural resources into the hands of the citizenry. Thomas Jefferson was perhaps more influential in crystallizing this philosophy in the new nation than anyone else. It was his conviction that an agrarian society made up of small landowners would furnish the most stable foundation for building the nation (8, pp. 59–68). This concept has received support up to the present and, against growing economic pressures in recent years, through government programs that have encouraged the conventional family farm. This point is clearly relevant to the subject of this article because it explains how the natural resources of the nation came to be controlled not by a few aristocrats but by many citizens. It explains how decisions that ultimately degrade the environment are made not only by corporation boards and city engineers but by millions of owners of our natural resources. This is democracy exemplified!

Challenge of the Frontier

Perhaps the most significant interpretation of American history has been Fredrick Jackson Turner's much criticized thesis that the western frontier was the prime force in shaping our society (9). In his own words,

If one would understand why we are today one nation, rather than a collection of isolated states, he must study this economic and social consolidation of the country. . . . The effect of the Indian frontier as a consolidating agent in our history is important.

He further postulated that the nation experienced a series of frontier challenges that moved across the continent in waves. These included the explorers' and traders' frontier, the Indian fron-

60

tier, the cattle frontier, and three distinct agrarian frontiers. His thesis can be extended to interpret the expansionist period of our history in Panama, in Cuba, and in the Philippines as a need for a continued frontier challenge.

Turner's insights furnish a starting point for suggesting a second variable in analyzing the cultural basis of the United States' environmental crisis. As the nation began to expand westward, the settlers faced many obstacles, including a primitive transportation system, hostile Indians, and the absence of physical and social security. To many frontiersmen, particularly small farmers, many of the natural resources that are now highly valued were originally perceived more as obstacles than as assets. Forests needed to be cleared to permit farming. Marshes needed to be drained. Rivers needed to be controlled. Wildlife often represented a competitive threat in addition to being a source of food. Sod was considered a nuisance—to be burned, plowed, or otherwise destroyed to permit "desirable" use of the land.

Undoubtedly, part of this attitude was the product of perceiving these resources as inexhaustible. After all, if a section of timber was put to the torch to clear it for farming, it made little difference because there was still plenty to be had very easily. It is no coincidence that the "First Conservation Movement" began to develop about 1890. At that point settlement of the frontier was almost complete. With the passing of the frontier era of American history, it began to dawn on people that our resources were indeed exhaustible. This realization ushered in a new philosophy of our national government toward natural resources management under the guidance of Theodore Roosevelt and Gifford Pinchot.

Samuel Hays (10) has characterized this movement as the appearance of a new "Gospel of Efficiency" in the management and utilization of our natural resources.

The Present American Scene

America is the archetype of what happens when democracy, technology, urbanization, capitalistic mission, and antagonism (or apathy) toward natural environment are blended together. The present situation is characterized by three dominant features that mediate against quick solution to this impending crisis: (i) an absence of personal moral direction concerning our treatment of our natural resources, (ii) an inability on the part of our social institutions to make adjustments to this stress, and (iii) an abiding faith in technology.

The first characteristic is the absence of personal moral direction. There is moral disparity when a corporation executive can receive a prison sentence for embezzlement but be congratulated for increasing profits by ignoring pollution abatement laws. That the absolute cost to society of the second act may be infinitely greater than the first is often not even considered.

The moral principle that we are to treat others as we would want to be treated seems as appropriate a guide as it ever has been. The rarity of such teaching and the even more uncommon instance of its being practiced help to explain how one municipality can, without scruple, dump its effluent into a stream even though it may do irreparable damage to the resource and add tremendously to the cost incurred by downstream municipalities that use the same water. Such attitudes are not restricted to any one culture. There appears to be an almost universal tendency to maximize self-interests and a widespread willingness to shift production costs to society to promote individual ends.

Undoubtedly, much of this behavior is the result of ignorance. If our accounting systems were more efficient in computing the cost of such irresponsibility both to the present generation and to those who will inherit the environment we are creating, steps would undoubtedly be taken to enforce compliance with measures designed to conserve resources and protect the environment. And perhaps if the total costs were known, we might optimistically speculate that more voluntary compliance would result.

A second characteristic of our current situation involves institutional inadequacies. It has been said that "what belongs to everyone belongs to no one." This maxim seems particularly appropriate to the problem we are discussing. So much of our environment is so apparently abundant that it is considered a free commodity. Air and water are particularly good examples. Great liberties have been permitted in the use and abuse of these resources for at least two reasons. First, these resources have typically been considered of less economic value than other natural resources except when conditions of extreme scarcity impose limiting factors. Second, the right of use is more difficult to establish for resources that are not associated with a fixed location.

Government, as the institution representing the corporate interests of all its citizens, has responded to date with dozens of legislative acts and numerous court decisions which give it authority to regulate the use of natural resources. However, the decisiveness to act has

thus far been generally lacking. This indecisiveness cannot be understood without noting that the simplistic models that depict the conflict as that of a few powerful special interests versus "The People" are altogether inadequate. A very large proportion of the total citizenry is implicated in environmental degradation; the responsibility ranges from that of the board and executives of a utility company who might wish to thermally pollute a river with impunity to that of the average citizen who votes against a bond issue to improve the efficiency of a municipal sanitation system in order to keep his taxes from being raised. The magnitude of irresponsibility among individuals and institutions might be characterized as falling along a continuum from highly irresponsible to indirectly responsible. With such a broad base of interests being threatened with every change in resource policy direction, it is not surprising, although regrettable, that government has been so indecisive.

A third characteristic of the present American scene is an abiding faith in technology. It is very evident that the idea that technology can overcome almost any problem is widespread in Western society. This optimism exists in the face of strong evidence that much of man's technology, when misused, has produced harmful results, particuarly in the long run. The reasoning goes something like this: "After all, we have gone to the moon. All we need to do is allocate enough money and brainpower and we can solve any problem."

It is both interesting and alarming that many people view technology almost as something beyond human control. Rickover put it this way (11):

It troubles me that we are so easily pressured by purveyors of technology into

62

permitting so-called "progress" to alter our lives without attempting to control it—as if technology were an irrepressible force of nature to which we must meekly submit.

He goes on to add:

It is important to maintain a humanistic attitude toward technology; to recognize clearly that since it is the product of human effort, technology can have no legitimate purpose but to serve man—man in general, not merely some men; future generations, not merely those who currently wish to gain advantage for themselves; man in the totality of his humanity, encompassing all his manifold interests and needs, not merely some one particular concern of his. When viewed humanistically, technology is seen not as an end in itself but a means to an end, the end being determined by man himself in accordance with the laws prevailing in his society.

In short, it is one thing to appreciate the value of technology; it is something else entirely to view it as our environmental savior—which will save us in spite of ourselves.

Conclusion

The forces of democracy, technology, urbanization, increasing individual wealth, and an aggressive attitude toward nature seem to be directly related to the environmental crisis now being confronted in the Western world. The **Judeo-Christian tradition has probably influenced the character of each of these forces. However, to isolate religious tradition as a cultural component and to contend that it is the "historical root of our ecological crisis" is a bold affirmation for which there is little historical or scientific support.**

To assert that the primary cultural condition that has created our environmental crisis is Judeo-Christian teaching avoids several hard questions. For example: Is there less tendency for those who control the resources in non-Christian cultures to live in extravagant affluence with attendant high levels of waste and inefficient consumption? If non-Judeo-Christian cultures had the same levels of economic productivity, urbanization, and high average household incomes, is there evidence to indicate that these cultures would not exploit or disregard nature as our culture does?

If our environmental crisis is a "religious problem," why are other parts of the world experiencing in various degrees the same environmental problems that we are so well acquainted with in the Western world? It is readily observable that the science and technology that developed on a large scale first in the West have been adopted elsewhere. Judeo-Christian tradition has not been adopted as a predecessor to science and technology on a comparable scale. Thus, all White can defensibly argue is that the West developed modern science and technology *first*. This says nothing about the origin or existence of a particular ethic toward our environment.

In essence, White has proposed this simple model:

I	II	III
Judeo-Christian tradition →	Science and technology →	Environmental degradation

I have suggested here that, at best, Judeo-Christian teaching has had only an indirect effect on the treatment of our environment. The model could be characterized as follows:

I	II	III	IV
Judeo-Christian tradition →	1) Capitalism (with the attendant development of → science and technology) 2) Democratization	1) Urbanization 2) Increased wealth 3) Increased population → 4) Individual resource ownership	Environmental degradation

Even here, the link between Judeo-Christian tradition and the proposed dependent variables certainly have the least empirical support. One need only look at the veritable mountain of criticism of Weber's conclusions in *The Protestant Ethic and the Spirit of Capitalism* to sense the tenuous nature of this link. The second and third phases of this model are common to many parts of the world. Phase I is not.

Jean Mayer (*12*), the eminent food scientist, gave an appropriate conclusion about the cultural basis for our environmental crisis:

It might be bad in China with 700 million poor people but 700 million rich Chinese would wreck China in no time. . . . It's the rich who wreck the environment . . . occupy much more space, consume more of each natural resource, disturb ecology more, litter the landscape . . . and create more pollution.

References and Notes

1. J. O. Hertzler, *Social Institutions* (McGraw-Hill, New York, 1929), pp. 47–64.
2. L. A. White, *The Science of Culture* (Farrar, Straus & Young, New York, 1949), pp. 121–145.
3. M. Weber, *The Protestant Ethic and the Spirit of Capitalism*, translated by T. Parsons (Scribner's, New York, 1958).
4. L. White, Jr., *Science* 155, 1203 (1967).
5. E. B. Fiske, "The link between faith and ecology," *New York Times* (4 January 1970), section 4, p. 5.
6. R. A. Nisbet, *The Sociological Tradition* (Basic Books, New York, 1966), pp. 21–44. Nisbet gives here a perceptive discourse on the social and political implications of the democratic and industrial revolutions to the Western world.
7. It should be noted that a slower and less dramatic process of democratization was evident in English history at a much earlier date than the French revolution. Thus, the concept of democracy was probably a much more pervasive influence in English than in French life. However, a rich body of philosophic literature regarding the rationale for democracy resulted from the French revolution. Its counterpart in English literature is much less conspicuous. It is an interesting aside to suggest that perhaps the industrial revolution would not have been possible except for the more broad-based ownership of the means of production that resulted from the long-standing process of democratization in England.
8. F. Thistlewaite, *The Great Experiment* (Cambridge Univ. Press, London, 1955).
9. F. J. Turner, *The Frontier in American History* (Henry Holt, New York, 1920 and 1947).
10. S. P. Hays, *Conservation and the Gospel of Efficiency* (Harvard Univ. Press, Cambridge, Mass., 1959).
11. H. G. Rickover, *Amer. Forests* 75, 13 (August 1969).
12. J. Mayer and T. G. Harris, *Psychol. Today* 3, 46 and 48 (January 1970).

Attitudes on Pollution and Growth in Hamilton, or "There's an awful lot of talk these days about ecology"*

GILBERT WINHAM

Good government requires the capacity to make hard choices. Nowhere is this dictum more evident than in the area of environmental policy. Government officials today are pressed by the public to reduce environmental pollution. At the same time they are also expected to maintain high growth rates and to increase employment opportunities. Too often these demands are simply inconsistent.

How much economic growth is antithetical to pollution abatement is a matter of conjecture. Experts do not agree on the subject. Spokesmen from industry contend that pollution is a technical problem which will be reduced when sufficient attention and resources are committed.[1] Undoubtedly there are instances where this advice is correct. However, others counter by saying that pollution is endemic in modern industrial life, and that to maintain present growth levels is certain to cause further deterioration of our environment.[2] This position has been taken by some economists who question the value of increasing gross national products,[3] or who propose thinking of the economy as a closed rather than an open system.[4]

The controversy over economic growth versus pollution abatement will obviously occupy knowledgeable observers for some time to come. Meanwhile what may be more important for public policy is the prevailing attitudes towards growth and pollution in the general population, and the policy-makers' perceptions of these attitudes. Public attitudes are seldom the principle component of public policy, yet they are a factor which is weighed in the decisions of popularly elected leaders. This is particularly true on questions such as growth or pollution which involve considerations of "public taste." This point is corroborated by

---

*Statement by Hamilton Mayor Vic Copps before City Council, while discussing a controversial land exchange deal between the city and two major steel firms. Mr. Copps' remarks, as cited in the *Spectator*, were: "There's an awful lot of talk these days about ecology. Our greatest problem in this city isn't ecology. It is unemployment. This deal will help ease that problem." "Turkstra Bid Fails to Oust Elliott," *Spectator* (December 1, 1971) 3.

The data used in this paper were gathered in a survey carried out by the author and his students at McMaster University. The author is indebted to his students and collaborators for their insights in constructing the survey design, and for their efforts in seeing the project through. A report on this project was earlier made to members of Hamilton City Council.

[1]This observation is made in a Special Report to *Business Week*: "The Trade-Offs for a Better Environment," *Business Week*, April 11, 1970, pp. 63–78.

[2]Donella H. Meadows, Dennis L. Meadows, Jorgen Randers, and William W. Behrens, III, *The Limits to Growth: A Report for the Club of Rome's Project on the Predicament of Mankind* (Washington, 1972).

[3]Edward J. Mishan, *The Costs of Economic Growth* (London, 1967).

[4]Kenneth E. Boulding, "The Economics of the Coming Spaceship Earth," in Henry Jarrett, ed., *Environmental Quality in a Growing Economy*, Essays from the Sixth RFF Forum (Baltimore, 1966).

CANADIAN JOURNAL OF POLITICAL SCIENCE, September, 1972, Vol. 3, pp. 389-401.

environmental scientists, who widely assume that public action on environmental problems is dependent on changing public attitudes.[5]

When the question comes to public attitudes, we are aware of the widespread concern about pollution, but what is the public's view on the so-called trade-off between more jobs and less pollution? How willing is the public to accept privations to have less pollution? Finally, will the public voice support for specific pollution control measures, and if so what general conclusions can be drawn from such verbal support?

I. Methodology

Data for this analysis were generated in a city-wide survey in Hamilton, Ontario, between November 1970 and January 1971. The survey included direct interviews with 685 Hamilton residents based on a questionnaire which took about thirty minutes to administer. The sample for the survey was drawn in order to reflect accurately the population characteristics of the city. The general procedure was to randomly select households from Hamilton as a whole, and to randomly select individuals for interviewing from the selected households.

Households were drawn from the city directory which lists all residences alphabetically by street. The city directory was used rather than voters' or other lists because it is more representative of the population, and because residence lists are less prone to error than tallies of individuals. The city directory was sampled, using every fifth page, and numbers were laid on the households (to 19,190) on the selected pages. Non-dwelling units such as businesses, schools, and hospitals were eliminated from the tally. One thousand householders were selected on the basis of random number generation. Information was collected on the sex and age of individuals age twenty-one or over in each household chosen. The persons selected for interviewing within the households were randomly chosen, in order to insure that young and old, male and female, had an equal chance of being selected.

Allowing for vacant residences, or those destroyed by urban renewal or converted to businesses, the final sample included 956 individuals. Interviews were completed with 72 per cent of this number. Of the remainder, 16 per cent were contacted but refused the interview, 10 per cent were unreachable after three return calls, and 2 per cent were not interviewed because of illness, language difficulty, or other reasons.

II. Attitudes on pollution and growth

As a background to the Hamilton findings, it is apparent from recent survey results that pollution has leaped into prominence as a public concern in a manner matched by few other issues. National polls in both Canada and the United States find pollution contending for the top position among domestic problems.[6] In both countries current readings are much higher than in the mid-1960s. Surveys on

[5]See, for example, Paul R. and Anne H. Ehrlich, *Population Resources Environment* (San Francisco, 1970), 256.
[6]See reports of CIPO and AIPO polls in the *Toronto Daily Star*, Dec. 2, 1970, and the *Chicago Sun-Times*, May 14, 1970.

Les attitudes envers la pollution et la croissance à Hamilton

On analyse dans cet article les attitudes du public envers la pollution et la croissance économique, en prêtant une attention particulière à l'ampleur du soutien que le public accorde aux mesures anti-pollution et à sa volonté de réduire la pollution même si c'est au prix de certains sacrifices. Les données proviennent d'un échantillon au hasard composé de 685 résidents de la ville de Hamilton, en Ontario. Selon les conclusions générales qui s'en dégagent, l'opinion publique est fortement favorable à une augmentation de la croissance économique, tout en s'inquiétant du problème de la pollution. L'analyse montre que ces deux attitudes sont contraires et que l'opinion pourrait bien se diviser un jour au sujet de la croissance et de la pollution.

Les attitudes envers la pollution conduisent généralement à favoriser des mesures anti-pollution, même si les individus doivent en subir les coûts et les inconvénients. Les attitudes envers la croissance conduisent à préférer des mesures opposées. Par exemple, les personnes qui estiment que la pollution est le principal problème de la ville ont tendance à vouloir interdire la circulation des automobiles dans le centre-ville, tandis que celles qui sont plutôt favorables à un développement industriel accéléré s'opposent à cette mesure. Il y a toutefois une exception : les personnes qui sont favorables à la croissance acceptent plus ou moins de payer le prix de la lutte à la pollution. Cela suggère que les mesures anti-pollution qui consistent à imposer des coûts aux individus sont probablement mieux acceptées par les électeurs que celles qui tendent à ralentir le taux de croissance économique ou à modifier les modes de vie économique.

Enfin, les données semblent indiquer que les attitudes anti-pollution ont une base fragile, surtout lorsqu'elles viennent en conflit avec les attitudes envers la croissance économique. Les données montrent aussi que le sentiment anti-pollution se manifeste moins à l'occasion d'un problème réel (par exemple, l'expansion de l'aéroport d'Hamilton) qu'à l'occasion d'un problème artificiel, et que ce sentiment se rencontre surtout chez des gens qui sont moins aux prises que d'autres avec les problèmes de la pollution.

pollution have also been taken in several major North American cities over the past decade, including Toronto, Buffalo, Los Angeles, St Louis, and Seattle.[7] While specific questions differ from questionnaire to questionnaire, these surveys corroborate nationwide reports regarding mass concern for pollution.

Data from the 1970–1 Hamilton survey are generally consistent with national trends, although concern levels are somewhat higher in Hamilton. In this survey respondents were asked three questions measuring their concern for pollution. Two involve choosing the major problem facing Hamilton and Canada respectively, from cards with nine problems listed each (see Table I). The third question asked how concerned respondents felt they were over pollution. The percentage responses were: extremely concerned, 41 per cent; concerned, 49 per cent; and not too concerned, 10 per cent.

The data from Table I show that pollution heads the list of problems for Hamilton residents. Furthermore, Hamiltonians quite sensibly view pollution as more serious in the city than in Canada overall, with the figures on unemployment apparently making up the difference. The concern for pollution is a recent phenome-

[7]See, for example, Andris Auliciems and Ian Burton, "Perception and Awareness of Air Pollution in Toronto," Working Paper #13, National Hazard Research, University of Toronto, 1970.

TABLE I

CHOICE OF MAJOR PROBLEM* (percentages)

Canada		Hamilton	
Crime prevention	10	Welfare	10
Foreign ownership	3	Urban renewal	3
Pollution	32	Crime prevention	6
Unemployment	25	Pollution	41
Quebec separatism	6	Unemployment	17
Sale of resources and energy		Rapid growth	2
to the US	4	Not enough parks and	
Cost of living	12	recreational facilities	2
Overpopulation	2	Inadequate housing	7
Taxes	6	Cost of living	11
No answer	1		
	100		100

*This question was asked first in order not to bias responses. The question was: "There are many problems facing our country (city) today. Which of the ones on the list do you think are most important, and should get first priority. You should choose three ... Now, which ONE (of these three) do you think is *most* important?"

non, since a 1968 pre-election survey in Hamilton failed to turn up any comparable interest in pollution.[8] Because of the worsening economic situation after 1970, one might expect more recent data would show an increase in the figures for unemployment, possibly at the expense of those for pollution. Whether the concern over pollution, which developed quickly in Hamilton, will continue in future years is a matter of conjecture at this point.

The conclusion from the Hamilton survey is that pollution is a high priority concern of the residents of Hamilton. An equally prominent conclusion is that Hamiltonians favour further growth and development of the city, and do not at this time regard growth as a policy problem.

The question concerning community problems (Table I) shows that rapid growth was least frequently selected – and by a wide margin – as a major problem facing Hamilton. On the positive side, respondents were asked what they felt the city should work for in the next decade. Four out of every five favoured increased industrial and land development, as well as improved cultural and educational opportunities. Given the distributions in Table II, there is some question whether respondents made a clear distinction between material development, such as increased industrialization, or cultural development, such as improved education. What this question does point out is that growth in a generic sense is a high priority value among the respondents, and there is no gainsaying that the material component of growth is equally important to the public as the non-material.

In comparing attitudes on growth with those on pollution, it can be inferred

[8]Gilbert R. Winham and Robert B. Cunningham, "Party Leader Images in the 1968 Federal Election," this JOURNAL, III no 1 (March 1970), 37–55. The question was: "What are the problems facing Canada that the government should do something about?" The major issue areas were coded as follows: cost of living 26 per cent, housing 22 per cent, taxes 22 per cent, social welfare 18 per cent, French-English unity 16 per cent, and unemployment 14 per cent. Respondents could name more than one issue. Of the total sample, 14 per cent declined to mention any issue. Pollution was not mentioned often enough to warrant coding.

TABLE II

RESPONSES ON GROWTH QUESTIONS (percentages)
"Do you think Hamilton as a city should work for these following things in the next ten years?"

	Yes	No	Don't know
Increased industrial development (that is, more industries and more jobs)	79	19	2
Improved cultural opportunities (for example, live theatre, music)	81	17	2
Improved public and private education	77	20	3
Increased land development (for example, more housing units and shopping areas)	80	18	2

TABLE III

MAJOR PROBLEM (POLLUTION) AND INDUSTRIAL DEVELOPMENT (percentages)

	Industrial development	
	Yes	No
Major problem		
Pollution	36 (193)	59 (78)
Others	64 (343)	41 (54)
	100 (536)	100 (132)
	N = 668	
	Gamma = −.439;	
	χ^2 significant at .001	

that the public views these factors as being connected with each other.[9] Persons who favoured industrial growth in the sample were proportionately less likely to pick pollution as the major problem in Hamilton, and vice versa. This relationship, which is strong and statistically significant, is demonstrated in Table III. While there may be an agreement among experts about whether growth and pollution are related, attitudes on growth and pollution clearly are related in public opinion, and this may be a significant fact for future public policy.

One can speculate from the data in Table III that the potential exists for a major cleavage in the population over growth and pollution. At present a majority of the sample (421, or 61 per cent) are consistently "growth-minded" (that is, pro-growth, unconcerned about pollution) or consistently "ecology-minded" (that is, anti-growth, concerned about pollution). Of course, within these figures the absolute number favouring increased growth substantially exceeds the number concerned about pollution. Furthermore, of those concerned about pollution, most (193, or 71 per cent) favour increased growth at the same time, which puts them in an ambivalent position compared with the general trend in the sample. If the problems associated with growth and pollution become more serious in the future – and there is ample evidence to argue this position – it is possible that the middle

[9]Subsequent analysis uses the question on industrial development (industries and jobs) as the indicator for attitudes towards growth.

TABLE IV

MAJOR PROBLEM (UNEMPLOYMENT) AND INDUSTRIAL
DEVELOPMENT (percentages)

	Major problem	
	Unemployment	Others
Industrial development		
Yes	91	78
No	9	22
	100 (115)	100 (553)
	N = 668	
	Gamma = .367;	
	χ^2 significant at .001	

TABLE V

RELATIONSHIP BETWEEN FEAR OF LOSING JOB AND MAJOR PROBLEM
(POLLUTION) AND INDUSTRIAL DEVELOPMENT (percentages)

	Major problem		Industrial development	
	Pollution	Others	Yes	No
Lose job				
Yes	27	44	39	29
No	73	56	61	71
	100 (264)	100 (377)	100 (512)	100 (127)
	N = 641		N = 639	
	Gamma = −.350;		Gamma = .219;	
	χ^2 significant at .001		χ^2 significant at .05	

position of "pro-growth anti-pollution" may become increasingly untenable. It is primarily this group that now prevents attitudes from being polarized.

There is some evidence that anti-pollution and pro-growth attitudes receive differential support in the community. In the first place the public's view towards unemployment is clearly related to attitudes on pollution and growth. By definition those who chose pollution as the major problem in Hamilton did not choose unemployment, and of those who chose unemployment first there was a distinct tendency to be pro-growth (see Table IV). Secondly, respondents were asked whether they felt anti-pollution measures would result in unemployment.[10] Thirty-five per cent answered affirmatively, and this group was composed disproportionately of blue collar workers and less affluent individuals. Comparing this question with responses on pollution and growth, it is apparent that fear of job loss was negatively related to choosing pollution as a major problem, and positively (although weakly) related to favouring growth (see Table v).

On certain socio-economic variables, attitudes towards pollution generally received differential support from the Hamilton sample. Youth, high income, and white collar occupational status are associated with a tendency to choose pollu-

[10]The question was: "Do you think people will be forced out of their jobs if companies are required by government to cut back on pollution?"

TABLE VI

AGE, INCOME, OCCUPATION AND MAJOR PROBLEM (POLLUTION) (percentages)

	Age		Family income		Occupation		
	40 or under	Over 40	$8000 or less	Over $8000	White collar	Blue collar	Other*
Major problem							
Pollution	45	36	35	48	51	38	32
Others	55	64	65	52	49	62	68
	100 (341)	100 (327)	100 (398)	100 (266)	100 (194)	100 (380)	100 (99)
	N = 668		N = 664		N = 673		
	Gamma = .169		Gamma = −.248		Gamma = .235		
	χ^2 significant at .05		χ^2 significant at .001		χ^2 significant at .001		

*Includes retired.

TABLE VII

EDUCATION AND MAJOR PROBLEM (POLLUTION) AND INDUSTRIAL
DEVELOPMENT (percentages)

	Education	
	Less than Grade 12	Grade 12 and over
Major problem		
Pollution	33	53
Others	67	47
	100 (411)	100 (252)
	N = 663	
	Gamma = −.403; χ^2 significant at .001	
Industrial development		
Yes	84	74
No	16	26
	100 (410)	100 (250)
	N = 660	
	Gamma = .292; χ^2 significant at .001	

tion as a main problem (see Table VI). This finding is generally consistent with surveys in North America over the past decade.[11] However, differential support is not the case for attitudes on growth. There were no statistically significant relationships between attitudes favouring industrial growth and age, income, or occupation. The one exception to this pattern was education. Education strongly differentiates the attitudes on pollution and growth, and in an opposite direction (see Table VII). Respondents with higher education show a pronounced tendency to select pollution as a major policy problem, while on the other hand they disproportionately disfavour increased industrial growth.

To sum up the evidence so far, it would appear that attitudes towards pollution are more complex than they appear at first glance. No one is "for" pollution today,

[11]See Cecile Trop and Leslie L. Roos, Jr., "Public Opinion and the Environment," in Leslie L. Roos, Jr., ed., *The Politics of Ecosuicide* (New York, 1971), 52–63.

but a substantial majority is for increased growth, and rightly or wrongly pollution and growth are probably viewed as trade-offs by the mass public. Anti-pollution sentiment, which is differentiated by socio-economic variables, apparently contends with a widespread and generally undifferentiated support for continued material development of the society. Such support is deeply woven into the fabric of mass opinion. For example, in answer to the question "Do you think Hamilton will be a better place to live in ten years, and why?" 72 per cent (N = 496) of the Hamilton sample were optimistic about the future. Coding the remarks of the optimists showed there were three times more articulated responses (N = 166) dealing with some aspect of economic development (for example, physical improvements, better employment) than for the next articulated reply (less pollution).

III. Attitudes on policy variables

The analysis was carried further by posing several policy related questions dealing with pollution control. The object of these questions was to examine whether the public was willing to accept privations to have less pollution. This tactic is useful in that it shows whether broad concerns are consistent with operational attitudes,[12] but results must be interpreted cautiously. For example, a willingness to pay tax for pollution control may be more tangible than a generalized concern over pollution, but it still is an opinion which under some circumstances may not be translated into behaviour.

The policy questions were of two types: those dealing with costs, and those dealing with economic life style (particularly transportation). In the first category, respondents were asked if they would pay increased costs for emission control devices on automobiles, and pay extra anti-pollution taxes. Questions in the second category queried opinions on banning automobiles in downtown Hamilton, and on expanding the Hamilton airport. In all save the airport case, the anti-pollution position was taken by a substantial majority of the sample (see Table VIII). This finding in itself would suggest the public is serious about some aspects of pollution control, at least as far as this can be assessed through public opinion surveys.

Responses on the policy questions were compared to the general questions of choosing pollution as a major problem, and of supporting industrial growth. If no relationship occurred between these variables, then responses on the policy questions might be isolated occurrences and not part of any general attitudinal orientation. However, if relationships do occur, we have some evidence that people move from general attitudes to more specific concerns – specifically, a willingness (or unwillingness) to accept privations for pollution control.

The cross-tabulated data show that there are positive relationships between choosing pollution as a major problem and supporting measures for pollution abatement (see Table IX). Albeit, the direction of these relationships was hardly unexpected. However, the findings are consistent throughout, and it appears that concern about pollution in the public takes on an additional importance in so far

[12]For further discussion, see James W. Prothro and Charles M. Grigg, "Fundamental Principles of Democracy: Bases of Agreement and Disagreement," *Journal of Politics*, XXII (May 1960), 276–94.

TABLE VIII

RESPONSES ON POLICY VARIABLES (percentages)

	Yes	No	Don't know
Experts tell us that emission control devices may cost $150 per car. Would you be willing to pay this cost if it effectively reduced air pollution?	85	8	7
Experts claim that Hamilton's sewage disposal system contributes to water pollution in Lake Ontario. Would you be willing to pay extra taxes if it meant pollution from this source could be reduced?	78	10	12
Do you think Hamilton and other cities like it should try in the next decade to ban automobiles from downtown areas, and use only public services for inner city transportation?	62	36	2
Are you in favour of establishing a major airport in the Hamilton area (specifically, at Mount Hope)?	53	44	3

TABLE IX

MAJOR PROBLEM (POLLUTION) AND
POLICY VARIABLES (percentages)

	Major problem	
	Pollution	Others
Emission control		
Yes	91	85
No	9	15
	100 (272)	100 (390)
	N = 662	
	Gamma = .287;	
	χ^2 significant at .05	
Extra tax		
Yes	85	75
No	15	25
	100 (272)	100 (397)
	N = 669	
	Gamma = .317;	
	χ^2 significant at .01	
Ban autos		
Yes	73	57
No	27	43
	100 (271)	100 (390)
	N = 661	
	Gamma = .345;	
	χ^2 significant at .001	
Favour airport expansion		
Yes	46	59
No	54	41
	100 (269)	100 (386)
	N = 655	
	Gamma = −.256	
	χ^2 significant at .001	

TABLE X

INDUSTRIAL DEVELOPMENT AND POLICY VARIABLES
(percentages)

	Industrial development	
	Yes	No
Emission control		
Yes	87	91
No	13	9
	100 (530)	100 (129)
	N = 659	
	χ² *not* significant at .05	
Extra tax		
Yes	79	86
No	21	14
	100 (527)	100 (130)
	N = 657	
	χ² *not* significant at .05	
Ban autos		
Yes	59	82
No	41	18
	100 (527)	100 (132)
	N = 659	
	Gamma = − .518;	
	χ² significant at .001	
Favour airport expansion		
Yes	58	42
No	42	58
	100 (526)	100 (128)
	N = 654	
	Gamma = .301;	
	χ² significant at .001	

as it is linked to the operational attitude of being willing to do something about pollution.

The findings on relationships with industrial growth are mixed (see Table x). Persons favouring growth tended to favour airport expansion, and were opposed to changing Hamilton's transportation system. However, there were no significant relationships between favouring growth and the positions taken on paying for pollution control. The findings of this table bear some significance for future environmental policy. They suggest that those who favour growth are unconcerned about the increased costs of pollution abatement, but are less willing to slow economic development or change life style to facilitate anti-pollution measures. An interpretation of these data would be that future pollution control policies that create direct costs to the community may be more acceptable to the public than those which raise indirect costs in the form of decreased growth.

In the above analysis, the most important variable is the airport question. First, unlike the other policy variables, airport expansion is a real and not a fabricated issue. Whether Hamilton should undertake a major expansion of its airport is a continuing issue in city politics, and it is obvious that this issue is typical of many that cities are now facing. Second, unlike the other variables, the majority response to the airport issue was not favourable to the anti-pollution position. Table IX has shown a significant relationship between choosing pollution first and opposing airport expansion. This, however, simply means that among those respondents who chose pollution first the percentage of those opposed to the airport is higher than among those who did not choose pollution. The relationship says nothing about the absolute number for or against, which is the more important factor in public policy. This can be put another way. In the overall sample there were 275 respondents who chose pollution first before other problems. Less than two out of four of them opposed the airport, while three out of four supported banning automobiles from Hamilton, an issue which is at present hypothetical. Where were the anti-pollution persons on a real issue? Was the airport not seen as an issue which involved pollution, or were anti-pollution attitudes simply not strong enough to lead respondents to oppose airport expansion?

The question of whether the airport was viewed as a pollution issue can quickly be put to rest. Following the question regarding their support for airport expansion, respondents were asked whether they felt establishing a major airport would significantly add to the city's level of pollution. Sixty-six per cent answered affirmatively, and there was a strong relationship in the overall sample between opposing the airport and viewing the airport as a polluter (gamma = $-.718$; χ^2 significant at .001).

The reason why anti-pollution sentiment drains away on the airport issue is because this issue raises the question of economic growth. Attitudes favouring growth were significantly related to those favouring airport expansion, which undoubtedly acted in a way to cross-pressure many in the overall sample. On this issue attitudes towards growth were apparently the more important factor. Given this analysis, it is interesting to speculate what would happen if the proposal to ban automobiles became a live possibility. On the one hand, three out of five respondents presently support a ban. On the other hand, the relationship between favouring growth and favouring a ban is negative and strong. The most realistic expectation – based on the airport case – is that support for banning automobiles would fade if the issue became real.

Some additional analysis regarding airport expansion showed that it triggered concerns about growth in the public that apparently were dormant on other issues. For example, the question about Hamilton's future referred to previously was cross-tabulated with the policy variables. This produced negative results with one exception. There was a strong and significant relationship between being optimistic about Hamilton's future and favouring airport expansion (gamma = .427; χ^2 significant at .001). Considering that the open-ended responses to this question had a strong economic development dimension, it is clear that the growth aspect of the airport constituted an important element of its popularity with the sample.

A second concern triggered by the airport question was the spectre of losing jobs to anti-pollution cutbacks. That subset of respondents who supported the airport even though they thought it would cause increased pollution was isolated

(N = 186), and their views were compared against the marginals of the overall sample. There were few substantial differences, with one notable exception. Forty-six per cent of the subset felt anti-pollution cutbacks might cause unemployment, as compared to 35 per cent in the sample. Apparently fear of job loss is an attitude which is not held by many, but is nevertheless important because it surfaces on real as opposed to hypothetical issues.

IV. Summary and discussion

Choices between pro-growth and anti-pollution policies are hard decisions for governments to make. Such choices are not any easier for the mass public. The conclusion from this study is that public opinion overall prefers more growth and less pollution, but that individuals who support further growth tend to be unconcerned about pollution, while those concerned about pollution are less likely to favour economic growth. Underlying attitudes on pollution and growth generally lead to opposite policy preferences on environmental issues. Thus, for example, persons choosing pollution as the major urban problem tend to support banning automobiles from the inner city, while those favouring increased industrial development oppose the policy. The one exception is the relative willingness of persons holding pro-growth attitudes to pay anti-pollution costs. This exception suggests that pollution control policies that raise money costs may be somewhat more popular with the electorate than those which seek to change growth rates or economic life style. Finally where pro-growth and anti-pollution attitudes conflict there is some evidence that anti-pollution support on a real issue (namely, the expansion of Hamilton's airport) is less than on the other hypothetical issues posed in the questionnaire. It seems "talk" about ecology may not necessarily be backed up with action when it affects our material well-being.

Public opinion surveys are useful because of the speculation they arouse. Public opinion can change – even substantially – from one survey to the next. What is more enduring than the exact statistics are patterns and relationships between attitudes, and the political importance that can be inferred from them.

Observing the Hamilton data and the broader scene, it is probable that the concern over pollution *per se* has reached a peak as a force in the public consciousness. The public has become sensitized to pollution in a remarkably short time, which has already brought about shifts in public priorities. However, concern about pollution has risen within a framework of traditional preferences for growth, increased production, and material amenities. It is not likely that the preferences in this framework have changed much, and it is clear they contend with views on pollution when the matter gets down to policy issues. If environmental thinking is to remain a factor in public opinion in the future, it will depend more on people changing their attitudes on growth than on their becoming more alarmed about pollution.

This analysis has found that when issues get serious the anti-pollution position tends to be less decisive. This could be because underlying preferences for less pollution are not as strongly held as preferences for increased growth. There are indications that the concern people feel about pollution is an intellectualized concern, and is not deeply woven into the fabric of their everyday lives. The groups most concerned about pollution – the affluent, well-educated, and white collar workers – are not the groups one expects would experience the most pollution, and the survey evidence confirms that those living in the most polluted areas in Hamilton are less rather than more concerned about pollution than others.[13] Consistent with this explanation, the mass media is often cited as having "caused" the recent public awareness of ecology. Although this interpretation is facile, it is quite possibly true in Hamilton where the large increase in concern between 1968 and 1970 was coincident with vigorous coverage of pollution issues by the local newspaper. To summarize, anti-pollution attitudes may not be an intrinsically strong or durable segment of public opinion, and if the anti-pollution argument is pushed to an extreme there could well be a "backlash" that some observers have warned about.[14] To date the concern over pollution has raised important questions in the public consciousness about the effect of our material life style on the environment. If the talk about ecology is to have an impact on policy in the future, the discussion will probably have to shift to more fundamental questions about the desirability of maintaining that life style itself.

[13]An air pollution map prepared by Ontario's Air Management Branch, Department of Energy and Resources Management, divided the city into five areas according to monthly dust fall for the year 1969. Respondents living in less polluted areas more frequently chose pollution as the major problem, and this relationship held even after controlling for education and income. More memorable, however, than the numerical data was the response of one industrial area resident. The air was bad enough, he claimed, to peel the paint from his automobile in two years, but his main concern was unemployment.

[14]Peter F. Drucker, "Saving the Crusade," *Harper's Magazine*, 244 (Jan. 1972), 66–71.

Up and down with ecology— the "issue-attention cycle"

ANTHONY DOWNS

AMERICAN public attention rarely remains sharply focused upon any one domestic issue for very long—even if it involves a continuing problem of crucial importance to society. Instead, a systematic "issue-attention cycle" seems strongly to influence public attitudes and behavior concerning most key domestic problems. Each of these problems suddenly leaps into prominence, remains there for a short time, and then—though still largely unresolved—gradually fades from the center of public attention. A study of the way this cycle operates provides insights into how long public attention is likely to remain sufficiently focused upon any given issue to generate enough political pressure to cause effective change.

The shaping of American attitudes toward improving the quality of our environment provides both an example and a potential test of this "issue-attention cycle." In the past few years, there has been a remarkably widespread upsurge of interest in the quality of our environment. This change in public attitudes has been much faster than any changes in the environment itself. What has caused this shift in public attention? Why did this issue suddenly assume so high a priority among our domestic concerns? And how long will the American public sustain high-intensity interest in ecological mat-

THE PUBLIC INTEREST, Summer, 1972, No. 28, pp. 38-50.

ters? I believe that answers to these questions can be derived from analyzing the "issue-attention cycle."

The dynamics of the "issue-attention cycle"

Public perception of most "crises" in American domestic life does not reflect changes in real conditions as much as it reflects the operation of a systematic cycle of heightening public interest and then increasing boredom with major issues. This "issue-attention cycle" is rooted both in the nature of certain domestic problems and in the way major communications media interact with the public. The cycle itself has five stages, which may vary in duration depending upon the particular issue involved, but which almost always occur in the following sequence:

1. **The pre-problem stage.** This prevails when some highly undesirable social condition exists but has not yet captured much public attention, even though some experts or interest groups may already be alarmed by it. *Usually, objective conditions regarding the problem are far worse during the pre-problem stage than they are by the time the public becomes interested in it.* For example, this was true of racism, poverty, and malnutrition in the United States.

2. **Alarmed discovery and euphoric enthusiasm.** As a result of some dramatic series of events (like the ghetto riots in 1965 to 1967), or for other reasons, the public suddenly becomes both aware of and alarmed about the evils of a particular problem. This alarmed discovery is invariably accompanied by euphoric enthusiasm about society's ability to "solve this problem" or "do something effective" within a relatively short time. The combination of alarm and confidence results in part from the strong public pressure in America for political leaders to claim that every problem can be "solved." This outlook is rooted in the great American tradition of optimistically viewing most obstacles to social progress as *external* to the structure of society itself. The implication is that every obstacle can be eliminated and every problem solved *without any fundamental reordering of society itself*, if only we devote sufficient effort to it. In older and perhaps wiser cultures, there is an underlying sense of irony or even pessimism which springs from a widespread and often confirmed belief that many problems cannot be "solved" *at all* in any complete sense. Only recently has this more pessimistic view begun to develop in our culture.

3. **Realizing the cost of significant progress.** The third stage consists of a gradually spreading realization that the cost of "solving" the

problem is very high indeed. Really doing so would not only take a great deal of money but would also require major sacrifices by large groups in the population. The public thus begins to realize that part of the problem results from arrangements that are providing significant benefits to someone—often to millions. For example, traffic congestion and a great deal of smog are caused by increasing automobile usage. Yet this also enhances the mobility of millions of Americans who continue to purchase more vehicles to obtain these advantages.

In certain cases, technological progress can eliminate some of the undesirable results of a problem without causing any major restructuring of society or any loss of present benefits by others (except for higher money costs). In the optimistic American tradition, such a technological solution is initially assumed to be possible in the case of nearly every problem. Our most pressing social problems, however, usually involve either deliberate or unconscious exploitation of one group in society by another, or the prevention of one group from enjoying something that others want to keep for themselves. For example, most upper-middle-class whites value geographic separation from poor people and blacks. Hence any equality of access to the advantages of suburban living for the poor and for blacks cannot be achieved without some sacrifice by middle-class whites of the "benefits" of separation. The increasing recognition that there is this type of relationship between the problem and its "solution" constitutes a key part of the third stage.

4. **Gradual decline of intense public interest.** The previous stage becomes almost imperceptibly transformed into the fourth stage: a gradual decline in the intensity of public interest in the problem. As more and more people realize how difficult, and how costly to themselves, a solution to the problem would be, three reactions set in. Some people just get discouraged. Others feel positively threatened by thinking about the problem; so they suppress such thoughts. Still others become bored by the issue. Most people experience some combination of these feelings. Consequently, public desire to keep attention focused on the issue wanes. And by this time, some other issue is usually entering Stage Two; so it exerts a more novel and thus more powerful claim upon public attention.

5. **The post-problem stage.** In the final stage, an issue that has been replaced at the center of public concern moves into a prolonged limbo—a twilight realm of lesser attention or spasmodic recurrences of interest. However, the issue now has a different relation to public attention than that which prevailed in the "pre-problem" stage. For

one thing, during the time that interest was sharply focused on this problem, new institutions, programs, and policies may have been created to help solve it. These entities almost always persist and often have some impact even after public attention has shifted elsewhere. For example, during the early stages of the "War on Poverty," the Office of Economic Opportunity (OEO) was established, and it initiated many new programs. Although poverty has now faded as a central public issue, OEO still exists. Moreover, many of its programs have experienced significant success, even though funded at a far lower level than would be necessary to reduce poverty decisively.

Any major problem that once was elevated to national prominence may sporadically recapture public interest; or important aspects of it may become attached to some other problem that subsequently dominates center stage. Therefore, problems that have gone through the cycle almost always receive a higher average level of attention, public effort, and general concern than those still in the pre-discovery stage.

Which problems are likely to go through the cycle?

Not all major social problems go through this "issue-attention cycle." Those which do generally possess to some degree three specific characteristics. First, the majority of persons in society are not suffering from the problem nearly as much as some minority (a *numerical* minority, not necessarily an *ethnic* one). This is true of many pressing social problems in America today—poverty, racism, poor public transportation, low-quality education, crime, drug addiction, and unemployment, among others. The number of persons suffering from each of these ills is very large *absolutely*—in the millions. But the numbers are small *relatively*—usually less than 15 per cent of the entire population. Therefore, most people do not suffer directly enough from such problems to keep their attention riveted on them.

Second, the sufferings caused by the problem are generated by social arrangements that provide significant benefits to a majority or a powerful minority of the population. For example, Americans who own cars—plus the powerful automobile and highway lobbies—receive short-run benefits from the prohibition of using motor-fuel tax revenues for financing public transportation systems, even though such systems are desperately needed by the urban poor.

Third, the problem has no intrinsically exciting qualities—or no longer has them. When big-city racial riots were being shown nightly on the nation's television screens, public attention naturally focused

81

upon their causes and consequences. But when they ceased (or at least the media stopped reporting them so intensively), public interest in the problems related to them declined sharply. Similarly, as long as the National Aeronautics and Space Administration (NASA) was able to stage a series of ever more thrilling space shots, culminating in the worldwide television spectacular of Americans walking on the moon, it generated sufficient public support to sustain high-level Congressional appropriations. But NASA had nothing half so dramatic for an encore, and repetition of the same feat proved less and less exciting (though a near disaster on the third try did revive audience interest). So NASA's Congressional appropriations plummeted.

A problem must be dramatic and exciting to maintain public interest because news is "consumed" by much of the American public (and by publics everywhere) largely as a form of entertainment. As such, it competes with other types of entertainment for a share of each person's time. Every day, there is a fierce struggle for space in the highly limited universe of newsprint and television viewing time. Each issue vies not only with all other social problems and public events, but also with a multitude of "non-news" items that are often far more pleasant to contemplate. These include sporting news, weather reports, crossword puzzles, fashion accounts, comics, and daily horoscopes. In fact, the amount of television time and newspaper space devoted to sports coverage, as compared to international events, is a striking commentary on the relative value that the public places on knowing about these two subjects.

When all three of the above conditions exist concerning a given problem that has somehow captured public attention, the odds are great that it will soon move through the entire "issue-attention cycle" —and therefore will gradually fade from the center of the stage. The first condition means that most people will not be continually reminded of the problem by their own suffering from it. The second condition means that solving the problem requires sustained attention and effort, plus fundamental changes in social institutions or behavior. This in turn means that significant attempts to solve it are threatening to important groups in society. The third condition means that the media's sustained focus on this problem soon bores a majority of the public. As soon as the media realize that their emphasis on this problem is threatening many people and boring even more, they will shift their focus to some "new" problem. This is particularly likely in America because nearly all the media are run for profit, and they make the most money by appealing to the largest

82

possible audiences. Thus, as Marshall McLuhan has pointed out, it is largely the audience itself—the American public—that "manages the news" by maintaining or losing interest in a given subject. As long as this pattern persists, we will continue to be confronted by a stream of "crises" involving particular social problems. Each will rise into public view, capture center stage for a while, and then gradually fade away as it is replaced by more 'fashionable issues moving into their "crisis" phases.

The rise of environmental concern

Public interest in the quality of the environment now appears to be about midway through the "issue-attention cycle." Gradually, more and more people are beginning to realize the immensity of the social and financial costs of cleaning up our air and water and of preserving and restoring open spaces. Hence much of the enthusiasm about prompt, dramatic improvement in the environment is fading. There is still a great deal of public interest, however, so it cannot be said that the "post-problem stage" has been reached. In fact, as will be discussed later, the environmental issue may well retain more attention than social problems that affect smaller proportions of the population. Before evaluating the prospects of long-term interest in the environment, though, it is helpful to analyze how environmental concern passed through the earlier stages in the "issue-attention cycle."

The most obvious reason for the initial rise in concern about the environment is the recent deterioration of certain easily perceived environmental conditions. A whole catalogue of symptoms can be arrayed, including ubiquitous urban smog, greater proliferation of solid waste, oceanic oil spills, greater pollution of water supplies by DDT and other poisons, the threatened disappearance of many wildlife species, and the overcrowding of a variety of facilities from commuter expressways to National Parks. Millions of citizens observing these worsening conditions became convinced that *someone* ought to "do something" about them. But "doing something" to reduce environmental deterioration is not easy. For many of our environmental problems have been caused by developments which are highly valued by most Americans.

The very abundance of our production and consumption of material goods is responsible for an immense amount of environmental pollution. For example, electric power generation, if based on fossil fuels, creates smoke and air pollution or, if based on nuclear fuels, causes rising water temperatures. Yet a key foundation for rising living standards in the United States during this century has been the doubling of electric power consumption every 10 years. So more pollution is the price we have paid for the tremendous advantages of being able to use more and more electricity. Similarly, much of the litter blighting even our remotest landscapes stems from the convenience of using "throwaway packages." Thus, to regard environmental pollution as a purely external negative factor would be to ignore its direct linkage with material advantages most citizens enjoy.

Another otherwise favorable development that has led to rising environmental pollution is what I would call the democratization of privilege. Many more Americans are now able to participate in certain activities that were formerly available only to a small, wealthy minority. Some members of that minority are incensed by the consequences of having their formerly esoteric advantages spread to "the common man." The most frequent irritant caused by the democratization of privilege is congestion. Rising highway congestion, for example, is denounced almost everywhere. Yet its main cause is the rapid spread of automobile ownership and usage. In 1950, about 59 per cent of all families had at least one automobile, and seven per cent owned two or more. By 1968, the proportion of families owning at least one automobile had climbed to 79 per cent, and 26 per cent had two or more cars. In the 10 years from 1960 to 1970, the total number of registered automotive vehicles rose by 35 million (or 47 per cent), as compared to a rise in human population of 23 million (or only 13 per cent). Moreover, it has been estimated that motor vehicles cause approximately 60 per cent of all air pollution. So the tremendous increase in smog does not result primarily from larger population, but rather from the democratization of automobile ownership.

The democratization of privilege also causes crowding in National Parks, rising suburban housing density, the expansion of new subdivisions into formerly picturesque farms and orchards, and the transformation of once tranquil resort areas like Waikiki Beach into forests of high-rise buildings. It is now difficult for the wealthy to flee from busy urban areas to places of quiet seclusion, because so many more people can afford to go with them. *The elite's environmental deterioration is often the common man's improved standard of living.*

Our soaring aspirations

A somewhat different factor which has contributed to greater concern with environmental quality is a marked increase in our aspirations and standards concerning what our environment ought to be like. In my opinion, rising dissatisfaction with the "system" in the United States does not result primarily from poorer performance by that system. Rather, it stems mainly from a rapid escalation of our aspirations as to what the system's performance ought to be. Nowhere is this phenomenon more striking than in regard to the quality of the environment. One hundred years ago, white Americans were eliminating whole Indian tribes without a qualm. Today, many serious-minded citizens seek to make important issues out of the potential disappearance of the whooping crane, the timber wolf, and other exotic creatures. Meanwhile, thousands of Indians in Brazil are still being murdered each year—but American conservationists are not focusing on that human massacre. Similarly, some aesthetes decry "galloping sprawl" in metropolitan fringe areas, while they ignore acres of rat-infested housing a few miles away. Hence the escalation of our environmental aspirations is more selective than might at first appear.

Yet regarding many forms of pollution, we are now rightly upset over practices and conditions that have largely been ignored for decades. An example is our alarm about the dumping of industrial wastes and sewage into rivers and lakes. This increase in our environmental aspirations is part of a general cultural phenomenon stimulated both by our success in raising living standards and by the recent emphases of the communications media. Another cause of the rapid rise in interest in environmental pollution is the "explosion" of alarmist rhetoric on this subject. According to some well-publicized experts, all life on earth is threatened by an "environmental crisis." Some claim human life will end within three decades or less if we do not do something drastic about current behavior patterns.

Are things really that bad? Frankly, I am not enough of an ecological expert to know. But I am skeptical concerning all highly alarmist views because so many previous prophets of doom and disaster have been so wrong concerning many other so-called "crises" in our society.

There are two reasonable definitions of "crisis." One kind of crisis consists of a rapidly deteriorating situation moving towards a single disastrous event at some future moment. The second kind consists of a more gradually deteriorating situation that will eventually pass some subtle "point of no return." At present, I do not believe either of these definitions applies to most American domestic problems. Although many social critics hate to admit it, the American "system" actually serves the majority of citizens rather well in terms of most indicators of well-being. Concerning such things as real income, personal mobility, variety and choice of consumption patterns, longevity, health, leisure time, and quality of housing, most Americans are better off today than they have ever been and extraordinarily better off than most of mankind. What is *not* improving is the gap between society's performance and what most people—or at least highly vocal minorities—believe society *ought* to be doing to solve these problems. Our aspirations and standards have risen far faster than the beneficial outputs of our social system. Therefore, although most Americans, including most of the poor, are receiving more now, they are enjoying it less.

This conclusion should not be confused with the complacency of some super-patriots. It would be unrealistic to deny certain important negative trends in American life. Some conditions are indeed getting worse for nearly everyone. Examples are air quality and freedom from thievery. Moreover, congestion and environmental deterioration might forever destroy certain valuable national amenities if they are not checked. Finally, there has probably been a general rise in personal and social anxiety in recent years. I believe this is due to increased tensions caused by our rapid rate of technical and social change, plus the increase in worldwide communication through the media. These developments rightly cause serious and genuine concern among millions of Americans.

The future of the environmental issue

Concern about the environment has passed through the first two stages of the "issue-attention cycle" and is by now well into the third. In fact, we have already begun to move toward the fourth stage, in which the intensity of public interest in environmental improvement must inexorably decline. And this raises an interesting question: Will the issue of environmental quality then move on into the "post-problem" stage of the cycle?

My answer to this question is: Yes, but not soon, because certain characteristics of this issue will protect it from the rapid decline in public interest typical of many other recent issues. First of all, many kinds of environmental pollution are much more visible and more clearly threatening than most other social problems. This is particularly true of air pollution. The greater the apparent threat from visible forms of pollution and the more vividly this can be dramatized, the more public support environmental improvement will receive and the longer it will sustain public interest. Ironically, the cause of ecologists would therefore benefit from an environmental disaster like a "killer smog" that would choke thousands to death in a few days. Actually, this is nothing new; every cause from early Christianity to the Black Panthers has benefited from martyrs. Yet even the most powerful symbols lose their impact if they are constantly repeated. The piteous sight of an oil-soaked seagull or a dead soldier pales after it has been viewed even a dozen times. Moreover, some of the worst environmental threats come from forms of pollution that are invisible. Thus, our propensity to focus attention on what is most visible may cause us to clean up the pollution we can easily perceive while ignoring even more dangerous but hidden threats.

Pollution is also likely to be kept in the public eye because it is an issue that threatens almost everyone, not just a small percentage of the population. Since it is not politically divisive, politicians can safely pursue it without fearing adverse repercussions. Attacking environmental pollution is therefore much safer than attacking racism or poverty. For an attack upon the latter antagonizes important blocs of voters who benefit from the sufferings of others or at least are not threatened enough by such suffering to favor spending substantial amounts of their money to reduce it.

A third strength of the environmental issue is that much of the "blame" for pollution can be attributed to a small group of "villains" whose wealth and power make them excellent scapegoats. Environmental defenders can therefore "courageously" attack these scapegoats without antagonizing most citizens. Moreover, at least in regard to air pollution, that small group actually has enough power greatly to reduce pollution if it really tries. If leaders of the nation's top auto-producing, power-generating, and fuel-supplying firms would change their behavior significantly, a drastic decline in air pollution could be achieved very quickly. This has been demonstrated at many locations already.

Gathering support for attacking any problem is always easier if its ills can be blamed on a small number of "public enemies"—as is shown by the success of Ralph Nader. This tactic is especially effective if the "enemies" exhibit extreme wealth and power, eccentric dress and manners, obscene language, or some other uncommon traits. Then society can aim its outrage at a small, alien group without having to face up to the need to alter its own behavior. It is easier to find such scapegoats for almost all forms of pollution than for other major problems like poverty, poor housing, or racism. Solutions to those problems would require millions of Americans to change their own behavior patterns, to accept higher taxes, or both.

The possibility that technological solutions can be devised for most pollution problems may also lengthen the public prominence of this issue. To the extent that pollution can be reduced through technological change, most people's basic attitudes, expectations, and behavior patterns will not have to be altered. The traumatic difficulties of achieving major institutional change could thus be escaped through the "magic" of purely technical improvements in automobile engines, water purification devices, fuel composition, and sewage treatment facilities.

Financing the fight against pollution

Another aspect of anti-pollution efforts that will strengthen their political support is that most of the costs can be passed on to the public through higher product prices rather than higher taxes. Therefore, politicians can demand enforcement of costly environmental quality standards without paying the high political price of raising the required funds through taxes. True, water pollution is caused mainly by the actions of public bodies, especially municipal sewer systems, and effective remedies for this form of pollution require higher taxes or at least higher prices for public services. But the major costs of reducing most kinds of pollution can be added to product prices and thereby quietly shifted to the ultimate consumers of the outputs concerned. This is a politically painless way to pay for attacking a major social problem. In contrast, effectively combatting most social problems requires large-scale income redistribution attainable only through both higher taxes and higher transfer payments or subsidies. Examples of such politically costly problems are poverty, slum housing, low-quality health care for the poor, and inadequate public transportation.

Many ecologists oppose paying for a cleaner environment through higher product prices. They would rather force the polluting firms to bear the required costs through lower profits. In a few oligopolistic industries, like petroleum and automobile production, this might work. But in the long run, not much of the total cost could be paid this way without driving capital out of the industries concerned and thereby eventually forcing product prices upwards. Furthermore, it is just that those who use any given product should pay the full cost of making it—including the cost of avoiding excessive pollution in its production. Such payment is best made through higher product prices. In my opinion, it would be unwise in most cases to try to pay these costs by means of government subsidies in order to avoid shifting the load onto consumers. We need to conserve our politically

88

limited taxing capabilities to attack those problems that cannot be dealt with in any other way.

Still another reason why the cleaner-environment issue may last a long time is that it could generate a large private industry with strong vested interests in continued spending against pollution. Already dozens of firms with "eco-" or "environ-" in their names have sprung up to exploit supposedly burgeoning anti-pollution markets. In time, we might even generate an "environmental-industrial complex" about which some future President could vainly warn us in his retirement speech! Any issue gains longevity if its sources of political support and the programs related to it can be institutionalized in large bureaucracies. Such organizations have a powerful desire to keep public attention focused on the problems that support them. However, it is doubtful that the anti-pollution industry will ever come close to the defense industry in size and power. Effective anti-pollution activities cannot be carried out separately from society as a whole because they require changes in behavior by millions of people. In contrast, weapons are produced by an industry that imposes no behavioral changes (other than higher taxes) on the average citizen.

Finally, environmental issues may remain at center stage longer than most domestic issues because of their very ambiguity. "Improving the environment" is a tremendously broad and all-encompassing objective. Almost everyone can plausibly claim that his or her particular cause is another way to upgrade the quality of our life. This ambiguity will make it easier to form a majority-sized coalition favoring a variety of social changes associated with improving the environment. The inability to form such a coalition regarding problems that adversely affect only minority-sized groups usually hastens the exit of such problems from the center of public attention.

All the factors set forth above indicate that circumstances are unusually favorable for launching and sustaining major efforts to improve the quality of our environment. Yet we should not underestimate the American public's capacity to become bored—especially with something that does not immediately threaten them, or promise huge benefits for a majority, or strongly appeal to their sense of injustice. In the present mood of the nation, I believe most citizens do not want to confront the need for major social changes on any issues except those that seem directly to threaten them—such as crime and other urban violence. And even in regard to crime, the public does not yet wish to support really effective changes in our basic system of justice. The present Administration has apparently concluded that a relatively "low-profile" government—one that does not try to lead the public into accepting truly significant institutional changes—will most please the majority of Americans at this point. Regardless of the accuracy of this view, if it remains dominant within the federal government, then no major environmental programs are likely to receive long-sustained public attention or support.

Some proponents of improving the environment are relying on the support of students and other young people to keep this issue at the center of public attention. Such support, however, is not adequate as a long-term foundation. Young people form a highly unstable base for the support of any policy because they have such short-lived "staying power." For one thing, they do not long enjoy the large amount of free time they possess while in college. Also, as new individuals enter the category of "young people" and older ones leave it, different issues are stressed and accumulated skills in marshaling opinion are dissipated. Moreover, the radicalism of the young has been immensely exaggerated by the media's tendency to focus attention upon those with extremist views. In their attitudes toward political issues, most young people are not very different from their parents.

There is good reason, then, to believe that the bundle of issues called "improving the environment" will also suffer the gradual loss of public attention characteristic of the later stages of the "issue-attention cycle." However, it will be eclipsed at a much slower rate than other recent domestic issues. So it may be possible to accomplish some significant improvements in environmental quality—if those seeking them work fast.

PUBLIC OPINION AND ENVIRONMENTAL QUALITY
A Reappraisal

TIMOTHY O'RIORDAN

In accordance with policies established under the Air Quality Act of 1967, the Massachusetts State Public Health Department instructed a technical advisory commission to recommend suitable air quality standards for sulphur dioxide and particulate emissions for the Boston metropolitan area. In due course, the commission tabled its report and was amazed to discover that a considerable body of public opinion demanded standards that were 25 to 35% better than their recommended levels for these two classes of emissions. Two public hearings were held; both were well attended and widely publicized. In light of this powerful expression of public concern, the commission agreed to tighten up its proposed emission standards, but only to a level considerably lower than the vociferous public groups had requested. When questioned later on why he did not heed more fully the demands of these groups, the chairman of the commission stated that he did not regard the public as "competent" to testify about the standards, since "they didn't understand what the numbers meant." He went on to say that all the commission wanted was some expression from public

AUTHOR'S NOTE: *The author is grateful to the National Advisory Committee on Water Resources Research, Department of Energy, Mines and Resources, Ottawa, for funding part of this research.*

ENVIRONMENT AND BEHAVIOR, June, 1971, Vol. 3, pp. 191-213.

opinion that the public wanted "pure air," and the technical people would decide how to achieve it (Lockeretz, 1970).

This story highlights a number of issues relating to the broad question of public opinion and environmental quality.

(1) To what extent should public opinion influence technical judgments which affect the nature of the environment in which all of us live?

(2) To what extent is the opinion expressed that of a public knowledgeable of the issues and competent to make judgments?

(3) To what degree are the views of the participating groups representative of the general public will (if such a thing exists and can be measured)?

(4) How can we resolve the growing conflict between the "expert," who believes his professional judgment should be paramount and seldom considers the "lay" public competent to advise on questions of technical speciality, and some members of the public, who are becoming dissatisfied with the traditional posture of accepting technical opinion and who wish to be directly involved in the decision-making process?

(5) Assuming that the public's view should be considered, in what way can this be identified and most suitably incorporated into the decision-making process?

A CASE STUDY

Behind all these questions, of course, is the basic issue of what exactly the role of public opinion is in environmental quality decision-making. This is a much easier question to ask than it is to answer, but before attempting to develop a general model, I would like to clarify the nature of the relationship and some of the problems involved a little further by use of a case study with which I was involved in 1969.

Situated on the southern shores of Shuswap Lake in southern British Columbia are two small communities—namely Salmon Arm Village (population 1,800) and Salmon Arm District Municipality (population 4,200) (Figure 1). Despite their geographic contiguity, the two settlements are amalgamated and thus are administered by two separate councils. During the period 1966-1969, both councils were grappling with the problem of how best to treat and dispose of their municipal sewage. The village, being smaller and more densely settled, was serviced by a partial system of sewers which collected septic tank effluent and discharged it without further treatment directly into the lake near the municipal wharf (Figure 2). The district, on the other hand, was unsewered and serviced by individual septic tanks. In 1966, a group of residents living in a closely settled area of the district immediately to the southwest of the village became alarmed at the spectacle of surface seepage from their septic tanks. There was a distinctly unpleasant smell in the neighborhood, and residents expressed anxiety over the quality of their drinking water (Salmon Arm Observer, 1966c).

The district council could see no low-cost solution to this problem, other than that of persuading the village to extend its sewerage to this neighborhood (Salmon Arm Observer, 1966b). Though the village was initially willing to do this, the two councils could not agree upon a satisfactory financing formula (Salmon Arm Observer, 1966a). Meanwhile, the problem got no better, and under pressure from both trade and private citizens' groups, both councils decided to embark on separate new sewage treatment and disposal schemes. Each council hired its own consulting firm, and each of these prepared a separate scheme for secondary treatment of the effluent with lake discharge.[1] These were the lowest-cost solutions, which were in keeping with provincial pollution control policy.[2] These proposals can be seen in Figure 2.

While these proposals were being considered, however, Skaha Lake in the Okanagan Valley south of the Shuswap experienced a major algal bloom (see Figure 1). This bloom was an unpleasant manifestation of entrophication or accelerated biological enrichment, and its occurrence has been extensively investigated elsewhere (Vollenweider, 1968). Although there is no complete agreement on the matter, it is now generally conceded that nitrates, phosphates, and a number of micronutrients play an important role in controlling algal growth. Such nutrients are not removed by conventional secondary treatment processes, and, at a rate depending upon the flushing action of the lake water receiving the effluent, gradually build up over time (Stein and Coulthard,

93

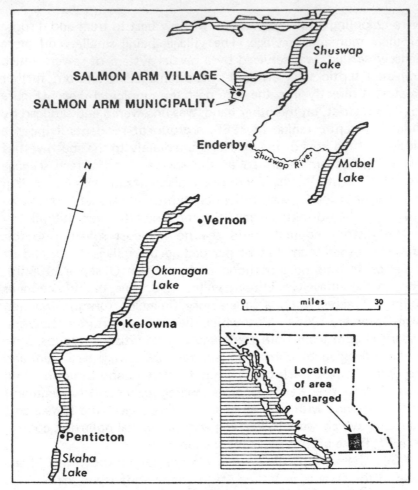

Figure 1: LOCATION OF SHUSWAP LAKE, THE SALMON ARM COMMUNITIES AND THE OKANAGAN VALLEY, B.C.

1968). The Skaha bloom was the first of its kind in British Columbia and attracted much press comment (Vancouver Sun, 1967). Both in 1967 and in the succeeding year, when a bloom also occurred, it was estimated that tourist revenue in the Okanagan Valley dropped by a third—a loss of some $5 to $7 million each year (Osoyoos Chamber of Commerce, 1969).

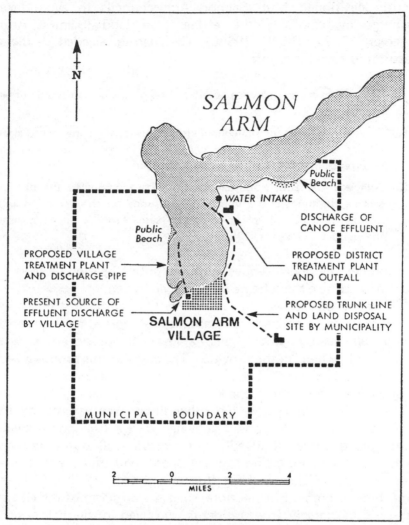

Figure 2: THE VARIOUS PROPOSALS CONSIDERED BY SALMON ARM VILLAGE
AND THE SALMON ARM DISTRICT MUNICIPALITY FOR THE TREAT-
MENT AND DISPOSAL OF MUNICIPAL SEWAGE

Naturally, the residents of the Salmon Arm area were concerned that such an occurrence might also afflict the Shuswap. In late 1967 and early 1968, the Shuswap Rural Ratepayers Association and the Salmon Arm and District Ratepayers Association frequently petitioned both Salmon Arm councils to avoid lake discharge by disposing the effluent on land (Salmon Arm Observer, 1967a, 1967b, 1968b). The District acceded to these pressures for three reasons:

(1) The ratepayers groups were voters and taxpayers and so could not be ignored.

(2) Three of the seven district councillors had personally experienced algal blooms elsewhere and argued persuasively in council that such an occurrence must not happen in Shuswap Lake.[3]

(3) Although the B.C. Pollution Control Board permitted the district scheme, it imposed a number of conditions on the operation and maintenance of the plant to ensure satisfactory effluent quality (Salmon Arm Observer, 1967c).

In addition, the board requested that a public hearing be held in the district before the scheme be finally approved.

Before the public hearing took place, the district instructed its consultants to examine the feasibility of spreading untreated sewage on nearby sandy soils, a low-cost solution that was practiced elsewhere in the province. The costs of this proposal and of other solutions by the two councils are presented for comparative purposes in Table 1.

The village council, on the other hand, was assured by its consultants that the proposed activated sludge (secondary treatment) plant, while admittedly not removing all nutrients, was acceptable to the Pollution Control Board, and that the lake was large enough to absorb the effluents without any ill effect for some time to come. Furthermore, since the criticism of the village scheme came largely from residents who lived in the district and beyond, the council did not feel the same political pressure to act as did the district.[4]

For a period of eighteen months, the two councils remained stalemated; the village council refused to consider land disposal of raw sewage, citing the dangers of health hazard and land subsidence as serious obstacles (Salmon Arm Observer, 1968a). The district council, on the other hand, was equally steadfast in its

TABLE 1
ESTIMATED TOTAL CAPITAL COST, OPERATING COST
AND ANNUAL COST AND ANNUAL TAXATION PER HOUSEHOLD
FOR VARIOUS PROPOSED SEWAGE TREATMENT SCHEMES[a] ($)

Municipality	Total Capital Cost	Operating Cost	Annual Cost	Cost per Household
Salmon Arm Village: secondary treatment.plant lake disposal	320,000	24,600	40,000	65
Salmon Arm District: land disposal lagoon	220,000	12,000	25,000	104
Salmon Arm District and Village: tertiary treatment	420,000	36,000	N/A	N/A
Salmon Arm District and Village: land disposal lagoon	379,000	18,500	47,000	59 (V) 90' (D)
Salmon Arm District and Village: secondary treatment and land disposal	519,000	27,000	66,700	83 (V) 120 (D)

N/A Not available
(V) Cost to Salmon Arm Village
(D) Cost to Salmon Arm District

a. This information is based on best estimates by the town clerks of the three municipalities involved, and should not be considered as final figures. Figures for the initial District proposal for lake discharge were not available.

refusal to permit any form of lake discharge. The obvious compromise was a joint scheme for secondary treatment and land disposal, but neither council seriously considered this move initially, because it was assumed the public would not be willing to pay the additional costs. Although the basic issues associated with entrophication and sewage disposal were outlined in the local newspaper, the members of both councils admitted they had made little personal attempt to discover just what the public *did* feel about the matter, nor had they ever clearly stated the relative costs of the alternative proposals in terms which the public could understand—namely increased taxes.

In the summer of 1969, the author sampled the opinions of a cross-section of the local population[5] and discovered the following:

(1) There was widespread concern over the future quality of Shuswap Lake. The lake was not only a tourist attraction, and therefore a valuable component of the local economy, but was extensively used by local residents for recreational purposes (Table 2). Furthermore, as can be seen from Table 3, though a majority of those interviewed felt that the lake was not particularly polluted at present, 81% felt that its quality would deteriorate in the future.

(2) There was considerable disapproval regarding the decision by the village to discharge secondarily treated effluent into the lake. Of the combined sample from both communities, 74% were opposed to this decision (54% strongly opposed). Furthermore, it appeared that a substantial number of the public based their judgments on a thorough understanding of the situation; over 41% clearly knew of the relationship linking sewage disposal and entrophication. (The local newspaper probably contributed largely to this high degree of awareness; over 65% stated that the newspaper was a "most important source" for providing them with information on the problem).

(3) The interest in preserving the lake was sufficiently strong that a large number of respondents felt prepared to pay substantial amounts for sewage treatment; 56% stated that they were willing to pay at least $60 per year (a 12% increase in local taxes); and 20%, $120 per year (a 25% increase in local taxes). These figures should perhaps be regarded more as an expression of residents' desire to preserve a clean

TABLE 2

SUMMER USE OF SHUSWAP LAKE COMPARED WITH OTHER
SUMMER ACTIVITIES AS EXPRESSED BY A SAMPLE
OF LOCAL RESIDENTS (in percentages)

	Frequently[a]	Seldom[b]	Never
Swimming	66.2	13.9	19.9
Fishing	36.8	32.7	30.5
Boating	30.5	33.1	36.4
Water Skiing	17.7	21.4	60.9
Camping	22.9	27.8	49.3
Hunting	21.8	24.1	54.1
Hiking	15.4	22.2	62.4
Golf	8.6	13.2	78.2

a. More than once per week.

b. Once or twice per month.

98

TABLE 3
OPINION OF SALMON ARM RESIDENTS TO NEARBY
LAKE WATER QUALITY (in percentages)

(a) Quality of Skaha/Shuswap Lake at present:	
Very dirty	4.1
Dirty	23.7
Neither dirty nor clean	58.6
Clean	9.8
Very clean	6.8
(b) Quality of Skaha/Shuswap compared with past:	
Better	0.8
Same	32.3
Worse	44.7
Don't know	22.2
(c) Future quality of Skaha/Shuswap compared with present:	
Better	2.3
Same	4.9
Worse	81.2
Don't know	11.6

lake than as a specific statement of willingness to pay for pollution control, since at the time of the interview, the actual costs had not been made public.

(4) Despite the fact that so many people held reservations over lake discharge, few had publicly expressed their concern via any of the normal channels (Table 4). This inaction was perhaps partly explained by the fact that a surprising number doubted if any form of political action would influence the local council (Table 5). In addition there was a notable expression of personal political inefficacy; 30% felt that, individually, they could do nothing to influence the course of events with regard to the control of water quality on the lake (Table 6).

In October 1969, the results of this poll were presented to a joint meeting of the two Salmon Arm councils at the same time the district council received a report from its consultants that land disposal of either raw or treated sewage was technically feasible. In light of these findings, the two councils agreed to embark on a joint project whereby secondarily treated effluent would be pumped onto the nearby beachland for disposal (Salmon Arm Observer, 1969).

TABLE 4
POLITICAL ACTION TAKEN BY A SAMPLE OF SALMON ARM RESIDENTS IN RELATION TO DETERIORATING WATER QUALITY (in percentages)

	Yes	No
Letter to local council	2.6	97.4
Letter to M.L.A.	4.9	95.1
Letter to M.P.	3.0	97.0
Joining an action group	12.4	87.6
Letter to local paper	1.9	98.1
Phoning radio station	2.3	97.7
Attending public meetings	21.1	78.9

TABLE 5
EFFECTIVENESS OF POLITICAL ACTION TO CONTROL WATER QUALITY DETERIORATION AS EXPRESSED BY A SAMPLE OF SALMON ARM RESIDENTS (in percentages)

	Effective	Not Effective	Don't Know
Letter to local council	24.1	54.5	21.4
Letter to M.L.A.	20.3	58.6	21.1
Letter to M.P.	23.7	52.6	23.9
Joining an action group	46.6	33.1	20.3
Letter to local paper	26.7	50.0	23.3
Phoning radio station	20.7	54.9	24.4
Attending public meetings	39.5	39.1	21.4

TABLE 6
RESPONSE BY A SAMPLE OF SALMON ARM RESIDENTS TO THE STATEMENT "I FEEL THAT MY CONCERN HAS VERY LITTLE EFFECT IN INFLUENCING THE AMOUNT OF POLLUTION IN SHUSWAP/SKAHA LAKE AND THAT SUCH INTEREST THAT I HAVE DOESN'T DO ANY GOOD" (in percentages)

Strongly agree	7.5
Agree	23.7
Neither agree or disagree	26.6
Disagree	21.4
Strongly disagree	18.8

Figure 3 portrays schematically the sequence of events which led to the final Salmon Arm decision. With a number of minor modifications, this diagram would seem to be applicable to a large class of environmental quality issues. It is based upon the work of Wengert (1955) and Kasperson (1969a, 1969b) and it visualizes a decision process evolving from group struggle. Initially, an environmental stress is perceived by a special interest group (either public or private) as imposing a threat to its accustomed way of life. This stress may appear in the form of a perceived shortage of a resource, such as water or timber, or a sudden catastrophe, such as flood or hurricane, or a gradually deteriorating condition which is regarded as increasingly undesirable, such as air or water pollution. This stress may be communicated directly to the decision maker (the politician) or may pass from the threatened group directly to a reasonable public agency (for example, in the United States the local office of the Corps of Engineers; in certain cases a large private organization may be responsible for the first decision, largely through internally derived expert advice—i.e., with minimal discussion at the political level). If the political pressure exerted by such a group is sufficient to create stress upon the decision maker, he will seek expert advice from a consultant or a public agency as to possible alternative courses of action. Normally, the professional experts contacted at this point are limited both in their terms of reference and in the cost ceilings for their proposals, and, due to the specialized nature of their training or the traditional practices of the organizations for which they work, offer a relatively narrow range of alternatives (see National Academy of Sciences, 1966). Rarely in the past have deliberations included any specific public discussion, though it is possible for the decision maker to parry potentially adverse community reaction by publicly extolling the merits of one or more of the proposed alternatives and emphasizing the urgency, seriousness, and need for low-cost solution of the problem. Not infrequently, the consultant's recommendation of a particular alternative is adopted by the responsible decision-making body. This is Decision 1 on the diagram, and may be the final decision.

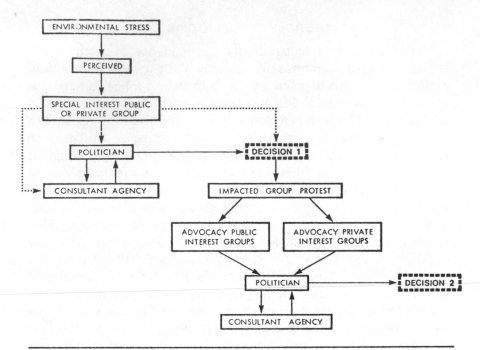

Figure 3: A SCHEMATIC REPRESENTATION OF POLITICAL CONFLICT OVER ENVIRONMENTAL QUALITY ISSUES

However, in many cases concerning environmental quality, such decisions do not take fully into account the wider environmental impact of the proposed action, or the opposition from impacted groups. Such groups, acting either in their own self-interest or from an advocacy standpoint for general environmental protection, are sometimes capable of exerting considerable political opposition against a proposal. Sometimes the groups are private interest groups protecting their self-interest—for example, when industry protests the excessiveness of a pollution control program—or they may be public antipollution or environmental control organizations advocating stiffer general pollution control policies or countering a specific proposal to dam a valley or carry out logging in a national park; sometimes they are the same groups who initiated the original political pressure and who were not satisfied with Decision 1. If the political pressure exerted by one or more of such groups is sufficient to create political conflict, the

102

decision maker may seek to resolve this conflict by requesting his advisers (new advisers or the same ones as before) to take a second look at the alternatives in question (including the possibility of taking no action at all). This result is Decision 2, which usually incorporates some degree of "public opinion," however that may be defined. In some instances, the politician may seek to diffuse potential group opposition by such methods as (a) launching a public relations campaign to point out the merits of the proposed scheme, (b) using his technical advisers as scapegoats, (c) issuing partial or misleading information, (d) announcing a detailed investigation regarding the issue, or (e) holding a public hearing, hoping to divide and weaken the opposition by encouraging the different groups to present separate and sometimes conflicting briefs.[6] Such tactics may, of course, backfire, but they are not uncommon strategies to mollify potential public protest.

LESSONS FROM THE MODEL

What can we learn from this model and from the Shuswap case study—in particular, about the role of public opinion and environmental quality? I think there are six factors which we should bear in mind.

(1) Resource management is essentially a process of pluralistic group bargaining, and the "public interest" is really the residue of this conflict rather than the positive expression of the public will. This point is clearly made by Wengert (1955).

(2) Group conflict is predominantly issue-oriented, and its major point of entry into the struggle is "post facto." This, of course, focuses the action and heightens the conflict but is hardly conducive to rational debate.

(3) The vast majority of the general public never participate in this process, particularly concerning broad policy questions, though their presence is always considered in the sense that they hold the sanction of the vote. Nevertheless, as illustrated by the Shuswap study, their views cannot and should not be ignored, for though the majority may be "silent," they are not *necessarily* indifferent to questions of

103

environmental quality. That silence may be as much a function of political inefficacy and limited information as it may be to the holding of mild preferences.

(4) Public protest is largely identified with a variety of advocate groups. In the case of the "conservation" advocate group (such as anti-pollution organizations or "save the beaches" associations, and so on), the membership may constitute a tiny faction of the general public who may be involved for a variety of selfish or altruistic reasons (O'Riordan, 1971) but it is spearheaded by a highly committed leadership that is capable of arousing very strong passions (Hendee et al., 1969).

(5) The role of professional consultants is a highly important one in this process and, regardless of popular criticism of their advice, their influence will continue to be important.

(6) The final decision is frequently a compromise falling somewhere between the extreme positions taken by the various advocate groups. This process of incrementalism and bargaining to achieve what is desirable rather than what is optimal has been well presented by Chevalier and Cartwright (1966) and Holden (1966). In some cases, there is no room for compromise, for example, the preservation of scenically or historically unique sites (though part of the site may be protected), and consequently the conflict may be prolonged and very bitter (Freeman, 1969).

RESEARCH NEEDS

It will be readily apparent that the arrangement as presented in Figure 3 is not a very satisfactory one for making environmental quality decisions. Communication and information channels between the decision makers and those who are affected by such decisions are imperfectly developed; the professional advisers are as wary of public involvement as a vociferous section of the public is of the adequacy of technical judgment; protest usually develops around issues rather than around broad questions of policy; and we have little idea of the representativeness of the advocacy groups. The real challenge is to try and improve the process and still make it workable, given the complexity of environmental issues and the very real difficulties of identifying and evaluating public opinion.

In what ways do we identify and evaluate public opinion with regard to environmental issues at present? Apart from analyzing the various interest group positions through public hearings, letters to newspapers, and petitions, probably the most popular method (and the one used in the Shuswap study) is the so-called public "attitude and perception" survey (Breslow, 1962; de Groot and Samuels, 1962; Medalia, 1965; Frederickson and Magnas, 1968; Auliciems and Burton 1970; Sewell and Burton, 1971). By and large, what these studies have generated is an expression of individual cognition and opinion. Generally, respondents have been asked to rank the relative importance of air or water pollution in the context of other community issues such as unemployment, crime, and housing availability. In addition they have been asked how they identify such pollution, what sources are most to blame and how much they are willing to pay to see it reduced (or eliminated) in the form of increased taxes, higher prices on goods, or both.

Such studies are valuable in that, assuming good questionnaire design and minimal interviewer bias, they do solicit views of the "silent majority," which otherwise would go entirely unrecorded. They also permit the investigator to comment on the relative concern over environmental issues in the community sampled vis-à-vis other issues at the time of the survey. They are further useful in identifying how people are reacting to environmental management programs and in discovering just how much they know or don't know about various local issues of importance. For example, they often reveal quite interesting misperceptions. In a recent study of air pollution in Toronto, Auliciems and Burton (1970) found that most respondents identified air pollution most readily in visual or olfactory terms (for example, particulate matter, oil refinery smells) and that the potentially more hazardous gaseous pollutants (sulphur dioxide, carbon monoxide, and various oxides of nitrogen), which are not so readily identifiable by the primary senses, were not regarded as so serious.

Although these gases were not observed in levels giving rise to any physiological ill-effects, the same study recorded that thirty percent of the interviewed sample nevertheless complained of respiratory and eye irritation, leading the authors to the conclusion that factors other than the presence of pollutants were influencing people's judgments. Studies such as these help us identify misperceptions and assist us in designing further studies to ascertain how and why these arise. In addition, such studies can be quite useful as part of a public education campaign, for they highlight areas where more information is required.

By their very nature, however, such studies are of fairly limited usefulness in helping us to solve the basic question of how we can incorporate public opinion more effectively into the decision-making process, principally because they do not allow us to get down to the really basic issues. Surely, what we are really trying to discover is the *intensity* of an individual's feelings about an environmental quality issue measured in terms of how much he is willing to sacrifice in money (via taxes or higher prices), time (in educating and informing himself), and effort (in responsible political participation and in self-discipline) in order to achieve more desirable levels of such quality. When he is asked to rank various community problems, we have little idea how much he is willing to trade off between these issues. For example, given that, say, 83% of an interviewed sample answer that air pollution is the "number 1" problem, how much are they willing to see their general taxes rise, or to accept a cutback in, say, the schools or roads program to meet improved air quality standards? Apart from the obvious difficulties of deciding normatively what degree of pollution control would be "desirable," very few people have any real idea of how much they will be committed to in this regard. The result is that, when faced with this kind of question, many who state that pollution is most serious tend to be noncommittal when it comes to paying for its control. Thus, in the Toronto study (Auliciems and Burton, 1970), although 83% felt that pollution control was extremely important and ranked it first on a list of community issues, 41% of the sample were either not prepared to pay for the control of this pollution or not willing to commit themselves to a specific figure.

In light of these remarks, it would seem appropriate that we focus our attention on more detailed small-group studies to try and elucidate how the public evaluate various levels of environmental quality. For example, we need to know a lot more about how people react to various kinds of information, what incentives are necessary to arouse their interest, and to what extent they are likely to react under varying conditions. Thus, if we were to make a lot more information available over a large number of issues of public concern, how much of this can people absorb and for how long? In what way can the information be distilled to make it more digestible? What media of information presentation is most suitable to maintain interest and attention? There is little doubt that the media do affect public opinion particularly in creating short-lived but intense public feeling over specific issues, but how the media can be used more effectively in the area of information presentation is still the subject of much research.

Secondly, we need to develop better techniques to assess how people trade off various kinds of amenity and disamenity. In essence, what we are really after is the nature of an individual's indifference curve between two or more amenity factors such as less traffic noise and convenient access to a local park. In Britain, the Social and Community Planning Research Council (1970) has devised an "amenity trade off" game in which participants are asked to allocate a certain sum of money to improve various amenities in their neighborhoods and to rate these preferences against their evaluation of existing conditions. The game holds much promise, but requires sophistication, especially in the avoidance of price tags for various levels of amenity.

Thirdly, using specific groups and more detailed attitude-scaling techniques, much can be learned about how users react to changing environmental conditions. For example, in the recreational field, the studies by Lucas (1964), Hendee et al. (1968), and Shafer (1968; Shafer and Meitz, 1969) have thrown some light on the manner in which recreationists respond to such factors as increased crowding, deteriorating ecological surroundings, or alternative management proposals. Studies such as these are proving vital for future management decisions regarding the use of recreational sites. For example, Hendee et al. (1968) discovered there were noticeable attitude differences between dedicated wilderness lovers and casual visitors to the same wilderness area in their motivations, their behavior, their tolerance of crowding, and their view of existing and proposed management measures. The former group was far more resistant to any form of "management" and was far less tolerant of crowding than was the latter, yet the latter group comprised eighty percent of the total sample. So for whom do we manage these wilderness areas—the "sensitive" minority or the "tolerant" majority? The resolution of this dilemma will not be easy, but at least recreation managers have a better idea of the problem as a result of these user-attitude studies, and various management alternatives can be identified and proposed to user groups in a more meaningful way.

However, all these attitude and perception studies assume some predictable correlation between the verbal expression of behavior and the actual deed. Yet, such an assumption flies in the face of a considerable body of literature which doubts that such a connection exists (see Deutscher, 1966). This in itself is a very serious methodological problem, for the majority of such public opinion studies rely extensively upon this relationship, and, indeed, recommend public policy changes on the basis of the evidence gained. We appear to be a long way from understanding all the factors influencing human behavior, nor can we readily predict how individuals or groups will react, even if they express an attitude shift (Festinger, 1964). Perhaps more empirical analysis of group behavior under varying experimental conditions (e.g., various degrees of air pollution in simulated conditions) and eventually in more complex and realistic environments might provide some valuable clues.

Fourthly, we need to know a lot more about the life cycles of environmental advocacy groups. There is ample literature dealing with interest groups and voluntary associations (Warriner, 1961; Milbraith, 1965; Hagedorn and Labovitz, 1968; Alford and Scoble, 1968a, 1968b), but to date we have little information on the proliferation of antipollution groups that have sprung up in the past two years. Harry et al. (1969) have pointed out that wilderness preservation conservationist groups tend to be largely composed of the upper-socioeconomic elite in terms of income, education, and occupation, and that the active members of such groups tend to confine their political activities largely to the conservation preservation ethic. Do these findings hold for the antipollution groups, the save the beaches associations, or other instrumental or expressive groups dedicated to the resolution of specific issues or improved public policies? Are the members of these latter groups better informed on environmental issues or more passionate, or both, than the public at large? To what extent do the views of these groups reflect the broad mass of public opinion? What factors motivate people to join such groups, and to what extent are individuals participating or peripheral to its activities? What are the tactics of the various kinds of environmental action groups? Is there any relationship between the tactics employed and the objectives pursued (Chant, 1970; De Bell, 1970a, 1970b)?

The Shuswap case study showed that the instrumental rate-payers groups were remarkably representative of local opinion *in that particular issue* and indicated that, though a surprising number of people were pessimistic about the efficacy of their own opinions in a local pollution issue, nevertheless a large number placed the greatest faith in the political power of such pressure groups (Table 5).

CONCLUSIONS

Given research along these lines, we might be in a better position to assess more critically the role of public participation in resource allocation. It would undoubtedly be desirable to amend Figure 3 to involve public opinion *before* final decisions are made, and it would appear that the dialogue that should take place should be based on as much information as is reasonably possible, to provide an adequate understanding of that information, a willingness on the part of resource managers and professional advisers to incorporate public opinion in their deliberations, and a reasonable sense of trust among all the participants involved.

Whether such an ideal state of affairs can ever be achieved is, of course, the major question, for there are a number of pitfalls along this path. For one thing, not everyone can get excited about pollution control. A number of studies (Frederickson and Magnas, 1968; Swan, 1970) have shown that underprivileged groups would sooner see funds directed into welfare and equity programs. This is a legitimate complaint that is frequently overlooked in the antipollution rhetoric and underlines the need to enmesh environmental quality programs with other important social and economic objectives. For another, not everyone wishes to be involved in the deliberations of all public issues (until or unless the impact of such an issue directly and adversely affects them). For yet another, it may not be possible for everyone who is interested to have a sufficient grasp of a complex issue so as to be capable of making a sound judgment. Multiply this by a number of disparate but equally complex issues, and the difficulties are further compounded. A sort of information indigestion could all too easily occur. Finally, and of very real concern, is the fact that, by requesting public response, the environmental manager is faced with so many alternative suggestions and conflicting demands that to make any decision at all within a reasonable space of time becomes impossible. In any case, by the time he is actually able to announce his decision, he may be confronted by a sudden change of the collective public heart; after all, it was only ten or so years ago that a few "crank" conservationists were talking about environmental quality!

Some of these potential difficulties can be tackled. For example, environmental education is still in its infancy and, as it grows, the reservoir of public knowledge and awareness will expand enormously (see Grimshaw and Briggs, 1970: though we should be careful of attitude "brainwashing" and the moral arrogance of the environmentalists that conservation, solitude, wilderness, and the like are a "good" ethic. Some people may not see it this way; do we ignore them?). Secondly, it is not impossible to visualize new kinds of participating techniques, where televised simulation models are linked via a computer to the viewer's telephone. By dialing certain combinations of numbers, the viewer could record his preferences, discover how these would affect the future, and learn of the implications of his wishes. Thirdly, we are just beginning to think about an "environmental tax" (the effluent charge is an example of this [Kneese and Bower, 1968; Dales, 1968]), which would be imposed on various forms of environmental use in proportion to the amount of environmental inconvenience imposed. The revenue from this tax could be used to "bribe" *in certain cases* those who are affected by such use. Such bribes would have to be in the form of equivalent compensation, not merely replacement value. This idea would not always be suitable, for example, in cases where priceless amenity was involved (though here the environmental tax could be set prohibitively high); but in cases where sacrifices do have to be made, it could be used to transfer payments from the gainers to the losers, something we have not been very good at in the past. Certainly, this would help to reduce potential opposition, but it is not a panacea.

So really we are only at the beginning of a long road, strewn with potholes. But there are signs for optimism. An increasing number of public agencies are committed to public information and participation programs (for example, the Susquehanna River Basin study by the Corps of Engineers). More and more politicians recognize the need to sound out and incorporate public opinion in their decision-making calculi over environmental matters, and with the growing success of multidisciplinary environmental study centers, the professional resource managers of the future are likely to be responsive to ecological issues and to public opinion. However, in the final analysis, success will depend upon our individual and collective desire to seek better standards of environmental quality, a determination which will require that we clearly recognize the sacrifices we must make in the reduction of other desirable objectives such as material wealth and individual freedom. If we cannot make such a commitment, then surely public opinion will continue to be inconsistent, shifting, and unclear, and hence the value of public opinion analysis as a guide for long-term public policies in environmental management will be increasingly called to question.

NOTES

1. Since the district was faced with the cost of providing a sewerage system as well as a treatment plant, it was keen to minimize the cost of the treatment plant. The secondary treatment process its consultants recommended was the spyrogester system, a less efficient system than the standard activated sludge or trickling filter process. A similar spyrogester system was installed in Canoe, a small settlement in the northern part of the municipality in 1967 (see Figure 2).

2. The Provincial Pollution Control Board is responsible for establishing standards and issuing permits for all waste discharges in the province. All discharges into inland waters are required to be of secondary treatment standard.

3. Based on personal interviews with all aldermen.

4. Upon receiving a letter of protest from the Shuswap Rural Ratepayers Association over the proposed village scheme, one village alderman is reported to have exclaimed, "Who are these people anyway? They do not pay taxes and so have no right to criticise" (Salmon Arm Observer, 1967b).

5. The sample consists of 266 interviews drawn randomly from the electoral lists of both communities (total p = 6,000). This represents about 4% of the total population. It is extremely difficult to test for the representativeness of the sample compared with the socioeconomic characteristics of the total population as the relevant census information covers a far larger area than the two Salmon Arm municipalities. However, by drawing randomly from election lists, it was hoped that a reasonably representative sample of the opinions of the voting and tax-paying public would be produced.

6. Recently, for example, the B.C. Pollution Control Board granted a permit to a mining company to dispose of 9.3 million gallons per day of copper mine tailings into a convenient outlet. The minister responsible for this decision admitted that the permit had been guaranteed to the company before the public hearings had been held, since the company had invested a considerable sum on its development. The public hearings were therefore a sham (Vancouver Sun, 1971).

REFERENCES

ALFORD, R. A. and H. M. SCOBLE (1968a) "Sources of local political involvement." Amer. Pol. Sci. Rev. 42, 4: 1192-1206.

——— (1968b) "Community leadership, education and political behavior." Amer. Soc. Rev. 33, 2: 259-272.

AULICIEMS, A. and I. BURTON (1970) "Perception and awareness of air pollution in Toronto." Natural Hazards Research Working Paper 13. University of Toronto.

BRESLOW, L. (1962) Air Pollution: Effects Reported by California Residents. Berkeley: University of California Department of Health.

CHANT, D. A. [ed.] (1970) Pollution Probe. Toronto: New Press.

CHEVALIER, M. and T. J. CARTWRIGHT (1966) "Towards an action framework for the control of pollution." Paper D30-1 in Canadian Council of Resource Ministers, National Conference on Pollution and our Environment. Ottawa: Queen's Printer.

DALES, J. H. (1968) Pollution, Property and Prices: An Essay in Policy Making and Economics. Toronto: Univ. of Toronto Press.

DE BELL, G. [ed.] (1970a) The Environmental Handbook. New York: Ballantine.

——— (1970b) The Voter's Guide to Environmental Politics. New York: Ballantine.

DEUTSCHER, I. (1966) "Words and deeds: social science and social policy." Social Problems 13: 235-254.

FESTINGER, L. (1964) "Behavioral support for opinion change." Public Opinion Q. 28, 4: 404-417.

FREDERICKSON, A. G. and H. MAGNAS (1968) "Comparing attitudes toward water pollution in Syracuse." Water Resources Research 4, 5: 877-889.

FREEMAN, A. M., III (1969) "Advocacy and resource allocation decisions in the public sector." Natural Resources J. 9, 2: 166-175.

GRIMSHAW, P. W. and K. BRIGGS (1970) "Geography and citizenship: pupil participation in town and country planning." Geography 55, 3: 307-314.

DE GROOT, I. and W. S. SAMUELS (1962) People and Air Pollution: A Study of Attitudes in Buffalo, N.Y. Washington, D. C.: Department of Health, Education and Welfare.

HAGEDORN, R. and S. LABOVITZ (1968) "Participation in community organizations by occupation: a test of three theories." Amer. Soc. Rev. 33, 2: 272-283.

HARRY, J., R. GALE, and J. HENDEE (1969) "Conservation: an upper-middle class social movement." J. of Leisure Research No. 3: 246-254.

HENDEE, J., R. P. GALE, and J. HARRY (1969) "Conservation practices and democracy." J. of Soil and Water Conservation 24, 6: 212-215.

HENDEE, J., W. R. CATTON, Jr., L. D. MARLOW, and C. F. BROCKMAN (1968) "Wilderness users in the Pacific Northwest: their characteristics, values and management references." Forest Research Paper PNW-61. Portland, Ore.: Department of Agriculture.

HOLDEN, M., Jr. (1966) "Pollution control as a bargaining process." Publication 9. Cornell University Water Resources Center.

KASPERSON, R. E. (1969a) "Environmental stress and the municipal political system: the Brockton water crisis of 1961-66," pp. 480-496 in R. E. Kasperson and J. V. Minghi (eds.) The Structure of Political Geography. Chicago: Aldine.

——— (1969b) "Political behavior and the decision-making process in the allocation of water resources between recreational and municipal use." Natural Resources J. 9, 2: 176-211.

KNEESE, A. V. and B. T. BOWER (1968) Managing Water Quality: Technology Economics Institutions. Baltimore: Johns Hopkins Press.

LOCKERETZ, W. (1970) "Arrogance or clean air." Science 168, 3932: 651-652.

LUCAS, R. C. (1964) "Wilderness perception and use: the example of the boundary waters Canoe area." Natural Resources J. 3, 3: 394-411.

MEDALIA, M. Z. (1965) "Community perception of air quality: an opinion survey in Clarkston, Washington." Publication 999-AP-10. Department of Health, Education and Welfare.

MILBRAITH, L. W. (1965) Political Participation. Chicago: Rand McNally.

National Academy of Sciences (1966) "Alternatives in water management." Publication 1648. National Research Council Committee on Water.

O'RIORDAN, T. (1971) "Factors affecting the perceptions and attitudes of participants in decision making in resources management: a strategy for public involvement," in W. R. D. Sewell and I. Burton (eds.) Attitudes and Perceptions in Resources Management. Ottawa: Queen's Printer.

Osoyoos Chamber of Commerce (1969) Personal communication (July).

Salmon Arm Observer (1969) October 30.

——— (1968a) December 18.

——— (1968b) January 4, February 14, February 21.

———.(1967a) September 14, September 28, November 16.

——— (1967b) November 9.

——— (1967c) August 24, August 31.

——— (1966a) September 22.

——— (1966b) September 8.

——— (1966c) June 16.

SEWELL, W. R. D. and I. BURTON [eds.] (1971) Attitudes and Perceptions in Resources Management. Ottawa: Queen's Printer.

SHAFER, E., Jr. (1968) "Perception of natural environments." Environment and Behavior 1, 2: 71-82.

——— and J. MEITZ (1969) "Aesthetic and emotional experiences rate high with northeastern wilderness hikers." Environment and Behavior 1, 2: 187-198.

Social and Community Planning Research Council (1970) "What will you pay for amenity?" Economist (May 23): 76-77; (June 6): 64.

STEIN, J. and J. COULTHARD (1968) Report of Investigations into Okanagan Lake Water Quality. Victoria: B.C. Department of Lands, Forests and Water Resources.

SWAN, J. (1970) "Response to air pollution: a study of attitudes and coping strategies of high school youths." Environment and Behavior 2, 2: 127-152.

Vancouver Sun (1971) January 28: 26.

——— (1967) August 27, August 29, August 31, September 7.

VOLLENWEIDER, R. A. (1968) "The scientific basis of entrophication with particular emphasis on phosphorous and nitrogen as factors causing entrophication." Publication DAS (CSI) 68-27. Organization for Economic Cooperation and Development. Paris.

WARRINER, C. K. (1961) "Public opinion and collective action: formation of a watershed district." Administrative Sci. Q. 6, 3: 333-359.

WENGERT, N. (1955) Natural Resources and the Political Struggle. New York: Doubleday.

114

Concern for Environmental Rights
Among College Students*

By RILEY E. DUNLAP, RICHARD P. GALE
and BRENT M. RUTHERFORD

RECENT SURVEYS show that most Americans are in favor of "saving the environment." Opinion polls indicate strong endorsement for cleaning up the landscape, protecting natural resources, stopping pollution, and preventing over-population (1). Moreover, this pro-environment sentiment appears to have had some effect in recent elections (2). But despite the widespread existence of favorable attitudes toward environmental protection, it is clear that a national commitment to solve environmental problems will run head-on into many traditional values and time-honored practices. The preservation of natural resources will have to achieve primacy over the concern for economic growth and development. The prevention of pollution will have to overcome the inherent tendency of industry to minimize production costs. And programs to control population growth will entail a revision of the belief that the determination of family size is an inalienable right. In short, it would appear that efforts to bring about *fundamental change* in major areas of environmental abuse will meet stiff opposition (3).

Given the deep entrenchment of these practices and values which (directly or indirectly) encourage environmental abuse, it becomes highly questionable whether *meaningful* reforms can be carried out. Recently, however, some segments of the American public appear to have gone beyond a simple desire to "save the environment," and have developed a commitment to pursue solutions which openly challenge established practices and values. The most visible manifestation of this development is on college campuses, where many students have adopted "environment" and "ecology" as their "cause." If any segment of the population is willing to assert the primacy of environmental concerns and to challenge traditional values such as those emphasizing economic growth, it would seem to be the new generation of ecologically aware students.

To date, however, little systematic information is available on the degree of student commitment to the environmental movement (4). Media ac-

* This is a revision of a paper presented at the annual meeting of the Pacific Sociological Association, Honolulu, Hawaii, April, 1971. We wish to thank the Center for Ecological Studies at the University of Oregon for providing funds for data collection. Thanks are also due Ronald G. Faich for his helpful comments on an earlier draft.

AMERICAN JOURNAL OF ECONOMICS AND SOCIOLOGY, January, 1973, Vol. 32, pp. 45-60.

counts of specific environmental campaigns, detailed information on specific environmental organizations, and surveys of Earth Day "protest incidents," do not enable us to gauge the extent of commitment among college student populations (5). In an effort to obtain more systematic data, we recently surveyed a sample of university students on environmental issues. Specifically, we were interested in the degree to which they are willing to assert the primacy of pro-environment policies over established practices and dominant values which conflict with the maintenance of a quality environment. To accomplish this, we inquired about the students' attitudes on environmental issues, obtained information on their past involvement in environmental campaigns, and looked for indications of future commitment in their responses to a series of hypothetical situations involving environmental abuse.

I

DATA COLLECTION PROCEDURES

THE SURVEY was conducted at the University of Oregon, a liberal arts university with an enrollment of approximately 15,000, which is located in the small urban area of Eugene-Springfield. The survey was carried out in May of 1970, approximately one month after the National Environmental Teach-In of April 22nd ("Earth Day"), when nationwide interest in the environment was very high.

A sample of the Oregon student body was drawn from the Spring-term registration list. One name was selected from each page by use of a table of random numbers. Foreign students were excluded, and a total of 300 graduate and undergraduate students were selected, approximately 2 per cent of the student body. The total sample was compared to the university population on the variables of sex, year in school, and campus residence, and was found to be very representative.

Questionnaires were mailed to the sample members and, a week later, postcard reminders were sent out. A total of 237 usable questionnaires were returned, representing a 79 per cent response rate. The non-respondents were compared to the respondents on the variables mentioned above, and were found to be similar. Thus, our respondents should provide, within probability limits, an accurate representation of the Oregon student body.

II

ATTITUDES TOWARD ENVIRONMENTAL ISSUES

ALTHOUGH ENVIRONMENTAL CONCERN has been manifest on a wide range of specific issues, most environmental action has dealt with three

116

broad areas of concern—conservation of natural resources, prevention of pollution, and control of population growth. Several items in the questionnaire focused on the conflict between pro-environment practices and traditional practices in these three areas, as well as the conflict between the concern for environmental welfare and economic priorities in general.

Conservation of natural resources is the oldest environmental issue. Conservationists have focused on a wide range of issues, such as seeking governmental protection of vast areas of land and urging a policy of "wise use" for forests, grazing lands, and mineral resources (6). Nearly all such programs concerning natural resources inevitably raise questions, either explicitly or implicitly, regarding the autonomy of private (individual or corporate) property rights relative to the rights of larger social collectives (7).

The position of our student sample on the issue of public versus private control over natural resources was tapped by the following item:

1. *Where natural resources are privately owned, society should have* NO *control over what the owner does with them.*

Few students endorse this laissez-faire perspective, as only 12 per cent express agreement with the statement, while 83 per cent disagree and 5 per cent are undecided (8). However, when we cast this conflict of public versus private rights into more concrete terms, by introducing the possibility of forced sale of private property for public use, many more students side with the property owner as indicated by their responses to the following item:

2. *Preservation of areas for public use justifies government purchase of private property even when the owners do* NOT *wish to sell.*

Almost half (46 per cent) of the students disagree, indicating their opposition to the use of condemnation as a method of asserting public rights over private property. Only 39 per cent indicate agreement, and an additional 15 per cent are undecided. Thus, although nearly all of the students feel that society should have some control over privately owned natural resources, many stop short of endorsing actual condemnation, the most extreme manifestation of societal control over private property in our society.

That many of the students fail to endorse the use of condemnation should not, however, be interpreted as a serious handicap for environmentalists, since relatively few environmental protection programs require the condemnation of private property. In contrast, a large number of such programs do require monitoring and regulating private concerns to prevent the despoliation of natural resources. These programs rest on the premise that the public has the right to exert *some* control over the use of private property, and such a premise is strongly endorsed by our sample. The students are clearly opposed to allowing private concerns to exploit their property with little thought given to the consequences for future use.

The second general area of interest is pollution control, and we focused on industrial pollution since it is surely one of the most critical environmental problems. Despite widespread concern, efforts to control industrial pollution have met with only limited success (9). Government regulations, usually written with the help of the industry in question, typically impose standards which are "economically feasible" rather than "technologically possible." When such standards are developed, a generous amount of time is allowed for their implementation, and even once adopted, enforcement may be minimal and permissive (10). Clearly a much more unyielding posture is required of governmental agencies if industrial pollution is to be controlled effectively. Such a posture is definitely supported by our sample, as indicated by their responses to the following item:

3. *Industries should be forced to shut down if they refuse to meet government pollution standards.*

An impressive 81 per cent of the students agree with this statement, while only 13 per cent disagree, with 6 per cent undecided. Endorsement of this statement indicates both agreement with the idea that governmental regulation of industry is legitimate, and further, that government should adopt strong sanctions when industry fails to conform to existing regulations.

Yet, such a stringent position is difficult to maintain in practice, as legal injunctions causing shut-downs lead to loss of jobs. In fact, industry's most effective weapon in opposing strict pollution controls is to raise the "payroll versus pollution" argument, and assert that rigid enforcement of "unfeasible" regulations will force plant closures and put people out of work. Pressure generated by such threats, particularly when the possibility of an industry leaving the community is also raised, has generally discouraged strict enforcement and permitted industries to continue operating on the promise that they are "working on the problem." However, students' responses to an item which poses the "pollution versus payrolls" dilemma indicate that industry's threats may become less effective. The item states:

4. Even if an industry is causing substantial pollution, it should NOT *be forced to stop operations if it would put people out of work.*

Only 20 per cent of the sample are willing to put payrolls before pollution by agreeing with this statement. A large majority, 68 per cent, disagree with the statement, indicating that their commitment to controlling industrial pollution overrides their fears about the consequences of strict enforcement (11). This ready endorsement of *strong* governmental control of industrial pollution challenges the traditional ideal of limited government in general, and limited regulation of industry in particular. Responses to items 3 and 4 clearly indicate that the students are willing to support new, tougher programs and regulations aimed at controlling industrial pollution.

The third area of concern, population control, has become a central issue for many environmentalists. It has also turned out to be a very emotional issue, as programs designed to control population growth have been met with cries that the determination of family size is a private matter, not subject to regulation (12). Yet, such a belief is strongly challenged by our sample, as evidenced by their responses to the following statement:

5. A married couple should have as many children as they wish, as long as they can adequately provide for them.

Only 21 per cent of the sample agree with this statement, while 72 per cent disagree with it, and 7 per cent are undecided. What is even more critical, however, than whether the students are in favor of people having as many children as they wish, is the extent to which they will support specific measures designed to discourage large families. The following item summarizes one such proposal which has received considerable public attention (13):

6. The number of children a couple can claim as tax deductions should be limited to TWO, *except for families having more than two children before the new law is put into effect.*

Surprisingly, 70 per cent of the sample agree with this proposal, while only 22 per cent disagree, with the remaining 8 per cent undecided. In other words, the students not only reject the *principle* of unlimited family size, but seem willing to translate their beliefs into specific measures designed to encourage small families.

The discussion of the first two general areas of environmental concern, resource preservation and pollution control, implied a conflict between environmental and economic priorities. Since we believe that the widespread tendency to place economic considerations before environmental considerations represents the most formidable hurdle for proponents of "environment first" policies, we wanted to pose this conflict in a more explicit manner for the students (14). Therefore, we included the following item:

7. *More emphasis should be placed on society's environmental rights and less placed on individuals' economic rights.*

The responses of the students are consistent with their pro-environment responses to the previous items, as 71 per cent express agreement with that statement, while only 18 per cent disagree, and 11 per cent are undecided. We also tried to present the environment-economic conflict in somewhat less abstract terms by juxtaposing environmental and economic rights at the individual level. The conflict at this level was expressed in the following way:

8. *One person's right to a clean environment is* NOT *as important as another's right to gainful employment.*

Here the students are even more likely to assert the primacy of environmental considerations. Thus, 77 per cent disagree with this statement, while only 13 per cent agree, and 10 per cent are undecided. In short, responses to these two items indicate the students feel the time has come to place more emphasis on "environmental rights," and less on economic rights.

In summary, the responses to these eight items reflect a great amount of concern for the welfare of the environment by the members of the sample. Except on the issue of condemnation of private property, the students strongly endorse policies designed to reduce environmental abuse. It must be remembered, however, that the eight items deal with several areas of environmental concern. Therefore, before concluding that a large majority of the students *consistently* favor more emphasis on environmental welfare, we must determine whether the responses in these different areas are empirically linked. In other words, we need to know if students who take a pro-environment position on one item tend to take a similar position on the other items.

III

THE CONCERN FOR ENVIRONMENTAL RIGHTS SCALE

THE QUESTION of response consistency leads directly to a consideration which is central to attitude measurement—the extent to which several individual items can be treated as a unidimensional scale. Although the eight items refer to several different areas of environmental concern, in each one the respondent must choose between the "rights" of individuals and society to a good environment, and the rights of individuals, families, industries, or other entities to pursue policies which may result in personal or economic gain at the expense of environmental quality. In other words, a person must choose between the primacy of environmental interests and the primacy of other interests, ranging from the desire to have as many children as one wishes, to allowing industry to minimize production costs by disposing of untreated wastes. Given the conceptual commonality of the eight items, it seems logical to expect that students who take a position favoring environmental rights on one item will tend to do so on the other items. In other words, we have reason to believe that we can legitimately combine the eight items into a single scale.

We formed a summated rating scale, by assigning directionality to the items, and then summing the students' scores on all eight items (15). We then used several quantitative techniques designed to assess the appropriateness of combining the items into a scale.

The first procedure, the computation of corrected item-to-total correlations, provides a measure of internal response consistency (16). For the eight items, all item-to-total correlations are positive, ranging from 0.34 to 0.58, and average 0.45 (all are statistically significant beyond the .01 level). Another measure of internal consistency is Cronbach's *alpha,* which provides the mean of all possible split-half reliabilities (17). In the present case, *alpha* is 0.76, which is quite substantial for an eight-item scale (18).

More precise examination of response consistency involves an analysis of the item structure. An inter-item correlation matrix was constructed and all correlations are positive and average 0.29, ranging from 0.15 to 0.65 (all are statistically significant beyond the .05 level). Furthermore, factor analyzing the inter-item correlation matrix yields information strongly supportive of uni-dimensionality (19).

Lastly, analysis indicates that the total scores assigned to respondents are sufficiently varied so that item responses appear to be systematic rather than random. A Hoyt analysis of variance shows that the null hypothesis of random differences among respondents can be rejected at less than the .01 level (F = 4.09, df = 236 and 1652) (29). Thus, score differences from respondent to respondent are in all likelihood systematic rather than random differences.

In sum, the foregoing evidence indicates that students who take a position favoring environmental rights on one of the eight items are very likely to do so on the others. Therefore, it seems appropriate to treat the eight items as a unidimensional scale, and in the following analyses we shall refer to this new variable as the Concern for Environmental Rights Scale (CERS).

In order to facilitate tabular presentation, we divided the sample into approximate quartiles on the CERS (21). In the following discussion we will consequently refer to scores on this variable as ranging from 1 (low) to 4 (high).

IV

ENVIRONMENTAL CONCERN AND ENVIRONMENTAL ACTION

A PERENNIAL QUESTION concerning the study of attitudes is their relationship to actual behavior (22). Two facts of this relationship are the linkage of attitudes to past behavior, and their utility in predicting future behavior. In the present research we are particularly interested in the relationship between the strong environmental commitment which our student respondents reflect on the attitudinal items in the Concern for Environmental Rights Scale, and their actual involvement, both past and future, on behalf of the environment.

First, we asked the students if they had ever taken action on an environmental issue, and a surprising 50 per cent indicated that they had. Their experiences are highly related to the specific environmental issues which attained prominence on the University of Oregon campus during 1969–70. Thus, when asked to name the specific issue on which they *first* became involved, one quarter of the students who had taken some action mentioned opposition to U.S. Forest Service plans to allow timber cutting in a virgin forest area near Eugene. Almost as frequently mentioned (by 22 per cent) was a campaign to halt U.S. Army plans to store nerve gas in Oregon. A wide variety of other issues was mentioned, with some type of pollution problem most widely cited (by 18 per cent). We also asked what specific action was taken the first time the students became involved on an environmental issue. A majority of those who had been active mentioned types of action which require neither expertise, in terms of detailed knowledge of an issue, nor a sustained commitment. Thus, of the students who have taken action, 27 per cent indicate attending a rally or demonstration as their first action, and 25 per cent mention signing letters or petitions. Less typical activities are direct physical action such as cleaning up an area (18 per cent), and types of action which call for considerable commitment, such as speaking to groups (8 per cent), organizing a campaign (5 per cent), and picketing or sitting-in (3 per cent).

As we expected, past action on behalf of the environment is strongly related to students' concern for environmental rights. As the data in Table 1 show, students who have high scores on the CERS are much more likely to have taken action than are those with low scores. For example, of the students with a score of 3 or 4, 65 per cent have taken action, while only 36 per cent of those with scores of 1 or 2 have taken such action.

In a similar vein, we inquired about the students' past participation in the various environmental organizations active on the University of Oregon campus during 1969–70 (23). We were surprised to find that 32 per cent of the sample indicate participation in at least one organization,

TABLE 1

Per Cent of Students Who Have Taken Action on an Environmental
Issue by Score on the Concern for Environmental
Rights Scale

	Score on the Concern for Environmental Rights Scale			
	1 (low)	2	3	4 (high)
% Who have taken action	34%	37%	66%	64%
	(56)	(65)	(58)	(56)

$x^2 = 20.39$, df $= 3$, P $< .001$

although in many cases the extent of activity is surely limited to such minimal actions as signing petitions. Involvement in these campus environmental organizations is also strongly related to concern for environmental rights, as indicated by the data in Table 2. Among the students with high scores (3 or 4) on the CERS, 43 per cent have participated in at least one of the campus environmental organizations, while among those with low scores (1 or 2), only 21 per cent have participated in one of these organizations (24).

V

COMMITMENT TO FUTURE ENVIRONMENTAL ACTION

THE PRECEDING DISCUSSION focused on past environmental action by the members of our sample. Generally the type of action in which they participated only slightly extended beyond traditional "middle class politics." Petitions, letter and telephone campaigns, and peaceful demonstrations aimed at mobilizing popular support were used, based on the assumption that the influence of an aroused public would be sufficient to produce a favorable outcome. However, if the premise underlying this paper is correct—that an unequivocal commitment to halt environmental abuse will sharply conflict with existing dominant values and practices—then measures necessary to dissuade abusers of the environment from continuing their harmful practices will have to extend beyond the traditional tactics of middle class politics. At least that is what past experience would indicate, as exemplified by the Civil Rights Movement (25). It was not until their demands were backed up by strong action, primarily peaceful (but illegal)

TABLE 2

Per Cent of Students Who Have Participated in a Campus
Environmental Organization by Score on the
Concern for Environmental Rights Scale

	Score on the Concern for Environmental Rights Scale			
	1 (low)	2	3	4 (high)
% Active in organization	9%	32%	39%	47%
	(56)	(65)	(59)	(57)

$x^2 = 21.19$, df = 3, P < .001

sit-ins, that meaningful legislation and other changes desired by Black people came about. We would not be surprised if environmentalists were similarly forced to take such strong actions to bring about change (26).

To obtain an indication of students' willingness to employ stronger tactics than those traditionally used in environmental campaigns, we presented our sample with several hypothetical situations of the type which frequently interest environmentalists. The two most pertinent and realistic are the following:

9. *The Forest Service announces a timber sale in a previously uncut area which has many recreational values.*

10. *A large industry is polluting the air and tells an environmental agency that it is "economically unfeasible" to install pollution abatement equipment before 1975.*

The students were asked what action, if any, they would be willing to take on each issue. They were presented with a list of tactics, ranging from letter writing to "illegal demonstrations, such as sit-ins, possibly leading to arrest," and asked to indicate the tactics they would be willing to use in order to obtain a favorable outcome on each issue. We were especially interested in the number of students indicating a willingness to resort to illegal sit-ins, since it is the most "extreme" tactic listed, and has seldom been used by environmentalists.

Surprisingly, very few students (less than 4 per cent) say they would take *no action* on the two hypothetical issues. What is perhaps even more

TABLE 3

Per Cent of Students Willing to Engage in Sit-Ins by Score on
the Concern for Environmental Rights Scale

	Score on the Concern for Environmental Rights Scale			
	1 (low)	2	3	4 (high)
% Willing to sit-in on:				
Timber sale issue [a]	6%	13%	23%	33%
	(53)	(64)	(57)	(57)
Industrial pollution issue [b]	18%	30%	36%	49%
	(55)	(64)	(58)	(57)

[a] $x^2 = 16.26$, df = 3, P < .001

[b] $x^2 = 12.67$, df = 3, P < .01

surprising, however, is that 19 per cent of the sample indicate a willingness to resort to sit-ins to prevent the sale of timber in a recrational area, and 33 per cent indicate a willingness to take similar action to prevent the continuance of industrial pollution. Although it is certainly the case that many of these students would not actually convert their expressed commitment into action, if only a fraction did so it would represent a very large number of demonstrators.

This willingness to resort to strong tactics is highly related to students' concern for environmental rights, as evidenced by the data in Table 3. Only 9 per cent of those with low scores (1 or 2) on the CERS are willing to sit-in to protest the sale of timber by the Forest Service, while 28 per cent of those with high scores (3 or 4) say they would sit-in. Similarly, only 24 per cent of the students scoring low on the CERS indicate a willingness to sit-in to prevent an industry from delaying installation of pollution abatement equipment, while 43 per cent of those with high scores express a willingness to sit-in. In short, students' concern for environmental rights is again seen to be highly related to environmental action, although this time at the hypothetical level.

VI

CONCLUDING REMARKS

WE BELIEVE the significance of the foregoing results lies in the fact that the students' concern for the environment, a concern which is strongly related to actual behavior, extends beyond simple endorsement of currently popular "save the environment" platitudes. Faced with decisions between environmental welfare and traditional concerns such as economic priorities, a large majority of the students consistently give primacy to environmental considerations. We doubt that adult populations, faced with these decisions, would place similar importance on the welfare of the environment. Consider for example, the responses of a cross-section of Oregonians to a recent Louis Harris survey (27). Fifty-three per cent volunteered "pollution" as one of the 'two or three most serious problems" facing their own community, and 98 per cent felt pollution was one of the most serious problems facing the state of Oregon. Yet, when later asked if they would favor a new industry coming into their community if it meant an increase in pollution, over half (55 per cent) were in favor of a new industry even if it caused a "slight" increase in pollution, while one-third were in favor of a new industry even if it caused a "large" increase in pollution (28). We expect our sample of students would have given very different responses.

Our data suggest that students (29), unlike much of the public, will give strong support to *meaningful* environmental reforms, even when such reforms challenge traditional priorities such as economic interests. But significant reforms will be difficult to achieve, and will come about only through the application of considerable pressure by concerned environmentalists. A critical question, then, becomes the extent to which this deep commitment to environmental quality held by students will be translated into sustained action.

As we indicated above, many students have already become involved in environmental action, although their involvement has generally been minimal and sporadic. Channeling students' concern for the environment into effective action on its behalf will depend, in large part, on the ability of environmentalists to include opportunities for student participation in campaigns on specific issues. As we noted above, almost half of the Oregon students who have taken action on an environmental issue first became involved in one of two specific campaigns (to prevent logging of a virgin forest area and to prevent the Army from shipping nerve gas to Oregon) which were well publicized on campus. Furthermore, the fact that the students express a *generalized* environmental concern, rather than a concern with specific areas such as population or conservation, becomes especially important since it implies that the *types* of problems focused on by environmentalists will not be a critical factor in determining student support. Our data clearly suggest that students will be receptive to a wide range of environmental issues.

Severe problems lie in the path of a major re-orientation of our society's environmental policies, but the fact that college students—who provided the vanguard of the civil rights and peace movements—are deeply committed to halting environmental degradation offers some hope (30). And since their attitudes concerning the importance of environmental welfare, especially their willingness to de-emphasize economic considerations, seem to cohere nicely with dominant values in the growing "counter culture" (31), it is probable that students will increasingly reject those traditions and practices in our society which encourage environmental abuse.

1. For example, see "Gallup Survey on Conservation," *National Wildlife*, 7 (April–May, 1969), pp. 18–19; "New Conservation Poll," *National Wildlife*, 8 (December–January, 1970), pp. 18–19; Robert S. Diamond, "What Business Thinks: The Fortune 500-Yankelovich Survey," *Fortune*, Vol. 81, pp. 118–19; Arvin W. Murch, "Public Concern for Environmental Pollution," *Public Opinion Quarterly*, 35 (Spring, 1971), pp. 100–106; and Rita James Simon, "Public Attitudes Toward Population and Pollution," *Public Opinion Quarterly*, 35 (Spring, 1971), pp. 93–99. In a 1970 national poll concerning top domestic priorities, 53 per cent of a Gallup sample said that reducing air and water pollution was one of the three problems which should receive governmental attention in the next two or three years. In 1965, only 17 per cent attributed as much importance to pollution reduction. See *Gallup Opinion Index*, Report No. 60, June, 1970, p. 8.
2. See "Earth Watch," *Saturday Review*, December 5, 1970, pp. 64–65.
3. Preventing litter is one of the few environmental "issues" which does not challenge traditional values. Consequently, there has been little opposition to efforts to "educate

the public" to clean up highways, use litter barrels, and so one. In fact, industry, as well as government, appears willing to sponsor such campaigns, and is quick to laud the efforts of citizen groups concerned with litter. How society will eventually confront the more basic problem of solid waste disposal is far more controversial. Efforts to solve a re-defined "litter problem" may enjoy far less industrial support when solutions such as banning nonreturnable containers, limiting elaborate packaging, and recycling paper, glass, and metals are actively pursued.

4. There have been, however, several polls of student opinion on environmental issues. See, for example, "How Students See the Pollution Issue," *Business Week*, February 7, 1970, pp. 86–88; *Gallup Opinion Index*, Report No. 55, January, 1970, pp. 20, 24; Alan E. Bayer, Alexander W. Astin, and Robert F. Boruch, "College Students' Attitudes Toward Social Issues: 1967–70," *Educational Record*, 52 (Winter, 1971), pp. 52–59; and "Playboy's Student Survey," *Playboy*, September, 1970, pp. 182–184. In the *Playboy* survey of 7,300 college students "the environment" was superseded only by "the war in Indochina" and "racial conflict" as the "single most important issue" facing our nation.

5. For example, see S. V. Roberts, "Better Earth: Report on Ecology Action Group, Berkeley, California," *New York Times Magazine*, March 29, 1970, pp. 8–9; W. B. Devall, "Ecology Action: The Roots of a Social Movement," paper presented at the Annual Meeting of the Pacific Sociological Association, Disneyland, Calif., 1970 (mimeo: Dept. of Sociology, Humboldt State College, Arcata, Calif.); and Alexander W. Astin, "New Evidence on Campus Unrest, 1969–70," *Educational Record*, 52, (Winter, 1971), pp. 41–47.

6. It is important to distinguish between two types of conservationists: the proponents of "conservation-wise-use" programs, and the backers of "conservation-preservation" policies. The former, exemplified by Theodore Roosevelt and Gifford and Amos Pinchot, seek more effective management of federal lands to conserve timber, water, grazing land, and other resources. The latter, typically members of voluntary organizations such as the Wilderness Society and the Sierra Club, are more concerned with the preservation of the natural environment for its own sake. For histories of the early conservation-wise-use movement, see Samuel P. Huntington, *Conservation and the Gospel of Efficiency* (Cambridge, Mass.: Harvard Univ. Press, 1959), and Elmo R. Richardson, *The Politics of Conservation: Crusades and Controversies, 1897–1913*, University of California Publications in History, Vol. 70, 1962. The more recent conservation-preservation movement which directly led to the contemporary environmental movement, is discussed in Roderick W. Nash, *Wilderness and the American Mind* (New Haven, Conn.: Yale Univ. Press, 1967).

7. For interesting perspectives on the conflict between private rights and the public interest in decisions relating to natural resources see Allen V. Kneese, "Protecting Our Environment and Natural Resources in the 1970's," in *The Environmental Decade* (Action Proposals for the 1970's), (Washington, D. C., Government Printing Office, 1970). For a perceptive view of some of the problems of our existing land ethnic, see Lynton K. Caldwell, "The Ecosystem as a Criterion for Public Land Policy," *Natural Resources Journal*, Vol. 10, 1970, pp. 203–221.

8. On each item the students were presented seven response categories. In addition to an "undecided" category, both agreement and disagreement were presented with three levels of intensity—"completely," "mostly," and "slightly." In this paper we discuss the responses in the simplified form of agree, undecided and disagree.

9. See J. Clarence Davies III, *The Politics of Pollution* (New York: Pegasus, 1970), and Ted Caldwell and Leslie L. Roos, Jr., "Voluntary Compliance and Pollution Abatement," pp. 236–267 in Leslie L. Roos, Jr., ed., *The Politics of Ecosuicide* (New York: Holt, Rinehart and Winston, 1971).

10. See Ralph Nader, "The Profits in Pollution," *The Progressive*, April, 1970, pp. 19–22, and Caldwell and Roos, *ibid.*

11. The students' response to the "payroll versus pollution" issue should not necessarily be interpreted as indicating a lack of concern with unemployment. They may very well feel that this is an industry ploy, and that when confronted with the choice of curtailing pollution or halting operations most industries will choose to stay in business.

12. Criticism of such programs has come from both the Left and the Right. For example, see Murray Bookchin, "Toward an Ecological Solution," *Ramparts*, May 1970, p. 10 and Gary Allen, "Ecology: Government Control of the Environment," *American Opinion*, May, 1970, p. 12.

13. This summarizes the proposal which was introduced in 1970 by Senator Robert Packwood of Oregon.

14. See Kenneth E. Boulding, "The Economics of the Coming Spaceship Earth," pp. 96–101 in Garrett De Bell, ed., *The Environmental Handbook* (New York: Ballantine/ Friends of the Earth, 1970) and Karl William Kapp, "Social Costs of Business Enterprise," pp. 82–90 in Marshall I. Goldman, ed., *Controlling Pollution: The Economics of a Cleaner America* (Englewood Cliffs, N. J.: Prentice-Hall, 1967). Senator Gaylord A. Nelson has noted how our legal system is biased against environmental considerations: "Our Anglo-Saxon common law tradition has focused protection on economic or personal injury. We are learning now, however, that environmental damages can be just as severe." See "The 'New Citizenship' for Survival," *The Progressive*, April, 1970, p. 36.

15. The scoring for items 1, 4, 5 and 8 was reversed since disagreement with them reflects a concern for environmental welfare. We purposely reversed the wording of one item in each of the four areas in an effort to avoid response set bias. Since there are 7 response categories for each item (see footnote 8) we assigned a "7" for the most pro-environment response and a "1" for the least pro-environment response. Thus, for the eight items, total scores can range from 8 to 56. The actual scores do in fact range from 8 to 56, with a mean of 41.8 and a standard deviation of 8.65. For a description of summated rating scales see Jum C. Nunnally, *Psychometric Theory* (New York: McGraw-Hill, 1967), chap. 14.

16. See George W. Bohrnstedt, "A Quick Method for Determining the Reliability and Validity of Multiple-Item Scales," *American Sociological Review*, Vol. 34, 1969, pp. 542–548.

17. See Andrew R. Baggaley, *Intermediate Correlational Methods* (New York: John Wiley & Sons, 1964), pp. 63–65 and Bohrnstedt, ibid.

18. Since reliability is partially dependent on number of items, if our scale was twice its present length, with the eight additional items equal in quality to the original ones, *alpha* would equal 0.86. See Baggaley, *ibid.*, pp. 79–80.

19. The pattern of successive eigenvalues emerging from a principal components analysis is indicative of a single dominant factor and subsequent error factors: 3.05, 1.13, 0.89, 0.86, . . . , 0.29. Moreover, no item is correlated less than 0.49 with the first factor, and the eight correlations average 0.61.

20. See Cyril Hoyt, "Test Reliability Estimated by Analysis of Variance," *Psychometrika*, Vol. 6, 1941, pp. 153–160.

21. The range of scores and number of cases for each of the approximate quartiles are as follows: lowest: 8 to 35 (N = 56), second: 36 to 42 (N = 65), third: 43 to 48 (N = 59), highest: 49 to 56 (N = 57).

22. For example, see Stephen M. Corey, "Professed Attitudes and Actual Behavior," *The Journal of Educational Psychology*, Vol. 28, 1937, pp. 271–280 and Howard J. Ehrlich, "Attitudes, Behavior, and the Intervening Variable," *The American Sociologist*, Vol. 4, 1969, pp. 29–34.

23. Eight organizations, concerned with a wide variety of environmental issues, were active during 1969–70. Three are local chapters of national organizations. Planned Parenthood and Zero Population Growth are concerned with the population problem, and the Sierra Club is a national environmental organization which began as an outdoor recreation and conservation-preservation organization. Four of the organizations, which are either local or state-wide in scope, were organized to deal with specific environmental problems. Save French Pete was organized to block Forest Service plans to log a virgin forest area 60 miles east of the campus. The Future Power Committee successfully campaigned to delay temporarily a planned municipal nuclear power plant. Nature's Conspiracy is a student organization which obtained its impetus from the Save French Pete campaign, and is concerned with a wide range of conservation problems. On the regional level, People Against Nerve Gas (PANG) carried out a successful campaign to prevent the Army from storing nerve gas in an eastern Oregon weapons depot. The eighth

organization is the University Outdoor Program, a student-run recreation organization which supplied the nucleus of activists for the Save French Pete campaign.

24. The strong relationship between score on the CERS and actual behavior on behalf of the environment is evidence that the scale has criterion validity. See Bohrnstedt, *op. cit.*, p. 542.

25. See, for example, Lewis Killian and Charles Grigg, *Racial Crisis in America* (Englewood Cliffs, N. J.: Prentice-Hall, 1964), and Donald Von Eschen, Jerome Kirk, and Maurice Pinard, "The Conditions of Direct Action in a Democratic Society," *Western Political Quarterly*, 22 (June, 1969), pp. 309–25.

26. One instance in which this has happened is in Santa Barbara, where good middle-class citizens, frustrated over their failure to "get oil out," occasionally resorted to surprisingly strong tactics. See Harvey Molotch's excellent account of events in "Oil in Santa Barbara and Power in America," *Sociological Inquiry*, Vol. 40, 1970, pp. 131–144.

27. "The Public's View of Environmental Problems in the State of Oregon," (New York: Louis Harris and Associates, 1970).

28. When we consider only those sample members who have college educations (and therefore more comparable to our student sample) the proportions favoring new industry decline, but not a great deal: 46 per cent of the college-educated adults will accept new industry if it causes a "slight" increase in pollution and 28 per cent will accept new industry even if it causes a "large" increase in pollution.

29. We realize the danger involved in generalizing from a study of one campus to students in general. However, we do *not* feel that University of Oregon students are atypical in their concern for the environment. Although there has been considerable interest and involvement in environmental issues at Oregon, this is also true of many colleges and universities. See Peter R. Janssen's survey of environmental action on U.S. campuses in "The Age of Ecology," pp. 53–62 in John C. Mitchell and Constance L. Stallings, eds., *Ecotactics: The Sierra Club Handbook for Environmental Activists* (New York: Pocket Books, 1970), and Astin, *op. cit.*

30. The importance of strong student support for the civil rights, peace, and environmental movements can be seen in a broader context. Historically a wide variety of phenomena, ranging from important social "causes" to fads (in music and dress, for example) appear to have spread to the larger society after first gaining popularity on college campuses.

31. See Theodore Roszak, *The Making of a Counter Culture* (Garden City, N. Y.: Doubleday, 1969). More recent, and wider ranging, exposition of the development of a new "consciousness" in American youth are presented by Charles A. Reich, *The Greening of America* (New York: Random House, 1970), and Philip Slater, *The Pursuit of Loneliness* (Boston, Mass.: Beacon Press, 1970).

The Land Ethic Realized: Some Social Psychological Explanations for Changing Environmental Attitudes[1]

Thomas A. Heberlein

Changing environmental attitudes from an economic to a moral orientation are discussed in terms of the activation of moral norms to guide and evaluate behavior. In controlled experimental situations, increasing levels of two variables (awareness of the negative interpersonal consequences and ascription of responsibility) increased the likelihood that moral norms influenced behavior. Changes in the social system are discussed which have increased both our awareness of, and the actual adverse consequences stemming from, a strict economic approach to the environment. Other modifications have made decision-makers responsible for these consequences. These changes have fostered the current moral fervor concerning the natural environment.

The rapid ascendance of the environmental crisis is probably attributable to the general moral turbulence of the sixties and the breadth of its popular appeal. The scenario for moral indignation had been gradually worked out in the earlier civil rights and war protest movements. It was a simple matter to apply these techniques to a new content area—the environment. While only some had been adversely affected by discrimination and the war, nearly everyone had experienced undesirable environmental change. This undoubtedly added to the scope of the movement. These, however, were merely precipitating causes necessary for the rise, and for that matter the decline, of such a movement. The important question is what happened to per-

---

[1] This paper is a revision of a paper originally presented at the meetings of the Rural Sociological Society in Washington, D.C., in August 1970. The author would like to thank Gilbert F. White and Shalom Schwartz for commenting on earlier drafts. The author of course takes full responsibility for the conclusions and generalizations in the article.

JOURNAL OF SOCIAL ISSUES, 1972, Vol. 28, pp. 79-87.

ceptions of the environment such that environment became a moral issue and a potential subject for such a movement. To answer this we shall examine some conditions which lead people to both make and evaluate decisions on the basis of moral standards, and then suggest how these same mechanisms were at work in society prior to the environmental crisis.

Traditionally, a strict laissez-faire economic orientation served as the basis for man's relationship to the natural environment. Appropriate behavior toward the natural world was behavior which was most expedient for the individual decision-maker. Adverse or favorable consequences for others of the decision were lumped into a residual category labelled "externalities" and were not part of the decision. As Leopold (1948) suggested two decades ago: "There is yet no ethic dealing with man's relationship to the land and to the animals and plants which grow upon it. Land . . . is still property. The land relationship is still strictly economic, entailing privileges, but not obligations."

A change from this tradition is evident. Decisions based solely on economic efficiency for the decision-maker and which entail deleterious consequences for the environment are being questioned in the public forum. Moreover, individuals in their own everyday management decisions are willing to incur greater costs in terms of time and effort to preserve the quality of the environment when they purchase non-leaded gasoline and returnable bottles, or when they bundle and recycle newspapers. The ethical standard which appears to be influencing these decisions is multifaceted and difficult to state succinctly. Leopold himself (1948) probably best summarized it when he said: "A thing is right when it tends to preserve the integrity, community, and beauty of the natural environment. It is wrong when it tends otherwise."

One aspect of this change is that it rejects the notion that man is separate from and superior to the natural world (White, 1967). Man is viewed as part of nature; he is inextricably related to the natural world. Rejecting this belief leads to a change in our view of the effect of environmental degradation on man. When man becomes part of the natural world, he is in some way diminished when it is disrupted. Under a strict economic orientation, the adverse effects on men present or future had little weight in the decision-making process—economic efficiency for the decision-maker was the sole criterion for evaluation. By eliminating the man-nature distinction, it is assumed that mankind is injured when the integrity, stability, or the beauty of the biotic community is disrupted, whether from oil spills, carbon dioxide increases in the atmosphere, or sanitary land fills. The real or potential threats of any decision for the biotic community and, hence, the human community are becoming as important as economic efficiency. Leopold labelled this change, which he had hoped for and which we are gradually realizing, as a change from the economic to the ethical: making decisions concerning the natural environment on the basis of morality rather than economics.

MORAL DECISIONS AND MORAL NORMS

To understand why this change has occurred, it is helpful to consider how one goes about making decisions based on morality. According to Schwartz (1970a) moral decisions are supposed to have three characteristics. First, moral decisions necessarily lead to interpersonal actions having consequences for the welfare of people affected by them. Second, decisions are classified as moral only when the person who makes them is perceived to be the responsible agent, that is, to have chosen the action knowingly and willingly when he could have done otherwise. Finally, the actions resulting from moral decisions and the agent held responsible for them are evaluated as good or bad according to the consequences the actions have for other's welfare. Culture specifications of what constitute good and bad interpersonal behavior, i.e., moral norms, are the reference points for these decisions.

Schwartz has been interested in the conditions which activate existing moral norms so that they influence behavior. For example, in our culture it is normative to help people in distress; yet, in many everyday as well as in a few notable instances, this norm has failed to influence behavior. In his investigations Schwartz found that two variables are crucial to the activation of norms. Norms will be activated and influence behavior when the decision-maker is aware of the consequences of his action for others and when he feels personally responsible for the action and its consequences (Schwartz, 1968a, 1968b). More recent work has indicated that experimentally increasing people's perception of the consequences of their choice for others and of their personal responsibility leads to increasing the incidence of volunteering for self-sacrificing behavior (Schwartz, 1970b).

Littering Behavior

Decisions guiding behavior which has an environmental impact appear to fit the same model. In a field experiment I examined littering behavior (Heberlein, 1971). Littering can be viewed as a behavior which is economically expedient for the individual. Carrying litter or searching out a proper receptacle is more costly for the individual than merely tossing away the unwanted object. The more noxious the litter and the more inaccessible appropriate modes of disposal, the greater the cost of not littering. A decision to refrain from littering involves bearing higher economic costs by adhering to cultural standards of appropriate behavior; it is essentially a moral decision.

It was hypothesized that the antilittering norm expressed in public sentiment, advertising campaigns, and laws (Keep America Beautiful, 1968) would be activated to influence behavior when the decision-maker was aware of the negative consequences of this action and felt personally responsible for these consequences. To test this theory, handbills urging voter registration were distributed to people who were strolling down the street in a resort community. Those who were observed to litter (i.e., to toss away the handbill) in a specified distance were interviewed (N = 36), as well as a randomly sampled control group of nonlitterers (N = 41). Without taking space here to describe controls and checks on this experiment (for which see Heberlein, 1971), it can be stated that there was strong support for the hypothesis. The zero-order correlation between awareness of consequences and littering behavior was $-.43$ ($p < .0005$) and those who ascribed responsibility to themselves were also less likely to litter (r = $-.31$, $p < .015$). The joint effects of ascribing responsibility and awareness of consequences yielded a multiple correlation of .49, with each variable accounting for a significant amount of the variance. These relationships suggest that when persons both are aware of the consequences of their action and feel personally responsible they will behave according to moral norms rather than economic expedience.

While the paradigm discussed was developed to explain the activation of moral norms, it may explain the *generation* of moral norms as well. When a decision necessarily leads to actions which have consequences for others and the person who makes the decision is perceived to be responsible, a moral norm is activated to define (in the case of the decision-maker) or to evaluate (in the case of those affected by the decision).

In a decision of this type when no specific norm applies, it is plausible that a new norm will be generated or an old but similar norm will be modified to accommodate the situation.

ENVIRONMENTAL ACTIONS AS MORAL DECISIONS

In this section I will attempt to show that the physical environment became a moral issue precisely because actions which had an effect on the environment came to fit this model. Until recently, decisions to discharge wastes into the environment were seen to have few negative consequences for others, or at least the ratio between negative consequences and the benefits of the decision was very small. Furthermore, decision-makers were not seen as personally responsible for these outcomes.

Consider decisions for industrial development early in our country's history. Most human consequences in terms of profits, jobs, and the conversion of raw materials into goods were positive. Since the rivers and air were clean, the slight additional effluent or smoke had relatively minor negative effects. Also, low population density downstream or downwind kept the sum total of adverse effects on human beings low. So, with a relatively unpolluted environment in conjunction with a low population density, the perceived human consequences were minimal.

To understand why the perceived responsibility of the decision-maker was minimal, we might briefly consider what kinds of situations lead people to be held responsible for their actions, both by themselves or by others. Schwartz (1970a) has reviewed a number of studies in terms of how various situational variables affect the ascription of responsibility. These variables fall into two related categories: (a) people are likely to hold themselves personally responsible if there are no others to whom blame can be shifted, and (b) people hold themselves responsible if they feel that they had some degree of choice in the decision. If decisions and actions are dictated or constrained by some force outside the individual—such as role restraints, actual coercion, or simple lack of alternatives—he is less likely to hold himself responsible or to be held by others as responsible for the consequences of his action. The plea, "I had no choice," is sufficient to shed responsibility.

The Role of Science and Technology

Technology has altered the responsibility of the decision-maker for the negative interpersonal consequences of his decision. In our early industrial and urban development, decision-makers had little choice but to pollute since there were no alternatives open to them. If one were going to build a paper or steel mill, dumping waste directly into the environment was about the only solution available to the decision-maker. In the past, then, the decision-makers were not responsible for the negative consequences of their decisions nor were these consequences particularly serious. Technology has effectively increased the number of alternatives open to the decision-maker. Pollution is no longer a necessary evil of the industrial process; it has become an option that can be expressed in terms of economic costs. For the first time the choice not to pollute has become a realistic option. Technology has made the decision-maker responsible.

In a recent survey of water users in Denver, over 85% of the respondents felt that the top level management of a company which disposed wastes in the water supply had both alternative actions and responsibility for the negative consequences of the pollution (Heberlein, 1972). Analysis of the relationship between perception of alternatives and attribution of responsibility for several roles suggested that although there is a small direct relationship between these variables, perception of alternatives is a necessary condition for attribution of responsibility.

The responsibility engendered by the availability of alternatives helps explain a perplexing matter. As Ableson (1971) noted, "One of the odd features of the emotional peak [of the environmental crisis] is that it occurred at a time when most of the important components of pollution had leveled off or declined." Herfindahl and Kneese (1965) corroborate the assertion about pollution levels by pointing out that since 1940: "Rivers have been cleared of their grossest floating materials; cities have substantially reduced the particulate matter in the atmosphere." A change in public attitudes before such effective action would have been extremely unlikely *since the action itself is necessary to establish the availability of alternatives.* The modification of the quality of the environment is the proof that the manager has alternatives; this in turn is what makes the manager responsible.

The other condition, the awareness of the negative consequences of environmental decisions, has been enhanced by science just as responsibility has been increased by technology. One of the effects of the scientific enterprise is to establish links between supposedly unrelated events. In this decade we have seen the links exposed between such diverse events as bug control and the thickness of egg shells, between smoke and heart failure. Management decisions which are economically rational for one individual may spell disaster for those far distant in time and space. Science has shown us these disasters. This caveat is the unifying factor of most of the popular journalism concerning the quality of the environment. Our daily newspapers trumpet the ways in which economically rational decisions spell doom for someone else. Science has been expanding our awareness of the real effects which are external to the decisions in a single economic unit, until the effects of the externalities are seen as violations of the cultural commitments to the health and welfare of the population.

The combination of increased population, increased pollution, and scientific research which has spelled out the adverse effects of pollution, has dramatically increased the negative consequences for others which stem from a strict economic approach to decisions involving the environment. Technology, furthermore, has made the decision-maker responsible for these adverse effects, since he knowingly and willingly chose them by avoiding the alternatives which it has produced. All of these things have acted to make environmental decisions into moral decisions, and we see the generation of moral norms to guide these decisions. Norms, or expectations about behavior, usually have sanctions to enforce them. These range from very informal to the formal or legal proscriptions. Legal sanctions are beginning to be generated and enforced; one suspects, although there are no hard data available, that the same is true for informal sanctions.

This approach to the generation of moral norms is corroborated by some additional empirical work. Schmitt (1964) examined the conditions under which people would invoke moral norms to gain outcomes favorable to them. When, he asked, will person A use a moral justification to get person B to modify his behavior? Person B was described as either willing or unwilling and either able or unable to perform the activity solicited by person A. His findings were that knowing that person B was *unwilling* and *able* explained 44% of the variance for A's invocation of moral norms to gain B's compliance. In the unwilling/able situation, moral obligation was invoked significantly more often than in the willing/able, unwilling/unable, and willing/unable situations. This parallels our previous arguments. Technology, by giving the decision-makers alternatives by which they can decide to reduce pollution, has placed them in the able but (if they don't decide to use them) unwilling group from the perspective of those who are affected adversely by their decisions. In response to the decision-maker's being placed in this group, we can expect, from Schmitt's data, that those who wish to modify the behavior of the decision-makers will invoke moral norms.

Schmitt also found that moral obligation is invoked more often when a person lacks alternatives for obtaining what he desires. This helps explain the fervor which surrounds environmental decision-making. One cannot obtain a clean environment by stopping only one polluter, the way one can obtain a car from only one dealer. To achieve the goal, all polluters must be stopped. And they are not interchangeable the way auto dealers are for the car buyer; it is in that sense that there is no alternative source of supply for a clean environment. Consequently, the invocation of moral norms is more likely.

Conclusion

Generalization from bits and pieces of laboratory findings, field experiments, and limited surveys to major social events is always risky business. Simple bivariate relations which account for only modest proportions of the total variance may not reasonably be adequate to interpret complex systems full of simultaneous causation and feedback loops. The conclusions of this paper should be taken with that degree of tentativeness which is inherent in a science that tries to explain complex natural phenomena.

The upshot of this analysis is that while technology and to a lesser extent science have been the villains of the environmental crisis, paradoxically they have enhanced the necessary conditions for a change in public attitudes. Science has helped increase awareness of consequences; while technology, by providing alternatives, has made the decision-maker responsible. These have placed normally innocuous and routine decisions into a domain where they are evaluated by moral rather than economic standards. It is not unlike the myth of the phoenix, for out of those things which caused the ashes of pollution have sprung the impetus for social change. The ethic which Leopold longed for appears to be rising from the very things which made the ethic necessary.

REFERENCES

Ableson, P. H. Changing attitudes toward environmental problems. *Science,* 1971, **172**, 3983.

Keep America Beautiful, Inc. Who Litters and Why. Mimeographed, 1968.

Heberlein, T. A. Moral norms, threatened sanctions, and littering behavior. Unpublished doctoral dissertation, University of Wisconsin, 1971.

Heberlein, T. A. Perception of alternatives and attribution of responsibility for a water pollution problem. Paper presented at the meeting of the Rural Sociological Society, Baton Rouge, Louisiana, August 1972.

Herfindahl, O. C., & Kneese, A. W. *Quality of the environment: An economic approach to some problems in using land, air, and water.* Washington, D.C.: Resources for the Future, 1965.

Leopold, A. *A Sand County almanac.* New York: Oxford University Press, 1948.

Schmitt, D. The invocation of moral obligations. *Sociometry,* 1964, **27**, 299–310.

Schwartz, S. H. Awareness of consequences and the influence of moral norms on interpersonal behavior. *Sociometry,* 1968, **31**, 355–369. (a)

Schwartz, S. H. Words, deeds, and the perception of consequences and responsibility in action situations. *Journal of Personality and Social Psychology,* 1968, **10**, 232–242. (b)

Schwartz, S. H. Moral decision making and behavior. In J. Macauley & L. Berkowitz (Eds.), *Altruism and helping behavior.* New York: Academic Press, 1970. (a)

Schwartz, S. H. Elicitation of moral obligation and self-sacrificing behavior: An experimental study of volunteering to be a bone marrow donor. *Journal of Personality and Social Psychology,* 1970, **15**, 283–292. (b)

White, L., Jr. The historical roots of our ecological crisis. *Science,* 1967, **155**, 1203–1207.

SECTION III

ENVIRONMENTAL DECISION-MAKERS

PREFACE TO SECTION III

ENVIRONMENTAL DECISION-MAKERS

To a certain degree we are all environmental decision-makers. In our personal habits, the products that we buy and the policies that we support (or fail to oppose) we all are involved in making decisions which ultimately may affect the quality of our environment. Clearly, though, there are some whose decisions are more weighty than others, whose actions directly and significantly influence our surroundings. These "key" decision-makers deserve special attention. We need to know more about the basic values and perspectives of these individuals, how they are shaped, and how they in turn shape environmental policy. Craik's overview more-or-less defines this field of study and touches on some of the evidence that is now available to us. Kraft and Sewell examine specific sets of decision-makers - Congressmen, engineers and public health officials - while Ingram speaks more generally of how the flow of information can affect the decision-making process. Those few selections can only suggest the kind of evidence that we need to fully understand the decisions that shape our environment, for better or for worse.

The Environmental Dispositions of Environmental Decision-Makers

By Kenneth H. Craik

By Kenneth H. Craik

abstract

ABSTRACT: A new interdisciplinary field of research has recently emerged which studies how persons comprehend the everyday physical environment, how they use it, how they shape it and how they are shaped by it. In seeking an objective understanding of the behavioral aspects of the total personal-societal-environmental system, professional environmental decision-makers, such as architects, urban planners and natural-resources managers, are strategic choices for psychological study. Within this context of environmental design and management, research is being directed toward clarifying the implicit assumptions about environmental behavior held by decision-makers, overcoming social and administrative distances from clients, and conducting systematic follow-up evaluations of the behavioral consequences of planning and design decisions. However, subtle and precise study of man-environment relations will require the development of psychological techniques providing a comprehensive and differentiated description of any person's orientation to the everyday physical environment. Methods for measuring individual differences in environmental dispositions are reviewed and their potential usefulness for advancing knowledge of the interplay between human behavior and the physical environment is illustrated.

ANNALS OF THE AMERICAN ACADEMY OF POLITICAL AND SOCIAL SCIENCE, May, 1970, Vol. 389, pp. 87-94.

144

IN Cambridge, a Harvard student checks his written directions, observantly proceeds afoot along the prescribed route, that is:

Quincy Square: south along Bow Street to Mt. Auburn Street; left to Banks Street; right to far (south) side of Peabody Terrace; right through housing to Memorial Drive; right to Dunster House, . . .

then records his impressions of that urban pathway on a standard descriptive check list, while, in a grove of the Harvard Forest in western Massachusetts, a landscape architect similarly describes the rural pathway he has just traversed, that is:

Begin at Route 32 one-half mile south of Connor Pond. Just beyond the parking lot on left, take wagon road that angles off highway to right. Follow down road as it becomes a narrow track, crossing brook and heading down through forest in a southwesterly direction. Continue beyond wooden structure (right) to red tape in grove at bottom.[1]

In northeastern Minnesota, visitors within the Boundary Waters Canoe Area indicate on a map the point at which they consider they had entered the wilderness, while in Ciudad Guayana, a rapidly developing industrial city in Venezuela, residents locate its most memorable features on maps they themselves have sketched.[2] In Frontier, Nebraska, a Great Plains farmer creates a story in response to a picture of a farmer harvesting wheat as a storm approaches on semiarid acreage not unlike

his own.[3] In Boston, a blindfolded person is moved through the financial district in a wheelchair, as he records his impressions of the soundscape of the city.[4] In Victoria, residents are asked whether they discern air and water pollution in their own urban environment.[5] In Salt Lake City and on the Louisiana State University campus, the interiors of major libraries and other public rooms are systematically assessed by panels of architects and typical users.[6] In Berkeley, forest-management experts view a landscape scene and make inferencess about its likely appearance ten years hence, while in San Francisco, architects and planners attempt to specify what social goals they sought, by means of what design decisions, for a public housing project.[7]

These diverse and geographically scat-

[1] David Lowenthal, et al., An Analysis of Environmental Perception: Interim Report (Washington, D.C.: Resources for the Future, Inc., 1967).

[2] Robert C. Lucas, "Wilderness Perception and Use: The Example of the Boundary Waters Canoe Area," Natural Resources Journal 3 (January 1964), pp. 394–411; Donald Appleyard, "Why Buildings Are Known: A Predictive Tool for Architects and Planners," Environment and Behavior 1 (December 1969), pp. 131–156.

[3] Thomas F. Saarinen, Perception of the Drought Hazard on the Great Plains, University of Chicago Department of Geography Research Paper No. 106 (Chicago: University of Chicago, 1966).

[4] Michael Southworth, "The Sonic Environment of Cities," Environment and Behavior 1 (June 1969), pp. 49–70.

[5] D. R. Lycan and W. R. Derrick Sewell, "Water and Air Pollution as Components of the Urban Environment of Victoria," Geographical Perspectives (Spring 1968), pp. 13–18.

[6] John B. Collins, "Perceptual Dimensions of Architectural Space Validated against Behavioral Criteria" (Ph.D. dissertation, University of Utah, 1969); Joyce Vielhaucr Kasmar, "The Development of a Semantic Scale for the Description of the Physical Environment" (Ph.D. dissertation, Louisiana State University, 1965).

[7] Kenneth H. Craik, "Human Responsiveness to Landscape: An Environmental Psychological Perspective," in Gary J. Coates and Kenneth H. Moffett, eds., Response to Environment, Student Publication of the School of Design, Vol. 18 (Raleigh, N.C.: North Carolina State University, 1969), pp. 168–193; Clare Cooper, Some Social Implications of House and Site Plan Design at Easter Hill Village: A Case Study (Berkeley: Center for Planning and Development Research, University of California, 1965).

tered events did not occur simultaneously but they all took place within the recent past, and they serve to illustrate the varied and sometimes ingenious strategies being employed in efforts to increase our understanding of the ways in which persons interact with their everyday physical environment.[8]

The interplay between human behavior and the physical environment engages a complex and little understood network of personal, societal, and physical variables. Not surprisingly, a growing consensus that this intricate system has gone awry is fostering a scientific examination of its behavioral aspects.

STUDYING ENVIRONMENTAL DECISION-MAKERS

In modern technological societies, responsibility for environmental policy-formation and decision-making is concentrated, to an unknown extent, within professional and institutional roles and positions. Remarkably little is known about environmental decision-makers such as architects, urban designers, transportation planners, landscape architects, natural-resources managers, and conservationists. Does their comprehension of the physical environment differ from that of their clients and other constituents, and, if so, what are the implications of these differences? What working assumptions about man-environment relations guide their decisions, and how accurate are they? What behavioral and social goals, if any, do they seek by means of what physical designs and management policies and with what success? What unintended behavioral, social, and environmental consequences result from their decisions?

There are plenty of reasons for advancing the hypothesis that environmental decision-makers differ from their clients in their perception, interpretation, and evaluation of the everyday physical environment. In addition to the impact of technical training, Alan Lipman has pointed to the increasing social and administrative distances which separate contemporary architects from their clients.[9] In undertakings of ever larger scale, such as retirement communities and new towns, environmental designers serve a clientele drawn from the full spectrum of society, yet often deal directly only with intermediary agents, such as private developers and governmental committees.

Indeed, a growing body of empirical evidence supports the hypothesis. In Ciudad Guayana, Donald Appleyard found that design and planning specialists differed not only from its native inhabitants, but also among themselves in their comprehension of the city.[10] Robert Hershberger has reported differences between architectural students and other university students in their criteria for evaluating scenes within the built environment.[11] Demarcations of the wilderness region made by visitors to the Boundary Waters Canoe Area bear little relation to its administrative borders.[12] Herbert Gans' well-known report delineated the discrepancies in appraisals rendered by inhabitants and urban renewal experts of the viability and resources of Boston's West End.[13]

[8] Kenneth H. Craik, "Environmental Psychology." in Kenneth H. Craik et al., New Directions in Psychology: 4 (New York: Holt, Rinehart, and Winston, 1970), pp. 1–122.

[9] Alan Lipman, "The Architectural Belief System and Social Behaviour," British Journal of Sociology 20 (June 1969), pp. 190–204.

[10] Donald Appleyard, "City Designers and the Pluralistic City," in Lloyd Rodwin et al., eds., Regional Planning for Development (Cambridge, Mass.: MIT Press, 1969).

[11] Robert G. Hershberger, "A Study of Meaning and Architecture" (Ph..D dissertation, University of Pennsylvania, 1968).

[12] Robert C. Lucas, "The Contribution of Environmental Research to Wilderness Policy Decisions," Journal of Social Issues 22 (October 1966), pp. 116–126.

[13] Herbert J. Gans, The Urban Villagers: Group and Class in the Life of Italian-

Future research must be directed toward systematic analysis of the implications of these differences. In any man-influenced transformation of the physical environment, the basic questions remain: Who participated in this physical transformation? what beliefs and assumptions operated? what ends were sought? and what were the behavioral and social consequences? Pioneering in this research design, Clare Cooper's case study of a public housing project (1) identified the social goals of the designers and the design decisions by which they hoped to achieve them and (2) appraised, in a follow-up study of the completed and inhabited settlement, how pertinent the objectives were to its occupants and how well they were realized.[14] Despite the tendency of environmental designers to consider every project unique, scientific understanding of these man-influenced transformations will require comparable study of samples of projects drawn from the same class, for example, samples of shopping centers, churches, and playgrounds.

If available knowledge of the ways in which environmental decision-makers comprehend and evaluate the physical environment is limited, similar information about their clients is no more abundant, although its importance is now recognized.[15] Further, F. J. Langdon and Serge Boutourline have argued that the notion of environmental management must be interpreted broadly:

the building superintendent who monitors the heating and air conditioning and the restaurant manager who adjusts the sound and lighting systems may have an impact comparable to the architect's, while Gilbert White has noted that every farmer in a flood or drought plain plays a part in water-resource management.[16] The increasing degree to which broad environmental policy is becoming a major public, and perhaps political issue highlights the participation of every person in environmental decision-making. Expanding the scope of research in another direction, an environmental decision-maker's comprehension of the environment must be fully explored and analyzed, beyond the domain of any immediate professional concerns. For example, water-resources engineers, trained to intervene in and control environmental processes, are surprisingly reluctant to advocate large-scale weather-modification and heedful of possible unforeseen consequences.[17]

IDENTIFYING AND ASSESSING ENVIRONMENTAL DISPOSITIONS

Clearly, a basic task for the study of man-environmental relations is the development of psychological techniques yielding a comprehensive and differentiated description of *any* person's orientation to the everyday physical environment.

Americans (New York: Free Press of Glencoe, 1962).

[14] Cooper, *Some Social Implications of House and Site Plan Design at Easter Hill Village.*

[15] F. J. Langdon, "The Social and Physical Environment: A Social Scientist's View," *Journal of the Royal Institute of British Architects* 73 (October 1966), pp. 460–464; Gilbert F. White, "Formation and Role of Public Attitudes, in Henry Jarrett, ed., *Environmental Quality in a Growing Economy: Essays from the Sixth RFF Forum* (Baltimore: Johns Hopkins University Press, 1966), pp. 105–127.

[16] Langdon, "The Social and Physical Environment"; Serge Boutourline, "The Concept of Environmental Management," *Dot Zero IV* (September 1967), pp. 1–7; Gilbert F. White, "The Choice of Use in Resource Management," *Natural Resources Journal* 1 (January 1961), pp. 23–40.

[17] W. R. Derrick Sewell, "The Role of Attitudes of Engineers in Water Management," in Fred L. Strodtbeck and Gilbert F. White, eds., *Attitudes toward Water: An Interdisciplinary Exploration* (Chicago: University of Chicago Social Psychology Laboratory and Department of Geography, forthcoming).

As a beginning, a person can be characterized on the basis of a specific kind of response to a given class of environmental settings. For example, when 237 beach-users along Lake Michigan individually evaluated fourteen photographs of beach scenes, two distinct preference types could be identified: persons fond of beaches with natural scenery and fans of city swimming beaches.[18]

At a second level, a person's general disposition toward a class of environmental settings can be assessed. On a questionnaire measuring individual differences in the environmental disposition, "wildernism," a person receives points for deeming certain features and activities of wilderness recreation important—for example, Alpine meadows, native wild animals, back-packing, and sleeping outdoors—and points for considering the others relatively unimportant —for example, developed resort facilities, camp-sites with plumbing, power-boating, and cutting Christmas trees. Scores on the wildernism scale are positively related to (1) membership in conservation organizations, (2) the frequency of visits to wilderness areas, and (3) preferences for management policies within wilderness areas.[19] The breadth of this environmental disposition, and the capacity of the wildernism scale to predict other aspects of a person's orientation to the physical environment, can be gauged only by further empirical validational research.[20]

Ultimately, we must seek to attain the differentiated assessment of persons across a standard array of environmental dispositions. The comprehensive description of a person's interpersonal traits requires a multivariate approach, assessing such dimensions of personality as dominance, nurturance, sociability, and tolerance. Similarly, an array of environmental dispositions must be identified and assessed to afford an equally comprehensive description of this heretofore neglected realm of personality.

George McKechnie's recently developed Environmental Response Inventory, while still in preliminary form, serves to illustrate this direction of research.[21] The preliminary inventory consists of 218 items expressing various ways in which persons may relate to the everyday physical environment. In completing it, an individual simply indicates whether each item is descriptive of his views and typical behavior. On the basis of data derived from a sample of university faculty and students in Berkeley and Davis in California, Corning, New York, and Middletown, Connecticut (378 males; 365 females), ten preliminary scales were developed for males and ten for females, by means of factor analysis. These tentative scales of the Environmental Response Inventory assess such dispositions as pastoralism, urbanism, stimulus-seeking,

[18] George L. Peterson and Edward S. Neumann, "Modeling and Predicting Human Response to the Visual Recreation Environment," Report from the Department of Civil Engineering, Northwestern University (Evanston, Ill.: Northwestern University Department of Civil Engineering, 1969).

[19] John C. Hendee, William R. Catton, Jr., Larry D. Marlow, and C. Frank Brockman, *Wilderness-users in the Pacific Northwest: Their Characteristics, Values, and Management-Preferences,* United States Department of Agriculture Forest Service Research Paper PNW-61 (Portland, Oregon: Pacific Northwest Forest and Range Experiment Station, 1968).

[20] The same applies, of course, to the beach-preference procedure, which may have broader relevance than is indicated here.

[21] George E. McKechnie, "The Environmental Response Inventory: Preliminary Development," Report from the Institute of Personality Assessment and Research, University of California (Berkeley: University of California, Institute of Personality Assessment and Research, 1969).

environmental adaptation, environmental well-being, abstract conservationism, environmental security, and modernism.[22]

Two scales of the Environmental Response Inventory will illustrate its characteristics and potential usefulness. Analysis of the data from both male and female samples yielded a scale assessing an environmental disposition which may be best termed pastoralism. In general, the scale's content conveys a deeply personal orientation toward the natural environment and away from the urban development: This disposition is expressed by items related to everyday behavior and experience,

I occasionally take a walk in the rain just for the experience.
I usually try to catch at least a glimpse of the setting sun.

by items embodying sentiments and preferences,

It makes me sad to see all the animals in cages at the zoo.
I would rather have tax money spent on conservation than on traffic control.

and by items dealing with attitudes and beliefs,

Buildings made of metal and glass express a disrespect for human nature.
The stress and strain of urban life has led to increased rates of mental illness.

Urbanism is a second environmental disposition identified in both male and female samples, assessed by such items as:

Every child should have the opportunity to enjoy the excitement of a large city.
I enjoy riding on crowded subways.
If I lived in a large city, I would make good use of its cultural benefits.

[22] For a review of current research on environmental dispositions, see Kenneth H. Craik, "Assessing Environmental Dispositions," Paper presented at the Annual Meeting of the American Psychological Association, Washington, D.C., September 4, 1969.

In the male sample, the pastoralism and urbanism scales are quite independent, showing a correlation of $-.04$. Thus, a man's status on one environmental disposition provides no basis for predicting his status on the other. This is not so clearly the case in the female sample, in which the obtained correlation was $-.45$. A generally successful effort is being made to develop environmental scales whose intercorrelations are low.

Membership in conservation organizations is positively associated with pastoralism and urbanism, while membership in organizations whose aims are to improve the quality of the urban environment is positively correlated with urbanism.[23] Thus, for research purposes, persons can be identified in the general population who share environmental dispositions possessed by members of voluntary environmental organizations but who lack those other personality characteristics that lead to active participation in community life. Furthermore, by making use of the additional information afforded by examining combinations of scale scores, meaningful differentiation among members of conservation organizations may also be made through use of the Environmental Response Inventory. For example, members whose highest scores are obtained on the pastoralism and urbanism scales may differ on policy stances from those whose highest scores occur on the pastoralism and stimulus-seeking scales.

The adequacy of these new scales for assessing broad environmental dispositions must be appraised by determining empirical relationships across many modes of response to many classes of environmental settings. Does the pastoralism scale relate to preference for swimming beaches with natural scenery? Do persons scoring high on urbanism

[23] McKechnie, "The Environmental Response Inventory," pp. 35–39.

and environmental adaptation, but low on pastoralism, display a markedly non-wildernist orientation to the wilderness environment? Considering the wonderfully diverse forms of human response to the physical environment, the task is obviously formidable and inherently open-ended: When encountering the varied environmental settings of their daily experience, how do high scorers on each scale differ from low scorers in the elements and attributes they attend to, the environmental vocabularies they possess, the images and concepts they employ, the beliefs they hold, the inferences they make, and the evaluations they render? It would be misguided to examine only, for example, the orientation to beaches of high scorers on the pastoralism scale and that of high scorers on the urbanism scale to air pollution; indeed, it may be just those other possible combinations, for example, the urbanite's response to the hinterland or the pastoralist's response to the urban setting, which will yield new understanding of the interplay between human behavior and the everyday physical environment.

As the environmental scales are psychometrically refined and acquire expanded meaning through the kinds of research already suggested, investigation of the acquisition and development of the various environmental dispositions will become appropriate. Not surprisingly, the male pastoralism scale is correlated positively with number of years spent on a farm and negatively with reports of having been "closely cared for and guarded" as a child, while the male urbanism scale is correlated negatively with number of years spent on a farm or living in a small town, but positively with the number of years spent living in an urban location.[24] However, the psychological factors which mediate between these background variables and

[24] *Ibid.*, pp. 35–39.

differential strength of environmental dispositions have been little studied and are not understood in any systematic way. In addition, strikingly different personality patterns are associated with the various environmental dispositions.[25] How nonenvironmental personality factors serve to foster and sustain the differential development and strength of environmental dispositions also warrants further research. The extent to which special programs of experience and training can alter environmental dispositions and behavior would serve as a focus for complementary research. Programs which introduce urban children to the forest environment and rural children to the urban environment offer promising contexts for such investigation.

Research on environmental dispositions is destined to promote a greater appreciation of the personal order that exists in an individual's daily multifarious responses to his complex and varied physical environment and, by affording comprehensive descriptions of the full range of environmental decision-makers, to advance more subtle and precise scientific study of man-environment relations.

THE INTRICACY OF THE PERSONAL-SOCIETAL-ENVIRONMENTAL SYSTEM

An important social institution in the state of California, its legislature, recently took action within the context of man-environment relations by passing Senate bill 206, the aim of which is to foster the development of conservation-education programs in local school districts. Testimony at hearings on the bill suggests the existence of two distinct, although hardly incompatible, approaches to conservation education.[26]

[25] *Ibid.*, pp. 35–61.
[26] California, Senate, Committees on Natural Resources and Education, Transcript of Joint Hearings on a Program of Conservation-Edu-

150

The well-established tradition of outdoor education stresses respect and understanding of nature, advocates direct contact with the nonurban outdoors as a means of conservation education, and focuses largely upon personal experience. The newly emerging ecological approach stresses the interrelationship of organisms and environment and the possibility of remote and unforeseen consequences of human action, advocates a more conceptual emphasis in conservation-education, dealing with the quality of the urban as well as nonurban environment, and focuses upon public policy. The current potency of the environmental issue on the university campus indicates that manpower pools representing both the ecological orientation and the outdoor orientation may be available for recruitment as conservation teachers in the public school system.[27] Can these distinctive orientations to conservation education be documented by empirical research? Would exemplars of the two approaches differ in their environmental dispositions and other personality characteristics? Would they seek different aims and develop different educational programs? Would their programs have differential impacts upon the environmental orientations of their pupils? What long-term societal and environmental consequences might follow from the distinctive impact of such orientations upon the younger generation? Consideration of the agents, aims, techniques, and consequences of this mode of environmental socialization reveals the intricacy of the personal-societal-environmental system, but at the same time, its openness to scientific scrutiny.

cation for the Department of Education, Sacramento, California, March 16, 1966.

[27] See, for example, Gladwin Hill, "Environment May Eclipse Vietnam as College Issue," *The New York Times,* November 30, 1969.

INFORMATION CHANNELS AND ENVIRONMENTAL DECISION MAKING

HELEN M. INGRAM

Information is a political tracer element that delineates the channels of communication within a decision making process. Up until this decade, the channel from environmental interest to decision makers was negligible. Information on the economic efficiency or the regional development effects of actions affecting natural resources was much more salient than intelligence on environmental impact. In recent years, attempts have been made to generate more information upon the implications of natural resources policy and feed it into the decision making process. In particular, the National Environmental Policy Act[1] is expressly aimed at accounting for environmental impacts of governmental decisions.

The theory of this article is that the incremental and fragmented process by which decisions are actually made imposes important restraints upon the flow of information. The initial task is to catalogue and describe these restraints, then to identify the factors that affect channels of communication. What determines which facts decision makers take into consideration? What motivates the generation and transfer of information? This article will discuss the answers to these questions and the possibilities of improving the current environmental information basis.

FACTORS AFFECTING WHAT DECISION MAKERS HEAR

Classical formulations of problem solving involve the identification and ranking of goals, the cataloging of methods of achieving those goals and the investigation of the consequences of each alternative. Unfortunately, formulations do not provide an accurate description of decision making.[2] Such a policy making process would compel a decision maker to reach out for all the related information to his problem and analyze it. The decision making strategy that Lindblom and Braybrooke call disjointed incrementalism is a better approximation of the real world.[3] Only policies which differ incrementally from the status-quo are seriously considered, and, in consequence, decision makers focus upon a quite limited number of alternatives in making

---

1. National Environmental Policy Act of 1969, 42 U.S.C. 4321 *et seq.* (1970).

2. Lindblom, The Policy Making Process Ch. III, (1968); Dror, Public Policy Making Reexamined 86-87 (1968).

3. Braybooke & Lindblom, A Strategy of Decision: Policy Evaluation as a Social Process 81-110 (1963).

Reprinted with permission from 13 Natural Resources Journal 150-169 (1973), published by the University of New Mexico School of Law, Albuquerque, NM 87131.

choices. Further, not all the consequences of any alternative are, in fact, taken into account. There is a tendency among decision makers to concentrate on the direct and immediate effects of decision, discounting the remote, and imponderable, the intangible, and the poorly understood. The practical decision-making strategy dictates that a decision maker attend to the short run consequences in hope that the long run will take care of itself—or that some other decision maker in another setting will take care of it.

The information needs of decision makers are restricted in this incremental and disjointed decision-making process. They are not required to listen to all the interests that may have a stake in any decision or to collect and weigh data on all possible impacts. Furthermore, they are barraged by more information than they can actually use in the limited choices they are comfortable in making. Information overload is a likely problem. The fact is that the receptivity of decision makers is screened by a number of considerations.

THE ISSUE CONTEXT affects what information the decision makers are receptive to. Over time, participants in a policy area develop a particular fix or conception of the dimensions of the issues involved. Information is sorted out and used in decision making on the basis of that conception, and data which related to another way of thinking about the issue is never really considered. Aaron Wildavsky explains the reluctance of the Eisenhower Administration to attend to the political dangers of the Dixon-Yates controversy in terms of the operative issue context. The Republican Administration conceived of the issue as a public versus private power controversy. Although there were numerous signals that the issue was likely to explode as a question of conflict of interest, agency offficials and Presidential advisers failed to take the cues. The information which might have proceeded early warning was filtered out.[4]

The issue context of water quality was for years a matter of health, and information about the spread of communicable disease through water supply overshadowed data about aesthetics, recreation, and wildlife habitat. Water quality officials in the Department of Health, Education and Welfare were such captives of the issue context that they were unable to adjust to the changing dimensions of the question. Ultimately the inability of these decision makers to receive and process new categories of information led to the loss of HEW jurisdiction over water quality programs.

Public works has been the issue context of a number of natural

4. Wildavsky, The Analysis of Issue-Contexts in Decision-Making, Revolt Against the Masses (1971).

153

resource policies, particularly water development. A dam, a levee, or an irrigation project has been seen as a means to give local economies a shot in the arm. One Congressman, a senior member of the House Public Works Committee, expressed the following conception of the water development issue:

> A member of Congress from an arid western state, where dependable water supply has held back both industries development and agricultural production, may perform his most effective service for the economic future of his region by the promotion of soundly conceived water resource developments. For a lawmaker representing a coastal area it may be the building of a sea wall to protect his town from the ocean's occasional ravages. If he serves a locality where recurrent flood hazards exist, his primary project may be the approval and eventual completion of a needed flood control measure by the Corps of Engineers.[5]

The relevant information when water projects are conceived in such terms includes the development possibilities of particular projects and the strength and unity of local support. Environmental implications are unlikely to be particularly salient.

THE SOURCE OF INFORMATION, evaluated in terms of the decision maker's goals and interests, is a factor in determining its receipt and consideration. A decision maker can not simply make judgments, he must concern himself with building support for his decisions. He must take care of his ability to influence, and attend to the consequences of choices he makes upon his future ability to influence. A decision maker is most apt to listen to information emitting from his constituency upon which he depends for continuing support. The antennae of Congressmen are directed toward picking up the preferences of individuals and groups important to their renomination and reelection. Agencies relate particularly to communications flowing from the groups served by agency programs—groups which ordinarily assist the agency's protecting or extending its authority budget and jurisdiction. Officials in the Soil Conservation Service (SCS) listen attentively to local soil and water conservation districts on proposed small watershed projects. The approval and active backing of local sponsors is crucial to agreements on cost sharing where local beneficiaries are required to pay back some portion, and continuous local efforts are necessary to push a project through the complicated authorizations and funding processes.[6] The same attention is not directed by the SCS to information sources apart

---

5. Wright, You and Your Congressman 49 (1965).
6. Allee & Ingram, Authorizations and Appropriations Processes for Water Resources Development, Report to National Water Commission (1972).

from the local sponsors. The frustration of the environmental agencies from their inability to get access to the decision making process in the SCS (and also the Corps of Engineers) was expressed by Nathaniel P. Reed, Assistant Secretary of the Interior for Fish and Wildlife and Parks before a Congressional hearing on channelization.

> A large portion of the morale problem within my Department is the result of rarely being listened to when we offer relevant recommendations to other agencies on this problem. It is discouraging for our biologists and field personnel to stand by helplessly and watch the wetlands resource succumb to the dredge bit or dragline bucket with little or no regard for the natural system.[7]

Sources of information which are not supporters of decision makers, but which hold a recognized veto position over actions are heeded. Once environmental groups had collected substantial numbers of sympathetic Congressmen and Senators sensitive to their appeals, their reception by Interior and Public Works Committees changed markedly. Indicative perhaps is the fact that the mailing list for announcements of hearings and activities of the House Public Works Committee expanded from less than a dozen to more than 180 environmental organizations in the decade of the 1970's. The concern of federal construction agencies for developing public participation programs is a function of their interest in forestalling the stalemates which have occurred in recent years with local conservation groups.

In actuality, regulated groups often veto decisions of the governmental agencies assigned the task of regulating them. In the long run, enforcement of regulation depends upon voluntary compliance. Because of physical and political constraints, regulators cannot take punitive action against every violator of standards if the violations are widespread. Consequently, the setting of standards, and the choice of whom to prosecute for non-compliance depends not only upon what it is reasonable to expect of the regulated industry, but also what the adverse consequences would be if the industry were prevented through enforcement action from carrying on its trade. Matthew Holden has convincingly described pollution control as a bargaining process.[8] Command of relevant information is a powerful resource which polluting industries have in bargaining. Holden says,

> To tell a firm to stop a certain discharge practice is to tell it to assume a cost which it has been able to pass on to someone else.

7. Statement of Nathaniel P. Reed, Assistant Secretary of the Interior for Fish and Wildlife and Parks, *Before the House Government Operations Subcommittee,* 91st Cong., 2d Sess. (1971).

8. Holden, Jr., Pollution Control as a Bargaining Process: An Essay on Regulatory Decision-Making (Cornell Water Resources Center, Oct. 1966).

Yet this cannot be done without reference to whether or not the firm can afford to do so. In general, only the firm or industry itself is likely to have the relevant information on such matters as the importance of the firm or industry in the political economy, the nature of the product and process, and the related possibilities for technical adaptation. And the firm or industry is likely to be secretive, both because of the uses which its competitors might make of such information and because of the uses which public officials might make of it.[9]

Regulators must establish a fund of good will, common interest and established links of communication with the regulated. In the end, this often means that regulating agencies are more receptive to information from the regulated industry than from environmental groups. Understandably then, the Federal Power Commission, attuned to the electric industry's case for new sites, was not sensitive to information from conservationists about the consequences of licensing power plants such as Storm King until the courts directed the Commission to take the environment into account.[10]

CONTENT OF INFORMATION affects its reception by decision makers. Dexter has illustrated the fact that a Congressman hears most often from those who agree with him, and that some men automatically interpret what they hear to bolster their own viewpoints.[11] Agencies, too, seek out information which supports actions toward which they are already inclined. In his case study of the planning process within the Army Corps of Engineers on the DelMarVa Waterway, Leonard Shabman noted that the Corps paid meticulous attention to the Bureau of Sports Fisheries and Wildlife and the Bureau of Outdoor Recreation reviews of the Pocomoke Canal, a structure the Corps had no enthusiasm to build. A memo in Corps files affixed to unfavorable comments read, "This is exactly what we hoped to get from BOR. Beautiful example of interagency coordination."[12]

Decision makers are particularly receptive to categories of information which justify and legitimize their decision making process.[13] Cost benefit analysis is favored information to legislators and natural resource agencies. The ratio of benefits to costs provides a rationale for not pursuing certain projects while at the same time the economic

9. Id. at 33.
10. Scenic Hudson Preservation Conference v. Federal Power Commission, 354 F.2d 608 (2d Cir. 1965).
11. Dexter, The Representative and His District, New Perspectives on the House of Representatives 3-28 (1963).
12. Shabman, DelMarVa Waterway Report, Cornell U. Water Resources & Marine Sciences Center (1972).
13. Downs, Some Thoughts on Giving People Economic Advice, 9 Am. Behavioral Scientist 30-32 (1965).

tool is flexible enough to supply a justification to projects which have strong support. As Herbert Marshall put it, "one of the principal uses of benefit/cost analysis is to clothe politically desirable projects in the fig leaf of economic respectability."[14] Decision makers have a strong preference for kinds of information which can be applied to politically viable solutions. Dean Schooler has pointed out that physical technologies produced by the physical, medical, biological and engineering sciences are favored by policy makers over behavioral technologies which emerge from the political, social, economic and psychological sciences. Behavioral technologies have the disadvantage to the decision maker of implying new life styles, shifts in values and changed patterns of behavior which are likely to produce conflict.[15] It is far more difficult, for instance, to focus on the behavioral requirements for reducing the demand for electric energy than to concentrate upon a technical solution such as fusion to generate more energy for everybody.

In a politically controversial situation, a decision maker is likely to be receptive to information content which places the issue in new terms amenable to settlement. An illustration can be found in the Central Arizona Project debate revolving around the Grand Canyon dams.[16] The Bureau of Reclamation, historically a hydroelectric power agency, would never have considered the financial support of coal fired steam plants as a possible alternative to dams had not the conservationists drawn a stalemate on the issue in Congress.

CHARACTERISTICS OF THE DECISION MAKER affect the information that is received. The background and experience of a decision maker screens his receptivity in favor of disciplines and facts with which he feels familiar and comfortable, and the recruitment patterns of an agency affects its ability to collect and assimilate data. The dominance of engineers in federal construction agencies has affected their bias toward construction solutions and their lack of receptivity to environmental concerns. Indicative of the balance, in the Army Corps of Engineers the Civil Works Study Board found that of the 622 professionals whose sole responsibility was planning, 91 percent were engineers.[17] Organizational militancy affects the kind of data collected and the way it is fed into the decision-making process. In his study of the Forest Service, Ashley Schiff found that research on

---

14. Marshall, Politics and Efficiency in Water Development, Water Research 294 (1965).

15. Schooler, *Political Arenas, Life Styles and the Impact of Technology on Policymaking*, 1 Policy Sciences 275-87 (1970); Science and Public Policy (1971).

16. A case history can be found in H. Ingram Patterns of Politics in Water Resources Development: A Case Study of New Mexico's Role in the Colorado River Basin Bill, (1969).

17. Civil Works Study Bd. of the Senate Committee on Public Works, 89th Cong., 2d. Sess. Civil Works Program of the Corp of Engineers (Comm. Print 1966).

controlled burning and the effect of vegetal cover on stream flow was heavily influenced by the doctrines which administrators found useful in promoting the agency. Research was too closely identified spiritually and structurally with "the cause" to impartially identify and investigate problems of forestry management.[18] For similar reasons, the multidisciplinary staffing of the Soil Conservation Service has not affected any particular receptivity to alien ideas. The SCS is a very unified organization with strong centralized control.[19] The agency's pattern of a "universalist" (what the well grained soil conservationist should be) is of the same cut regardless of discipline or area of the country.

RULES AND REGULATIONS structure the formal behavior of organizations and give legitimacy to whatever information collected and transmitted according to the rules that is actually considered by the agency. It is doubtful, however, if rules can build certain information into the decision making process than would otherwise not be considered. If the rules require that a decision maker consider data which imply large policy changes, then the decision maker is likely to bend the rules to fit the incremental strategy which is both more comfortable and safe.

The Fish and Wildlife Coordination Act of 1958[20] is ambitious in its stated purposes. Equal consideration for fish and wildlife conservation along with other features of water resources development such as navigation, flood control and irrigation is supposed to take place. The rules in every construction agency require it to consult with the federal bureau and state game and fish departments whenever they propose major water development projects. There is no provision that conservation agency recommendations be accepted, however, and in practice conservation viewpoints affect decisions only when it suits the construction agency, or when a coalition of interests lends some muscle to the conservation viewpoint.[21]

LEARNING CAPACITY affects a decision maker's receptivity to information. This complex notion merits a more lengthy discussion than is possible here, but in general learning capacity is related to the amount of uncommitted inner resources.[22] An individual can restructure the way he responds to external information, provided he has certain resources to invest. He must command sufficient intellectual and emotional capability to recognize the inappropriateness of his present actions, and he must not be under stress. In the same way an

18. Schiff, Fire and Water; Scientific Heresy in the Forest Service (1962).
19. Hardin, The Politics of Agriculture 66 (1952).
20. 16 U.S.C. 661 et seq. (1964).
21. Allee and Ingram, supra note 6, at ch. 3 & 7.
22. For extended theoretical treatment see Deutsch, Nerves of Government (1966).

organization can, with adequate competent staff and budget and time, alter its reception of information. The process of adjusting to new sources of information is typically slow. Decision makers repeatedly encounter troublesome opposition and conflict and seek out ways to deal with negative feedback. Decisions are altered marginally and tentatively, as the decision maker tests for a more positive response. Through numerous incremental adjustments new channels of communciation are established.

Decison makers, including resource agencies, differ in their ability to learn. Among them, the Army Corps of Engineers demonstrates better than average flexibility. It is responding to local conflict with an energetic public participation program, and is increasingly receptive to non-structural solutions to flood control problems. The chief's offiice has directed Corps divisions to come up with new plans directed toward urban problems. Most important, the Corps has responded to pollution with planning studies of regional waste management. This capacity to innovate is associated to some extent with the fact that the organization has some surplus resources. The size of its program, for instance, gives the Corps leeway to experiment. Nearly three-quarters of all federal water development is under the aegis of the Corps.

TIMING of information affects the nature of its reception. Chances are that decision makers will be most receptive to new information during the sorting out phase of an emerging issue. If a decision maker is uncertain about the values involved in the question, and about his risks and options, he is apt to be relatively open to all suggestions which appear helpful. Information is likely to have its greatest impact early in the planning process while the need for an airport, highway, dam, power plant or pipeline is still being discussed, and before a site is selected. Once the issue has been placed in a context, the decision maker will follow routine patterns and listen to regular sources.

FACTORS AFFECTING WHAT INFORMATION IS GENERATED AND TRANSMITTED

In a democratic society it is an accepted value that individuals and groups will have the opportunity to participate in or be represented in decisions that affect them.[23] However, in the real world of fragmented, inconsistent and often incoherent policy, not every interest group participates in decisions that affect its concerns. The focus of interests is likely to be upon those decision points and decision makers where access and impact can be most easily achieved.

23. Fox, *Strategic Considerations in Attaining Water Planning Goals*, J. Water Pollution Control (1966).

The effective means of expressing most interests in the political system is through organizations, including interest groups and agencies oriented toward particular interests. Whether or not an interest group or an agency spokesman for an interest voices its concern in decision-making depends upon its perception of the potential costs and benefits involved in generating and transmitting information. Such organizations' calculus is constrained by the hierarchy of importance among decisions affecting its interest and the budget of resources it has to expend in participating in decision making.[24] The following factors affect an interest group's or interest oriented agency's willingness to generate and transmit information reflecting its concerns.

THE PERCEPTION OF THE DECISION and what is at stake affects what information is generated and transmitted. An organization's evaluation of what is at issue is a function of its goals and perceptions. The core interest of the traditional conservation movement represented by such organizations as the Izaac Walton League, National Parks Association, Audubon Society, Wilderness Society, National Wildlife Federation, and Sierra Club is the preservation of natural areas through parks and other reserves. The decisions made by natural resource agencies are perceived as essentially developmental decisions fostering growth of particular industries and regions. For the most part decisions made by such agencies as the Bureau of Reclamation, the Corps of Engineers, and the Bureau of Public Roads is outside the purview of conservation. It is only when a park, wild river, or trout stream is threatened that the actions of these agencies become relevant.

The newer envirnomental groups, emerging in the 1970's have tended to focus on individual family consumptive decisions rather than governmental actors. The public has been directed to stop littering, use returnable bottles, use pollution free detergents, buy non leaded gasoline, reduce water and pesticide use, tune up autos and so on. Some observers see both the traditional conservation groups and new environmentalists currently altering their focus toward a wide range of public decisions. Governmental action is seen as a way of preserving the environment, and changes in present government decisions are viewed as essential if environmental quality is to be achieved.[25] A new assessment by environmental groups of the role of public decisions in reaching environmental goals will foster the

24. Shabman, Decision Making in Water Resources Investment and the Potential of Multi-Objective Planning: The Case of the Army Corps of Engineers ch. 4 (Cornell Water Resources and Marine Sciences Center 1972).

25. Morrision, Hornback, & Warner, The Environmental Movement: Some Preliminary Observations, Social Behavior, Natural Resources, and the Environment, (forthcoming).

generation of different kinds of information designed to influence political actors.

An interest group or an agency expressing a particular interest will react first to what it perceives as imminent and direct effects upon its interest and will react later, with a lower order of effort, to questions with an indirect and remote impact. The direct impact of a dam, highway, or power plant is experienced in jobs, growth and profits. The indirect environmental implications are less immediate and much harder to predict. Partly for this reason, development interests have traditionally had more communications links with natural resources decision makers than have environmental groups. Because of the remote impact of planning decisions, conservation interests have not been motivated to make much of an input into planning studies. Nothing happens to many plans, even authorized ones, as illustrated by the fifteen billion dollar backlog of authorized water projects. If plans come to fruition, it is often far in the future. The average time for the planning and construction of civil works projects by the Army Corps of Engineers is currently seventeen years and eleven months. Construction agency planners have not traditionally made much effort to present their plans as important and immediate to conservation groups outside the regular constituency of the agency. Like other parts and decision making, the incremental strategy has restricted the scope of planning.

THE EXPECTED IMPACT of information affects whether it will be transmitted and its content. The corollary of the notion that decision makers hear what they want to hear is that organizations will transmit information to decision makers when they believe it will get a hearing. The crucial points for stopping a dam or highway for conservation interests have not been on the local level where development benefits have their strongest appeal or within agencies whose mission it is to build public works. Instead it has been the national political leaders including members of Congress who have been open to conservationist persuasion. As a result opposition interests which fail to show up at agency hearings have a habit of surfacing later when projects reach a national decision making arena. The tremendous increase in citizen's suits attests to the willingness of environmental interests to prepare a case for whatever decision makers, in this case the judges, they perceive to be sympathetic.

Federal review agencies which express conservationist and recreation interests, including the Bureau of Sports Fish and Wildlife, the National Park Service, and the Bureau of Outdoor Recreation, focus their comments on what they believe is achievable in the incremental process of decision making. Reviews tend to be pro-forma unless the proposed project threatens an important interest. Even then the message of these agencies is seldom outright opposition since past experience has shown it is usually unsuccessful. Instead reviewers suggest changes in design and location of the project, and mitigating and compensating features such as recreational access and facilities, a wildlife sanctuary, fish hatchery, fish ladder etc.

It is possible, of course, that environmental interests may despair of influencing particular decision makers and use public hearings to appeal to the broader citizen audience. In such cases environmental groups will talk past decision makers with a general message aimed at rallying supporters to the cause, and impart little to the decision maker which relates to the choices he has at hand.

The *RESOURCES* of an organization affect what information it can generate and transmit. Unity and cohesion are important resources.[26] The environmental movement has suffered from fragementation and internal division. The number of groups is growing as well as membership. The Council of Environmental Quality estimated that there are over 5,000 environmental organizations in the United States.[27] These groups differ in their conceptions of environmental quality. A unified strategy, even on limited specific issues, is often impossible for them to agree upon and execute. Very often environmental groups are in competition for another important resource, membership. Up until recently lack of numbers has been a resource limitation. The Sierra Club, for instance, had only 30,000 members in 1966. A great deal of the energy and resources environmental groups have has been plowed back into the organizations in membership and fund raising drives.

The older conservation organizations have been mainly national organizations with a national appeal, but with only a few members scattered in localities. As a result, it has been much more possible to mount a national campaign than to stop a project on the local level. Thus the National Parks Association could cause the Bureau of Reclamation proposal to build Echo Park Dam great difficulties in Congress in the 1950's but could not dent the staunch support of Utah residents.[28]

Data base and expertise is a requirement for meaningful participation in natural resources decisions. Much of the debate on issues such as nuclear reactor safety, thermal pollution, air and water quality measurements, etc. takes place in technical terms. Environmental groups have solicited the aid of biologists and foresters in testimony

---

26. Truman, The Governmental Process 167 (1955).
27. Council on Environmental Quality, Letter from Staff, 1973.
28. Stratton & Sirotkin, The Echo Park Controversy (1959).

on clear cutting and have hired economists to do benefit cost analysis of water projects. The availability of experts on the staff or within the membership is a valuable resource. Without specialists, an organization can not substantiate an independent position or even interpret data which comes in from outside.

Lack of adequate staffing and budget have been persistent problems for the Bureau of Sports Fish and Wildlife in voicing the conservationist position. Up until a few years ago the River Basin Studies Division which has been assigned to review water development proposals of the Army Corps of Engineers, the Bureau of Reclamation, and the Soil Conservation Service were dependent upon the lead construction agency to fund their evaluations. Today about half the budget for BSF and W review comes form outside. These budgetary restraints are compounded by other resource limitations which affect the kind of reviews it makes. A division handbook describes the difficulty of the River Basin Studies Planner.

> Usually he is operating against a deadline, frequently a short one—nearly always shorter than the lead planning agency—and often with less adequate tools and manpower. Nearly always, too, he has less adequate basic data and information than much that is available to the lead agency . . . The parameters dealt with by the RBS and lead agency planners are of different orders of complexity, variability and recognized utility. Thus the basic data on climate and hydrology have been long recognized as valuable to Man's welfare, while comparably basic data on fish and wildlife populations and their dynamics not only are less widely valued, but they are far more difficult to obtain.[29]

The National Environmental Policy Act[30] (NEPA) was designed to alter the existing channels of communication in policy making affecting the environment. The principal thrust of Section 102 (2) (C) was to establish a new "action-forcing" provision to assure detailed research and full consideration of environmental impacts in decision making.[31] Judged by the number of court cases which environmental organizations have won under NEPA directing government agencies to comply, the legislation has been a success. Citizen's suits have produced court orders blocking or delaying a variety of projects including the Alaska oil pipeline, dams, highways, nuclear and

29. River Basins Studies Division, Bureau of Sports Fisheries and Wildlife, Procedures & Techniques of Fish and Wildlife Analysis & Planning.

30. National Environmental Policy Act of 1969, 42 U.S.C. 4321 et seq. (1970). (hereinafter cited as NEPA).

31. Report on the Administration of the National Environmental Policy Act, Comm. on Merchant Marine and Fisheries, H.R. Rep. No. 316, 92nd Cong., 1st Sess. (1971).

hydroelectric power plants, canals and logging in national forests.[32] There is considerable difference, however, between sand in the wheels of progress on specific projects and actually altering the patterns of communication in decision making. What impact has NEPA had on what decision makers actually hear, and what information is actually generated and transmitted?

Section 102 of NEPA requires that all agencies of the Federal Government prepare detailed environmental impact statements on proposals for legislation and other major actions significantly affecting the environment. In impact statements agencies are directed to consider: (1) the environmental impact of the proposed action; (2) any adverse environmental effects which cannot be avoided should the proposal be implemented; (3) alternatives to the proposed action; (4) the relationship between local short-term uses of man's environment and the maintenance and enhancement of long-term productivity; and (5) any irreversible and irretrievable commitments of resources involved in the proposed action should it be implemented. In the process of preparing impact statements, federal agencies are to consult with other federal agencies which have jurisdiction, by law or special expertise, with respect to any environmental impact involved. Environmental statements and accompanying comments are to be made available to the President, the Council on Environmental Quality (CEQ) and the public and are to accompany proposals throughout the review process. The Council has issued guidelines, and each federal agency has developed or is working on formal procedures for preparing and processing 102 statements.

NEPA AND DECISION MAKERS

The *ISSUE CONTEXT,* or the framework in which a decision maker conceives a problem and the information he considers relevant is built up over time and experience and is highly resistant to change. The incremental model of decision making suggests that decision makers relate closely to past experience. They consider only alternatives which differ marginally from those taken into account in previous decisions. The informal rules of decision which dictate what information is relevant and what can be dismissed are only loosely related to the formal rules and procedures with which the decision maker complies on paper. It is unreasonable to expect, then, that an alteration of formal procedure such as NEPA could, by itself, accomplish much change in issue contexts in established programs. There is ample evidence of a reluctance to change decision making procedure even formally. A number of Congressmen and administra-

---

32. Zeldin, *Will Success Spoil NEPA,* Audobon 106-11 (July 1972).

tors see NEPA as introducing additional red tape.[33] The initial failure of agencies to comply with the procedural requirements of the act has led to a great deal of litigation. A spate of bills were introduced into the 92nd Congress to provide specific exemptions from NEPA.[34] And, even as agencies adjust to procedural requirements, and they are presently on the whole complying, it is still possible for decision makers to favor information on development rather than environmental impact. Although the environmental impact statement on the Alaska pipeline acknowledged severe environmental effects, the Secretary of the Interior recommended approval of the pipeline on the basis of economics and national security.

NEPA requires that an agency preparing an impact statement obtain the comments of other Federal, State and local agencies having jurisdiction or special expertise on any environmental impacts involved. Under the Freedom of Information Act,[35] the agency must make draft statements and comments available to the public and any individual or organization may comment. The Council of Environmental Quality receives statements and may also comment. Theoretically, then, agencies have broad sources of environmental information to call upon. Whether these SOURCES are actually considered in decision making depends partly upon the agency's evaluation of their political significance. No agency, including the Council on Environmental Quality (CEQ), is authorized to veto a project proposed by another agency on the basis of an adverse environmental statement. CEQ prepares guidelines and monitors the preparation of environmental statements. Under the law,[36] it may, but is not required to comment. As part of the President's staff, CEQ can recommend that the President reject a project. This option was exercised in halting the Cross Florida Barge Canal, but otherwise has not often been used. As Presidential advisers, the informal persuasion of agencies by the CEQ may be effective. Chairman Russell Train told a Congressional Committee, "if we are troubled by a proposed action, either in whole or in part, we generally say so—and there have been cases, to my knowledge, proposals that have been withdrawn, never see the light of day, if you will, I think because of our reaction."[37] However, in its

---

33. *Hearings on Red Tape—Inquiring into Delays and Excesssive Paperwork in Administraton of Public Works Programs Before the Subcommittee of Investigations and Oversight of the Committee on Public Works*, 92nd Cong., 1st. Sess. (1971).

34. For a partial listing see National Wildlife Federation, Conservation Report No. 12, (Apr. 14, 1972).

35. 5 U.S.C. 22(1964).

36. NEPA.

37. *Hearings on the Administration of the National Environmental Policy Act Before the Subcomittee on Fisheries and Wildlife Conservation of the House Committee on Merchant Marine and Fisheries*, 91st Cong. 1st Sess. 13 (1971).

review of the implementation of NEPA in seven agencies, the Comptroller General's office found that much of the formal and informal guidance given by CEQ to Agencies focused on the inclusiveness and quality of particular statements, not upon the procedure whereby statements were integrated into decision making.[38]

Under its own legislative mandate, the Environmental Protection Agency (EPA) has a particular responsibility to review impact statements from the perspective of its broad environmental concerns. Responsiblity is different from vigorous effort, which the General Accounting Office Report, cited above, found wanting. The causes for failure to generate and transmit information relate to EPA's own perspectives and resources and will be discussed below. Whether or not EPA could become a significant source of environmental information is related in part to its strength in Congress, the White House and with its own environmental constituency.

Court decisions are of increasing concern to agencies. Failure to satisfy the courts has cost agencies troublesome delays. Up until the present the courts have concentrated upon the procedure required by NEPA, not the substance of decision making. If this stance is maintained the courts will become less salient as agencies meet the necessary procedures. In the *Calvert Cliffs*[39] decision, a U.S. Court of Appeals held that if a decision is reached procedurally without individual consideration and balancing of environmental factors, conducted fully and in good faith, the courts will examine the weight of environmental information in the decision making process. Historically, however, courts have been reluctant to second guess agencies on the substance of decisions.

Environmental considerations were given formal recognition in NEPA. As a result, environmental data gained stature and credibility with decision makers. However, agencies are reluctant to take information which is likely to produce conflict and make decisions more difficult to reach. It is logical to expect that an agency will include in draft and final statements the data which best supports its own decisions and decision making process. Left to their own devices, without external oversight, impact statements are likely to become justifications to environmentalists of what the agency has determined to do.

NEPA promises to alter the *CHARACTER OF DECISION MAKERS*, and in the long run the changes it makes in agency

---

38. Comptroller General, Report on Improvements Needed in Federal Efforts to Implement the National Environmental Policy Act of 1969 (1972).

39. 449 F.2d. 1109 (D.C. Cir. 1971).

recruitment and personnel can significantly alter channels of communication. It takes life scientists to write environmental statements, and biologists are being brought into federal agencies in significant numbers. The Bureau of Reclamation, for example, has placed at least one G.S. 14 biologist in each of its regions to supervise the preparation of environmental impact statements. How much effect newly recruited individuals with environmental expertise have upon the receptivity of each to environmental concerns will vary according to the success with which the agency inculcates its traditional orientation and mission into its personnel and its learning capacity.

The charge of Sec. 102 (a) (A) of NEPA to all agencies is a "systematic, interdisciplinary approach which will insure the integrated use of the natural and social sciences and the environmental design arts in planning and decision making." Despite the recruitment of life scientists, many agencies are as yet unable to comply. There is a paucity of funds to attract sufficient numbers of qualified people. More important, agency prospectives are currently too narrow to undertake a broad environmental overview. For instance, the Rocky Mountain Center on the Environment found that one Forest Service "102" statement had utilized an "interdisciplinary team" of six timber management specialists.[40]

Environmental impact statements are apt to be *post hoc* evaluation, prepared after decision makers have settled upon a course of action. A specific project or action has become the center of attention in the decision making process by the time an environmental impact statement is introduced. The interest by this time within the agency and among their organizational backers is often to build support for the proposal, not to re-examine goals and needs. The General Accounting Office found that for the seven agencies they reviewed, impact statements were prepared in stages as proposals moved up the organzational levels toward the final stages of review. As a result a lower level did not have the benefit of all environmental aspects of a proposal prior to advancing it to the next organizational level. In some agencies, such as the Bureau of Reclamation and the Corps, even top officials did not have a completed statement when reviewing proposals.[41] The Administration, Congress and the public are allowed 90 days after publication of a draft statement and 30 days from the final statement to react before an agency can take action.[42] By this time it is likely that options are so narrowed and the proposal has accumulated such support that stopping it is difficult and costly.

---

40. Hansen, NEPA: Problems and Outer Limits, (1972).
41. Comptroller General, *supra* note 38.
42. NEPA.

NEPA requires a statement presenting detailed information about every action with substantial effect upon the environment. It is possible that environmental interests will be prompted by this information into an awareness of stakes which were previously remote. The environmental impact statement may serve as alarm which activates distracted and latent groups. Whether or not environmental groups react to the warning and attempt to establish channels of communication with agencies depends on their view of agency receptivity. Certainly such organizations have focused on impact statements as a means to get court delays. Courts have demonstrated their receptivity to environmental groups. Whether or not they are also perceived as a means to communicate with agencies in decision making is partly a function of the ability of environmental groups to generate and transmit information.

A central question which experience will finally decide is whether environmental agencies and groups have *ADEQUATE RESOURCES* to make their views known to decision makers on the basis of environmental statements. Certainly conservation oriented agencies already engaged in making reviews of projects are likely to feel that NEPA has afforded them additional resources. The Bureau of Sport Fisheries and Wildlife and the Bureau of Outdoor Recreation are given additional legal basis for their claim of a say in actions affecting their interests. They now review impact statements as well as proposed actions in areas where they already have review prerogative, and may consult in the preparation of environmental statements. These agencies however, still suffer from long-standing budgetary and staffing restraints which NEPA by itself cannot change.

The volume of §102 statements circulated for comment and review on the national level threatens to become very large. By November, 1971 draft or final environmental statements for 2040 actions had accumulated at CEQ.[43] A peak of 50 final and draft statements per day was anticipated. The Corps of Engineers' permit program's for waste discharges under the 1899 Refuse Act [44] could alone generate some 7,000 permits per year and, unless the law is amended, environmental impact statements are required on each one. Such numbers place a great strain on agencies such as CEQ and EPA and constitute an information overload.

The Council of Environmental Quality, as most staff agencies of the President tend to be, is a very small organization. Its present staff is at

43. Council on Environmental Quality, 1, 102 Monitor, no 10, 1971.
44. 33 U.S.C. 407, 411, 413 (1970).

30 professionals, and many of these engage in matters apart from §102 statement reviews. At the beginning of 1972, only one man covered all statements on environmental impacts of water projects proposed by the Corps, the Bureau of Reclamation and the Soil Conservation Service. Unless some federal conservation agency or environmental group brings a particular project to the reviewer's attention, environmental impact statements are apt to get no more than general oversight. CEQ's outlook upon its reponsibilities with regard to §102 statements are bound to be affected by the fact that the agency is designed to serve the President. It is unlikely that the President desires or can afford to become involved in large numbers of controversies over governmental activities detrimental to the environment. In consequence, CEQ is unlikely to openly challenge very many governmental actions.

In light of the other demands upon its attention, the Environmental Protection Agency also faces severe limitations in regard to its review of environmental statements. EPA is a young agency, created in 1970, and much of its resources are taken up in establishing its own internal organization. Further, EPA has a number of difficult regulatory programs to administer including water and air pollution, control of pesticides, radiation protection, and solid wastes management. It is likely that these activities have a priority over environmental impact statement review. The experience with EPA's handling of Environmental Impact Statements has been that the agency is very slow. EPA's first listing of comments on statements was published in the Federal Register on January 18, 1972, approximately two years after the enactment of NEPA. The agency has complained to the CEQ that the quality of statements was poor, but with the exception of the Atomic Energy Commission, EPA has not yet sent guidelines to other federal agencies setting forth the type of information needed for EPA to carry on its review responsiblities.[45]

Environmental interest groups have problems similar to those of environmental agencies in exploiting NEPA. A survey of member organizations of the Natural Resources Council of America, a large coalition of groups, revealed that none had the necessary personnel to conduct an in-depth review of the volume of environmental statements anticipated on specific projects. It was estimated that one man-day was necessary simply to determine the adequacy of an impact statement concerning a Corps of Engineers project and one-half man-day for a simple highway impact statement. An in-depth review would take much more staff time, varying according

---

45. Comptroller General, *supra* note 38.

to the complexity of the subject. In all cases it would be necessary for the reviewer to have detailed information of his own.[46]

Independent detailed information about the impact of a proposed government action upon the environment most likely will come from local environmental interests familiar with the project area. The number of local environmental groups has increased impressively, and the growing membership of national groups has strengthened their local base. While a few years ago national interest groups called attention to impending degradations, now local groups exist to strongly oppose actions harmful to the environment on the local level. Communication between national and local levels on environmental statements remain a problem. Local groups will probably have to signal national organizations about projects proposed by field offices of federal agencies so that particularly important environmental statements can be sifted out and monitored. *Timing*, too, remains a significant problem for effective communications from environmental groups. The Rocky Mountain Center on the Environment estimates that it takes 80 to 90 days to react to a §102 statement. Agencies may well have taken action before interest groups can generate and transmit information.[47]

CONCLUSIONS

The National Environmental Policy Act of 1969 is being hailed as effective by its friends and foes alike. The *National Audubon* magazine has called it the "first effective environmental law of the land," while Senator Gordon Allott has said that it is a means of promoting mischief and should be reviewed,[48] and Secretary of Interior Rogers Morton has blamed NEPA for the delay in the department's activities to overcome the energy crises.[49] Most of these reactions are based upon the achievements of citizen lawsuits compelling government agencies to comply with the procedural requiremens of the Act. Evaluated in terms of the long. term effectiveness in forging new channels of communication to broaden the environmental information base upon which public policy is made, proclamations of success are not yet warranted.

NEPA has been examined here from the perspective of the incremental process of decision making. A great deal of relevant information is ordinarily outside the purview of any decision maker

---

46. Natural Resources Council of America, Report of the Ad Hoc Committee On Environmental Impact Statements (mimeo) (Aug. 12, 1971).

47. Hansen, *supra* note 40.

48. Zeldin, *supra* note 32.

49. *Hearings on Fuel and Energy Resources Before the House Interior and Insular Affairs Comm.*, 92nd Cong., 2d Session (1972).

who typically concentrates upon marginal alt[...]
quo. Information becomes relevant to the decis[...]
becomes convinced that it will help him, or that he [...]
ignore it. New rules and regulations are not likely, by th[...]
force a decision maker to take into account interests and con[...]
would not otherwise consider, despite the claims of NEPA's spo[...]
that its provisions are action forcing. Instead, NEPA may facilitate
change in communications channels where decision makers are
already in search of alternatives to avoid the conflict with environmentalists which have made their past patterns of decision-making
uncomfortable. Realistically, it should be expected that receptivity to
environmental interests will come about incrementally and unevenly
among government agencies. The extent to which it happens depends
upon the continuing strength and activity of environmental interest
groups. The passage of NEPA can be viewed as an outcome of past
failures of environmentalists to get the ear of decision makers. It will
take the sustained effort of environmentalists to make it work.

essional
...les Toward
...nvironment

Michael E. Kraft

The recently published The Limits to
Growth, the final report of the U.S. Commission
on Population Growth and the American Future,
and the final proposals for the upcoming United
Nations Conference on the Human Environment in
Stockholm present at least one important curiosity.[1] On the one hand they confirm our suspi-
cions that environmental calls to alarm over the
past several years and proposals for fundamental
changes in our social, economic, and political
practices are not unfounded; and on the other
hand, they point once again to the fact that --
without too much exaggeration -- very few political leaders and members of the public give
these issues much of their time and attention
and still fewer appreciate the full extent of
these problems and are willing to support the
degree of change implied. The puzzling situation of impending catastrophes eliciting little
worry or sense of urgency among our political
leadership is made especially significant by the
necessity of politics, broadly defined, to any
scheme of ecological change. However much we
might like instantaneous, non-political correc-
tions of our problems, the centrality of politics to ecological reform is inescapable. All
solutions -- and especially those fundamental in
nature -- to some extent involve public or governmental decision-making: the resolution of

ALTERNATIVES, Summer, 1972, Vol. 1, pp. 27-32; 34-37.

conflicting values and the shaping of collective
choice or public policy. Therefore, the rather
undramatic response of most political systems to
the challenge of the environmental crisis presents a highly suitable subject for political
analysis.

There is nearly an infinite variety of
particular questions one might investigate which
would shed some light on our ecological predicament and perhaps point to viable paths to an
ecologically sound future society. The research
reported here is intentionally narrowly focused
on congressional attitudes. Comments below
might be read with greater profit if other factors which shape politics and policy-making are
borne in mind: the overall institutional structure and the cultural and economic bases of the
American political system; the specific internal
structure and norms of Congress; and the values
and attitudes of major political actors and
their influence in the policy-making process --
the President, the bureaucracy, public opinion,
party and legislative leaders, and non-govern-
mental interest groups (including business,
labor, scientists, and various environmental organizations, among others).

Given the relative newness, scope, and
depth of ecological issues, one of the most obvious and central constraints on fundamental
change is the attitudes of major national political leaders and how those attitudes affect
willingness to support controversial and possibly radical policies. At this point in time the
anomaly of apparent inattention and misunder-
standing of ecological problems in the face of
abundant documentation of their reality presents
a question of particular interest. That environmental issues are on the political agenda is
undeniably true in 1972; that they are supported
in principle by almost everyone is equally evident. However, neither is a guarantee that
these issues are seriously attended to, fully
understood, or given a high priority by all
those who share in policy-making. In fact, to
attend to environmental issues is not as easy as
it seems. Political leaders, especially at the
national level of government, are busy; they are
subjected to inordinate demands on their time
and routinely face multiple and competing social
problems and "crises", many of which in their

173

view are equally or more important than environmental ills, especially in the short-run. There simply is very little time for or personal profit in philosophical contemplation of our ecological future.

Further, ecologists and environmentalists seem determined to ignore a lesson learned often in recent years -- namely, that scientific knowledge and political feasibility may on occasion collide head on. Proposals of policy recommendations, however well supported by facts or justified by the public interest, amount to very little if not *listened to, believed, and acted on by those in position of power.* We have a long and instructive history of the use, nonuse, and misuse of social and scientific knowledge in major, controversial policy decision in the United States, a country presumably quite high on a scale of rationality and dedication to science. A consideration of actions in policy areas as diverse as foreign policy (e.g., the Indochina war), urban policy (e.g., crime control or welfare reform), and civil liberties (e.g., reform in drug and abortion laws) reminds us that political leaders and the public as well act not infrequently on the basis of personal emotions and ideological prejudices, or simply out of ignorance of available scientific evidence.[2] There is no reason to think that ecological issues will escape this pattern; indeed, the politics of population limitation is a good example of these forces at work.

Since these conflicts do exist, proposals for radical and controversial ecological change must consider political belief and willingness to act as important -- and perhaps as the most significant -- factors affecting the extent and speed of that change. In this paper I want to draw attention to two variables which shape the policy preferences of congressmen and their willingness to favor ecological priorities: attention paid to environmental problems and the way in which those problems are viewed and defined. The assertion underlying this discussion is that the greater the attention paid to environmental problems by relevant political elites and the greater their tendency to think about these issues in terms of ecological threats -- as opposed to limited pollution control, conservation, or recreational-aesthetic

174

problems -- the more likely they are to support and actively promote sound ecological policies. Without more attention to the entire range of environmental problems and more widespread and informed ecological awareness or consciousness among political elites, the likelihood of speedy or adequate policy-making is rather slim.

STUDY DESIGN

A few words on the nature of the study may be useful. This research was motivated by a feeling that too often we rely on questionable journalistic accounts and intuition to inform ourselves about environmental politics and con- straints on change. I think it advisable to supplement the flood of environmental writing to date with more reliable, empirical evidence on these matters, in particular on the actual con- ditions in our political institutions where key decisions are made or not made. The more we understand the intricacies of politics, the greater our ability to choose strategies intelli- gently and to influence whatever changes pos- sible.

Between mid-January and early April, 1970 interviews were conducted with nearly the entire membership of five sub-committees in the House of Representatives and one in the Senate, all of which dealt primarily or heavily with environ- mental issues. Congress at that time, in my judgment, was more of an innovator or initiator in environmental affairs than the executive. It was playing a substantially more significant role than the executive branch in calling atten- tion to these issues, launching ideas and giving them visibility, in setting the political agenda. This was done largely through the publicity at- tendant to a series of subcommittee hearings. Since the kinds of ecological change called for most often (national and international planning or ecomanagement, a limit to economic growth, population limitation and in general a move to- ward global ecological equilibrium) require further national legislation, Congress obvious- ly is a highly relevant body on that basis as well.

One major reason for this investigation was to evaluate the claims of critics that eco- logical problems were not understood or given a high priority of attention by leading political

175

decision-makers. Given the internal organization of Congress, a subcommittee focus was the most efficacious means of studying environmental attitudes among those who might both have developed ideas about environmental issues and be in a position to shape Congressional policy. It is generally conceded that almost all significant policy-making in Congress takes place in its committees and subcommittees and not on the floor (this is especially true in the highly structured and specialized House of Representatives.). Thus, the sample was not random, nor strictly speaking, representative of the Congress as a whole, but was *intentionally biased toward congressmen more likely to be involved with these issues, attentive, informed and receptive to an ecological frame of thought than their colleagues.*

The five subcommittees in the House were Science, Research and Development of the Science and Astronautics Committee, headed at that time by Emilio Daddario of Connecticut; Conservation and Natural Resources of the Government Operations Committee, chaired by Henry Reuss of Wisconsin; Rivers and Harbors of the Public Works Committee (water pollution legislation) chaired by John Blatnik of Minnesota; Public Health and Welfare of the Interstate and Foreign Commerce Committee (air pollution) chaired by John Jarman of Oklahoma -- though effectively handled by Paul Rogers of Florida on air pollution issues; and Fish and Wildlife Conservation of the Merchant Marine and Fisheries Committee (which handled the National Environmental Policy Act in the House), chaired by John Dingell of Michigan. The Senate subcommittee on Air and Water Pollution of the Public Works Committee, headed by Edmund Muskie of Maine completed the sample. I will refer below only to the House, though insofar as such a generalization is proper, the Senate was not very different.

Forty-five interviews were held with Members of the House. In a number of additional cases, interviews with personal staff, legislative and administrative assistants, proved adequate substitutes. Other interviews were conducted with committee staff personnel, journalists, and interest group representatives. The interviews were semi-structured with open-ended questions. Almost all were tape-recorded with the permission of the congressmen and a guarantee of anonymity on my part; this procedure produced little observable reduction in the frankness of their response.

ATTENTION AND ENVIRONMENTAL ISSUES

The overwhelming diversity and abundance of issues and communication demands on congressmen and the press of immediate day-to-day affairs, combined with an obvious shortage of time and energy, create a condition of selective attention. A survey of the number and variety of public problems facing a congressman at any one point in time -- or simply a visit to Capitol Hill -- is sufficient to demonstrate this highly important fact.[3] Analyses of congressional behavior -- indeed of almost all political behavior -- for some reason take little notice of this constraint on possible or feasible political action. Yet, as "insiders" frequently tell us, episodic or marginal attention to most public problems and to the details of legislation is the norm rather than the exception. If this is true, then one would expect that day-to-day demands and more immediate or pressing issues will tend to shift ecological problems to the back burner as far as congressmen are concerned. Future issues, abstract, technical, or bewildering problems -- typical of more serious ecological threats (e.g., population growth, ecosystemic effects of pollution, or unlimited economic growth itself) -- are likely to be selected out for relative inattention or low priority concern. Most politicians do not have the time, or possibly the inclination, to ponder such problems. Rather, they are geared to respond to immediate constituent demands, to specific legislative proposals, to current situational pressures -- and further, to do so in a way that maximizes their probability of re-election and least antagonizes possible sources of political opposition. Congressmen, then, are quite naturally more often concerned with the economic status of their districts and getting re-elected every two years than with issues like the environment. They also are more at home with established and familiar issues than with those newly emergent.

Given these conditions and habits, relative inattention to ecological problems, a lack of information, and a superficial understanding of what ecological change means (in terms of demands for fundamental economic and social changes) are likely results. And this ecological illiteracy leads to a strong probability of inadequate policy-making from the perspective of serious environmentalists. To those who would point to the popularity of "ecology" and "environment" since 1970, I would suggest the value of skepticism. *There is very little evidence that this superficial political popularity has produced serious changes in understanding of and concern for ecological problems over the last few years.*

There are, then, substantial reasons to expect a low level of attention as measured by time spent on environmental problems and the centrality of such issues in the complex of concerns facing a congressman. One also expects different congressmen to respond differently. Not all are alike on environmental issues, no more than all are doves or hawks, or all liberals or conservatives. Congressmen can be differentiated according to the saliency of environmental issues, much as scholars have done with respect to legislative "roles". Since saliency is an important factor shaping an individual's attitudes and policy preferences, this seems a worthwhile exercise. Presumably, a highly attentive and well-informed congressman will *perceive* ecological problems and *act* on them differently than those who scarcely consider these issues at all.

It would not be much of an exaggeration to assert that the politics of ecology turns to a great extent on *who attends to what, how and with what effects*. This perspective raises some very different questions than the more traditional notion of politics as who gets what, when, and how -- i.e., of decision-making -- and questions not always raised by those who study attitudes of political elites but ignore variable saliency or intensity of opinions.

Two independent empirical measures of the degree of attention paid to environmental issues were made; one was through personal interviews and the other through content analysis of the *Congressional Record*. The two measures are both approximate indicators of this rather complex concept, but do correlate highly with each other. Both represent an attempt to assess en-

178

vironmental saliency on as systematic a basis as possible to minimize the inevitable bias in personal judgment in discussions of congressional behavior. The interview measure was based upon two specific questions and an analysis of the entire interview transcript. Each congressman was classified in terms of the saliency of those issues for him personally; that is, how central were environmental issues in his preoccupation with all political issues before Congress and the nation and how much time relative to other issues did he devote to environmental matters. Saliency was judged through a reading of the entire interview transcript in addition to the two questions specifically intended to draw out this information. One question used was "what do you feel is the most important domestic problem facing this country today?" Given the interview format and the initial letter requesting an interview on environmental issues, there is a built-in bias here toward environmentally-related answers. Yet, in spite of this, more than one-half of those asked mentioned no environmental problem in response to the question. The other question was "what type of issues here in Congress do you find you are spending most of your time on, any one or two areas in particular?"

The other measure was derived from an analysis of the annual index to the *Congressional Record* for the period 1967-1970 inclusive. Essentially a tabulation was made for the number of bills introduced, speeches made on the House floor, and articles inserted into the *Record* (a common practice) on environmental issues, environment being defined very broadly for this purpose to include conservation, resource use, pollution control, and various ecological issues. This number was then divided by the total bills, speeches and articles for all issues for the same period to get a measure of relative attention or saliency of environmental issues. The assumption underlying this analysis is that the relative number of bills, speeches, and articles on environmental matters over a four-year period tells us something about how a congressman allocates his time and energy and where his interests lie, especially when we use this measure only for broad comparisons among the sample. It should also be noted that through introducing

bills, making speeches, and otherwise participating in floor debate on such issues, Congress
is playing its crucial role of agenda-setting
for the nation: raising new ideas, propelling
them to national attention and creating the
basis for future policy change whatever the immediate impact.

FINDINGS

The personal interviews (using the overall measure) revealed that for only 28 percent
of the sample could environmental issues be legitimately characterized as "very salient" (i.e.,
a major area of concern and time allocation).
For 36 percent of the sample, these issues were
not at all salient. And for another 36 percent
they were moderately salient (ie., one of many
concerns but by no means a dominant one in terms
of time allocation). It is important to bear in
mind that the congressmen under consideration
here serve on subcommittees which deal with environmental measures (most subcommittees, needless to say, lack this close connection) *and*
that the interviews were obtained at the *height*
of the original surge of interest in environmental issues (early 1970).

The results of the content analysis of
the *Record* are similar, but too complex to discuss here except superficially. There was wide
variance in the degree of saliency for various
measures (bills, speeches, articles, and all
combined). The correlations between those measures and the interview measure were generally
high and confirm my intuitive feelings that both
indicators of attention to environmental issues
tap a genuine aspect of congressional behavior
in this regard. Those who revealed a high degree of personal attention and concern for environmental issues in the interview scored high
on the *Record* measures and, likewise, those who
admitted little attention to environmental issues in the interview scored low on the *Record*
measures.

It should come as no surprise to those
acquainted with congressional (and other political behavior) that few congressmen essentially
specialize in environmental issues and that
most give them rather marginal or limited attention if any at all. Even among our presumably
highly involved and attentive sample of congress-

men, however, there was an extremely wide variance in the saliency of these issues (even broadly and generously defined). There were some congressmen who were, indeed, highly active and attentive as revealed by both measures and by general consensus among relevant staff personnel on Capitol Hill. Typical of this group were John Dingell of Michigan, John Blatnik of Minnesota, Henry Reuss of Wisconsin, Paul McCloskey of California, Charles Mosher of Ohio, James Wright of Texas, John Saylor of Pennsylvania, and former Representative Emilio Daddario of Connecticut. These representatives, numbering from 25-35 percent of the particular sample in the House I studied, spent a good portion of their time on environmental issues, considered them highly important, were reasonably well informed and generally worked undramatically and unnoticed at solving these problems. They also tended to "hear" more than others from scientists and constituents on environmental issues, appeared to profit more from subcommittee hearings' testimony (frequently technical), and were much more likely to be concerned generally with national rather than local issues, which is highly unusual in the very parochial and locally-minded House. Ironically, given the usual complaints against the congressional seniority system, these members were also *higher in seniority* than their more apathetic colleagues. Many were chairmen or ranking members on their subcommittees. A position of power seems to have enabled those so inclined to act productively. Less senior representatives may have felt that any effort was not worthwhile (and they may been been right).

Other congressmen on the same subcommittees spent relatively little of their time on environmental issues, were not very active legislatively (measured by the number of bills introduced), and, in short, were not very attentive. Many of them scarcely took notice of the problems in spite of all the attendant publicity and popularity of these issues in early 1970. These congressmen were likely to confess that they were essentially more interested in other issues, from foreign policy to urban affairs. Consequently, they chose to devote their scarce resources to those ends rather than to environmental issues. Some spent very little time with the subcommittee at all (most had other committee assignments in addition to this one). Some appeared to spend little time on legislative matters of any type, other duties (such as constituency servicing) receiving more of their attentions. Others claimed they would have liked to spend more time with environmental issues but the press of more immediate demands and other obligations prevented them. All of these members were likely to be more concerned with local as opposed to national interests. They "heard" less from scientists and constituents on environmental issues, either due to less actual communication or less perception of it. They were often poorly informed on the nature of the problems, lacking even the rudimentary knowledge available to any interested reader of a national newspaper or news magazine. When they did speak out on environmental issues they were merely "going through the motions", not actually attempting to influence legislative policy-making.

The mere fact that some congressmen were less attentive than others to environmental issues is not in itself an astounding observation. The reason for emphasizing it here is to counter the false presumption on the part of many citizens and ecological activists that all congressmen -- or at least, certainly, those on appropriate committees -- are in fact "paying attention", are concerned, are well-informed, are hard-working, and therefore are, or will be, responsive to the full range of ecological problems as soon as they are brought to light. The data reported here suggest that only with great imagination can such a view of Congress be supported. We might expect the same of other legislative and executive bodies where constraints on time and energy create similar conditions of selective attention. *Consciously and unconsciously information is perceived and adapted to screen out the politically undigestible and personally unimportant. Those less involved with these issues will not likely be as well informed, will not hear as much, or be as receptive to, scientific advice or constituency opinion, will be less inclined to believe in the seriousness of the "crisis", and in general will likely be less conscious or aware of ecological problems.* To judge from the present sample of representatives, these individuals are more likely to vote against "pro-environment" measures than those who are highly attentive, especially when those measures are controversial, costly, or not greatly popular with their constituents.

A more realistic view of the congressional process than normally put forth regarding environmental issues is that attention and concern are highly variable. Therefore, one ought to ask *who* attends, *how* he attends, *why* he does so, and what the *political effect* of this attention is. Further, part of any strategy for political change should stress keeping environmental issues before politicians -- high on the political agenda -- with persistently high levels of attention. Different techniques of appeal or influence will have varied effects on different congressmen. In some cases, one is attempting to persuade a man to change his mind; in others, one is trying to activate a potential supporter to give more of his time and energy.

The casual assumption that political leaders will foster ecological change without such prodding or encouragement is highly unrealistic given the constraints under which they must work -- limited resources of time, energy, and political capital, and excessive, pressing, and conflicting demands. Unless already predisposed to attend to and concern themselves with ecological issues by personal nature, previous experience, or current political situations (as was the case with most of the highly attentive and ecologically-minded group reported here), intense and persistent constituent demands may be one of the few ways to encourage indifferent politicians to act in a more ecologically sound fashion. On something of an optimistic note we can suggest that it may even be easier for voters to influence a congressman to shift positions on matters of relatively minor interest to him. The cost to the congressman in such a case is likely to be far less than the benefits derived from his change.

ENVIRONMENTAL ISSUE-ORIENTATION

To recognize the existence of or to pay attention to environmental problems and legislation to whatever extent is not necessarily to perceive and define those problems in an ecological framework, nor to favor automatically comprehensive political change. Attention may be highly variable as noted; it can also be very selective in its particular focus, shaped by one's conceptualization of what the problems really are. When asking *who* attends to environmental problems, then, it is equally important to ask *how* one attends to them, how he defines the nature of the problems facing us. A major factor in the making of environmental policy is the distinction between how professional ecologists define the extent and severity of various threats and how non-expert politicians understand and believe in their reality or importance.

As anyone who has followed environmental issues over the past few years knows, there are a variety of conceptualizations of environmental problems, their seriousness and their causes. Some observers are prone to equate ecology with aesthetic values or the "quality of life". There is the older strain of conservationist thought, putting great emphasis on conservation of national resources, wildlife, virgin forests, wild rivers, and the like. There are those who seek primarily greater recreational values in clean lakes and streams and open spaces or who take "environment" to mean inner-city living conditions. The recent pollution-control movement has generated a class of followers in itself. And of course there are those like Paul Ehrlich, Barry Commoner and other ecologists who are most concerned with ecosystemic threats: with population growth, unrestrained economic growth, and the environmental impact of human technology. Whatever their particular differences they share a view of ecological problems based upon a systemic or holistic view of the world, the interrelationships between man and his natural surroundings, and a time perspective which includes an assessment of likely *future* developments and threats as well as presently evident dangers.[4]

Among both the public and politicians there is a great diversity of viewpoints, of definitions of or concern for various environmental problems. They may all represent important concerns but such diversity is also indicative of fundamental disagreements over the priority of problems, estimates of the severity of threats, the necessity of governmental policy, and over the degree of change mandated by the "environmental crisis". Because this is one of the most significant aspects of the politics of ecology, especially as regards the more basic

and less visible problems, congressmen in the
sample were asked to venture definitions of what
"environmental quality" (the phrase most commonly used in 1970) meant to them. (The question
was: "As you know, the phrase 'environmental
quality' is used quite a lot today. What does
this phrase mean to you personally?") In addition, the entire interview transcript, covering
a number of questions on the specific problem,
their causes, and so forth, was analyzed using
the same criteria. Together with the variance
in attention, the results shed some light on the
impressive though little noticed differences one
finds among congressmen -- and by extension,
other political elites -- in environmental awareness and priorities.

FINDINGS

Though answers were diverse, three basic
types of orientation toward environmental problems seemed evident: a Recreational-aesthetic
orientation, a Pollution-control orientation,
and an Ecological orientation. These types are
implicit in many of the popular discussions of
ecological politics and are reasonably analyti-
cally exclusive. Particularly important is the
distinction between the Ecologically-oriented
congressmen and the others. As the case with
any typology of this sort the classification is
intended to capture *dominant modes of thought
which reflect basic variations in environmental
perspectives*. That it is not a perfect reflection of every congressman's thought on these issues is readily admitted. Nonetheless, the extensive open-ended discussions which form the
raw data for the construction of such a typology
are preferable to the artificiality of highly
structured questionnaires on environmental opinions.

A few examples of each type of issue-orientation will serve to illustrate the differences and point towards the significance of the
Ecological-orientation. The Recreational-aes-
thetic-orientation is typified by three Congressmen. A senior Southern Democrat: "purifying
the water and making the countryside better.
Beautification; I put a lot of emphasis on this,
on highway beauty, flowers, grass, trees. We
must preserve our environment, but make it better, purify it." A relatively junior Northern
Republican: "and you can see the dirt and junk

that surrounds it. And these people are talking
about Congress spending some money trying to
clean up our atmosphere. We have got to clean
it up where we are...leave that spot of ground
cleaner than the way we found it; then we could
have a cleaner America...and some pride in our
environment." An urban Northern Democrat:
"Well, to me personally it means what I have
known it to mean all my life...nice homes, clean
streets, clean alleys, fresh air, the kind of
life, environment, that people like to live in
and raise their children in."

This way of conceptualizing the issues
emphasizes appearance, cleanliness and a general
appreciation for the quality of life. Key terms
which appear frequently are "pure", "clean",
"decent", "quality", "beauty", and "countryside".
A prime feature in the thought of these congressmen is man's *use of* nature for *his purposes,*
aesthetic and recreational. Nature is considered *apart* from man and for *his* benefit, a distinctly non-ecological viewpoint. While this
way of thinking about environmental problems
does not necessarily imply an anti-environmental
position, it does turn out to be negatively correlated with ecological attitudes and roll-call
behavior on some recent issues. While only a
few of the congressmen interviewed presented
themselves as against environmental issues (it
was surprising that anyone did), the Recreational-aesthetic type was the least involved and
concerned.

Traditional conservationist sentiments
may or may not fall into this category, depending upon the *purpose* of the conservation and understanding of the connection of preservation of
endangered species and the like to *ecological*
concerns (e.g., for ecosystem stability).

It is also worth noting that critics of
the environmental movement (left and right and
both "humanists" and industrialists) frequently
define environment or ecology in this fashion.
The reason, one suspects, is that such labeling
eases the propagandistic intent of the critics
to dismiss the significance of environmental
problems altogether. This is especially true of
those commercial advertisements which tell us
(with a double irony) how container manufacturers or oil companies are ecologically-minded by
virtue of their efforts to eliminate litter or

clean up beaches.

The Pollution-control-orientation is distinguishable from this attitude and can be illustrated by two examples. A junior Northern Democrat: "Well, in a negative way it includes the degrading of our environment by the pollution of our air, water and soil, to the point where we are creating unhealthful conditions....In a positive way, I would say it is a movement to curb this erosion of air and water and land and the corruption of it, the pollution of it." A senior Northern Republican: "It has a wide application. It could mean emission of gases from automobiles, air pollution from factories; it could mean stream pollution...in rural areas streams are a place to dump pollution, to get rid of it."

This orientation stresses cleaning up air and water pollution, as is well known, has received a great deal of attention and has been a focus of much legislative activity in the past few years. Though in many ways an improvement over aesthetic, recreational and conservationist approaches to the environmental crisis, the Pollution-control orientation also suffers from grave weaknesses. Congressmen of this type rarely offer any reference to larger ecosystem relationships or to the biological effects of pollution except as they directly affect man and the quality of the air and water we ourselves use, especially in terms of human health and welfare. As another congressman defined it, this amounts to the "abatement of irritants". As with the Recreational-aesthetic orientation, this view of environmental problems is primarily anthropocentric, based on the premise that the environment is primarily useful insofar as it benefits *man*.

A focus on *present, concrete, physical* problems rather than on *future, more abstract, less visible threats* is also typical. There is a tendency among this group towards a more technological solution to the problems, toward engineering and public works projects to "solve" the pollution and remove the "irritants". Such a view encourages politics as usual as though "pollution" were merely another routine public problem susceptible to the same incremental, moderate approach characteristic of most contemporary policy-making. The disagreements (some severe to be sure) are over the amounts of money to be spent, the strength of pollution-control measures (e.g., in the 1971-72 controversy over the water pollution control bill) and the particular mechanisms of administration. As Margaret and Harold Sprout put it, this is typical of the American engineering or pragmatic approach; it represents a "manipulative way of viewing the world" through "tunnel vision" which ignores systemic interrelationships and long-term effects of actions, while concentrating on discrete instrumental tasks.[5] Such an "ideology" also expresses great faith in human technology and engineering, and continues a tradition of belief in human omnipotence over nature.

Rarely is someone of either of these two orientations likely to suggest our attitudes, culture, or social structure, our pattern of consumption in an affluent technological society, population growth, economic growth, or the private enterprise or market system of economic choice as fundamental causes of "pollution". Put otherwise, policies are considered only within currently "feasible" limits which do not make great demands upon present socio-economic practices. Further, there is rarely likely to be a concern for what is happening beyond the borders of the United States. Without too much exaggeration, we might consider this to be representative of the brunt of present public policy approaches in the U.S. and probably the dominant public view of recent years.[6] Needless to say, from an ecological perspective, these approaches are greatly deficient.

The difference between these two types of response and the Ecological-orientation can be illustrated by the following two congressmen. A senior Western Republican: "Environmental quality means (pause) a meeting, a balancing of, and harmonizing with, nature, the problems of industrialization, population explosion and other causes of pollution of one kind or another, of all the environment; that includes water, air, land....It has been said that we could come to an end as a human race if we don't do something about stopping the poisoning of our own environment." And, at greater length, a junior Northeastern Democrat: "Well, the phrase 'environmental quality' means the capability of natural resources to support people. But above and beyond that, in my judgment, it has to do with the mores of the tribe. In other words, what kind of life do we want to live as individuals and can we afford to do it in a modern society? Environment has to do with sustaining life on this earth. Every single individual, with the recognition of the so-called industrial age we live in, is a polluter. Every single individual. It is no longer a question of whether we are going to regain nature as it was or the balance of nature. We have practically in large measure destroyed it in many areas. Whether or not we can resurrect it is a question."

In my estimation, these individuals reveal both a more thoughtful and more concerned environmental perspective than the others. On the whole, this orientation to the problems appears to be much closer to the new intellectual current stimulated by ecological thought. Much of the writing on ecology in recent years has stressed the need for an ecological consciousness and an environmental ethic. Such an ecological perspective is usually characterized by a recognition and understanding of the finite nature of Earth's resources and the fragile, complex nature of ecosystems which make human civilization intimately dependent on a balanced, harmonious relationship with natural processes. The holistic or systemic perspective is especially important for facilitating recognition of causes and problems beyond visible pollution and aesthetic irritants, for instance, population growth, or unlimited economic growth, and a willingness to act on them. It also suggests a Spaceship Earth or global view of man's problems in contradistinction to a national or parochial focus. As Lynton Caldwell has pointed out, "the problem of environmental control is basically conceptual. If the environment is not perceived as a complex interacting whole it will hardly be acted upon from this viewpoint."

Any adequate "solution" to the environmental crisis must be based upon ecological principles. The sooner we move in that direction the less costly will be the inevitable confrontation with ecological limits of the Earth. Yet, approaching political choice in holistic terms, being aware of *systemic* relationships and the aggregate ecological effects of our actions in the long-run, would be a fundamental -- indeed radical -- shift from most current decision-making. It is not at all clear that such comprehensive decision-making is either technically possible or politically feasible in the near future. But its significance for ecological change can hardly be minimized.

The Ecological-orientation (using the overall measure) was characteristic of slightly more than one-third of the sample, with very generous criteria for inclusion in this type. With more rigorous criteria perhaps only five or six representatives could be called strongly and consistently ecological in their orientation. The Recreational-aesthetic orientation was equally represented, with approximately one-third of the sample falling into this category. Put another way, slightly less than two-thirds could *not* be classified as ecological in their thought even through generous reading of their responses. And as I have tried to indicate, how problems are defined and how the causes of problems are understood dramatically affect policy preferences and willingness to support ecological priorities. By way of example, issue-orientation as measured here strongly correlated with key roll call votes on supersonic transport funding (1970-71), water pollution funding (1969) and recent attempts to strengthen the water pollution control act (1972).

Given the rather select nature of this particular group of congressmen, one must conclude, concerning the aggregate orientation of the sample, that it is *very far from the ideal of ecological reformers*. Presumably the U.S. House of Representatives as a whole would reveal a somewhat less "ideal" orientation. It is worth repeating that the sample was conservatively drawn to favor environmentally-oriented Members of Congress, that the time period in which the interviews were completed was favorable, *and* that the coding of answers was quite generous.

A similar conclusion can be drawn from answers to a question on the existence of an "environmental crisis". Most of the sample either rejected the notion altogether or gave highly qualified responses. Somewhat more than one-third agreed. (The question was: "Some scientists and others say we have an environmental crisis which may threaten the survival of life on this planet in 30, 50, or 100 years. Does the problem seem to you to be of such crisis proportions or is this an exaggeration?")

The tendency to agree was strongly associated
with our measure of environmental-orientation,
Ecologically-oriented Members being far more
likely to agree than Recreational-aesthetically-
oriented Members.

CONCLUSION

What are we to make of these findings?
First, it is my impression (but only that) that
any changes in congressional behavior since 1970
are marginal. The thrust of the results would,
I think, be the same if the survey was repeated
in 1972. One does hope, of course, that over
time, political leaders will come in greater
numbers to appreciate the need for an ecological
perspective. I see no great surge in this direction yet. A more significant question might
be: What is new or astounding about such findings? Can one realistically expect congressmen
to be revolutionary in their attitudes, well-informed on technical matters, and so open to
challenging new ideas?

It is certainly true that normally the U.
S. Congress is a centrist, moderate, and often
conservative body of politicians. This is due
largely to methods of electoral recruitment into
office, the internal norms within Congress, and
a distribution of power in that body which has
favored the more conservative elements. Change
comes about neither frequently nor speedily.
Congressmen are used to business as usual, conventional political values, and traditional ways
of doing things. In spite of some recent
changes, all of these factors reinforce the
overwhelming tendency toward preservation of the
status quo. In short, Congress is rarely innovative and almost always conservative in its actions; it reliably discourages the new and pro-
tects the old.

We might have expected the seriousness
and enormity of ecological problems to provoke
an unusual response. But the interviews, along
with other less systematic evidence, tend to
confirm the fears of environmental critics that insufficient attention, a lack of an ecological
perspective and inadequate commitment were typical of congressmen in early 1970 and continue to
be so. Throughout these interviews, virtually
no one suggested the need for any truly radical
or revolutionary changes in social or economic

191

behavior or a willingness to create appropriate
public policy. Optimism in our ability to handle environmental problems pervaded the sample.
There was virtually no sense of urgency or peril,
even among those who claimed to recognize an
"environmental crisis". Almost all policy recommendations were within what in American politics are the normally narrow confines of conventional political values and "reasonable" -- non-
controversial -- solutions.

The fact that ecological problems seem to
call for radical or fundamental changes in human
attitudes, behavior and institutional arrangements obviously presents a dilemma, especially
when the need is for immediate action, not in 30
or 50 years (both ecologists and population experts tell us that time is crucial). Congressional attitudes and a relative lack of receptivity to innovation constitute major obstacles to
the kinds of changes so often proposed by the
ecologically concerned. Both variables we have
studied here, attention and issue-orientation,
shape perception and evaluation of the problems
and influence willingness to support new priorities. Multiplied by probably similar conditions
in other political bodies, it is clear that political solutions to our ecological problems will
not be easily accomplished. The manifold biases
toward glacial political change cannot be overcome without more awareness of the problems confronting us and more widespread and serious concern on the part of key political leaders. Drastic actions will not be forthcoming on the basis
of moderate discomfort with occasional pollution
and aesthetic irritants. This is especially
true when "pro-environment" actions conflict
sharply with vested interests or highly cherish-
ed values, e.g., corporate profits, a high standard of living, personal freedom to do as one
pleases regardless of the consequences for the
environment, and so forth.

Unfortunately, the more threatening aspects of ecological instability are not immediately noticeable and do not impinge sufficiently
on our daily lives to motivate us to act in the
extraordinary fashion seemingly necessary. Perception of such threats is made all the more difficult by the limited ability of political leaders to devote more than casual attention to matters beyond the multitude of present day-to-day

demands and conflicts to which they are all subjected. An ecologically sound future depends
upon this situation being altered.

Our aggregate description of this sample
of representatives is also in one sense misleading. As with any aggregate account, it disguis-
es differentiation within the sample. One-
fourth to one-third of this sample *were* reasonably ecologically conscious and highly attentive
to environmental issues. They were also better
informed, more likely to profit from scientific
advice (to listen), more likely to take a long-
er-range view of man's plight than their colleagues, and more likely to agree that we do
have an "environmental crisis". If not exactly
radical and fully committed to an environmental
ethic, they were at least more receptive to common sense and to the obvious need for far-reaching innovation in the next few years than their
less aware fellow congressmen. And not surprisingly, the significant efforts toward innovative
environmental policy-making now being made in
the Congress are by and large led by congressmen
in this group. They are at this point in time
a *distinct minority*. They also face increasingly protracted and occasionally intense opposition from those less committed to environmental
priorities; for instance, a "backlash" is clearly under way in the halls of Congress in 1972,
part of which is aimed at the vitally important
National Environmental Policy Act of 1969 (NEPA).
If ecologically-aware congressmen can persuade
more of their apathetic and less conscious colleagues to take heed and support their efforts,
an otherwise gloomy prospect for ecological
change could be brighter. And if environmentally active citizens could be more aware of political reality and the not-so-obvious constraints
under which political leaders must operate, they
would be better able to exert whatever influence
they can command. In particular, they might concentrate on electing and supporting sympathetic
and innovative public officials, opposing those
less sympathetic to their cause, and engaging in
sustained, energetic, and sophisticated lobbying
for environmental goals. The election or defeat
of a few key congressmen on a significant committee can make a substantial difference. Environmentalists would be well advised in this vein
to bear in mind that the congressman who moves

boldly beyond the views of his constituents and the nation must not feel he is thereby sacrificing the security of his office. Few public leaders eagerly court their own early retirement. Until the public is much more environmentally concerned than at present, those pressing for radical changes must consider such matters. Congressmen must be shown that it is to their own advantage to support ecological change.

The findings reported here along with more impressionistic analysis of contemporary environmental politics suggest a strategy of ecological change based on vision and hope, but one equally rooted in persistent effort and attuned to a realistic and skeptical view of politics. In the critical game of politics, idealists and utopians are not as often rewarded as are realists who maximize their effectiveness through an understanding of political behavior and the potential for change. The more we learn of ecological motivation and behavior, the more we can combine utopian vision with effective politics. ∎

Notes

1. Donella H. Meadows, et al., *The Limits to Growth* (New York: Universe Books, Inc., 1972); "The Commission on Population Growth and the American Future," *Population and the American Future* (Washington, D.C.: U.S. Government Printing Office, 1972).

2. See Dean Schooler, Jr., *Science, Scientists and Public Policy* (New York: The Free Press, 1971) and Irving Louis Horowitz(ed.), *The Use and Abuse of Social Science* (New Brunswick, N.J.: Transaction Inc., 1971).

3. For some very perceptive comments on this phenomenon applied to Congress and other political bodies, see Lewis Anthony Dexter, *The Sociology and Politics of Congress* (Chicago: Rand-McNally, 1969).

4. For an overview of the substantive [...]
    cal problems see Barry Commoner, The [...]
    Circle (New York: Alfred A. Knopf, 197[...]
    Paul and Anne Ehrlich, Population Resou[...]
    Environment (San Francisco: W.H. Freeman [...]
    Co., 1970).

5. Margaret Sprout and Harold Sprout, Ecology
    and Politics in America: Some Issues and Al-
    ternatives, Monograph (New York: General
    Learning Press, 1971).

6. Two of Ralph Nader's study group reports are
    instructive on the nature of air and water
    pollution politics in the United States. See
    John Esposito, Vanishing Air (New York:
    Grossman Publishers, 1970); and David Zwick
    and Marcy Benstock, Water Wasteland (New
    York: Grossman Publishers, 1971). Also of
    value on recent American public policy are
    Environmental Quality, the second annual
    report of the Council on Environmental Qual-
    ity (Washington, D.C.: U.S. Government Print-
    ing Office, 1971); and Congress and the Na-
    tions Environment: Environmental Affairs of
    the 91st Congress, prepared by the Environ-
    mental Policy Division, Congressional Re-
    search Service, Library of Congress at the
    request of Henry M. Jackson, Chairman, Com-
    mittee on Interior and Insular Affairs,
    United States Senate (February 10, 1971).

7. Lynton Keith Caldwell, Environment: A Chal-
    lenge to Modern Society (Garden City,N.Y.:
    Doubleday and Company, revised edition, 1971).
    See also Caldwell's excellent In Defense of
    Earth: International Protection of the Bio-
    sphere (Bloomington, Indiana: Indiana Univer-
    sity Press, 1972).

EPTIONS AND

RS AND

LS

w. R. DERRICK SEWELL

One of the most significant characteristics of modern society is its
overwhelming dependence upon experts. This dependence appears
to stem from three main forces: the growing complexity of
problems faced by society, the fear of the individual that his own
judgment may result in disastrous consequences, and the salesman-
ship of the experts. Advances in science and technology have
produced problems which are beyond the capability of the
individual to handle on his own, because he feels he has either
insufficient knowledge or insufficient power. At one time, an
individual could repair his own automobile, design and build his
own house, or solve a family problem without advice from
outside. Those days have now gone. Bombarded with increasingly
complex gadgetry, by new discoveries about man and his physical
world, and by new ideas about how to do things, the individual
has turned to the expert to help him decide what course of action
to follow. The experts have helped promote this process both by
offering advice and by helping create problems to solve.

AUTHOR'S NOTE: *The research for this study was supported by grants from
Resources for the Future, Inc., Washington, D.C., and from the National
Advisory Committee on Water Resources Research, Department of Energy,
Mines and Resources, Ottawa, Ontario. The author wishes to thank those who*

ENVIRONMENT AND BEHAVIOR, March 1971, Vol. 3, No. 1, pp. 23-59.

There is considerable competition among experts for recognition, for some are accorded higher status than others (Sommer, 1963). Those who have attained the highest status are those who have specialized on problems relating to one or more of the following four areas:

(a) the development and use of technology;

(b) human health;

(c) human rights and obligations;

(d) finance.

It is in these areas that the average individual believes he has the least capability of understanding the problem or selecting a solution, that the personal costs of being wrong are especially high, and that the opportunity for the exercise of mysticism by experts is particularly great. As a consequence, it is the professionals that have the highest social status among experts, and among them, scientists, technologists, engineers, doctors, psychologists, lawyers, and economists appear to have attained the highest standing. This is reflected both in the salaries they earn and in the power they exercise, either as individuals or as groups. Increasingly they have assumed not only the responsibility for solving problems and recommending means for attaining goals, but also for defining the goals themselves.

The role of the professional has become institutionalized both in industry and in government. It is reflected in internal organization on the one hand, and in the process of decision-making on the other. Businesses and government agencies are now organized principally upon the basis of specialization, with divisions or departments established to handle particular processes or problems. The larger firms, for example, have a legal division, a

assisted in the study, notably Miss J. Elizabeth McMeiken and Mr. John Rostron of the University of Victoria, who undertook library research, carried out interviews, and contributed many useful ideas. He also wishes to acknowledge the helpful comments and criticisms of Dr. Harold D. Foster of the University of Victoria on earlier drafts of the paper.

financial division, a design division, a research division, and a marketing division. The same is true of government agencies (Corson and Paul, 1966). In the latter case, a whole department may be devoted to one particular kind of problem such as the management of fisheries or the construction of highways. Typically such divisions or departments are staffed by one kind of professional. Thus Departments of Water Resources are usually staffed by engineers, while Departments of Fisheries or Wildlife are manned mainly by biologists.

The exercise of professional expertise is also an integral part of the policy-making process. Professionals are called in at the various stages of problem definition, the analysis of alternative solutions, selection of solutions, and sometimes implementation as well. Typically, however, only a few types of professionals are involved. This is especially the case in the management of natural resources and in matters relating to the quality of the environment.

The specialization which has accompanied professionalization of management and policy-making has resulted inevitably in a compartmentalized or fragmented approach. This approach, however, is now being seriously challenged, both on conceptual and practical grounds. Those who challenge it suggest that its underlying assumptions are invalid. Reality, they point out, is not composed of a number of discrete facets which can be dealt with independently of each other. On the contrary, it is composed of a number of interlocking systems which together make up the physical and human environments. The causes of any problem, therefore, can only be identified by examining each of these systems and the interrelationships between them, and likewise the effectiveness of a solution can only be assessed by tracing the consequences in each system. Holism, therefore, is now advocated as the relevant approach to environmental quality problems (Nicholson, 1970; Shepard and McKinley, 1969; Watt, 1968).

Support for holism is based in part on the recognition of the interdependence of things, but also upon the fact that the fragmented approach has often failed to deal effectively with the problems at hand. Despite major inputs of expertise, for example, the condition of the environment has become progressively worse (de Bell, 1970; Cooley and Wandesforde-Smith, 1970). Today many of the nation's major bodies of water are so polluted that they constitute a severe hazard to human health, as well as to that of fish and wildlife. Costs of restoring them are staggering. The condition of the atmosphere in most major cities is also appalling and in some has reached crisis proportions. The solutions recommended by experts seem to have been ineffectual. Air pollution, for example, continues to increase despite the imposition of regulations and the installation of new devices on cars. The posting of signs that swimming is hazardous fails to keep bathers out of the water (Hewings, 1968). The construction of roads to wilderness areas tends to result not in the provision of wilderness experience, but in the opportunity to move the city temporarily out into the country. The Long Beach National Park on Vancouver Island, B.C., is an excellent example. Aiming to provide a national wilderness preserve, the Canadian federal government set aside a large uninhabited area on the west coast of Vancouver Island. Vigorous advertising of this "recreational paradise" and the provision of high quality access roads, however, have resulted in a massive influx of recreationists, most of whom are equipped with every modern convenience, including bathtubs and TV. The area has suddenly taken on the appearance of a temporary town. Its inhabitants have brought with them all the things they wished to leave behind—overcrowding, noise, and pollution! In this case, park planning has clearly failed to attain its intended objectives.

How has it come about that the experts have failed to diagnose problems correctly and offer effective solutions? Is it because they have a very constricted view of the problems with which they deal? Is it because they feel constrained to consider solutions other than those rooted in the conventional wisdom of their discipline? Is it because environmental experts appear to be more conversant with science and technology than with human behavior? The answers to these questions are not immediately clear for, as Craik (1970a) has pointed out, the perceptions and attitudes of environmental experts have never been studied in any systematic fashion. It seems, however, that with such answers we would be in a much better position to assess the role of various professionals in environmental decision-making, and, hopefully, to devise means whereby their contributions could be made more effective.

Two studies undertaken during the past three years at the University of Victoria have helped shed some light on how experts perceive the problems with which they deal, and the solutions which they recommend. These studies have also helped identify some of the factors which influence such perceptions. The research was intended to be exploratory, aiming principally to develop a methodology and to identify factors that might be examined in greater depth in subsequent investigations. Nevertheless, the findings do have some implications both for research and for public policy in the environmental quality field.

ENGINEERS AND PUBLIC HEALTH OFFICIALS

The studies were focused upon two groups of professionals who play critical roles in environmental quality management: engineers and public health officials. Both have a long tradition of involvement in this area. Problems resulting from alterations in the physical environment are typically referred to engineers, since they are believed to have the necessary training and experience to deal with them. This is especially the case with problems which affect man's economic well-being. Thus engineers are usually called in to deal with alterations in the environment stemming from natural hazards such as floods, hurricanes, or earthquakes to problems resulting from traffic congestion, industrial conglomeration, or mining operations. In such instances, economic costs can be clearly identified, and since the problems seem physical in origin, the expertise of the engineer is regarded as particularly appropriate (Gerstl and Hutton, 1966; Vallentine, 1967).

Public health officials have also been dealing with environmental quality problems for a long time (Brockington, 1961). The kinds of problems on which they work, however, differ from those involving engineers. Public health officials are mainly concerned with those aspects of environmental alteration that result in adverse effects on human health, such as the effects of disposal of industrial and municipal wastes into bodies of water.

200

The two groups of professionals play similar roles in the policy-making process. They act as technical advisers and administrators, and sometimes as decision makers as well. In these capacities, they are instrumental in defining the problems to be solved, determining the solutions to be considered, and, frequently, in selecting the strategy actually adopted. Inevitably, in doing so they give expression to their views as to what society wants and as to how it will react to what is provided.

The engineers' study was intended as a pilot investigation, designed to test methods of identifying attitudes and perceptions of a professional group. The emphasis was upon technique evaluation rather than on information collection. Its results provided guidance for the second study, which probed perceptions and attitudes of public health officials. In this case, a considerable amount of data was gathered, enabling much more sophisticated analysis. Sufficient information was obtained in the engineers' study, however, to enable some comparisons to be made with results of the public health officials' study.

ORGANIZATION OF THE STUDIES

The study of engineers was undertaken in the summer of 1967. It was based upon a sample of 30 engineers, specializing in water resources problems, and drawn from government agencies, firms of private consultants, and from universities, all in Vancouver and Victoria, B.C. Care was taken to include engineers involved at various levels of responsibility and having differing degrees of experience. The sample was believed to be reasonably representative of the universe from which it was drawn. There are approximately 359 engineers specializing in water problems in the two cities. The sample thus represented about 10% of the universe. It was randomly selected from lists of engineers supplied by the Association of Professional Engineers of British Columbia, which noted levels of responsibility and degrees of experience. Those selected were contacted first by telephone and then by letter. None refused to participate.

The public health officials' study was undertaken in the summer of 1969, based upon interviews with 40 officials who were located in the 20 health units which together cover the province of British Columbia. The sample was highly representative of the universe from which it was drawn, since it covered almost 95% of all those who could have been selected. A Medical Health Officer and a Public Health Inspector were selected from each health unit and then contacted by letter and by telephone. Only one unit refused to cooperate in the study. Its omission, however, did not bias the results unduly. The remainder of the sample covered officials from a wide spectrum of experience and interests and from a wide range of environmental conditions.

The Medical Health Officer (MHO) and the Public Health Inspector (PHI) work together as a team, but they perform quite separate functions. The MHO is ultimately responsible to the provincial Department of Health and to local Boards of Health. He is mainly an administrator, charged with the responsibility of interpreting government policy, and ensuring it is carried out. The Inspector is the field representative of the Department of Health and is generally regarded as "its eyes and ears" in the region in which he operates. He carries out various tests to determine water quality and acts as a sounding board to receive complaints and suggestions for policy change.

The various public health officials maintain contacts with each other through communication between health units and with their head office in Victoria. They also maintain contacts with personnel in other agencies, with representatives of industry, and with the general public (Figure 1).

The two studies were based upon interviews, guided by a questionnaire. In both cases, the interviews were conducted by a skilled interviewer and lasted about one hour. Open-ended and forced-choice questions were used. The answers were recorded in shorthand. In the case of the public health officials, more detailed information was sought on certain matters, and a questionnaire was left with the respondents to be mailed at their convenience to the researchers. Replies were received from all those who participated.

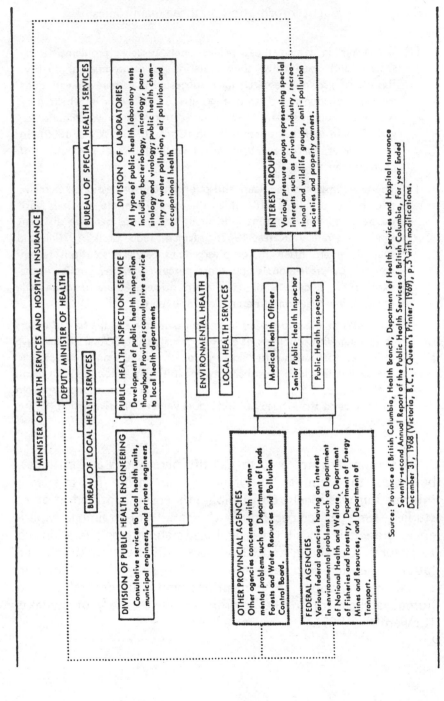

MINISTER OF HEALTH SERVICES AND HOSPITAL INSURANCE

DEPUTY MINISTER OF HEALTH

BUREAU OF SPECIAL HEALTH SERVICES

DIVISION OF LABORATORIES
All types of public health laboratory tests including bacteriology, micrology, parasitology and virology; public health chemistry of water pollution, air pollution and occupational health

INTEREST GROUPS
Various pressure groups representing special interests such as private industry, recreational and wildlife groups, anti-pollution societies and property owners.

BUREAU OF LOCAL HEALTH SERVICES

PUBLIC HEALTH INSPECTION SERVICE
Development of public health inspection throughout Province; consultative service to local health departments

ENVIRONMENTAL HEALTH

LOCAL HEALTH SERVICES

Medical Health Officer

Senior Public Health Inspector

Public Health Inspector

DIVISION OF PUBLIC HEALTH ENGINEERING
Consultative services to local health units, municipal engineers, and private engineers

OTHER PROVINCIAL AGENCIES
Other agencies concerned with environmental problems such as Department of Lands Forests and Water Resources and Pollution Control Board.

FEDERAL AGENCIES
Various federal agencies having an interest in environmental problems such as Department of National Health and Welfare, Department of Fisheries and Forestry, Department of Energy Mines and Resources, and Department of Transport.

Source: Province of British Columbia, Health Branch, Department of Health Services and Hospital Insurance Seventy-second Annual Report of the Public Health Services of British Columbia, For year Ended December 31, 1968 (Victoria, B.C.: Queen's Printer, 1969), p.5 with modifications.

Figure 1: PROVINCIAL HEALTH BRANCH ORGANIZATION: ENVIRONMENTAL HEALTH

The studies sought information on three main topics:

(1) The ways in which these professionals perceive problems facing society and specifically those relating to environmental quality. Results of previous research have suggested that there are variations among individuals and among groups in the ways in which they perceive problems, and that such differences may account for variations in their responses to them (Craik, 1970b; White, 1966). So far, however, there have been no in-depth studies of perceptions of professionals.

(2) The ways in which engineers and public health professionals perceive solutions to problems with which they deal. Here, too, previous work has revealed that different individuals and groups perceive different kinds of strategy (Kates, 1962; Saarinen, 1966; Craik, 1970a), and that there are often major divergencies between solutions recommended by professionals and those perceived by the public (Appleyard, 1969; Lucas, 1966). Here again, however, there has been little in-depth investigation of perceptions of experts.

(3) Attitudes of the two groups as to their own role and the role of others in dealing with problems of environmental quality. Other studies have indicated that views differ among individuals and among groups as to the extent to which responsibility for initiating action lies with them, their agency, the government, or the public at large. Views also seem to vary as to the efficacy of individual versus collective action (White, 1966).

It is important not only to identify perceptions and attitudes, but also to account for variations in them. To this end, information was sought on possible influences identified in other studies, such as socioeconomic characteristics, training, experience, present responsibilities, and views about man's relationship to nature (Kluckhohn and Strodtbeck, 1961; White, 1966). The latter dimension has been found to be a significant factor in explaining variations in perceptions and attitudes relating to human adjustment to the environment in a variety of contexts (Lowenthal, 1967).

The information gathered in the study was coded and subsequently punched onto computer cards. The data relating to engineers was subjected to simple techniques of correlation analysis and tests of significance. That relating to the public health officials was analyzed in greater detail, using three main phases of analysis, namely the development of correlation matrices, factor analysis, and stepwise multiple regression. A correlation matrix was developed to identify relationships between the different variables derived from the information gathered in the study. Significant intercorrelations were found among 66 of the 313 variables, and these were used in further analysis.

Factor analysis was used to examine data relating to

(a) perceptions of problems;

(b) perceptions of solutions;

(c) attitudes as to the roles of the public, public health officials, and the government, on the one hand, and factors hypothesized as possible influences and such perceptions and attitudes, on the other.

Stepwise multiple regression analysis was then used to determine the extent to which the influences identified in the latter case (designated independent variables) explained variations in the factors identified in the former case (designated dependent variables).

PERCEPTIONS OF PROBLEMS

An attempt was made to determine the views of the two groups of professionals as to what the major problems facing British Columbia are, and how environmental quality problems ranked among these issues. As indicated in Table 1, most of the public health officials identified environmental quality problems as the major issue facing the province, followed by various other social problems such as poverty, unemployment, and education. Air pollution and water pollution were seen as the major causes of

TABLE 1
PERCEPTIONS OF PROBLEMS

	Frequency of Mention	
	Public Health Officials	Engineers
Number One Problem Facing the Province		
Environmental quality	32	5
Social problems (poverty, unemployment, education)	20	20
Urban growth and transportation	9	15
Lack of health facilities	8	—
Politics	6	—
Drugs, alcoholism, crime	4	10
Quality of the Environment is Deteriorating in B.C.		
Air	35	10
Water	34	20
Land	26	—
Other	3	—
Measures of Water Quality		
Colli count	39	N1
BOD	36	N1
COD	18	N1
Visual characteristics	12	N1
Turbidity	12	N1
Taste	—	N1
Smell	—	N1
Major Concern About Water Quality		
Hazard to health	31	5
Impairment to aesthetic values	9	5
Increased costs of production	—	15

N1 = No information solicited.

environmental deterioration, followed by land pollution in various forms. Little mention was made, however, of such things as noise, billboards, or powerlines.

These results contrast somewhat with the findings of the engineers' study. In this case, problems of unemployment, labor unrest, and juvenile delinquency were seen as the major issues facing British Columbia. Environmental deterioration ranked far down the list. Of the various forms of pollution, water pollution was regarded as the most important. These findings, however, should be interpreted with caution. The engineers' study was undertaken in 1967, some two years before there was widespread public concern about environmental quality in British Columbia. If the study were undertaken today, the results might be quite different. It is interesting to note, nevertheless, that the close relationship between problems on which the respondent worked and the perceived importance of the problem observed in the case of the public health officials was not found in the case of the engineers.

Other indications of the ways in which professionals perceive problems are found in the terms in which they describe them and the means they use to identify them. Both groups of professionals in this study described environmental quality problems in technical terms, principally in terms of 'standards' used by the public health profession. Thus coliform counts and BOD levels were used to describe the degree of water pollution. Little mention was made, however, of parameters which are typically used by members of the general public to describe such pollution, such as color, smell, or taste.

It was also clear that both groups of professionals generally relied on measurements of physical attributes to assess the "seriousness" of a problem. The degree of public awareness or the extent of complaints was not normally regarded as an index of "seriousness." The public health officials noted that they did not usually go out to assess public awareness by surveys. The only measure they had was the number of complaints received by them or the number of letters to newspapers.

A final indication of the ways in which the two groups of professionals perceived water quality was in the extent to which they saw it as a health problem rather than as an impairment to aesthetic beauty or a cost of production. Interestingly, most of the public health officials saw it mainly as a health problem. Half the engineers viewed it as a factor increasing costs of production, and the remainder perceived it either as a hazard to health or as an impairment of aesthetic values.

PERCEPTIONS OF SOLUTIONS

The solutions proposed by the two groups were clearly influenced by the conventional wisdom and practices of their

207

respective professions. The public health officials felt that the way to handle environmental quality problems was to discuss the matter first with the offender and suggest he find means of reducing the pollution, and if he did not do so, to subject him to court proceedings (Table 2). This has long been the approach used by Departments of Public Health, but it has often been unsuccessful. The more powerful the offender, the more likely it is he will be able to ignore the regulations. Those interviewed were well aware of the fact that this had been the case in British Columbia, but most of them were uncritical of the policies and procedures used to combat pollution in the province (Table 2). Most of the officials were dissatisfied with present pollution legislation, but, in the main, their criticisms related to the lack of rigor of its application rather than to its relevance as a solution to the pollution problem.

There are various alternatives to legislation and regulation as strategies to deal with pollution, such as the imposition of charges

TABLE 2
PERCEPTIONS OF SOLUTIONS

| | Frequency of Mention | |
	Public Health Officials	Engineers
Strategy Generally Recommended		
Warning followed by litigation	40	2
Construction of facilities	—	28
Provision of subsidies	—	—
Imposition of charges	—	—
Public pressure	—	—
Present Legislation		
Adequate	3	15
Weaknesses of Present Approach		
Lack of staff and facilities	10	—
Lack of time, money and research	16	—
Inadequate enforcement	20	20
Suggested Improvements		
Enforcement and control	18	N1
Better testing facilities	11	N1
Improved criteria	9	N1

N1 = No information solicited.

for the use of water bodies, the provision of subsidies for effluent treatment, the development of nonpolluting processes or products, or the imposition of public pressure on polluters (Bower and Sewell, 1970). None of these, however, was mentioned (Table 2). Suggestions were offered for a more forceful attack on pollution problems, but these all reflected the generally conservative bias of the officials. Tougher standards, more finances for laboratory facilities, and higher fines for offenders were among the suggestions most frequently offered (Table 2). No radical departures from existing policies or procedures were suggested.

The engineers, too, perceived solutions in very conventional terms, reflecting standard practices of the profession, on the one hand, and an adherence to established government policy, on the other. Thus, the solution to declining water quality was generally perceived as the provision of additional water to increase the assimilative capacity of the water body, or installation of effluent processing facilities. Other alternatives, such as those noted above, were mentioned by a few of the engineers but were dismissed as being "unrealistic" or "unacceptable by the public." The engineers, too, seemed reasonably satisfied with present legislation and with the present approach to pollution problems in the province. Their main criticism was the lack of enforcement of regulations.

ATTITUDES AS TO ROLES AND RESPONSIBILITIES

Attitudes as to one's own role in dealing with problems, and the roles of others, appear to have an important bearing on one's perception of problems and on action proposed or taken (White, 1966; Lowenthal, 1966). The results of the engineers' study seemed to suggest that this was an especially important dimension (Table 3), and so it was decided to probe it in greater depth in the public health officials' study.

One indication of role assessment is the way in which an individual perceives his own job or agency in relation to other individuals or groups having responsibilities or interests in the same field. The public health officials were asked to list the various groups having an interest in environmental quality. As indicated in Table 3, health officials were mentioned by far the

209

TABLE 3
PERCEPTIONS OF ROLES

	Frequency of Mention	
	Public Health Officials	Engineers
Groups Concerned with Environmental Quality		
Health officials	28	—
Recreation and service clubs	19	—
Educators	14	—
Anti-pollution committees	13	—
Civic officials and chambers of commerce	12	—
Lakeshore property owners and rate payers associations	10	—
Provincial and federal agencies	4	—
Specific Roles		
Adviser	10	27
Decision maker	4	—
Adviser and decision maker	26	3
Consultations		
Internal		
Within own office or other regional offices	39	30
With head office	32	30
External		
Other provincial or federal agencies	16	10
Municipal councils	29	5
Private agencies	11	5
Other (pressure groups, etc.)	9	3
Perceived Opposition		
"Abnormal" minority groups	13	N1
Politicians	26	N1
Industrialists and developers	6	N1
Individual members of the public	10	N1
Attitude of PHO as to Areas of Responsibility		
Department of Health		
(1) all aspects of quality	20	N1
(2) sewage disposal and treatment	15	N1
(3) garbage disposal and treatment	11	N1
(4) recreation	3	N1
(5) ind. and comm. effluents	2	N1
(6) drinking water	4	N1
Pollution Control Board		
(1) all aspects of quality	3	N1
(2) sewage disposal and treatment	0	N1
(3) garbage disposal and treatment	1	N1
(4) recreation	2	N1
(5) ind. and comm. effluents	15	N1
(6) drinking water	0	N1

N1 = No information solicited.

most frequently, followed by recreation and service clubs, various anti-pollution groups, property owners' associations, and other government agencies. The groups noted in this list are those with whom the public health officials normally have to deal, and the frequency of mention may be a partial indication of their perceived importance.

Another indication is the extent to which the professional feels he is better equipped than others to handle the job assigned to him. As might be expected, both the public health officials and the engineers were convinced that their training and experience enabled them to deal with water quality problems better than others. Both suggested that the record clearly showed this to be the case. The officials pointed out that there had been no major outbreak of any communicable disease arising from poor water quality in the province since the first Public Health Act was passed in British Columbia in 1893. The engineers claimed that it was only where technology had been applied in British Columbia that major improvements had been achieved in water quality. The fact that it was now possible to swim at beaches in Vancouver was viewed as an excellent illustration of the efficacy of sewage treatment facilities.

The two groups of professionals saw themselves in a variety of roles in dealing with environmental quality problems. About 25% of the public health officials regarded their role as being that of a technical adviser (Table 3). Almost one-third of them, however, considered that they were decision makers as well as advisers. The need to make quick decisions in the field (within the broad limits imposed by law and policy) no doubt accounts for this view. In contrast, the engineers saw themselves principally as technical advisers, even though government engineers as well as consulting engineers were involved in the study. Only those concerned with issuing water licenses thought they had any kind of a decision-making role. The decision makers, suggested the engineers, are the politicians. As one of them put it: "They make the policy and to a considerable extent they interpret it too. Our role is generally defined by Terms of Reference which set out in detail what the task is, and what actions we are expected to perform in undertaking it."

A further indication of the way in which professionals perceive their role is the extent to which they feel that other groups have something useful to contribute to the solution of problems on

211

which they work. To this end, both groups were asked which other agencies or professions they consulted and how often, and in what ways they tried to assess public opinion. Contacts within an agency or a firm appeared to be very frequent (Table 3). Consultation among peers was, in fact, an integral part of practice in both professions. Beyond the agency or firm, however, contacts became much less frequent and were generally very formal.

Public health officials seem reluctant to contact officials in other agencies or to establish formal links with groups in the general public. At least two partial explanations might be offered for this reluctance. One is that continuous contacts with other agencies might lead to a sharing of responsibility. This, as the views expressed on the perceived roles of the Department of Health and the Pollution Control Branch seem to suggest, is clearly not what the public health officials want. They wish to retain complete jurisdiction over control of pollution, at least as far as health considerations are concerned, and are willing to concede only that part involving major industries, which the officials feel require much greater power to control than the Department of Health can exercise (Table 3).

Engineers are similarly jealous of the role they perceive for themselves. They, too, have very few continuous external contacts. The rationale given is that they are sufficiently aware of the overall picture to be able to cast the problem into a broad framework, and they only need to call in outside opinions when they require specialized advice on a certain aspect. They feel that they are much more likely to be effective in the decision-making process than many other types of professional because they are "precise and accurate, and have a reputation for offering workable solutions." They contrast the "practical view" taken by the engineer with the "idealism" that characterizes proposals of many other professions, notably planners. "Our projects usually get built," said one of the engineers, "whereas theirs usually end up on the shelf."

The engineers were even less anxious to establish direct and continuous links with the public than were the public health officials. Most of them thought that "the public is not well informed and therefore cannot make rational judgments" or that "consulting the public makes planning much more difficult, and generally it delays or even precludes any action being taken." Most of those interviewed thought that the conventional methods of consulting public opinion were satisfactory as guides, namely, the public hearing, the referendum, and the ballot box. "Here the public is presented with a clear choice of alternatives," said one of them. "Like any shopper you can decide whether to take it or leave it."

The problem of consulting public opinion poses a somewhat different problem for the public health official than it does for the engineer. The effectiveness of the former in performing his tasks depends very much upon the extent to which his recommendations and regulations are understood and accepted by the public, and the extent to which he is able to overcome opposition (real or imaginary) from various groups. One way of dealing with this problem is to carry out programs of public education through talks and lectures, and through encouraging the organization of anti-pollution groups. Many public officials engage in such activities. However, most of them seem to feel that they are facing a dilemma in this regard: if they educate the public, they may acquire increased support for their programs, but, at the same time, they may be offered more advice than they desire as to what those programs should be!

In summary, it seems that the perceptions and attitudes of the two groups of professionals studied have all the characteristics of a closed system. Their views seem to be highly conditioned by training, adherence to standards and practices of the respective professions, and allegiance to the agency's or firm's goals or mission. Both groups believe they are highly qualified to do their respective jobs and that they act in the public interest. Contact with representatives of other agencies or the general public, however, is considered either unnecessary or potentially harmful. There appears to be general satisfaction with past policies and practices, and few, if any, major alterations are suggested.

FACTORS CONDITIONING PERCEPTIONS AND ATTITUDES

The analyses of perceptions of problems, solutions, and attitudes as to roles and responsibilities tend to confirm impressions gathered from other indicators of these views—such as statements of leading engineers or public health officials in professional journals or in public hearings—and the courses of action they have recommended in the past to deal with certain problems. To an important extent, these perceptions and attitudes differ from those which appear to be held by other professionals and by members of the general public, as statements in the technical and popular press and at public hearings clearly testify. What then, are the factors that account for such divergencies in viewpoint? Are they rooted in the individual's training and experience, where he has lived, his interactions with others, or his views about the relationship of man to nature? Data were gathered on various factors which it was believed might have an influence upon perceptions and attitudes. These were examined by factor analysis to determine which were the most significant. Stepwise multiple regression was then used to discover the extent to which any of these factors could explain variations in the perceptions and attitudes.

As noted earlier, the factor analysis isolated some 21 variables reflecting perceptions and attitudes of public health officials. These are noted in Table 4 and fall into five main groups, namely those relating to:

(1) perceptions of problems;

(2) perceptions of solutions;

(3) role of the public;

(4) role of public health officials;

(5) role of other government agencies.

These were treated as dependent variables.

The analysis also revealed five main independent variables relating to possible influences upon perceptions and attitudes, namely:

(1) years in the profession;

(2) rank and mobility;

(3) distinction between Medical Health Officers (MHO) and Public Health Inspectors (PHI);

(4) nature over man;

(5) man over nature.

TABLE 4
SUMMARY LISTING OF DEPENDENT AND INDEPENDENT VARIABLES

Dependent Variables

Perception of Problems

1. Multiple quality criteria. (The range of criteria used in determining the extent of pollution.)
2. Pesticides, noise and purification. (Concern about problems of increasing use of pesticides, levels of noise, and the use of chlorination or fluoridation.)
3. Environmental quality and sewage disposal. (Sewage disposal seen as a major factor in environmental deterioration.)
4. Broad perspective. (Major issues and environmental quality problems perceived in a broad context.)

Perception of Solutions

5. Improved facilities. (The need for better laboratory facilities.)
6. Improved administration and standards. (The need for better administration and more rigorous application of standards.)
7. More meaningful water quality parameters. (The need to improve present bacteriological and chemical criteria.)
8. Adequate legislation. (Lack of dissatisfaction with present legislation.)

Role of Public

9. Dissatisfaction with role of public. (Public viewed as either apathetic or obstructive.)
10. Satisfaction with role of public. (Public viewed as well informed, active and nonobstructive.)
11. Opposition from vested interests. (Opposition received from pressure groups, especially property owners and rate payers.)
12. Organize groups. (Encouragement of local groups to obtain information and where appropriate, call for action.)

Role of Public Health

13. Water quality as a health problem. (Water quality viewed mainly as a human health problem and principally a responsibility of Department of Health.)
14. Intra-agency consultation. (Propensity to consult with colleagues within the agency.)
15. Extra-agency consultation. (Propensity to consult with people in other agencies or the general public.)
16. Adviser and decision maker. (Role viewed as a combination of adviser and decision maker.)
17. MHO as a health administrator. (MHO viewed as an administrator rather than as a physician or civic official.)

Role of Government

18. Water quality as department of health problem. (Water quality viewed as a problem that should be handled mainly by department of health.)
19. Focus on physical criteria. (Physical criteria viewed as relevant parameters in assessing water quality.)
20. Provincial versus municipal consultations. (Propensity to consult provincial rather than municipal officials on water quality matters.)
21. Consultations with other provincial and federal agencies.

TABLE 4 (Continued)

Independent Variables

Background and Professional Characteristics

1. Medical Health Officer/Public Health Inspector. (Distinction between the two posts.)
2. Rank and mobility. (Seniority and the extent to which the individual has transferred between posts.)
3. Years in public health.

Views Toward the Environment

4. Nature over man.
5. Man over nature.

The analysis revealed some important relationships between the two sets of factors.

YEARS IN THE PROFESSION

The hypothesis that the amount of time one spends in an occupation conditions one's perceptions and attitudes about the problems with which it is concerned was clearly borne out by the analysis. As Table 5 indicates, the concern of the public health official about environmental quality problems tends to decline the longer he has been in the profession, as do his desire to involve the public more directly in decision-making, his propensity to consult with others outside his agency, his concern about the effectiveness of present administrative arrangements, and his skepticism about the validity of water quality standards. It seems also that the longer an official has been in an agency, the less anxious he is to promote change in either its structure, its policies, or the matters with which it concerns itself. In the present study, it was mainly the younger, less-experienced officials who tended to be most aware of deteriorating environmental conditions and most skeptical about the ability of present administrative arrangements and policies to improve these conditions. It was they, too, who were the most anxious to provide the public with a more direct link into the planning and policy-making processes.

One possible interpretation of the findings is that the longer a public health official has been in the profession, the more likely he is to become adjusted to his physical and institutional environments. He is less prone to want to move elsewhere or to propose modifications to agency structure, standards of environmental quality, or public policies. So long as deterioration of environmental quality does not appear to be resulting in hazards to human health, the public health official does not feel any particular motivation to promote action or policy change. Modification of policies or expansion of responsibilities would obviously further complicate his task, a task which he believes is complicated enough already!

Years spent in public health appeared to be a good predictor of variations in perceptions and attitudes. As shown in Table 5, it accounted for more than 64% of the variance in ten significant dependent variables.

RANK AND MOBILITY

Several sociologists (Eiduson, 1962; Gerstl and Hutton, 1966; Gross, 1958) and others (Caldwell, 1967; Marshall, 1966) have suggested that an individual's view about the problems with which he deals and about his role in dealing with them are conditioned by his position in the employment hierarchy, and by his identification with the organization for which he works. It appears that those who occupy positions in the lower echelons generally feel divorced from responsibility for making decisions. They often develop an attitude of being a cog in a very large machine. As they ascend the ladder of responsibility, however, their feeling of commitment and of identification with the organization's goals seems to grow (Zytowski, 1968).

The extent to which an individual has moved from one post to another also appears to have an influence upon his perceptions and attitudes. In some occupations, notably the academic profession and industrial management, transfers from one location to another are a generally accepted means of moving up the hierarchy (Gerstl and Hutton, 1966; Caplow and McGee, 1958). In many government agencies, experience in the field is often a prerequisite for obtaining a post at the head office (Corson and Paul, 1966; Caplow and McGee, 1958). Having ascended to the top rung of the ladder, however, the individual then tends to become more sedentary. Generally there is nowhere else to go, except to another organization, and there is also the knowledge that others are anxious to reach the top positions. The individual, therefore, can be expected to defend both his own position and the aims and policies of the organization for which he works.

Seniority and mobility were found in the analysis to be closely related, and were combined into a single factor for the regression studies. This factor seems to have an important influence on perceptions of public health officials, accounting for more than fifty percent of the variance in six variables (Table 6). The more senior the official, the more likely it is that he has transferred at least five times, that he has a fairly narrow view of problems facing society, and that he identifies solutions in terms of the conventional practice of his agency. It seems also that seniority affects perceptions of the role of the public. The more senior officials are much more skeptical about involving the public in planning and policy-making than are the junior officials. Finally, it appears that seniority brings with it an increasing degree of dedication and commitment to the agency. The more senior officials spend a good deal of time outside their office hours informing themselves about environmental problems (such as through reading journals or attending meetings) and trying to inform the public.

These findings provide some interesting comparisons and contrasts with the results of the engineers' study. As in the case of public health officials, seniority is attained partly through experience acquired through working in a variety of places on a variety of problems. No characteristic patterns could be detected in transfers. It seems, however, that engineers may transfer at least three times before they settle into a post for more than five years. Like the senior public health officials, the senior engineers indicate both a close allegiance to the agency for which they worked and support for past recommendations made by it. In contrast to the public health officials, however, they tend to perceive a wider

TABLE 5

INFLUENCE OF YEARS IN THE PROFESSION: RESULTS OF MULTIPLE REGRESSION ANALYSIS

Dependent Variable Entering the Equation	Sign	R	R^2	Increase in R^2	T-value		Level of Significance
					To Enter Equation	In Final Equation	
Environmental quality and sewage disposal	-	.423	.179	.179	2.874	3.511	.005
Dissatisfaction with role of public	-	.585	.342	.163	3.041	2.176	.025
Extra-agency consultation	-	.633	.401	.059	1.868	2.714	.005
Improved administration and standards	-	.674	.454	.054	1.840	2.735	.005
Organize groups	-	.706	.498	.044	1.737	1.660	.10
Adviser and decision maker	+	.727	.529	.030	1.475	1.672	.05
Intra-agency consultation	-	.748	.560	.031	1.474	1.781	.05
Consultation with other provincial and federal agencies	+	.766	.587	.027	1.453	2.250	.025
Pesticides, noise, and purification	-	.786	.618	.031	1.546	1.437	.10
M.H.O. roles as a health administrator	-	.802	.643	.025	1.426	1.426	.10

TABLE 6

INFLUENCE OF RANK AND MOBILITY: RESULTS OF MULTIPLE REGRESSION ANALYSIS

Dependent Variable Entering the Equation	Sign	R	R^2	Increase in R^2	T-value To Enter Equation	T-value In Final Equation	Level of Significance
Broad perspective	-	.514	.264	.264	3.695	5.041	.005
Environmental quality and sewage disposal	+	.580	.336	.072	2.008	2.089	.025
Organize groups	+	.631	.398	.062	1.913	2.520	.02
Adviser and decision maker	-	.667	.445	.047	1.713	1.609	.10
Adequate legislation	+	.695	.483	.038	1.607	1.731	.05
Dissatisfaction with role of public	-	.717	.514	.031	1.452	1.510	.10
Pesticides, noise, and purification	+	.728	.530	.016	1.037	1.037	a

a. Statistically insignificant.

TABLE 7
INFLUENCE OF DISTINCTION BETWEEN MHO AND PHI: RESULTS OF MULTIPLE REGRESSION ANALYSIS

Dependent Variable Entering the Equation	Sign	R	R^2	Increase in R^2	T-value		Level of Significance
					To Enter Equation	In Final Equation	
Intra-agency consultation	+	.724	.524	.524	6.476	6.580	.005
Adviser and decision maker	+	.755	.570	.046	1.964	3.115	.005
Opposition with vested interests	+	.772	.596	.026	1.517	0.713	a
Dissatisfaction with role of public	+	.786	.618	.022	1.455	1.868	.05
Extra-agency consultation	-	.796	.634	.016	1.158	1.216	.10
Improved facilities	+	.802	.643	.010	1.003	2.319	.025
Environmental quality and sewage disposal	+	.811	.658	.015	1.132	1.064	a
Provincial versus municipal consultations	-	.818	.669	.011	1.021	1.290	.10
Focus on physical criteria	+	.828	.686	.017	1.264	1.469	.10

a. Statistically insignificant.

range of problems facing society, and their off-duty activities were much less related to their work. In particular, they were seldom involved in public lecturing or in organizing groups.

As noted earlier, responsibilities relating to public health in British Columbia are shared between Medical Health Officers and Public Health Inspectors. The essential difference between them is that the former are principally administrators, while the latter are the field representatives. This distinction appears to have an important bearing on their perceptions, attitudes, and behavioral responses. MHO's participate much more actively in intra-agency consultation than do PHI's, and especially with their head office. PHI's, in contrast, are much more frequently in contact with representatives of private industry and the general public. While MHO's are generally fairly skeptical about involving the public in policy-making, the PHI's tend to support such involvement.

The two groups also differed in their views as to their roles as advisers and decision makers. The former saw themselves as both advisers and decision makers, whereas the latter tended to consider themselves as advisers only. This, of course, reflects the kinds of functions which they perform in the agency, particularly in connection with environmental policy.

Differences in perceptions resulting from differences in functions performed by subgroups of a profession were also observed in the case of the engineers. The government engineers saw themselves as public servants, using their talents and training to promote the general welfare. All were strongly attached to the agency for which they worked and referred constantly to its goals, activities, and achievements. They spent much less time describing projects on which they had worked themselves. They contrasted their role with that of the consulting engineer. The latter, they thought, was brought in only to answer specific questions on a specialized topic and was not answerable to the public. "Consulting engineers," said one of the government engineers, "do not have to be as aware of government policy or of potential public reaction as we do. They are able to operate in a detached manner, whereas we have to be ready to field comments and criticisms long after the report is completed or the project is built."

The consulting engineers tended to concur with the government engineers' image of them. They, too, saw themselves as specialists on specific topics, participating as advisers in the planning and policy-making process when called upon to do so. They contrasted their role with that of the government engineer. The latter, they thought, carried out important functions as watchdogs, planners, and administrators, but their job was neither as challenging nor as precarious as that of the consulting engineer. As one of them suggested, "The consulting engineer can afford much less to be wrong than the government engineer."

MAN'S RELATIONSHIP TO NATURE

As noted earlier, several studies have shown that views about man's relationship to nature have an important bearing upon perceptions of and attitudes toward the environment. The views of the public health officials on this relationship were sought in several ways. First, the respondents were asked whether they thought technology had the answer to most problems faced by man. Next, they were asked for their views on three technological innovations now on the horizon and likely to alter the environment in important ways: namely the large-scale diversion of water from Alaska to Mexico (the NAWAPA scheme; Sewell, 1967); the purposeful modification of the weather (Fleagle, 1968); and the Supersonic Transport Plane (SST; Shurcliff, 1969). Finally, they were asked who should be put in charge of decisions about the control of nature. Their views in these connections were then correlated with their perceptions of problems, solutions, and responsibilities.

Opinion was sharply divided on the extent to which man is in control of nature and vice versa. Just over one-half of the public health officials felt that technology could not solve many of the major problems now faced by man (Table 8). The rationale given for this view was that there are some problems that are not amenable to the technological fix—like the Watts riot, poverty, or drug addiction—and that, in many cases, technological solutions create more problems than they solve. In contrast, those who felt that technology does have the answer pointed to the fantastic material progress made in the past three decades as a result of technological advances. To the technological optimists, the only limitations were money and the need to develop institutional means of ensuring the adoption of innovations.

Opinions were also divided on the desirability of the three technological innovations, with roughly half in favor of them and half against. Those who favored them spoke of improvements in income, additions to food supply, and more rapid communications. Those who were against them pointed out uncertainties as to impacts on the environment, and the lack of a clearly demonstrated need for the innovation.

Man now has the technological capacity to make vast alterations in the environment and perhaps even destroy it. To provide another indication as to attitudes toward the man-nature relationship, the respondents were asked to suggest a group of persons to whom they would entrust the control of technology and decisions as to its use. Opinion was divided on this matter, too (Table 9). Varying proportions of scientists and laymen were proposed. The only point of agreement was that no one would trust a group of politicians, a group of laymen, or a group of scientists to make such decisions!

TABLE 8
THE EFFICACY OF TECHNOLOGY

| | Frequency of Mention | |
	Public Health Officials	Engineers
Does Technology Have the Answer to all Problems?		
Yes	16	24
No	24	6
What Are its Deficiencies?		
Cannot deal with problems of human relations	15	6
Is limited by time or money	15	4
Creates problems	7	5

TABLE 9

ALLOCATION OF RESPONSIBILITY FOR CONTROL OF TECHNOLOGY

	n of Respondents	
	Public Health Officials	Engineers
Scientists	7	7
Politicians	8	1
Scientists and politicians	10	2
Scientists and the general public	15	20

The views of the public health officials on the role of technology were paralleled to a surprising degree by the views of the engineers. Knowing that the fundamental goal of the engineering profession is the control of nature, one would naturally assume that engineers would feel highly confident that technology has the answer to most problems, and that major technological innovations would be looked on with favor (Hertz, 1970). Analysis of the answers to the questions on technology reveals that while most engineers are confident about the ability of technology to solve human problems, they have reservations about the desirability of certain kinds of innovations. If anything, their reservations were even stronger than those of the public health officials (Table 10). There was general support for the SST, based on the view that reductions in travel time were still a desirable social goal. Some mentioned problems of noise, but these were believed to be surmountable. Attempts to alter the weather drew much less support, and most of the engineers thought such attempts should be strictly controlled, pending much better understanding of the processes involved. There was almost unanimous opposition to the proposed NAWAPA scheme, based partly on technical and economic considerations, but mainly on the fact that it involved export of Canadian water. Mention of the scheme seemed to trigger considerable emotion in many of the respondents, revealing a variety of attitudes about resource ownership, economic dependence, and so on.

TABLE 10
VIEWS ON THREE TECHNOLOGICAL INNOVATIONS

| | n of Respondents | |
	Public Health Officials	Engineers
Weather Modification		
Aware of the innovation	39	30
Is it feasible?	32	26
How far should we go?		
Do not attempt it	19	—
Small-scale	10	26
Large-scale	11	4
SST		
Advantageous innovation	9	18
Disadvantageous innovation	31	12
Advantages		
Increased speed of communication	9	16
Increased trade	4	7
Increased understanding	2	2
Challenge to the imagination	2	16
Disadvantages		
Noise	20	10
Space requirements	10	8
Jet contrails	2	2
Ecological disturbances	2	—
NAWAPA Scheme		
Advantageous innovation	18	8
Disadvantageous innovation	22	22
Advantages		
Solution to growing water needs	16	8
Source of revenue	8	6
Challenge to technology	6	8
Disadvantages		
Involves water export	22	22
Cheaper alternatives available	18	14
No demonstrated need	8	12
Potential ecological disaster	3	4

Views about man's relationship to nature appear to have an important influence on perceptions and attitudes. In the public health officials' study, those who regarded water quality mainly as a health problem, those who were skeptical about public involvement in environmental health decisions, and those who were particularly concerned about pesticides, noise pollution, and water purification tended to hold the view that nature is in control of man (Table 11).

TABLE 11
INFLUENCE OF VIEWS ON NATURE'S CONTROL OVER MAN: RESULTS OF MULTIPLE REGRESSION ANALYSIS

Dependent Variable Entering the Equation	Sign	R	R^2	Increase in R^2	T-value To Enter Equation	T-value In Final Equation	Level of Significance
Dissatisfaction with role of public	-	.315	.099	.099	2.045	1.424	.10
Water quality as a health problem	+	.412	.170	.071	1.771	1.852	.05
Adequate legislation	-	.492	.242	.072	1.858	1.179	a
Pesticides, noise, and purification	-	.522	.273	.030	1.209	1.412	.10
Extra-agency consultation	+	.547	.299	.027	1.142	1.050	a
Improved administration and standards	-	.565	.319	.020	0.964	1.053	a
Intra-agency consultation	+	.580	.336	.017	0.933	0.898	a
Opposition from vested interests	-	.591	.349	.013	.785	.785	a

a. Statistically insignificant.

The view that man is in control of nature, however, appeared to be an even better predictor of perceptions and attitudes. It accounted for 47% of the explained variance in nine significant variables (Table 12). Those who held this view also tended to feel that consultation beyond the public health unit is generally not essential, that public involvement often leads to unsatisfactory results, that present water quality criteria are valid, and that pesticides, noise, and water purification problems are not a matter for great concern. One possible interpretation of these results might be that the public health official not only sees man in control of nature, but also sees his own official role as occupying an especially vital position in helping man to deal with problems involving the physical environment. Believing that his background and experience furnish him with the necessary expertise, and that others are either less capable or disinterested in dealing with the problems with which he concerns himself, he feels a strong personal commitment to his job. At the same time, he is cognizant that other professionals, other agencies, and the general public are developing a concern about the environment. This poses a dilemma. On the one hand, it could mean that there will be vastly increased public recognition and support for his work. On the other, it could result in criticism, opposition, and perhaps an erosion of his position.

IMPLICATIONS OF THE RESULTS FOR
ENVIRONMENTAL QUALITY MANAGEMENT

The solution to the emerging environmental crisis will require at least three major changes in the present approach to environmental quality management. First, it will necessitate the adoption of a holistic rather than a fragmented view of the problem. Instead of water pollution being considered in isolation from air pollution or land pollution, and instead of the physical dimensions being considered apart from the human dimensions, a conscious attempt will need to be made to consider them together. Likewise, the overall effects of the adoption of any solution on the environment and on man will need to be taken into account in policy decisions.

TABLE 12
INFLUENCE OF VIEWS ON MAN'S CONTROL OVER NATURE: RESULTS OF MULTIPLE REGRESSION ANALYSIS

Dependent Variable Entering the Equation	Sign	R	R^2	Increase in R^2	T-value To Enter Equation	T-value In Final Equation	Level of Significance
Extra-agency consultation	-	.352	.124	.124	2.316	3.386	.005
Focus on physical criteria	-	.462	.213	.090	2.050	1.627	.10
Environmental quality and sewage disposal	+	.536	.287	.074	1.930	2.196	.025
Opposition with vested interests	-	.586	.343	.056	1.727	2.139	.025
Adviser and decision maker	-	.624	.389	.046	1.600	1.672	.05
Satisfaction with role of public	-	.642	.412	.023	1.153	1.416	.10
Pesticides, noise, and purification	-	.658	.433	.021	1.089	1.457	.10
Broad perspective	+	.674	.454	.021	1.088	1.157	a
Water quality as a health problem	+	.683	.467	.012	0.843	1.647	.10

a. Statistically insignificant.

Second, it will be necessary to involve the public much more directly in the planning process. It is already clear that the public feels alienated in this process, and that conventional means of consulting public opinion do not accurately reveal their preferences. Presenting the public with a few discrete alternatives has the advantage of simplifying the choice process, but unless the alternatives reflect the values held by the public rather than those of the planners, they may all be rejected.

Third, and as a corollary of the first two requirements, there will need to be changes in administrative structures, laws, and policies to ensure that a broader view is taken, enabling the various aspects of environmental quality problems to be considered in an integrated fashion, and ensuring that the public enjoys a satisfactory sense of participation.

The results of the two studies reported on here seem to suggest that such changes will not be easily accomplished. In fact, the likelihood is that they will be vigorously opposed. Holism, for example, is an antithesis to the approach upon which different professions depend for their recognition and is likely to be rejected by them. It is possible that some attempt will be made to broaden the viewpoint of certain professions by establishing training programs which expose members to ideas and methods of other disciplines, and by setting up formal and informal links among professions. This process is, in fact, already under way, generally under the banner of environmental science or environmental studies. Almost always, however, one discipline or profession dominates the scene, and only in rare instances does it appear that several professions can work together in a truly integrated fashion on a problem of mutual concern.

It also seems that professionals, particularly in the physical sciences and the natural sciences, are skeptical about involving the public in policy-making. For the most part, they appear to take the view either that the public is not well informed or that so many different opinions will appear that policy-making will become impossible. The alternative is to present the public with solutions conceived by the planners. The only choice then is to accept or reject them. If they are rejected, the problem remains unsolved. As the rows of unimplemented plans on planners' shelves testify, this is frequently the case.

Finally, it is clear that experts are not in favor of institutional change, especially if it means that their own role will be altered. Accordingly, they resist suggestions that new agencies should be established, new laws should be passed, new solutions should be tried, or that other professions should become involved. Such resistance appears to increase with seniority. There is, in fact, an inverse relationship between the perception of the need for change and power to accomplish it.

It is obvious that society will always need experts and expertise. The question now is the kinds of experts and expertise needed to solve environmental problems. Unless our present experts broaden their views and integrate their activities, they may well contribute more to the promotion of the environmental crisis than to its solution.

REFERENCES

APPLEYARD, D. (1969) "City designers and the pluralistic city," in L. Rodwin et al. (eds.) Regional Planning for Development. Cambridge, Mass.: MIT Press.

BROCKINGTON, C. F. (1961) "Organization and administration of health services," pp. 305-320 in W. Hobson (ed.) The Theory and Practice of Public Health. London: Oxford Univ. Press.

BOWER, B. T. and W. R. D. SEWELL (1970) Selecting Strategies for Management of Air Quality. Ottawa: Queen's Printer.

CALDWELL, L. (1967) Politics, Professionalism, and Environment. Bloomington, Ind.: University of Indiana Institute of Public Administration.

CAPLOW, T. and R. J. McGEE (1958) The Academic Marketplace. New York: Basic Books.

COOLEY, R. L. and G. WANDESFORDE-SMITH (1970) Congress and the Environment. Seattle: Univ. of Washington Press.

CORSON, J. and R. S. PAUL (1966) Men Near the Top. Baltimore, Md.: Johns Hopkins Press.

CRAIK, K. H. (1970a) "The environmental dispositions of environmental decision-makers." Annals of Amer. Academy of Pol. and Social Sci. (May): 87-94.

—— (1970b) "Environmental psychology," pp. 1-122 in T. M. Newcomb (ed.) New . Directions in Psychology. New York: Holt, Rinehart & Winston.

DE BELL, G. [ed.] (1970) The Environmental Handbook. New York: Ballantine.

EIDUSON, B. T. (1962) Scientists: Their Psychological World. New York: Basic Books.

FLEAGLE, R. G. (1968) Weather Modification: Science and Public Policy. Seattle: Univ. of Washington Press.

GERSTL, J. E. and S. D. HUTTON (1966) Engineers: The Anatomy of a Profession. London: Tavistock.

GROSS, E. (1958) Work and Society. New York: Thomas Y. Crowell.

HERTZ, D. B. (1970) "The technological imperative—social implications of professional technology," pp. 95-106 in Annals of Amer. Academy of Pol. and Social Sci. (May).

HEWINGS, J. (1968) "Water quality and the hazard to health." Natural Hazard Research Working Paper 3. University of Toronto Department of Geography.

KATES, R. W. (1962) "Hazard and choice perception in flood plan management." University of Chicago Department of Geography Research Paper 70.

KLUCKHOHN, F. R. and F. L. STRODTBECK (1961) Variations in Value Orientations. Evanston, Ill.: Row, Peterson.

LOWENTHAL, D. (1967) "Environmental perception and behavior." University of Chicago Department of Geography Research Series 109.

——— (1966) "Assumptions behind public attitudes," pp. 128-137 in H. Jarrett (ed.) Environmental Quality in a Growing Economy. Baltimore, Md.: Johns Hopkins Press.

LUCAS, R. C. (1966) "The contribution of environmental research to wilderness policy decisions." J. of Social Issues 22 (October): 116-126.

MARSHALL, H. (1966) "Politics and efficiency on water development," pp. 291-310 in A. V. Kneese and S. C. Smith (eds.) Water Research. Baltimore: Johns Hopkins Press.

NICHOLSON, M. (1970) The Environmental Revolution. London: Hodder & Stoughton.

SAARINEN, T. F. (1966) "Perceptions of the drought hazard in the Great Plains." University of Chicago Department of Geography Research Paper 105.

SEWELL, W. R. D. (1967) "NAWAPA: pipedream or practical possibility?" Bull. of Atomic Scientists (September): 8-13.

SHEPARD, P. and D. McKINLEY [eds.] (1969) The Subversive Science: Essays Towards an Ecology of Man. New York: Houghton-Mifflin.

SHURCLIFF, W. A. (1969) SST and the Sonic Boom Handbook. New York: Ballantine.

SOMMER, R. (1963) Expertland. Garden City, N.Y.: Doubleday.

VALLENTINE, H. R. (1967) Water in the Service of Man. Harmondsworth, Middlesex: Penguin.

WATT, K. E. (1968) Ecology and Resource Management. New York: McGraw-Hill.

WHITE, G. F. (1966) "Formation and role of public attitudes," pp. 105-127 in H. Jarrett (ed.) Environmental Quality in a Growing Economy. Baltimore Md.: Johns Hopkins Press.

ZYTOWSKI, D. G. (1968) Vocational Behaviour. New York: Holt, Rinehart & Winston.

SECTION IV

INDIVIDUAL AND COLLECTIVE ENVIRONMENTAL ACTION: THE ENVIRONMENTAL MOVEMENT

PREFACE TO SECTION IV

INDIVIDUAL AND COLLECTIVE ENVIRONMENTAL ACTION: THE ENVIRONMENTAL
MOVEMENT

Because of our focus on personal concern, so far we have dealt
primarily with individual behavior toward environmental issues.
Beyond this lies the question of how these individual behaviors may
become aggregated and organized into group action, and how all of
these forms of behavior in turn may stimulate official action.
What remains, in other words, is the study of the "environmental
movement" and its effect on policy. Although there has long been
an interest in conservation in our society, environmentalism has
only recently emerged as a mass movement. Since many of the problems that concern today's environmentalists have existed for some
time, we must ask why "environmentalism" has emerged so dramatically
at this moment in our history? Some suggest that this emergence is
due neither to a sudden crisis not to the abundance of new information about environmental deterioriation. Even more significant may
be the precedent of personal involvement in public issues set by
the civil rights and anti-war movements in the late 1950's and early
1960's, and the emergence of a popularized perspective on environmental problems epitomized by Rachel Caison's _Silent_ _Spring_ (1962).

Because the environmental movement is so new and apparently
so diverse, it raises a variety of other questions as well: What
is its connection with the earlier "conservation" movement? How
widespread and representative is it today? How effective has it

been in improving environmental quality, and by what means? And finally, what are its prospects for the future? In their brief review of "Conservation Politics and Democracy" Hendee, Gale and Harry suggest how increased urbanization and education have stimulated the more traditional segment of the movement - namely, conservation groups with both instrumental and expressive interests in preserving the environment. Still, the membership of these groups is relatively small and unrepresentative of the general population, a fact which raises some question about their role in a democratic society. In another study the same authors conclude that membership in the conservation-preservation movement comes largely from the urban, upper-middle class and as such it is "somewhat isolated ideologically from the mainstrams of both liberal and conservative political thought. They note that this isolation is reinforced by the conservationists' tendancy to concentrate their civic activities within their own field of interest, all of which places them at a political disadvantage, although it may help to reinforce their commitment to the cause. Devall's replication of their study suggests however, that conservationists are no more specialized in their outside activities than anyone else. He adds that membership in certain conservationist groups may act as a stepping-stone to wider participation in the environmental movement.

Both the earlier "preservationist" and the more contemporary environmental movement have left their legacy. Albrecht neatly categorizes their impact on various levels of culture and social organization. Yet this success has tended to raise its own opposition. As it has become apparent that environmental reform will not be achieved without substantial costs - perhaps even to our rate of economic growth - the environmental movement has passed from a "honeymoon" period of consensus to one of increasing conflict. Denton Morrison points out that this realization, and the elitist social composition of the movement itself, brings it into conflict not only with those economic interests that are most directly threatened by the costs of reform, but also with the less priviledged segments of society. The potential coalition of society's "top dogs" and "underdogs" threatens to block future environmentalist gains.

This bleak prospect is partly offset by Faich and Gale's study of the changing organizational goals of certain outdoor recreational groups, and the political implications of these changes. Despite its limited focus their study may have broad implications. It suggests the environmental movement's potential for transforming and absorbing existing social structures, and for mobilizing broader support for its goals. If it can realize this potential the environmental movement will certainly stand a better chance of realizing its aims in the future.

Conservation, Politics, and Democracy

JOHN C. HENDEE,
RICHARD P. GALE,
and JOSEPH HARRY

THE conservation movement is one of the major politico-economic developments in 20th-century America. Conservation organizations are effectual contestors in the country's policy-making arenas and influence the use of natural resources worth billions of dollars. National forests, national parks, state preserves, and all other public lands are particularly sensitive to their influence, but so are vast private and corporate-owned natural resources. Despite the impact of the conservation movement on our nation's past and its obvious implications for the future, surprisingly little is known about conservation organizations and their members.

From Wise Use to Preservation

The conservation movement began near the turn of the century when politically powerful eastern urbanites became concerned about assuring the wise development of the vast natural resources in the still virgin West. In this early era of progressivism the conservation philosophy promised equality for the common man and protection from the wasteful, monopolistic development of natural resources for profit by a few and encouraged preservation of natural resources for use by many (12). Hays (7) argued against the "political mythology of the people versus the interests" as the setting for the struggle and claimed instead that its essence was scientific, characterized by a zeal for rational planning to promote efficient development and use of all natural resources. However, wise use of resources and equitable distribution of benefits were implicit in both points of view and were reflected in major conservation measures of that era.

Under the leadership of President Theodore Roosevelt and Gifford Pinchot, the movement marked a radical change from the laissez-faire approach, which implied that natural resources were inexhaustible, to a philosophy emphasizing wise use. The withdrawal during Theodore Roosevelt's administration of 234 million acres of land (primarily in the West) from private entry for examination as to their appropriate future use reflected this philosophy. Most of this land was retained in public ownership, forming the basis for our national parks and forests of today (15).

Thus, the early conservation movement was dedicated to wise use of natural resources, not merely to their preservation. Nash (13) pointed out

JOURNAL OF SOIL AND WATER CONSERVATION, November/December 1969, Vol. 24, pp. 212-215.

that even the first preservation milestone, creation of Yellowstone National Park in 1872, was motivated by a desire for tourist development; and the second milestone, reservation of the New York State Forest Preserve in the Adirondacks and Hudson River, was motivated by fear for navigational water levels in the Hudson River and Erie Canal.

Wise use conservation was subsequently incorporated into the philosophy of land management agencies and helped bring about better planning of natural resources development. But the conservation movement of the mid-20th century represents a re-orientation rather than a revival of this early movement. The purely preservation aspects of conservation are becoming more prominent. Already a chasm exists between individuals promoting conservation for wise use and those promoting conservation for preservation and appreciative purposes.

These two perspectives now sharply oppose one another in the expanding debate over the future of the nation's resources and the quality of future environments, although supporters of both points of view might claim preservation of that quality as a long-range goal. Organized into citizen-based pressure groups, preservationists have increased their political, numerical, and financial strength and scored several major political victories. Creation of the Redwood and North Cascades National Parks, the Wilderness Act, the Land and Water Conservation Act, and the Wild and Scenic Rivers Act exemplify their recent success. Wise use conservationists, on the other hand, find considerable strength in resource management professions, such as forestry, and argue that " . . . the undisciplined advocacy of preservation of resources is completely faulty land use if the objectives are not in the interest of the public"

(5). However, as the number and political skills of preservationists increase, the preservation philosophy seems destined to become more important in the conservation movement. Ideological battles between use-oriented. and preservation-oriented conservationists are likely to increase. It is particularly important that the contemporary conservation movement is rooted in a great number of voluntary organizations whose ideology is that of preservation and not wise use.

Conservation Groups

The diversity and scope of voluntary organizations that sustain the preservation movement are illustrated by recent studies in the Pacific Northwest. A survey of wilderness visitors revealed that about 400 of the 1,350 respondents belonged to one or more conservation groups or outdoor clubs, representing a total of 218 different organizations (9). A subsequent survey of car campers and wilderness visitors in Washington revealed membership by about 20 percent of the 2,500 respondents in 258 different conservation groups or outdoor clubs.[1] The organizations to which these recreationists belonged ranged from small activity-oriented groups (boating, fishing, rock-collecting, etc.) with only incidental interest in conservation issues to large national organizations (Sierra Club and Wilderness Society) almost exclusively issue-oriented.

So vast is the network of groups and clubs, each pursuing its own special interest, that even those involved in the movement may be unaware of

[1] Hendee, John C. 1967. "Recreation clientele — the attributes of recreationists preferring different management agencies, car campgrounds, or wilderness in the Pacific Northwest." Unpublished doctoral dissertation on file in the College of Forest Resources Library at the University of Washington in Seattle.

its scope and potential political support if unified goals were established. Roger Hansen (6), executive director of the Colorado Open Space Foundation, recently summarized the problem: "A major reason for the failures of conservationists, in my opinion, has been their historical inability to weld themselves into an effective force, ready for battle on the great environmental issues of the day. Instead, there are dozens of diverse groups, each hawking its particular brand of conservation elixer. Meanwhile, back at the state or national capitol, a united and disciplined army of commodity groups, commercial interests, and power-hungry bureaucracies grind mercilessly down the road of unwise use of our environment."

Most observers of the conservation movement tend to focus exclusively on large national organizations and forget the many small groups who express similar concepts and values locally. When asked to estimate the number of groups encountered in the studies of recreationists in the Pacific Northwest, both professional resource managers and conservation leaders grossly underestimated the number of existing organizations.

Instrumental vs. Expressive Groups

Sociologists frequently classify voluntary organizations as "instrumental" or "expressive" according to their goals (10, 16). This dichotomy fits conservation groups and outdoor clubs rather well. Instrumental organizations pursue activities primarily as a means of achieving some goal, such as preservation of natural resources. Expressive organizations pursue activities for their own sake, such as specific types of recreation.

Although the instrumental-expressive dichotomy refers primarily to organizational goals, it may also describe the orientation of member participation. For example, the businessman who joins a country club to improve business contacts becomes instrumentally oriented in an essentially expressive organization. And the "little old lady in tennis shoes" may be expressively involved in instrumentally oriented conservation group activities.

Outdoor clubs typically promote conservation group activities, provide recreational facilities for members, and encourage the enjoyment of certain activities through educational programs. When these organizations do become instrumentally involved in conservation, they typically focus on protection of environments directly tied to those outdoor activities sponsored by the club.

Our analysis of several of these clubs indicated that officers strongly oppose greater involvement in instrumental conservation activities of a general nature and that typical organizational structures are conducive to spreading club policy formation among a broad membership base. Inasmuch as their instrumental activity is likely to be keyed to the expressive goals of the organization, members of outdoor clubs might be classified as *expressive conservationists*.

Although outdoor clubs frequently support conservation issues, the strength of the contemporary conservation movement is rooted in those organizations whose primary goals are to promote a preservation philosophy. The instrumental activity of these groups is frequently directed toward the protection of areas and environments that members themselves may not have visited. The acknowledged benefactor of these activities is "the public," and when expressive activities are sponsored, they are primarily designed to support the groups' instrumental objectives by making membership attractive and promoting com-

Wilderness, for years a focal point of political action by conservation organizations, merits preservation for preservation's sake, according to instrumental conservationists. Expressive conservationists support wilderness preservation for recreation opportunities in these areas.

munication and education among members.[2] To facilitate political effectiveness and maintain the desired ideological perspective, the executive committees of these organizations typically possess considerable autonomy and authority to make policy and represent the groups externally. Inasmuch as members of these conservation groups formally support and engage in instrumental conservation activities, they might be classified as *instrumental conservationists*.

Increasing Conservation Activity

Recent legislative successes show that instrumental conservation activities are both increasing and becoming more sophisticated. The little old lady in tennis shoes now wears high heels. She marches on the state capital or Washington instead of city hall. She

sends personal opinion telegrams instead of friendly, handwritten letters. She appears before legislative committees instead of local politicians or park rangers. And her testimony, in addition to featuring appeals to esthetic values, is likely to refer to cost-benefit analysis; recreation use statistics; and legal counsel on matters of *de jure* and *de facto* wilderness, previous legislation, and government regulations.

The expansion of the conservation movement is based in part on certain current social trends. First is the dramatic increase in outdoor recreation for expressive and appreciative uses of natural resources. Second are the structural changes occuring in American society that relate to increasing concern for the environment, for example, rising levels of education and urbanization.

Expressive and appreciative uses of natural resources have increased sharply during the past two decades, and this rapid growth seems likely to

[2] A representative of the Sierra Club recently stated that they sponsor hikes and other expressive activities partly as a strategy to get more people to know and love the land so they will fight for it.

continue. The resulting impact on resource management programs has been impressive. For example, Burch (2, 3) pointed out that before World War II campgrounds in national forests were developed primarily to concentrate campers in a few places and thereby protect the forest resource by reducing the threat of man-caused fires. With the overwhelming postwar increase in recreation use, providing campsites and other recreation benefits became a specific objective of national forest management rather than a byproduct of forest protection. Likewise, the Army Corps of Engineers now frequently includes recreation use as a justification for its projects.

This response, typical of virtually all public resource management agencies, has legitimized, encouraged, and increased the expressive and appreciative uses of natural resources and, to some extent, discouraged consumptive uses of the same resources. What this all adds up to is that now, more than ever before, nature appears to have acquired expressive meaning for the American people rather than being, as before, merely an object for consumptive use and conquest. There is little likelihood of reversing this trend.

Several studies suggest that outdoor recreation, at least in number of participants, is an urban-based phenomenon. Our data suggest this is particularly true for those activities that depend on an appreciation of the natural environment, such as wilderness visitation, nature photography, and more primitive forms of car camping, as opposed to activities not specifically appreciative, such as water skiing, swimming, or socializing with other campers (8, also see footnote 1). This suggests that participation in environmentally appreciative outdoor recreation activities — those appealing most to instrumental conservationists — are

strongly tied to the increasing urbanization of our society.

There is further evidence also of a link between urbanization and preservation perspectives. A study of wilderness users indicated that those with a purist-oriented concept as opposed to a development-oriented concept of wilderness are more likely to have been raised and to reside in urban areas (9).[3] A Pacific Northwest study of outdoor recreationists indicated that preservation — rather than use-oriented concepts of natural resources are associated with urban residence and upbringing (see footnote 1). Conversely, these same studies suggested that individuals raised in rural areas tend to be more use-oriented, prefer activities less concerned with appreciation of the environment, and are less likely to belong to conservation organizations.

Education appears to be a related factor. Although high levels of education are associated with participation in other types of voluntary organizations as well (17), members of conservation groups and outdoor clubs seem exceptional in this respect. Sixty percent of those reporting membership in a conservation organization or outdoor club were college graduates, and 40 percent had done post-graduate work. Those belonging to conservation groups tended to be more highly educated than those belonging to outdoor clubs, a phenomenon also reported in a later study.[4]

---

[3] Hendee, John C., Thomas Steinburn, and William R. Catton, Jr. "Wildernism-the development, dimensions, and use of an attitude scale." Paper presented at the Rural Sociological Society Meeting in San Francisco, California. August 16, 1967.

[4] Harry, Joseph, and Richard P. Gale. "The conservation movement: some preliminary data." Paper presented to the Pacific Sociological Society in Seattle, Washington, April 1969.

Membership in conservation organizations is thus likely to benefit from the trend toward higher levels of education in America. The strong association between higher education and instrumental involvement in conservation is also apparent in the intensity of the conservation movement on college campuses—a fact noted with alarm and bitterness by the adversaries of preservationists (1).

How Many Conservationists?

Only limited data are available on the proportion of Americans who belong to any type of voluntary organization (14, 17). Data on membership in conservation groups and outdoor clubs are even more limited. However, some inferences can be made from the outdoor recreationist populations that have been sampled.

A Pacific Northwest study revealed that about 20 percent of the wilderness users and less than 10 percent of the car campers belonged to either a conservation group or outdoor club (see footnote 1). Most of the wilderness users who belonged to a group were affiliated with a conservation organization, but only about half of the member car campers belonged to conservation groups; the other half belonged to outdoor clubs.

If wilderness visitors constitute about 5 percent of all campers and 20 percent of them belong to conservation organizations, then about 1 percent of all campers may belong to conservation organizations.[5] If, in addition, only 5 percent of the car campers belong to such groups, then the total of all campers involved would be 6 percent. An unpublished survey of outdoor recreation activities by the Bureau of Outdoor Recreation in 1965

indicated that about 10 percent of all Americans camp; thus, less than 1 percent of the total population may belong to instrumental conservation groups.

This estimate has several limitations. First, it does not account for possible regional variations; the studies on which it is based were conducted in the Pacific Northwest. Second, the estimate does not include the substantial number of persons who are active members of conservation organizations but who do not participate in outdoor recreation. Third, the estimate does not allow for multiple membership. In spite of these limitations the estimate has value in that it indicates there are relatively few conservationists in the total population.

The accomplishments of the conservation movement are somewhat remarkable in view of this relatively small portion of the total population that is formally involved. Opponents wail, "Never has so much been set aside for so few." Another perspective suggests that, like other social movements, a relatively few activists lead a passive but generally concerned public. The two or three million Americans formally involved in the conservation movement do constitute an important political entity. Organized conservationists may reflect merely "the tip of the iceberg," and thus justify their activity in terms of the long-range interests of the general public.

Are Conservationists Representative?

That organized conservationists typically reside in urban areas, are well educated, and are engaged in occupations placing them in somewhat elevated class positions seems pretty well established. That they are not representative of the general population is equally clear. However, they do command public audiences, are articulate in their appeals for public support,

[5] Between 6 and 7 percent of national forest recreation and about 3 percent of national park recreation took place in wilderness during 1960.

and they have demonstrated their political effectiveness. Certainly their class position contributes to their effectiveness, but the more critical question is whether organized conservationists are any less representative of the general population than other organized, political activist groups who represent other portions of the general public. They probably are not, since the highly educated professional and managerial segment of the public is the most involved in the political decision-making process on almost all issues (11).

Other factors may also contribute to the success of organized conservationists. The high degree of autonomy among the governing boards of conservation groups and the devices for maintaining organizational dedication to goals have already been mentioned. The intense personal commitment and missionary zeal of conservationists are important additional ingredients. Many of the most active conservationists resemble members of other movements that demand an almost exclusive commitment to the philosophy of the movement (4, 11). Conservationists may thus concentrate the extra-curricular use of their talents on conservation work alone, further contributing to the movement's success (see footnote 4).

Conservationists and Democracy

The fact that organized conservationists differ from the general population in education, income, and occupation calls into question the extent to which they represent the interests of a wider segment of the total population. Do only highly educated individuals desire extensive wilderness? Perhaps those occupying different class positions prefer increased employment in timber-related industries to new national parks or expanded wilderness. Maybe society in general does not want to pay the necessary

price for cleaner air, water, greenbelts, and the other steps toward a more livable environment that conservationists promote? Perhaps conservationists are operating in society's best interests representative or not? Such self-righteousness is, of course, a fundamental tenet of both conservationists and their adversaries.

Despite the social class bias of conservationists, they are, in one respect, more representative than many other politically successful lobby groups in that their strength is based on human rather than financial resources. Whereas most industries lobby on the strength of money provided as an essential cost of doing business, the conservation movement is sustained primarily by individual contributions of time and money by instrumental conservationists.

Like few other movements in a democratic society, the conservation movement has shown that a dedicated, vocal minority with relatively meager financial resources can influence legislation. Although some notable earlier successes cannot be ignored, only recently has Congress become highly responsive to the growing preservationist philosophy. In the past few partisan alliances, extremely limited financial resources, and an unwillingness to negotiate handicapped the ability of conservationists to command political power. Alliances with powerful leaders in the Senate and acceptance of political compromise were factors in recent legislative successes. Since the reputation of conservationists as "uncompromising Jeremiahs" is legendary, these recent successes may suggest a significant political awakening and increased appeal and acceptability of the movement among politicians.

REFERENCES CITED
1. Benneth, John C. 1967. *The engines of public opinion*. Am. Forest Products Industries, Inc., Washington, D. C. 12 pp.
2. Burch, William R., Jr. 1964. *Two concepts*

244

for guiding recreation management decisions. J. Forest. 62: 707-712.

3. Burch, William R., Jr. 1965. *The play world of camping: research into the social meaning of outdoor recreation.* Am. J. Sociol. 70(5): 604-612.

4. Coleman, James S. 1957. *Community conflict.* Free Press, Glencoe, Ill.

5. Connaughton, Charles A. 1969. *Preservation and conservation.* Am. Forests 75(3): 8.

6. Hansen, Roger P. 1968. *How Coloradoans win conservative battles.* Catalyst 2(4): 8-11.

7. Hays, Samuel P. 1965. *Conservation and the gospel of efficiency.* In Jan Burdon and Robert W. Kates [editors] *Readings in Resource Management and Conservation.* Univ. of Chi. Press, Chicago, Ill. pp. 202-203.

8. Hendee, John C. 1969. *Appreciative versus consumptive uses of wildlife refuges; studies of who gets what and trends in use.* Trans., 34th North Am. Wildlife and Natural Resources Conf. Wildlife Mgt. Inst., Washington, D.C.

9. Hendee, John C., William R. Catton, Jr., Larry D. Marlow, and C. Frank Brockman. 1968. *Wilderness users in the Pacific Northwest — their characterists, values, and management preferences.* Res. Paper PNW-61. Pacific Northwest Forest & Range Exp. St., Portland, Ore. 92 pp.

10. Jacoby, Arthur P., and Nicholas Badchuck.

1963. *Instrumental and expressive voluntary associations.* Sociol. & Social Res. 47: 461-471.

11. Kornhauser, William. 1959. *The politics of mass society.* Free Press, Glencoe, Ill. 256 pp.

12. McConnell, Grant. 1965. *The conservation movement — past and present.* In Jan Burton and Robert W. Katos [editors] *Readings in Resource Management and Conservation.* Univ. of Chi. Press, Chicago, Ill. pp. 189-201.

13. Nash, Roderick. 1968. *The American environment: readings in the history of conservation.* Addison Wesley, Reading, Mass. 236 pp.

14. Orum, Anthony M. 1966. *A reappraisal of the social and political participation of Negroes.* Am. J. Sociol. 72(1): 32-46.

15. Van Hise, Charles R. 1965. *History of the conservation movement.* In Jan Burton and W. Kates [editors] *Readings in Resource Management and Conservation.* Univ. of Chi. Press, Chicago, Ill. pp. 179-185.

16. Warner, W. Keith, and Sidney J. Miller. 1964. *Organizational problems in two types of voluntary associations.* Am. J. Sociol. 59(6): 654-657.

17. Wright, Charles R., and Herbert H. Hyman. 1958. *Voluntary association memberships of American adults: evidence from national sample surveys.* Am. Sociol. Rev. 23. 284-294.

Conservation: An Upper-middle Class Social Movement: A Replication

by W. B. Devall

From data on the Mazamas, a Pacific Northwest outdoor club of 1,600 members, Harry, Gale and Hendee (1969) indicate that the conservation-preservation movement draws its support from upper-middle class segments of the population; this may account for some of the political success of the movement. However, they argue that specialization of extracurricular memberships in conservation organizations and activities may be a political liability to supporters of preservation although it may reinforce their long term commitments to a difficult cause. Furthermore, it is argued that members who join an outdoor activity club may then develop a commitment to preservationist ideology and join preservationist organizations. Data collected from a sample of members of the Sierra Club reinforced the first conclusion and calls into question the latter two statements.[1]

The Sierra Club is one of the larger (80,000 members) and more influential conservation-preservation organizations. A sample survey of Club members was conducted by the author in May, 1969. A questionnaire was mailed to every sixtieth name on the roster of adult members (twenty-one years and older). In addition, questionnaires were sent to all chapter and group chairmen in the Club. Out of 1,232 questionnaires mailed, 907 were returned (a 74 percent return).

The predominance of upper-middle class members of the Club is indicated by education, occupation, and income. Seventy-four percent of the respondents had at least a four-year college degree. Thirty-nine percent had an advanced degree. The high mean education of respondents is reflected in the occupational distribution of the sample. Forty-nine percent of the male respondents were "higher professionals," i.e., physicians, lawyers, college professors, engineers, and 21 percent were "lower professionals," i.e., school teachers, free lance writers, artists. Only 5 percent of the males were in clerical or sales occupations, owners of small businesses or unskilled workers.[2]

The income of respondents reflects both their occupation and education. Fifty-eight percent of the respondents said their family income was over $12,000 a year, and 30 percent said their income was over $18,000 a year. Only 2 percent

---

1. See William Devall, "The Governing of a Voluntary Organization: Oligarchy and Democracy in the Sierra Club," doctoral dissertation submitted to the University of Oregon, March, 1970.

○ W. B. Devall is assistant professor in the Department of Sociology, Humboldt State College, Arcata, California.

2. Members of the middle classes generally belong to formal voluntary organizations more than members of other classes. This much-replicated finding is cogently discussed by Charles Wright and Herbert Hyman in "Voluntary Association Membership of American Adults: Evidence from National Sample Surveys," *American Sociological Review*, 23 (June, 1958), pp. 284-294.

JOURNAL OF LEISURE RESEARCH, Spring, 1970, Vol. 2, pp. 123-126.

of the respondents, all college students, reported their income was less than $3,000 a year.

Harry, Gale and Hendee indicate that preservationists tend to specialize in the kinds of associations they join and thus are not able to capitalize on memberships in different types of associations. The data on the Sierra Club indicate only a third of the grassroots leaders (chapter and group chairmen) and a third of the members who are not Club leaders are active in a civic or community group. Thirty percent of the leaders and 31 percent of other respondents in the sample were members of churches. However 74 percent of the leaders and 58 percent of other members were members of a professional association, reflecting the preponderance of professionals in the Club. In the Hauskneckt study of memberships in voluntary organizations using a nationwide sample survey (1962), 21 percent of the respondents who were college-educated belonged to a church or religious organization, 51 percent belonged to a civic or service organization, and only 7 percent belonged to a political or pressure group. Twelve percent of the college-educated respondents in the Hauskneckt study belonged to an occupational or professional association. While Hauskneckt's classification may have been somewhat different from the one used in the present study, this comparison suggests that Sierra Club members may be as active or more active in many kinds of voluntary organizations as other college-educated people.

Sierra Club members are members of and active in other conservation organizations and outdoor clubs. Forty percent of the sample belonged to one or more conservation organizations besides the Sierra Club and 13 percent belonged to one or more other outings organizations. Thirty seven percent of the leaders and 21 percent of the other members said they were active in one or more conservation organizations besides the Sierra Club. Respondents listed over 200 other conservation and outdoor clubs to which they belonged.

The conservation-preservation movement is a very diffuse movement and includes hundreds of small organizations dealing with a specific project (e.g., the Committee to Save the Tule Elk) or a specific area (e.g., the Desert Protective Association). An active preservationist may make a monetary contribution and therefore become a member of several conservation organizations each year. The diffuse nature of the movement is explored more fully by Devall (1970) and Hendee, Gale and Harry (1969).

Grassroots leaders of the Sierra Club tend to belong to other conservation organizations and to be more active in them than other members. This observation was made of the "conservationist" members of the Mazamas in Harry, Hendee and Gale's study. This may indicate that a small cadre of "active conservationists" provide much needed liaison and coordination to the movement. The leadership of the conservation-preservation movement and opinion leaders could be studied in order to explain the development of commitment to preservationist ideology.

Finally, the Sierra Club may serve as a recruiting organization for the whole preservationist movement. Those respondents who belonged to other preservationist organization (including the Wilderness Society, Audubon Society, California Planning and Conservation League, National Parks Association) tended to join the Sierra Club before the other groups. Furthermore, respondents who had joined the Sierra Club more recently said that they joined for the conservation activities rather than the outings. Of the respondents who had joined the Club within the last three years, 69 percent stated they joined primarily to support the conservation activities of the club, while only 25 percent of the respondents who had been in the Club ten years or longer said they joined primarily to support the Club's conservation program. Although some preservationists may be socialized to the preservationist ideology through their experience in outings clubs as indicated by Harry, Gale and Hendee, it may be that the recent upsurge in membership and activism in preservationist associations has come from people who do not have extensive outings experience. Further research is needed to explore the process by which respondents develop a commitment to a preservationist ideology.

In summary, the data on the Sierra Club support Harry's conclusion that conservation-preservation organizations draw members primarily from a segment of the upper-middle class. Active members of the Sierra Club tend also to be active in other conservation organizations. The Sierra Club may serve as a recruiting organization. People who are interested in the preservation movement may join the Sierra Club first and then become members of other preservationist organizations. Whether the conservation-preservationist movement can be characterized as an "extremist movement" of the upper-middle class (Harry 1969, p. 254) is questioned.

The respondents in the sample of Sierra Club members were no less likely to belong to other kinds of voluntary organizations than respondents in a nationwide sample survey. Their degree of participation in these other voluntary organizations was not tested in the present study. Furthermore, it is indicated that the stepping-stone hypothesis that people become active in outdoor clubs and then develop commitment to the preservationist ideology needs further study. It is suggested that the recent upsurge in membership in major preservationists organizations may have come from people who had a predisposition to the preservationist ideology and who may be instrumental conservationists interested in political action rather than from expressive conservationists who developed a commitment to preservationist ideology through their interest in outdoor experiences.

References

Devall, William. 1970. The organization and integration of a diffuse social movement. Paper delivered at Rural Sociology Meetings, Washington, D. C., August 1970.

Harry, Joseph; Gale, Richard; and Hendee, John. 1969. Conservation: an upper-middle class social movement. *Journal of Leisure Research.* 1 (Summer 1969): 255-261.

Hausknecht, Murray. 1962. *The joiners: a study of voluntary associations in the United States.* Totowa, New Jersey: Bedminster Press.

Hendee, John; Gale, Richard; and Harry, Joseph. 1969. Conservation, politics, and democracy. *Journal of Soil and Water Conservation.* 24 (November-December 1969): 212-214.

Jones, Holway. 1965. *John Muir and the Sierra Club: the battle for Hetch Hetchy.* San Francisco: Sierra Club.

Lundberg, George et al. 1968. Directed change: voluntary associations and social movements. Chapter 20 in *Sociology*. New York: Harper and Row.

Wright, Charles and Hyman, Herbert. 1958. Voluntary association membership of American adults: evidence from national sample surveys. *American Sociological Review*. 23 (June 1958): 284-294.

LEGACY OF THE ENVIRONMENTAL MOVEMENT
By Stan L. Albrecht

Introduction

The sociological literature on social movements suggests that they almost all go through a series of stages and that these stages form a somewhat consistent and repetitive "life cycle" (see, for example, Killian, 1964;
King, 1965; Zald and Ash, 1966). The genesis of the movement is usually
found in pockets of frustration or dissatisfaction with the present social
order or with the course of history that social order seems to be pursuing.
From the shared frustrations there may then develop a belief that a different
state of affairs is both desirable and possible. Frequently the social movement then evolves as an "enduring organization devoted to the attainment of
this vision" (Killian, 1964: 433). Values and goals are defined into a group
ideology, a structure emerges with its role definitions and division of
labor, and the movement enters the phase of its life cycle during which
its impact on the larger social order is likely to be at its highest peak.
The road from this juncture on is usually one of decline. The movement, or
significant portions of it, may be co-opted by the larger society, it may
be vigorously suppressed, or the original momentum may simply be lost and
though the movement itself may continue to survive, its influence becomes
virtually insignificant.

Mauss (1971: 192-195) has developed a more formalized model of this life
cycle process by proposing five rather specific stages through which the
movement progresses: 1) incipiency, or the genesis of the movement in response
to frustration, need deprivation, or whatever; 2) coalescence, involving the

ORIGINAL MANUSCRIPT, 1974.

250

coming together into a more organized and structured whole of the groups and individuals who are dissatisfied with current conditions and seek change; 3) institutionalization, which frequently involves both a society-wide coordination of the movement in an effort to attain its goals, and organization of the host society to cope with the movement in the form of co-optation or suppression; 4) fragmentation, resulting from either the movement's success or failure to achieve its goals, and 5) the demise of the movement as a viable force in the society.

A good deal of research and speculation has been directed toward the understanding of these phases in the history of social movements. This has been especially true of efforts directed toward understanding the conditions from which mass movements emerge, much of which was spurred by the writings of the mass society theorists of the 1950's and 1960's (see Kornhauser, 1959; Lipset, 1963; Fromm, 1965) who suggested that movements evolve out of conditions of alienation, anomie, and a break-up of primary group ties.

Few studies, however, have been devoted to an analysis of the impact that specific movements have had on the larger society from which they have emerged. As Killian (1964: 452) has noted, "The significance of social movements . . . lies not in their careers but in their consequences for the larger society and its culture. Unless a social movement results in significant social change, it becomes merely an interesting sidelight to history, a curiosity." This paper is an effort to select an important contemporary social movement (the environmental movement) and to assess some of the important impacts it has had on the larger society. It is recognized that selecting a movement that is still somewhat early in its career may be problematic since much of the impact of such a movement may lie yet in the future.

Nevertheless, it seems that the effects of the environmental social movement are already of sufficient consequence that they deserve our attention.

The Environmental Movement

There is already a rapidly growing literature on the nature and characteristics of the environmental social movement (see, for example, Hendee, Gale and Harry, 1969; Devall, 1970a, 1970b; Faich and Gale, 1971; Schnaiberg, 1971; Albrecht, 1972; Gale, 1972; Morrison, Hornback and Warner, 1972). While no attempt will be made here to review this body of literature, a few summary comments are in order prior to any discussion of legacy. The literature that has developed suggests rather clearly that the environmental movement has become one of the major politico-economic developments of 20th century America (Hendee, Gale and Harry, 1969). Schnaiberg (1971: 1), for example, argues that if we define success in the usual American context of size and rate of growth, the environmental movement is already more successful than such predecessors as the civil rights movement and the anti-Vietnam War movement. If this is, in fact, true, then this movement must be viewed as one of the important social movements of recent history. It has evolved out of a growing belief that the world faces an ultimate "eco-catastrophe" unless immediate and successful efforts are made to halt the deterioration of the environment, and has gone on to attract the support of hundreds of thousands of persons to its cause.

In terms of the life-cycle notion discussed earlier, the environmental movement is most probably now at or recently past its peak of influence and institutionalization. It is generally viewed as being a young movement (Gale, 1972), though most analysts in the area recognize that just as deterioration of the environment is not a new phenomenon, neither is public concern and action to try and halt that deterioration. In fact, there have been at least two or three other waves of environmental concern in American history (Harry, 1973). The most important of these until the present movement was that which evolved out of the Progressive Era of the late nineteenth century. According to Gale (1972), this early movement was characterized by two important and sometimes conflicting notions--"conservation-wise use and preservation." The conservation-wise use orientation stressed the idea of not necessarily preserving the bounties of the land, but conserving them or using them wisely for the best good of the people. This orientation frequently came into conflict with a more strictly preservationist view. The latter was frequently expressed by private citizens who were concerned about the destruction of the natural environment, the misuse of natural resources contained in that environment, and the disregard of the wildlife that inhabited it. Such concerns led to the formation of the Sierra Club in 1892 and to the first state Audobon Society in 1895 (Gale, 1972). Gale notes that while both those who held the conservation-wise use perspective and the preservationist perspective considered themselves conservationists, the management and development orientation of the former frequently conflicted with the preservation and protection orientation of the latter.

Whatever the characteristics of these early signs of environmentalism in this country, the present environmental social movement surpasses anything that has gone before. Launched in the fall of 1969 "with the nationwide coordination of activity culminating in the first Earth Day on April 22, 1970" (Gale 1972: 284), the movement has gone on to capture the attention of thousands, to mount successful political campaigns, and to convince much of the political and economic elite of the seriousness of the situation (Schnaiberg, 1971: 1). We will turn now to a more specific discussion of some of this legacy that the environmental movement is building in this country. We begin with some brief observations on the earlier conservation-preservation movement and then turn to the contemporary scene.

Some Impacts of the Preservation Movement - 1890-1910

As discussed above, with the passing of the frontier era in the late 1800's, there developed a growing realization in some circles that natural resources were, indeed, exhaustible (Moncrief, 1970). The early preservation movement helped to popularize this idea. Traditional emphasis had been on civilizing wilderness "in the name of prosperity and progress" rather than preserving it. One of the products of the early movement, then, was a change in attitude toward preservation of certain of nature's wonders for the benefit and enjoyment of posterity. As noted by Nash (1965: x), "In the closing decades of the nineteenth century the appreciation of wilderness, which previously had been confined to a small group of intellectuals, broadened to include increasing numbers of the American people." John Muir, who eventually founded the Sierra Club, played a major role in the popularization of the wilderness concept through his publications and tireless effort to share his concerns with his fellow-countrymen.

One of the major controversies of this period that did so much to arouse public concern over environmental issues, and a controversy in which John Muir and other early conservationists played important roles, was the move by the city of San Francisco to build a reservior for water supply purposes in the Hetch Hetchy Valley which had been included as a part of Yosemite Park. This case is particularly interesting because in it one sees the same issues being fought out that are present in most if not all of today's major environmental controversies (such as the SST or the Alaskan pipeline). The leaders of San Francisco argued that without the increased source of water that would be supplied by the new dam, the city could not continue to grow. Thus,

the issue then, as so frequently now, was one of continued growth vs.

environmental protection and preservation. According to Nash (1965: xi),

"The struggle over Hetch Hetchy seemed to many at the time to be symbolic

of a larger conflict between beauty and materialism, sentiment and the utilitarian

viewpoint, morality and irreligion. At stake, it appeared, was not just a

wild valley but whether Americans would ever be able to place the finer things

of life above the pursuit of the main chance." Though the environmentalists

were not successful in their efforts, the issue was highly publicized and

helped to generate broader national support for the environmentalists' goals.

Another of the outcomes of the controversies of this era, and certainly

a part of the legacy of this early movement, was the widespread acceptance

of the doctrine that in some instances the laissez-faire methods of obtaining

and utilizing natural resources would have to be modified to permit government

interference in such forms as the "withdrawal of public lands from private

exploitation and the wise management of these lands for the optimum economic

and social benefit of the people as a whole" (Jones 1965: 4). Probably no-

where did this developing doctrine create more controversy than in the State

of Colorado. Here, the conservation movement ignited one of the bitterest

political disputes between state and federal governments since the Civil War.

As McCarthy (1973: 27) has noted: "The conservation crusade, initiated by

American preservationists in the late 1870's and finally joined by the federal

government in the early 1890's for the purpose of saving . . . the vanishing

natural resources of the western public domain, gave rise to the critical

question of precisely where the rights of the states left off and the power

of the federal government began."

Colorado, like most of the other western states, was more concerned with attracting new settlers, exploiting mineral and forest resources within her borders, and clearing land for the growth of new towns and cities than with preservation. It should be recognized, of course, that the idea of exhausting the supply of land, forests, and other natural resources appeared almost incredible to many people, particularly in the western United States. Thus, angry westerners charged federal violation of "both the principle of state sovereignty and the 'rights' of American citizens to settle and establish 'civilization' where they pleased" (McCarthy 1973: 27).

Conservationists soon became aware that eastern legislators were much more willing to support the passage of bills setting aside vast tracts of western land for preservation than were westerners. Therefore, much of their effort was concentrated on Congress rather than on the states. Congress responded by passing several major preservation measures among the most important of which was the Forest Reserve Act of 1891 which gave the President of the United States the right to set aside public lands as forest reserves. McCarthy (1973: 27) notes that it became the reasoning of the federal government "that if the forests and waters and mineral wealth of the West were to be saved for the use of 'future generations', it would have to be done through federal regulation. The fact that western states like Colorado never agreed formed the crux of the conservation furor for the next two decades."

Numerous bills important to the conservationists were passed during this period, and their passage, at least in part, must be viewed as a part of the legacy of the early conservationists. The Yosemite National Park was set apart as a "forest reservation" in 1891. This was followed by several other national parks and wildlife refuges, the first of which was established on Pelican Island, Florida in 1903. In 1907, the "forest reserves" became "national forests" with the name change indicating, more than anything else, that these large tracts of land were now viewed as the continuing heritage of all of the American people.

The passage of many of these laws was aided by the fact that during part of this period the White House was occupied by a President who was among the most sympathetic of all American presidents to the cause of conservation, Theodore Roosevelt. In one of the most important steps in the history of conservation, President Roosevelt in May 1908 called a Conference of Governors of all the states to introduce a policy of "protection, preservation, and wise-use" of natural resources. This conference was later followed by the appointment of Conservation Commissioners in a majority of states and the appointment of a National Conservation Commission. Though the role of the state commissioners was greatly curtailed and sometimes abolished in states such as Colorado, the precedent had been set. And, though later presidents and congresses were less concerned with the causes of conservation, the groundwork was certainly laid upon which later efforts would build. This must be viewed as part of the legacy of the early environmental movement.

Legacy of the Contemporary Movement

The impacts of movements on the society from which they emerge vary from that of the successful revolutionary movement that overturns an existing social order to replace it with something new to the movement that fades rapidly or is quickly suppressed and which, therefore, may have little long-term impact at all. Nevertheless, probably all movements do have some impact. As Killian (1964: 454) notes: "Rarely does a social movement leave unchanged the structure of the group in which it arises." A movement the size of the contemporary environmental movement, then, should have major impact and this already appears to be the case. The changes in environmentally-related attitudes and behavior evident in the United States in the past two or three years border on the incredible. Certainly not all of these changes can be accredited to the environmental movement. Many of the more dramatic and recent changes in such things as the advertising policies of oil companies, electrical power companies, and other utility and related industries can more probably be traced to the reality[1] of the current "energy crisis." Even this, however, was foretold by the early spokesmen of the environmental movement, particularly those with scientific training. While it is no doubt impossible to prove any cause-effect relationship between the changes that have been occurring and the environmental movement, the two events are so closely related that it would be even more foolish to deny the role the movement has had in influencing some of these changes.

In the following sections, we will look briefly at the growing impact of the movement at the cultural and normative, and legal or legislative levels.

---

[1]The "reality" of the current gasoline shortage is now being widely questioned. For example, many people, including a growing number of congressmen, are suggesting that the shortage has been artificially created by the gas companies themselves in order to force up prices and eliminate the independent, cut-rate dealers. At this time there are major efforts developing for an investigation of the oil industry's role in the shortage. Despite this, one cannot deny the reality of the energy crisis when schools, businesses, and industry were forced to close in many states this past winter because distributors ran out of heating oil and other power-generating fuels.

1. Cultural and Normative Impacts of the Environmental Movement

Much of the legacy of the environmental movement is reflected in cultural and normative changes that have become evident in the American society during the past few years. Some of these changes have appeared on the broader societal level; others are reflected most clearly in individual life-styles. A few items that are indicative of these changes will be briefly discussed.

a. Societal Level. Perhaps the major change that can be observed at this level is the widespread interest that has been generated in environmentally-related issues. Data from the polls clearly show the suddenness with which Americans have become interested in and concerned about their environment. This issue came from almost nowhere to the point of being rated in some polls as a more serious concern than Vietnam, crime, or most any of the other issues that worried Americans in the late 1960's and early 1970's (Erskine, 1972). The environmental movement certainly played a crucial role in defining the environment as a significant problem for much of the American public. All across the country one now finds school children, social clubs, ladie's organizations, and so on, engaged in clean-up programs and in efforts to educate the public on matters concerning pollution, resource conservation, and related issues.

Another of the most basic societal changes has been the demand that we now consider more than just the economic effects of continued growth. This is clearly reflected in the defeat of plans to build supersonic airlines (SST) in the U.S. The question "what does it cost?" has come to have significance in other than financial terms. Strip-mining, which constitutes far the most efficient means of extracting coal and minerals from the earth, is now being outlawed in many states. The scars that the strip-mining leaves behind are now being considered as costs that are to be calculated in the cost-benefit equation. If nothing else, this has forced large industries and utility

companies to spend millions in P.R. campaigns to convince the American public

that they are concerned about the environment. Oil companies show pictures

of fishermen making trophy catches just below an active oil well to demonstrate

that they are having no negative effects on the eco-system. The major auto-

mobile company in the United States takes out full-page advertisements in the

New York Times containing two sentences:

DOES G. M. CARE ABOUT CLEAN AIR?

YOU BET WE DO!!

This is a far cry from the days when industry felt it could pollute with

impunity. While some of the changes probably go no deeper than the Madison

Avenue P.R. work, cases in which industries are being forced to clean-up have

become increasingly common occurrences.

Other important societal-level changes are evident in the political

arena. President Nixon's first Secretary of the Interior, Walter Hickel,

faced a most difficult time in gaining Senate confirmation because of his past

record on environmental issues. And though Hickel may have been chosen origi-

nally by Mr. Nixon because he was recommended by oil interests, the constant

prodding by the environmentalists seemed to contribute to his development of

a somewhat favorable environmental record during his brief stay in the cabinet.

Due in part to his efforts, Congress established five new national parks and

passed a wilderness bill which added 23 areas to the National Wilderness

Preservation System.

Environmentalists joined together during the 1972 national elections to

defeat a number of Congressmen that had compiled the poorest environmental

track records. Among these was the powerful chairman of the House Interior and Insular Affairs Committee, Wayne Aspinal of Colorado. Aspinal had received the label from the environmentalists of being perhaps the most notorious of the "dirty dozen" and this label plagued him continually in his unsuccessful run for re-election.

It seems quite clear that in the political arena the environmentalists have become an interest group of sufficient power that they cannot be ignored. As it has been rhetorically asked: "Is there now a politician anywhere who is in favor of smog, sewage-laden rivers, or the uncontrolled automobile exhaust?"

One also finds recent word additions to the vocabularies of many Americans that seem to have found their way into everyday argot through their initial emphasis by spokesmen of the environmental movement. Thousands of people from all walks of life now use the word "ecology," though few of them may be able to define it. "Energy crisis," "pollution," "eco-system," and similar words are bandied about by newscasters, politicians, and the man on the street. A new national symbol, Woodsey the Owl, has recently been created and one even hears Archie Bunker quoting "Give a hoot, don't pollute." It is hoped that Woodsey will have the same success that Smokey the Bear had in helping make the future generation of Americans (and perhaps the present one, too) aware of an important issue.

b. Individual Level. Important impacts of the environmental movement can also be seen in changes in the life-styles of many individual Americans. One sees this in the automobile driver asking for non-leader gasoline, the homemaker purchasing low-phosphate detergents, the teen-ager walking or riding a ten-speed instead of taking the family car.

Everywhere one sees individuals involved in personal efforts to "get back to nature." Certainly those actively involved do not constitute a majority of the population. However, it is no longer difficult to find persons who prefer "cross-country skiing or snow shoeing over snowmobiling (or even riding lift chairs), boots over trail bikes, and canoes over motor boats" (Baden, 1973: 2) More and more people seem to prefer retaining certain areas of the country as wilderness preserves or wild rivers rather than covering them over with four-lane highways and full-facility campgrounds where the hedonist-types can watch their color T.V.'s with "all the comforts of home."

It has been demonstrated that as incomes go up in this country, an increasing percentage of the income is spent on amenities such as outdoor recreation goods. It would be a serious mistake to imply that this in itself is a reflection of increased individual concern with the environment since few things have a more harmful environmental impact than do trailbikes and snowmobiles. However, as more Americans seek contact with the out-of-doors, some feel that this contact will ultimately increase concern with maintaining a high-quality out-of-doors.

Baden (1973) has assembled a series of tables that deomonstrate some of the points discussed above. Tables 1 and 2 are taken from his work in this area.

Table 1 shows the sudden and rapid rise in the use of national forest primitive and wilderness areas since about 1969. The number of visitor days spent in these areas increased by over two million in the four years of 1967-1971. These data make evident the growing interest in contact with the out-of-doors. They also make obvious future problems the forest service will face in managing such areas. Table 2 shows the equally rapid rise in imports of cross-country skis. (Until recently-at least 1972-all such skis sold in the U.S. were imported). Purchasers of cross-country skis (as opposed to down-hill types) are less likely to be jet-setters and more likely to be individuals

TABLE 1

Use of National Forest Wilderness and Primitive Areas, 1967-1971 (in 12 hr. visitor days)

Millions of 12 hr. Visitor Days

6.8 6.7 6.6 6.5 6.4 6.3 6.2 6.1 6.0 5.9 5.8 5.7 5.6 5.5 5.4 5.3 5.2 5.1 5.0 4.9 4.8 4.7 4.6 4.5

1967   1968   1969   1970   1971

Source: John Baden, "Neospartan Hedonism, Adult Toy Aficionados, and the Development of Bureaucratic Purgatory: A Casual Model," paper presented at the Meetings of the Pacific Sociological Association, Scottsdale, Arizona, May 1973. Baden's data are taken from a U.S. Forest Service report.

TABLE 2

Pairs of Cross-Country Skis Imported, 1967-1972

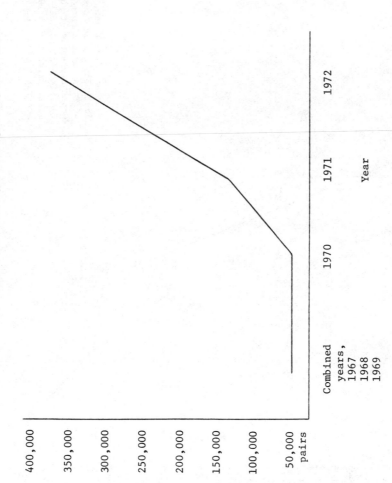

400,000

350,000

300,000

250,000

200,000

150,000

100,000

50,000
pairs

Combined
years,
1967
1968
1969

1970

1971

1972

Year

Source: John Baden, "Neospartan Hedonism, Adult Toy Aficionados, and the Development
of Bureaucratic Purgatory: A Casual Model," paper presented at the Meetings of the
Pacific Sociological Association, Scottsdale, Arizona, May 1973. Baden's data are from
the National Ski Touring Council.

264

interested in "getting back to nature."

It would probably not be too far-fetched to relate the recent communal movement in this country to the larger environmental social movement. Many individual participants in this movement are seeking to find a less material- istic relationship with the natural environment. One finds a majority of the communes being established in more isolated wilderness areas where their inhabitants can reject the symbols of the larger society, many of which, as items of conspicuous consumption, are seen as contributors to the environmental crisis. Here one can throw away the synthetic fabrics, the artificial foods, and can live with nature instead of having to subdue (and destroy) it.

2. Impacts at the Legal and Legislative Level

Many of the most significant of the changes wrought by the environmental movement are at the legal level. Numerous new laws have been passed, agencies created, and significant court decisions rendered. While it would require far too much space to document all of these, several of the most outstanding will be briefly discussed.

a. Air Pollution. Almost every year now brings several new bills deal- ing with the problem of air pollution. The Air Pollution Control Act of 1970 provided the means to establish nationwide air quality standards which are to be implemented in all of the states by May 31, 1975. In effect, states have been required to file plans indicating how they will meet the air quality levels that have been specified. For many urban areas, this has meant the development of transportation controls to reduce smog levels and numerous areas are now working on mass transportation plans to help implement this. Two-year delays approved earlier for some areas have recently been wiped-out by a federal appeals court thus requiring compliance with the mid-1975 deadline.

Some of the most far-reaching air quality laws have been directed at the automobile manufacturers. While in some instances, delays have been granted in meeting newly established exhaust emission requirements, the fact remains that by the mid-1970's the level of air pollution caused by the automobile will be greatly reduced.

b. Water Pollution. As with air pollution, the number of measures dealing with water pollution has increased rapidly in the past few years. The most far-reaching of these has been the Clean Water Act of 1972. This act seeks to end all water pollution by 1985 and calls for spending $24.6 billion in its first three years. Despite his claims of advocacy of environmental clean-up and protection, the Clean Water Act was vetoed by President Nixon. However, the veto was quickly overridden by wide margins in both the House and Senate.

c. Other Measures. Numerous other bills dealing with the environment have been passed or are under consideration. New standards are being set for noise pollution relating to such things as motor vehicles and construction equipment. Studies are underway to recommend air-craft and airport noise limits. Scenic highway bills have been passed directed at "visual pollution" and designed to bring about the removal of unsightly billboards along certain highways and streets. Laws now require that environmental, aesthetic, and social impacts be considered, along with the traditional economic impacts, of almost any type of development that occurs. To protect the interest of the general populace, public hearings are now required by law on most types of development before they are given approval.

d. The Courts. One of the most significant changes that has occurred in recent years has been the growing number of court suits directed at blocking developments that have possible negative environmental impacts. Citizens in many states can now go to court and challenge governmental policies which they view as having possible harmful consequences for the environment. Recent court decisions have given citizens this right even in cases where they cannot demonstrate personal financial loss or injury. Aesthetic values now constitute legitimate bases of argument in court cases.

With support from powerful elements of the environmental movement such as the Sierra Club and the Environmental Defense Fund, more and more citizens have been willing to take such action. As an example of this, members of the Navajo and Hopi Indian Tribes in the Southwest have joined with environmentalists in filing suit against the U.S. Government to block the development of a series of proposed coal-burning electrical power plants in their area. The Navajo and Hopi not only fear the effects of the power plants on vegetation, farming, and water supplies, but are also concerned with possible effects on religion, culture, and traditional life styles.

Certainly not all such efforts by the environmentalists have been successful. For example, in an important recent case the Sierra Club has been unsuccessful in its attempts to keep the U.S. Forest Service from allowing Walt Disney Productions to build a ski resort in Mineral King Valley in the Sierra Nevada. Nevertheless, the batting average is probably much higher than it would have been without the interest and concern the movement has generated.

e. New Federal Agencies. Several new federal agencies have been established in recent years both to monitor compliance with the numerous existing pollution and environmental protection laws and to help establish new policies. The most important of these are the President's Environmental Quality Council and the Environmental Protection Agency. The Environmental Quality Council was established by the National Environmental Policy Act of 1969. The stated purposes of this act were: "To declare a national policy which will encourage productive and enjoyable harmony between man and his environment; to promote efforts which will prevent or eliminate damage to the environment and biosphere and stimulate the health and welfare of man; to enrich the understanding of the ecological systems and natural resources important to the Nation; and to establish a Council on Environmental Quality."

Under the chairmanship of Russell Train, the Council has played an important role in defining issues and in prodding bureaucratic agencies to action.

Clearly the most active and powerful of the new agencies is the Environmental Protection Agency. The EPA was created to pull together a broad scattering of agencies in the anti-pollution field. Since its creation the EPA has shown little reluctance to take on even some of the country's most powerful firms over pollution issues. The roles of the EPA are many and varied. Environmental impact studies must be filed with and approved by the EPA before most developments such as new highways, dams, and power plants can be built. The agency sponsors a good-deal of much needed research on environmental questions and also plays an important monitoring role in checking to see that industries, cities, etc. are complying with environmental quality standards.

One of the most controversial of recent EPA proposals would cut gasoline consumption in the Los Angeles Basin by 86 percent. While many argue that such a move would totally paralyze the city, some EPA officials note that this drastic cut in consumption would be required to meet the standards established by the 1970 Clean Air Act. Air pollution levels defined as acceptable by this act were exceeded in Los Angeles on more than 220 days in 1971.

Summary and Conclusions

Concern with environmental issues has burst upon the American scene with surprising suddenness. Out of the concern (and also contributing to it) has evolved a social movement that has been classified by some as one of the major occurrences of this half of the twentieth century. Already this movement has grown into one of the largest social movements in our history and its impacts are reflected in the political arena, in broad-scale social change, and, on a more micro-level, in individual life-styles.

Despite such major changes, orientations toward the environment continue to vary greatly. This must be kept in mind in order to keep the current movement in its proper perspective. Within our own country, the crisis rhetoric of the environmentalists is loudly scoffed at by others. As has been noted, some right-wing groups have defined the environmental movement as a communist-inspired conspiracy designed to deny the United States access to minerals and resources vital to her survival (see Albrecht, 1972). Just as solemnly, some left-wing groups have seen the movement as an attempt by the power structure to draw attention away from more important social issues such as war and poverty. Many Black leaders in the country have tended to agree with this prognosis. To quote Richard Hatcher, Mayor of Gary, Indiana: "The nation's concern with environment has done what George Wallace was unable to do: distract the nation from the human problems of black and brown Americans" (quoted in Time, 1970). A number of citizens, who belong to neither the right nor the left, have probably wondered whether or not mankind will suffer "a whole hell of a lot if the whooping crane doesn't quite make it" (quoted in Time, 1970).

Despite such detractors, and whatever their reasons, the evidence that has been accumulated is rather clear in indicating that concern with the environment has increased at a rather rapid rate within the last decade. More and more Americans have come to see pollution, waste, resource depletion, and related issues as problems meriting concern and vigorous efforts directed toward their sollution. Whether or not this concern will last remains to be seen. Many critics see the environmental movement as simply a passing fad. Others have suggested that it will survive only if it is able to set priorities and establish goals that the mass of the American public can find meaningful and can support.

Whatever its future history, the legacy of the environmental movement discussed above is an important one. Further, the movement remains a vigorous one and it seems safe to predict that its effect on society will continue to be felt. Unlike the Vietnam War, we cannot erase the environment as social problem from the life and consciousness of most Americans by simply signing a treaty. The frustrations that the environmentalists have faced in their quest have caused the less committed to drop by the way but the more committed continue their efforts and continue to gain new recruits. Perhaps it is significant that, as Gale (1972: 296) notes: " . . . in spite of . . . feelings frustration on the part of many environmentalists, no environmental equivalents of Stokely Carmichel or Martin Luther King have stepped forward, no militant environmental organization has successfully challenged the leading role played by established organizations such as the Sierra Club and the Wilderness Society and no environmental campaign has brought about a nationwide mass mobilization. Further, the environmental movement has remained nonviolent, using public pressure as a means of forcing negotiation on specific environmental issues."

In sum, the environmental social movement is of such force now and will remain so for the foreseeable future that change will continue to be made, though perhaps with less fanfare. American society and the life-styles of the citizens living therein will continue to be affected. Thus, the legacy discussed above will be likely to continue to grow.

REFERENCES

Albrecht, Stan L.
    1972   "Environmental Social Movements and Counter-Movements: An
           Overview and an Illustration," Journal of Voluntary Action
           Research, 1 (October):2-11.

Baden, John
    1973   "Neospartan Hedonism, Adult Toy Aficionados, and the Develop-
           ment of Bureaucratic Purgatory: A Casual Model," paper presented
           at the Meetings of the Pacific Sociological Association, Scotts-
           dale, Arizona, May 1973.

Devall, W.B.
    1970a   "The governing of a voluntary organization: oligarchy and
           democracy in the Sierra Club." Ph.D. dissertation. University
           of Oregon.

    1970b   "Conservation: an upper-middle class social movement: a
           replication." J. of Leisure Research 2 (Spring):123-126.

Erskine, Hazel
    1972   "Polls: Pollution and its Costs," Public Opinion Quarterly,
           Spring 1972 (36:120-135).

    1972   "Polls: Pollution and Industry," Public Opinion Quarterly,
           Summer 1972 (36:263-280).

Faich, Ronald G. and Richard P. Gale
    1971   "The environmental movement: from recreation to politics."
           Pacific Sociological Review 14 (July):270-287.

Fromm, Erich
    1965   Escape From Freedom, N.Y.: Avon Books, 1965.

Gale, Richard P.
    1972   "From sit-in to hike-in: a comparison of the civil rights and
           environmental movements," pp. 280-305 in W. Burch; N. Cheek;
           and L. Taylor (eds.), Social Behavior, Natural Resources and
           the Environment, New York: Harper and Row, 1972.

Harry, Joseph
    1973   "Opportunities For Minority Power," paper presented at the Meetings
           of the Society for the Study of Social Problems, New York, 1973.

Hendee, John C., Richard P. Gale, and Joseph Harry
    1969   "Conservation, politics and democracy." J. of Soil and Water
           Conservation 24 (November/December):212-215.

Jones, Holway R.
    1965   John Muir and the Sierra Club, San Francisco: Sierra Club
           Publication.

Killian, Lewis M.
   1964   "Social Movements." Pp. 426-455 In Robert E.L. Faris (ed.),
           Handbook of Modern Sociology. Chicago: Rand McNally.

King, C. Wendell
   1965   Social Movements in the United States, N.Y.: Random House, 1965.

Kornhauser, William
   1959   The Politics of Mass Society, N.Y.: The Free Press, 1959.

Lipset, Seymour Martin
   1963   Political Man, Garden City, N.Y.: Doubleday and Co., 1963.

Mauss, Armand L.
   1971   "On Being Strangled by the Stars and Stripes," The Journal
           of Social Issues 27 (1):183-202.

McCarthy, G. Michael
   1973   "Retreat from Responsibility: The Colorado Legislature in
           the Conservation Era, 1876-1908," Rocky Mountain Social Science
           Journal 10 (April):27-36, 1972.

Moncrief, Lewis
   1970   "The Cultural Basis for our Environmental Crisis," Science 170
           (October 30, 1970):508-512.

Morrison, Denton E., Kenneth E. Hornback, and W. Keith Warner
   1972   "The environmental movement: some preliminary observations."
           pp. 259-279 in W. Burch; N. Cheek; and L. Taylor (eds.),
           Social Behavior, Natural Resources and the Environment.
           New York: Harper and Row, 1972.

Nash, Roderick
   1965   "introduction" to Holway R. Jones' John Muir and the Sierra
           Club, San Francisco: Sierra Club Publication, 1965.

Schnaiberg, Allan
   1971   "Politics, participation and pollution: The 'environmental
           movement'." Mimeo, Northwestern University.

Time Magazine
   1970   August 3, 1970, p. 42.

Zald, Mayer N. and Roberta Ash
   1966   "Social movement organizations: growth, decay and change."
           Social Forces 44 (March):327-341.

THE ENVIRONMENTAL MOVEMENT: CONFLICT DYNAMICS

Denton E. Morrison

1. ISSUES, CONTESTANTS, PROCESSES, TRENDS

The environmental movement has changed from a
movement of consensus to a movement of conflict.
Through and somewhat beyond Earth Day, April 22,
1970, the environment promised to be a crusade
that could integrate the country. Governments
and schools at all levels, private industry,
labor, the churches, the young, the old, liberal
and conservative quickly gathered on the band-
wagon led by the new environmental and older
conservation groups. There was agreement,
superficially at least, that the solution of
environmental problems was a matter of the
highest national priority. Partly this attitude was an over-optimistic over-reaction to
general weariness, and particularly mass-media
weariness, with the proliferation of several
conflict-generating movements on the scene:
the anti-war movement, the civil rights movement, the student movement, women's liberation,
and the farm worker's movement to name only the
most visible. Also involved were some dramatic
examples of pollution (for instance, the
Santa Barbara oil spill) that served as precipitating events for the movement.

The mood of consensus changed rather quickly
following the initial Earth Day. Fundamental to
this change was the fact that it soon became
apparent that environmental reforms shared the
common element of requiring substantial costs of
various sorts. Simultaneously came the revelation that costly environmental reforms would not
generally be undertaken by the voluntary participation of governments, firms, families and
individuals. Rather, the movement found it
necessary to employ power tactics, including
legal and other forms of coercion, to bring about
its reforms and the inevitable concomitant of
such tactics, conflict, followed.[1]

JOURNAL OF VOLUNTARY ACTION RESEARCH, Spring, 1973,
Vol. 2, pp. 74-85.

The Conflict Issues

The costs of environmental reform are not
necessarily long-term costs. Indeed, the very
essence of environmentalists' arguments is
that unless short-term environmental reform
costs are undertaken, the environment cannot in
the long-run continue to produce the benefits
we require of it (i.e., avoiding the costs of
environmental reform in the short-run will
court disaster in the long-run).

Some of the costs of environmental reform are
more or less straightforward economic ones:
higher costs for the production, distribution
and consumption of numerous goods and services;
costs for the research and development of new
environmental technology; the costs of insti-
tuting and operating new public agencies for
environmental management, regulation and law
enforcement. Less obvious, but perhaps of
equal or greater importance in the conflicts
involved, are the costs to individual, family,
corporate and public agency autonomy and freedom in decision-making: *it is increasingly
apparent that complete freedom and autonomy in
many crucial decision areas is to a substantial
extent incompatible with the long-term viability
of the environment.* Another environmental cost
is a qualitative one associated with the added
social complexity that must accompany the new
layer of social controls over environment.

The raising and debating of environmental
questions as "cost" questions has been a round-
about and somewhat unsatisfactory method of
leading society to grapple with the more fundamental and delicate question of the extent to
which environmental problems are important in
relation to other problems. Clearly, solutions
to some other problems must be deferred if
money, other resources, and social energy are
channeled toward the solution of environmental
problems.

Logically, then, policy decisions on environmental questions demand knowledge at various
levels:

(1) What are the *physical facts* of the case

(i.e., the nature and the extent of changes in
water, air, and land from its "natural" or
"desirable" state)?

(2) What are the health, survival, aesthetic,
or other *threats* to humans involved in these
environmental changes, and to whom and how many
are they threats?

(3) What are the alternative *means* for rec-
tifying the problem in various degrees?

(4) What are the *costs*, economic and otherwise, of various degrees of rectification by
various methods?

(5) In addition, when these extremely difficult but basically factual questions are answered,
there remains the essentially value-preference
and ultimately political question of what degree
of rectification, if any, *should* be undertaken,
by what method, on what scale, and at what rate?

Consequently, environmental debates inherently
involve a blurred mixture of physical/natural
science, social science (and particularly
economics) and ideology; they are not debates
that lend themselves to easy and enduring settlements.

Environmentalists have to date had a tendency
to view environmental changes as great in magnitude, broadly and seriously threatening, and to
call for total rectification by whatever means
is effective and at the fastest rate physically
possible (i.e., at whatever costs it takes to purify the air and water, restore the land). It has,
of course, been intrinsically impossible for anyone to be outspokenly against clean air or water,
or a good environment generally. Moreover, the
message of the broad and seriously threatening
nature of environmental problems came from the
prestigious ranks of science and was therefore
widely accepted as valid (another source of the
early consensus over environmental problems).

Consequently, most concrete environmental disputes have to date centered around attempts at
negotiating from the radical and idealistic pre-
scriptions of environmentalists on "5" above with

regard to the practicalities and social trade-offs involved in "3" and "4". Usually, these debates have surrounded more or less specific, piecemeal environmental reform issues, most often those connected with air and water pollution. Clearly the environmentalists have had a convincing early general offensive on points "1" and "2", but increasingly there has been a tendency for debates on environmental matters to push the questions back to these levels in specific terms. Indeed, it is only if the debate reaches these levels that costs can be meaningfully assessed (i.e., in relationship to benefits).

Both the increasing tendency toward debate of cost/benefit specifics and some indication of the failure of certain specific pollution reform measures -- for instance, the problematic aspects of the California emission controls in the Los Angeles area[2] -- have forced some environmentalists to a higher level of abstraction in constructing the environmental problem. Thus, there is among environmentalists a noticeable movement away from concern with solving specific problems of pollution and toward concern with the more fundamental problems of resource depletion and the carrying capacity of the earth.

In the last year or so, there has been among a segment of environmentalists an increasing disillusionment and skepticism as to the actual or probable outcomes of *specific environmental reforms*. There is also an increasing attraction to the notion that meaningful environmental change will take place only if there is substantial *societal redirection* in the form of basically reduced aggregate consumption patterns.

In particular, this change has been precipitated by the publication of the MIT Club of Rome report on *The Limits to Growth*.[3] The message of this report (regardless of its veracity) has not been news to some environmentalists. It only reinforced what they thought all along, and served to bring some others to their viewpoint. Similarly, it has reinforced the view of many skeptics outside the movement that environmental reform will not let you have your cake and eat it, that in the broadest sense the cost of environmental reform is the sacrifice of economic growth. *Increasingly, then, environmental battles are shaping up as battles over the desirability of growth.*

The Contestants

In the most general sense, the parties to environmental conflicts can be characterized as "environmentalists" and "growthists" (i.e., those tending to favor and those tending to oppose the costs to economic growth involved in environmental reform).[4] Naturally, this conceptualization greatly oversimplifies a complicated and varied social reality, and needs immediate elaboration and specification.

A. *The Environmentalists.* Insofar as environmentalists are involved in conflicts with growthists, two broad levels of movement organization are present: voluntary and institutional. Contrary to what is implied in much general writing on social movements, the environmental movement did not, at the start, and especially does not now, consist only or even mainly of individuals banding together in voluntary organizations to press for change.[5] The predominant image in social movement literature is one of voluntary movement organizations trying to break down, or at least get a foot into, the door of the "establishment." But for the environmental movement, the door was well ajar from the start.

While it is undoubtedly the case that the voluntary movement organizations provided the major initial impetus for change, it is also true that movement organizations very quickly came into being in major institutional areas and with the express blessing of the institutional leaders, particularly at all levels of government and education. But many industry, commerce, labor, religious, professional, and philanthropic organizations also quickly responded by establishing environmental committees, bureaus, agencies, personnel, and programs.

In the case of governments and universities, this quick and favorable response was doubtless because certain branches of these organizations, often ones that were the direct or indirect products of the earlier conservation movement, readily welcomed and nurtured public support to fan the coals under their own long-frustrated environmental programs. Also, institutional support was rapidly gained, in part, because the severe cost implications of environmental reform were not clearly recognized at first and many "establishment" people saw in the environment opportunities to co-opt youth and other potential social dissidents: the environment was seen as a "safe" issue (at least "safe" in relation to war, civil rights and campus issues) and also an important one.

In addition, institutional movement organizations rapidly emerged simply because the participants in the voluntary organizations, particularly those in the revitalized conservation groups, were an integral and potentially influential part of the institutions. It is, in fact, most interesting to observe the rapidity with which nearly every university in the country established environmental curricula, research programs and institutes, libraries, etc. When we compare this phenomenon with the slowness and controversy that surrounded the establishment of Black studies programs, Black culture centers, and so on, we get a clear clue to the establishment credentials of the environmentalists as well as to the early consensus around environmental issues.[6]

Indeed, the participants in the environmental movement (voluntary and institutional movement organization leaders, members, supporters, sympathizers) are, in composite, an elite, overdog group: scientists, professionals, government officials, teachers, educated citizenry, and those upwardly mobile toward such ranks, namely students.[7] Probably the most crucial point of their differentiation from growthists in personal characteristics is the high level and scientific character of their education (predominantly but not exclusively in the life sciences). But concomitant with this is their white race, their high occupational status and income level and, indeed, their prestige and power, all of which have been instrumental in allowing voluntary and institutional movement organizations, separately and together, rapidly to wield substantial power. (Similarly, both voluntary movement organizations and institutional movement organizations have been vehicles for upward income, status, and power mobility among those who have been able to identify their occupations and avocations with environmentalism.)

However, these characteristics do not in themselves predict environmentalist tendencies unless combined with a crucial situational variable typical of environmentalists, namely **their lack of direct dependence for a livelihood on organizations that are threatened by the costs of environmental reform.** All of these are, of course, only broad generalizations to which exceptions can easily be found. But they are visibly exhibited in their "ideal type" in the leaders of both the voluntary and institutional environmental movement organizations.

B. *The Growthists.* Growthists can be generally characterized as simply residual to the environmentalists (i.e., the rest of society). But the main, visible antagonists of the environmentalists are those who are the most immediately, directly, and severely threatened by the costs of environmental reform *and* who are sufficiently powerful to challenge environmentalists' pressures for change. Presently, then, the following growthist groups are those most engaged in conflicts with environmentalists: (1) mining and foundry, heavy manufacturing, lumber and paper, petroleum, chemical and automotive industries, plus agriculture; (2) utilities (natural gas, electricity, and waste disposal), including those publicly owned; and (3) land developers. These growthist groups, particularly the first, are generally and actively supported in their conflicts with environmentalists by a complex network of allied governmental, university and voluntary organizations, including labor and professional groups.

280

Since costs are typically passed on to those
in less competitive positions and to those who
are less organized to fight for their self-
interests, the poor, in general, as well as
consumers, in general, are threatened by the
costs of environmental reform. They are not
presently well prepared to challenge the environmentalists in meaningful conflicts, although they
provide peripheral support for the main growthist
combatants of environmentalism described above.
It is noteworthy, for instance, that Blacks and
the poor have on the whole been noticeably luke-
warm, if not outright hostile, to environmental
reform.

In part, this is because the environmental
movement has thus far focused mainly on rural
and wilderness-recreational features of the
natural environment, rather than on the work,
housing, shopping, transport, and recreational
environments of central cities -- environments
that are more salient to the poor as well as to
labor. Also, it is because increased costs for
utilities, autos, housing, and all consumer goods
create a stronger relative deprivation for those
who are not yet secure in their modest affluence.

But probably more central is the fact that anything that threatens economic growth also threatens the traditional means by which poverty is
reduced and economic security generated in our
society: new jobs and better pay levels at
existing jobs. This probably also explains some
ambivalence toward environmentalism in the women's
movement, despite obvious ideological overlap on
the abortion/family planning issue. The core
issue for all underdogs is equal jobs and equal
pay and this is threatened by the slowed-growth
economy implied in environmentalism. Hence, we
may expect to see some conflicts between environmentalists and underdogs that have growing,
organized power in their own movements, particularly urban Blacks and, to a lesser degree, women.[8]

The Processes

Conflicts between environmentalists and growthists are constantly in progress; several types

and arenas of conflict are involved:
(1) Voluntary movement organizations frequently conflict with specific, visible symbolically important growthist targets, usually polluters or land despoilers, in a variety of more or less *direct, informal, extra-institutional processes*. These include mostly on-site rallies, marches, protest demonstrations, sit-ins, picketing, delegations, petitions, and action-blockages, although some eco-guerrilla and mild sabotage tactics are on record. In general, however, the environmental movement has been singularly devoid of violence, property damage and other aggressively "disruptive" conflict processes that have been frequent in the anti-war and civil rights movements. Doubtless, this again reflects the characteristics and situations of the movement participants, as well as the fact that both voluntary and institutional movement organizations have had substantial *success* in engaging growthists in conflicts through institutional channels. Also important, of course, is the fact that environmental ideology is intrinsically anti-destructive of material resources.

Institutional conflict processes range along a continuum of directness and formality somewhat as follows:
(2) Environmentalists and growthists constantly employ *propaganda processes* in a battle for public opinion through all the mass media, as well as through special media such as movement and growthist magazines, newsletters, films, posters, and so on.
(3) Voluntary movement organizations actively engage growthists in conflicts involving *political processes* of election and legislative influence at all levels of government and to a lesser degree, in the corporate arena.
(4) Conflicts over the accuracy, completeness and proper interpretation of information about environmental problems pervade nearly every environmental conflict process, but conflicts over information which involve the *scientific processes* are especially focused between the research and educational agencies of the movement organizations (voluntary and institutional) and those more aligned with growthism in govern-

ments, universities and industries.

(5) Both voluntary and institutional movement organizations regularly conflict with growthists in and through hearings and meetings with public administrative, regulative, management and enforcement agencies that interpret, set and enforce specific, operational environmental policies. These conflicts involve various *policy determination and negotiation processes,* including debates, discussions, presentations, briefings and political pressures over the informational and ideological bases for decisions and interpretations. Often these conflicts involve inter-agency conflicts: government movement organizations contesting for power and authority with other governmental agencies representing growthist interests. (For instance, the Environmental Protection Agency [E.P.A.] conflicting with the Department of Agriculture or Commerce, or a state natural resources department with the highway department.) In cases where movement institutionalization has gone to the point where a government movement organization has gained power and authority over certain environmental administrative, regulatory or management areas, the movement organization often confronts industrialists or other growthists directly, as in the case of the E.P.A. and the auto manufacturers.

(6) Finally, both voluntary and institutional movement organizations are deeply involved in conflicts involving *legal processes,* with growthists in ongoing litigations at all levels of the court system.

Trends in Environmental Conflicts

Several closely related general trends in the processes of conflict between environmentalists and growthists are worth observing. Initially, it can be noted that there has been a tendency toward formalization in the conflict process over time (i.e., a general tendency for conflicts to move from "1" and toward "6" above). In part, this change is a result of the failure of the very early "participation" change strategies of the environmentalists (expecting that

283

informed people would voluntarily make changes).
It also results from the fact that the unique
characteristics and situations of environmentalists gave them unique opportunities for success
in power strategies aimed at achieving change
through institutional rather than noninstitu-
tional forms of coercion.

With the realization of general success in
influencing political candidates, legislation,
and the establishment of institutional movement
organizations for environmental management,
regulation and enforcement, it is now increasingly necessary for environmentalists to guard
against erosion of this great power potential
in specific policies, management decisions,
court decisions, enforcement proceedings, and
so on. In addition, the successes of the
environmentalists in getting favorable legislation (often of a quite vague and general
nature, as, for instance, the National Environmental Protection Act) has increasingly
allowed only the more formal administrative
hearing and court processes as the most salient
short-term recourse for growthists.

*Because of the increasingly formal character
of environmental disputes, environmentalists
have experienced a need for more sophisticated
information as well as for more sophistication
in political and legal tactics.* Consequently,
there is the accompanying trend for power to
flow into the hands of the larger state, regional,
and national voluntary and institutional movement
organizations. Together with an increasing
realization among environmentalists that effective environmental controls must follow the
geography of environmental problems rather than
local or state political boundaries, this has
caused environmental conflicts and victories to
escalate to larger scales of political and social
organization. Thus, governments and government
agencies (often institutional movement organizations) with larger jurisdictions are increasingly
involved in environmental conflicts with governments and government agencies of smaller jurisdiction, as well as with private growthists of both
large and small scale.

In this process, the institutional movement organizations, particularly those with federal, regional, and state jurisdictions, have gained in power, but they have also gained in their scope of public responsibility.

More and more they must play the role of mediating and compromising the more radical demands of the voluntary movement organizations and the interests of the growthists. Consequently, there is a tendency for the larger voluntary movement organizations, in particular, to conflict with the institutional movement organizations, and for voluntary groups to attempt to coalesce their power into court cases and court appeals, including requests for injunctions and stays against both growthist projects and the policies of institutional movement organizations.

In this conflict arena discrete "yes" or "no," "stop" or "go" decisions rather than compromises often result. This tends even further to polarize the voluntary movement organizations and the growthists and, increasingly, to polarize the voluntary against the institutional movement organizations, thus insuring continuing conflicts of growing complexity.

II. IMPLICATIONS AND SPECULATIONS FOR CLASS CONFLICT THEORY

Dahrendorf (1959) has analyzed the several reasons why Marxian-type class conflicts have not developed in capitalist economies. These reasons include the proliferation of inter-mediate ranks between workers and owners and the institutionalization of opportunities for upward mobility into these ranks as well as ownership ranks. Simultaneous with this, control has not concentrated in the hands of owners as Marx envisioned. Nor has wealth in any absolute sense. In part the latter is tied to the fact that industrial economies, particularly capitalistic ones, have been productive far beyond what was possible to foresee in the early stage of industrialization. The value of labor, it turns out, is as crucial in the consumption as in the production of this fantastic wealth.

Whatever exploitation of workers has been involved in this, it has also involved remarkable advances in the efficiency with which technology has been used in the extraction, harnessing, processing, distribution and consumption of natural resources. And, whether or not workers make gains relative to owners in this process, it is clear that both have made dramatic material advances in absolute material consumption terms.

These material advances have been made, we are now told on high authority, at great cost to the natural environment and to the long-term viability of the man-environment relationship, both in terms of pollution and resource depletion, Thus, a possible interpretation of social stratification as it relates to the industrialization process is that environmental exploitation has been a crucial factor in capitalist industrial societies in allowing the poor to come up without making the rich come down (i.e., environmental exploitation has prevented class conflict).

This is not to deny the presence or importance of "class" *antagonisms* along lines of wealth, ownership, or control differences in capitalistic societies. But these antagonisms are mainly over the terms on which cooperation is to take place. They have not involved fundamental attempts of workers to organize as a revolutionary class for the purpose of engaging in conflict with capitalists to appropriate industrial ownership, wealth, and control for workers -- the Marxian conception.[9]

Whatever relationships of antagonism and exploitation exist between the various strata of ownership, control, and wealth in modern industrial capitalism, *all* who are tied to this system share, to the extent that their ties are direct and to those segments of the economy most visibly involved in environmental exploitation, a common fate and a common interest in continued environmental exploitation. This suggests, in contrast with Marxist and other more general

notions of class antagonisms, that many of the
important industrial conflicts emerging in this
country around environmental issues will not be
between the various ownership, wealth, and control
strata of industry. Rather, such conflicts will
be between *all* those associated directly with
industries threatened by the costs of environmental reform and those who push those reforms,
the environmentalists.

More specifically, organized labor, management,
and ownership of threatened industries can be
expected to counter the actual and potential
consequences of environmental reform by forming
coalitions to counter environmentalist pressures.
Such coalitions are likely to receive broad public
support, particularly among those in the average
and lower economic strata (i.e., those in less
competitive economic situations whose economic
fate is correlated more closely than others with
the general health of industry and who also have
less eco-awareness).

This, of course, is a rather broad hypothesis,
one for which the evidence is not clear now and
will not be for some time. There are, moreover,
some reasons why it should not hold true -- and
some reasons against these reasons:

(1) It is possible that a sufficient number of
growthists will come to see environmental reforms,
despite the costs involved, as in their long-term
or even short-term interest. Obviously polluted
air and water is not a desirable situation for the
industries most responsible for the pollution,
either in terms of the climate of public opinion
in which they must operate or in terms of the
working or living environments that are created
by pollution.

However, those who control such industries,
particularly owners (stockholders) but also
managers, are often able to avoid the worst of
the pollution in their daily working and family
lives (air conditioned offices and homes in the
suburbs, if not in communities far removed from
the pollution source) and, particularly, in
their leisure lives. The latter is also
increasingly true for workers in such indus-

tries who have the affluence to enjoy a number
of long weekends and substantial vacations in
environments of their choice.

Those who control such industries, moreover,
control their employees politically in the
sense that the latter are not likely, ultimately, to bite the hand that feeds them, at
least if it feeds them well -- as is the case
in many of the threatened industries, for
instance automobiles and steel. (It may, in
fact, follow directly from the notion of
"externalized costs" that the most polluting
industries are the most profitable ones.)

In certain of the extractive industries
—for instance, fishing— the "tragedy of the commons"
(the tendency for unregulated public goods
to deteriorate) strikes more quickly and more
saliently and brings quick readiness to accept
environmental restraints, but industries where
this is likely to occur are relatively small
and unimportant. Even in lumbering there is no
reason to think that workers (or anyone else)
actually know how close the "tragedy" is;
managers and stockholders have skills and
resources that are substitutable in other
enterprises. The more common situation, then,
is the one in which huge firms and their stockholders are all too willing to shift their
financial and personnel resources from, say,
petroleum to strip mining and/or coal
gasification. In short, the environmentalists
claim that the tragedy is close, but for many
the tragedy of losing hard-won affluence is
more salient; for others the tragedy is viewed
as more or less deferrable.

(2) To some extent owners and managers of
threatened industries can recover the increased
costs of environmental reforms by increased
prices; organized labor can do the same by
pressing for higher wages. But these practices
are made problematic by anti-inflationary
controls. Also, the increased costs of some
environmental reforms such as the 1975 auto
emission controls are predicted to be so dramatic as to reduce demand and profits
substantially.

(3) Some industries will, naturally, be in a position to profit by research, development, manufacturing, construction and servicing related to demands for new environmental technology. Capital, management and labor can and doubtless will flow from threatened industries to these new growth areas. But the profit and job potentials of the antipollution industries are highly hypothetical at this time, and the cost threats to polluting industries very real. Also, the time involved in environmental-technological transfromations, for instance from auto commuting to mass transit, is such that the economic dislocations in immediately threatened industries will be severe for some time to come.[10]

(4) Certain segments of organized labor, even in environmentally threatened industries, have to date been strong supporters of certain environmental reforms (e.g., the United Auto Workers stand on the 1975 federal auto emissions standards). It remains to be seen, however, whether this support will extend to the rank and file of workers when the costs of such reforms become concrete, salient, and more genuinely threatening. Also, it remains to be seen whether such stands might, in a clinch, be softened in exchange for wage and fringe benefit concessions from management. It is most revealing that explicit, systematic arguments *against* the environmental viewpoint come mainly from the far left branches of labor. It is very clear in these arguments that contemporary Marxist labor theorists are upset in substantial measure *because* environmental pressures tend to unite capital and labor and thus ultimately play into capitalist interests (see Fuchs, 1970; National Caucus of Labor Committees, 1972).

Thus, the overall strategy of first preference for labor, management, ownership, and others whose fate is associated with threatened industries will be to engage in coalitions to resist environmental reforms. At a somewhat more abstract level this amounts to an assertion that the directness and degree of dependence on the industrial mode of production is more determinative of positions on emerging industrial conflict issues than ownership or nonownership of productive facilities -- the essence of what may be termed an "industrial - technological" rather than a Marxian "labor" theory of value and of class consciousness.

These groups in coalition and the environmentalists with whom they conflict, then, promise to constitute "classes" in Dahrendorf's specific, non-Marxian sense of groups in conflict over participation in or exclusion from *authority* over industrial policies (1959:138ff.)[11] But Dahrendorf's notion is not substantive or historical; it gives no clue as to the changing *basis* for authority claims in evolution of industrial society. In a general sense, then, the Weberian notion of the importance of understanding the increasing role of "rationality" in modern industrial society contributes as much to understanding environmental conflicts as Marxian or subsequent class conflict theories.

Neither the contestants, the issues, nor the processes of environmental conflict can be well understood without special reference to the role that certain *knowledge* developments play in these conflicts. The environmentalists, in fact, strive for and have significantly gained authority on the basis of their special claims to knowledge about ecological problems connected with industrial modes of production (i.e., what is rational long-term industrial policy). In effect, then, the environmentalists have offered an "ecological" theory of value and have shown in the process of gaining authority for their viewpoint the sense in which the "industrial-technological" theory has fallacies, and, indirectly, the sense in which that theory currently has superior explanatory power over the Marxian "labor" theory of value.[12]

Still, we should not lose sight of the general non-Marxian sense in which environmental conflicts both represent and can generate antagonisms along class lines (i.e., along lines of differences in wealth and correlated rank variables). Very simply, there are virtually no poor or working-class people represented among the environmentalists; on the other hand, average and lower economic strata constitute a

substantial proportion of the growthists. If
the fact that the affluent are also well
represented among the growthists somewhat blurs
and qualifies the class dimension of present
conflicts *between* growthists and environmentalists, we may expect that class-like
conflicts *within* growthist ranks will be
increased and perhaps somewhat less blurred if
and to the extent that environmentalists have
continued successes in introducing their
reforms.

If class conflicts have been historically
avoided, as hypothesized above, by, in effect,
"taking it out" on the environment, we may
expect class antagonisms to increase if and to
the extent that environmental reforms force the
curtailment of environmental exploitation. The
conflicts inherent in a system of relatively
fixed and unequally shared resources are, in
addition, likely to be accelerated when such a
system is imposed after a long period of
economic expansion and vertical mobility. Such
periods expand the absolute material expectations of poor and rich alike -- the familiar
relative deprivation notion (Morrison, 1971).

These conflicts cannot be expected to take
simple "have" *vs.* "have-not" lines, however,
because of the many economic differentiations
in the present system, the differential power
of various strata, and the differential and
sometimes conflicting bases of present strata
organizations. Blacks and women, for instance,
are likely to conflict with each other and .
with organized labor and all these are likely to
be in conflict with management and ownership and
over jobs and pay levels.

International Class Conflicts. At a broader,
macro-level of stratification, it is clear that,
just like the broad differences in social class
concern with environmental issues in the United
States, the poorer, less developed countries are
much less concerned with environmental problems
than are the richer, developed, highly indus-
trialized countries. There is, however, little

chance that the developing countries will become involved in conflicts with developed countries over environmental reforms pushed by the latter onto the former, despite some indications of such conflicts surrounding the recent Stockholm U.N. Conference on the environment.

Developed countries are increasingly and tightly linked to the developing countries in economic relationships in which natural resources move disproportionately in the direction of the developed countries (cf. Dean, 1971). These relationships are in large measure a way for developed countries to externalize environmental costs at the expense of developing countries. In fact, there would be a far greater short-term probability of conflict between developed and developing countries if the *latter* instituted stern environmental controls than if they do not. For this would very likely mean that they would cut off or greatly reduce resource flow to and/or greatly increase resource costs for the developed countries, many of which are dependent on developing countries for certain resources, particularly oil, natural gas, and other minerals.

Some conflicts of this kind are likely to arise if visible environmental degradation occurs in developing countries as a result of the tendency for developed countries to prohibit polluting industries within their own boundaries and thus shift demand for the products of such industries to developing countries. However, other conflicts with the general interests of developing countries may occur to the extent that substantial amounts of wealth of developed countries goes into environmental controls rather than purchase of the products of developing countries as the latter attempt to build their economies by export industries. The likelihood of this situation is enhanced by the balance of payments problem in the United States.

In the context of broader theories relating economy to social organization and social conflict, *the environmental problem is one of industrialism and not of capitalism*. Among industrial countries, it is the capitalistic

ones that apparently first experience or at least
first become aware of environmental problems
for two main reasons: (1) capitalist
economies are apparently more efficient at
productivity and thus at environmental
exploitation, with the attendant problems of
environmental degradation; and (2) such
countries generate a free scientific community
and a free and informed citizenry to identify
environmental problems and organize to press
for reforms. But it is clear that industrially
advanced capitalist and socialist countries are
much more alike than different in their
environmental problems -- although not
necessarily similar in their potential for
solutions.

III. *PROSPECTS*

Relative to other social movements, the
environmental movement has been uniquely
successful in bringing about or at least
setting the stage for rapid and substantial
changes. Achieving and, especially, concretely
implementing these changes has increasingly
involved environmentalists in conflicts with
growthists. There is little probability,
however, that the more radical change implications of environmentalism will come about
soon.

Partly this is because growthist opposition is
strong, probably overwhelmingly so. Many
environmentalists look upon this opposition as
an environmental "backlash" and there are some
evidences of a genuine backlash, a genuine
counter-movement.[13] To some extent, of course,
the forces that resist environmental reform
simply represent the status quo as it
encounters any change effort. This factor is
complicated by the crucial role of scientific
knowledge in undergirding the movement. Thus,
what is by some environmentalists interpreted
as resistance to environmental reform more
accurately represents the self-correcting
aspects of science at work in what amounts to a
closer scrutiny of environmentalists' claims.

But there is, in fact, more than just the normal defensiveness of entrenched social and economic interests in the resistance to environmental reform. At least some of the opposition to environmental reform represents and reflects *other* social reform movements that are as important to their promoters as environmental reform is to environmentalists. *Insofar as movements of the disadvantaged can attain their goals only in a context of economic growth, their programs will be incompatible with environmentalism.* We have tried to show why these forces, including the labor movement, will tend to coalesce with threatened economic interests in countering a common foe, the environmentalists. Naturally such a counter-movement cannot be overtly anti-environmental; instead it must stress the role of economic growth in solving society's problems and how environmentalism works against these solutions. It is noteworthy that the most systematic critique of environmentalism to date (Neuhaus, 1971) is framed in terms of the way environmentalism threatens the poor.

Increasingly, then, the growthists are better prepared for battles with environmentalists, including showdown battles in the courts. At the same time, some major voluntary movement organizations find their membership roles declining, and concomitantly, declining resources for such battles (cf., Barnett, 1972). With the growing realization of the cost implications of environmentalism, many individuals and organizations who were peripherally or superficially committed to the movement have dropped out. Similarly, the growth of conflict issues has brought out much ideological heterogeneity within the movement that was masked by the early euphoria over environment; there is much conflict within the movement over goals and means.

Consequently, the burden of carrying the environmental flag falls more and more to the institutional movement organizations where compromises with growthists rather than ideological purity are routinely necessary for organizational survival. Thus, environmental reform at a modest rate would probably continue in the short-run even if the voluntary movement organizations were not in the picture, but over time the institutional movement organizations will increasingly tend to be judged by voluntary environmentalists as co-opted by growthist interests. (Indeed, there is some basis in the existing research literature for the prediction that future studies will sustain such a judgment.[14] *This suggests that a hard core of voluntary environmentalists will be in continuing and even escalating conflict with growthists and with institutional movement organizations, but that the main future victories will not fall in the direction of the voluntary environmentalists.*

The above basically "structural" features of environmental conflicts can also be understood in their psychological dimension. The participants in the environmental movement are substantially integrated to society. Their commitment to environmental reform is genuine, but is not a commitment to radical reform.[15] Many environmentalists do not accept the anti-growth ideology that has recently stirred within the movement. Even those who have accepted it in the abstract are not willing to push its implications on a concrete level. This is basically because it is becoming increasingly apparent to all parties inside and outside the movement that the causes of environmental problems are at the same time the causes of many valued material comforts and conveniences that are integral to affluence.

In practice most environmentalists are no more willing than others to sacrifice or scale down dependence on these amenities. The affluent, however, including environmentalists, must do most of the changing in environmental reform, since affluence is directly related to disproportionate resource use and pollution creation. The poor, on the other hand, are those most ill-affected by the *de facto* operationalization of concrete environmental reforms, particularly those reforms that implement the no-growth philosophy. Thus, the dependence of environmentalists on industrial exploitation of the environment is less direct than that of others, but it is nevertheless clear and present. There is much truth in Pogo's observation that "we have met the enemy and he is us."

It is at least plausible that most environmentalists have difficulty with the dissonance created by knowing, on the one hand, that they are willing and continuing participants in life-styles that are disproportionately offensive to the environment and, on the other, are urging changes that logically should affect them more than others but that may in fact serve to keep those that are least offensive from achieving their legitimate economic aspirations. And in broad, international context, the citizens of the developed countries are, in the aggregate, identified with environmentalism.

Thus, both in terms of the way conflicts are structured between environmentalists and growthists, and the way they are resolved in the minds of environmentalists, the stage is set for the general deceleration of environmental reform in the short-run. As indicated above, this does not necessarily mean that the intensity of environmental conflicts will decrease. Indeed, the slowing of environmental reform will doubtless indicate to the hard core of environmentalists that environmental problems are likely to become more pressing over time. However, it does imply, if the analysis of this paper is correct, that a second set of conflicts engendered by environmental reforms, namely conflicts along traditional class lines, will be avoided in the short-run.

There is at least some basis for thinking that in the industrialization/modernization process, class conflict is in substantial measure prevented by environmental exploitation. But, if environmental exploitation leads inevitably to the necessity for restraints on such exploitation (as is implicit in environmentalists' claims), then it follows that environmental exploitation will be an important causal factor in an increase in class conflicts in the long-run.

It also follows that a society that is able to de-emphasize social stratification based on material wealth differentiations (there are of course many other bases for social stratification) *should have a much higher probability of developing sound environmental policies.* Paradoxically, then, this non-Marxian analysis of the basis of class conflict may imply a solution that is at least partly compatible with Marxian programmatic social outcome. Ecology is indeed a "subversive science" as one book title suggests -- much more so than most environmentalists or others imagine. (Shepard and McKinley, 1969)

This, of course, is a much too cursory and casual treatment of class conflict theory to constitute a refutation or reformulation. But it is clear that most stratification theory and research in sociology (including the large proportion of it that deals with class conflict) does not adequately consider the context of resource constraints or lack thereof in which the stratification system operates. Neither does such theory and research adequately consider the social composition or ideology of movements that push for and against such constraints. Just as emerging industrial society saw the growth of movements and ideologies addressed to the problems of the day, post-industrial society has created its own movements and ideologies. Both in intra- and international context environmental considerations and the movements related to such considerations promise to loom large in determining the future relations of social strata.

FOOTNOTES

[1] The change from consensus to conflict and other transformations the movement has undergone are further described and analyzed in Morrison, Hornback and Warner
(1972) and Morrison (1972).

[2] These controls have had the anticipated effect of reducing certain toxins in the air and the *unanticipated* effect of increasing others. The controls, moreover, have
been imposed on individual units (autos and other air
polluters) without any structural controls on the total
number of such units that can operate.

[3] Meadows *et al.* (1972). The same theme has been central
in other contexts, particularly in Ehrlich and Ehrlich
(1970) and Mishan (1970).

[4] The term "growthist" has not, to my knowledge, been used
to name environmental opponents, but is implicit in and
thus largely borrowed from Mishan's notion of "growtho-
mania" (1970:3-9).

[5] See, for instance, Zald and Ash (1966).

[6] For a detailed comparison of the civil rights and environmental movements see Gale (1972).

[7] For direct and indirect documentation of this point see:
Buttel (1972), Devall (1970), Harry *et al.* (1966), and
Zinger *et al.* (1973, p. 20). A recent news release
(Barnett, 1972) reported that 56 percent of the Sierra
Club members have graduated from college, 30 percent are
students, 14 percent are teachers and 18 percent have
Ph.D.'s.

[8] I cannot resist making explicit what is implicit in this
analysis, namely that the *simultaneous presence of several social movements on the current scene forces the
analyst's attention to the impossibility of adequately
understanding any of these movements in isolation from
the others*. The interrelationship of social movements
(as distinct from the relations of movements and counter-
movements) is a greatly neglected aspect of social movement theory and research. See Gans (1972) for a useful
analysis of these interrelationships.

[9] See Marshall (1938) for a useful discussion of these important differences in the nature of class antagonism.

[10]This point plus others in this section are concretely documented in Subcommittee on Air and Water Pollution (1971).

[11]Dahrendorf's specific definition is that "classes are social conflict groups the determinant of which can be found in the participation in or exclusion from the exercise of authority within any imperatively coordinated association" (1959:138). It is worth noting that part of what environmentalist-growthist conflicts are over is the extent to which it is imperative to have state coordination of private behavior with regard to environmental matters, and, in addition, whether the frame of reference for the "state" should be local, state, regional, national or international. The environmentalists are saying, in general, that a substantial degree of state control is necessary and that the scope of this control must eventually be international if environmental problems are to be solved.

[12]"Simply stated, an ecological theory of value would fix the worth of goods or services in terms of the units of the environment required to create them. The law would be this: the value of any activity would be high if very little of the environment were used or if the resources required for it were easily replenished" (Pearl and Pearl, 1971:37).

[13]For instance, the Western Environmental Trade Association is an industry-business-labor coalition formed in Oregon in 1971 to fight "environmental hysteria" that the leaders thought was harming the state's economy. Its vice president, Ed Whelan, also president of the Oregon AFL-CIO, charged that hundreds of millions of dollars of commerce had been delayed in Oregon because of "environmental McCarthyism employed by various self-proclaimed groups" (New York Times, 1971). See also Albrecht (1972) on environmental "counter-movements."

[14]See, for instance, Selznick's (1949) classic analysis of the Tennessee Valley Authority.

[15]Both Dunlap and Gale (1972) and Devall (1971) found that student eco-activists tend to be liberal but not far left in orientation.

Albrecht, Stan L.
1972   "Environmental Social Movements
            and Counter - Movements,"
            Journal of Voluntary Action
            Research 1 (October):2-11.

Barnett, Richard M.
1972   "Sierra Club goes defensive as
            drop-out rate soars." Lansing
            State Journal (July 18):A-8.

Buttel, Frederick H.
1972   The Relationship of Socioeconomic
            Characteristics of Wisconsin
            Residents to Pollution Concern
            (unpublished Master's thesis,
            rural sociology). Madison:
            University of Wisconsin.

Dahrendorf, Ralf
1959   Class and Class Conflict in
            Industrial Society. Stanford:
            Stanford University Press.

Dean, Heather
1971   "Scarce resources: The dynamics
            of American imperialism." Pp. 139-
            154 in K. T. Fann and Donald C.
            Hodges (eds.), Readings in U.S.
            Imperialism. Boston: Porter
            Sargent.

Devall, William B.
1971   "A report on college students
            active in the environmental
            movement" (unpublished paper).
            Arcata, California: Department
            of Sociology, Humboldt State
            College.

Devall, William B.
1970   "Conservation: An upper-middle
            class social movement: A
            replication." Journal of Leisure
            Research 2 (Spring): 123-126.

Dunlap, Riley E. and Richard Gale
    1972   "Politics and ecology: A
            political profile of student eco-
            activists." Youth and Society
            3 (June).

Ehrlich, Paul and Anne H. Ehrlich
    1970   Population, Resources, Environment:
            Issues in Human Ecology. San
            Francisco: W. H. Freeman and Co.

Fuchs, Sandor
    1970   "Ecology movement exposed."
            Progressive Labor 7,6 (Sept.):
            50-63.

Gale, Richard
    1972   "From sit-in to hike-in: A
            comparison of the civil rights
            and environmental movements."
            Pp. 280-305 in William R. Burch
            et al. (eds.), Social Behavior,
            Natural Resources and the
            Environment. New York: Harper
            and Row.

Gans, Herbert
    1972   "The American malaise." The
            New York Times Magazine (Feb.6):
            16 ff.

Hardin, Garrett
    1968   "The tragedy of the commons,"
            Science (Dec.) 162:1243-8.

Harry, Joseph, Richard P. Gale and John Hendee
    1969   "Conservation: An upper-middle
            class social movement." Journal
            of Leisure Research 1 (Summer):
            246-254.

Marshall, T. H.
    1938   "The nature of class conflict."
            Pp. 97-111 in T. H. Marshall (ed.)
            Class Conflict and Social Strat-
            ification. Ledbury: LePlay
            House, Institute of Sociology.
            Reprinted in S. M. Lipset and

R. Bendix (eds.), Class, Status
and Power. Glencoe: The Free
Press, 1953:81-87.

Meadows, Donella H. *et al*
    1972   The Limits to Growth. New York:
                Universe Books.

Mishan, E. J.
    1970   Technology and Growth: The Price
                We Pay. New York: Praeger.

Morrison, Denton E.
    1972   "The environmental movement moves
                on -- and changes." Paper
                presented at the Purdue University
                Water Resources Seminar.

    1971   "Some notes toward theory on
                relative deprivation, social
                movements and social change."
                American Behavioral Scientist
                14, 5 (May/June):675-690.

Morrison, Denton E., Kenneth E. Hornback and
W. Keith Warner
    1972   **"The environmental movement: Some
                preliminary observations and
                predictions." Pp. 259-279.
                William R. Burch** *et al.* **(eds.),
                Social Behavior, Natural Resources
                and the Environment. New York:
                Harper and Row.**

National Caucus of Labor Committees
    1972   "Blueprint for extinction: A
                critique of the zero growth
                movement." New York: National
                Caucus of Labor Committees.

Neuhaus, Richard
    1971   In Defense of People. New York:
                Macmillan.

New York Times
    1971   "Oregon Coalition Wary on Ecology."
                New York Times. (Dec. 26):34.

302

Pearl, Arthur and Stephanie Pearl
    1971   "Toward an ecological theory of
             value." Social Policy (May/June):
             30-38.

Selznick, Philip
    1949   TVA and the Grass Roots. Berkeley
             and Los Angeles: University of
             California Press.

Shepard, Paul and Daniel McKinley (eds.)
    1969   The Subversive Science: Essays
             Toward an Ecology of Man.
             New York: Houghton-Mifflin.

Subcommittee on Air and Water Pollution
    1971   Economic Dislocation Resulting from
             Environmental Controls: Hearings
             Before the Subcommittee on Air and
             Water Pollution of the Committee on
             Public Works, United States Senate.
             Washington, D. C.: Government
             Printing Office.

Zald, Mayer and Robert Ash
    1966   "Social movement organization:
             Growth, decay and change." Social
             Forces 44 (March):327-341.

Zinger, Clem, Richard Dalsemer and Helen
Magargle
    1973   Environmental Volunteers in
             America (Washington, D. C.:
             National Center for Voluntary
             Action).

THE ENVIRONMENTAL MOVEMENT

From Recreation to Politics

RONALD G. FAICH
RICHARD P. GALE

Seen from the perspective of leisure-time activity, the rapidly emerging environmental movement has several important implications for future research in the sociology of leisure. First, a number of people are expending substantial amounts of their nonwork time on behalf of the environment. Second, because much involvement is channeled through voluntary organizations, participation in the environmental movement must be considered within the context of the structure of voluntary organizations and their contribution to ongoing social movements. Third, the protection of areas for outdoor recreation is a major focus of the environmental movement.[1] The increasing public concern with environmental issues and the role that leisure-time organizations play in the movement suggest that social scientists interested in the sociology of leisure should direct some attention to the changing role of such organizations. Of particular interest in this regard would be the changing organizational goals of outdoor recreation groups and the political implications of these changes. The intent of this paper is to assess the limited previous research and theoretical development in this area, to report the preliminary results of a membership survey of a large outdoor recreation organization which is rapidly changing, and to suggest future needs in research and theory.

"The Environmental Movement: From Recreation to Politics," by Ronald G. Faich and Richard P. Gale is reprinted from PACIFIC SOCIOLOGICAL REVIEW, Vol. 14, No. 3 (July 1971) pp. 270-287 by permission of the Publisher, Sage Publications, Inc.

OUTDOOR RECREATION AND THE ENVIRONMENTAL MOVEMENT

Past research on outdoor-oriented leisure has focused mainly on the characteristics of recreationists (Burch, 1969), the specific activities engaged in (King, 1966), the frequency of outdoor recreation, and some of the motivations and meanings attached to it (Burch, 1965).

When previous investigators have examined the organizational memberships of outdoor recreationists, it has usually been limited to determining the proportion of recreationists who belong to some type of outdoor recreation group. Several studies report that about a third of the recreationists studied claim membership in some outdoor recreation or conservation group (Hendee et al., 1968; ORRRC, 1962; LaPage, 1967). Of secondary interest has been the diversity of organizations cited whenever recreationists are asked to list their recreation and conservation organization memberships. The 408 wilderness users in the Hendee et al. (1968) study belonged to 218 different groups, and many individuals cross-listed the same organization as both an outdoor recreation and a conservation organization. Although the Hendee group did not distinguish between outdoor recreation and conservation groups in their analysis, they did suggest a "stepping-stone" process whereby individuals initially joined local activity-oriented outdoor recreation groups, and later expanded their involvement in the conservation—now environmental—movement by joining large national organizations (Hendee et al., 1968: 21).

Most relevant to this paper is the body of research which places the study of outdoor recreation organizations in the context of the analysis of voluntary organizations. Variations of the instrumental-expressive distinction have been used to assess both the goals and the activities of the organization and the expectations and participation of the members of such organizations.[2] For example, Jacoby and Babchuk (1963: 468) describe a hiking club in which member participation was almost exclusively expressive, and members "apologized for the uselessness of their hiking club activities." Yet when the charter of the club and minutes of its meetings were examined, there was some evidence of instrumental action by the organization, although it was still considered primarily an expressive group by the investigators. In a later article, perhaps thinking of the same organization, Babchuk states, "But a hiking club by virtue of sending a resolution to a congressional representative on a conservation bill hardly qualifies by that token as an instrumental association" (Babchuk and Edwards, 1965: 155). It would be our contention that the environmental movement has probably changed the orientation of that hiking club, and that if Jacoby and Babchuk were to study the same club in 1971, they would find increased instrumental involvement, including, besides sending a resolution to a congressional representative, possible affiliation with a statewide environmental council, the solicitation of statements from congressional candidates on environmental issues, surveillance of a governmental agency with environmental responsibilities, and even possibly the filing of an injunction to protect a favorite hiking area.

In an attempt to categorize those outdoor recreation organizations which reflect varying degrees of instrumental involvement with environmental issues, Hendee et al. (1969) have applied the instrumental-expressive distinction to both organizations and their individual members.[3] The term "expressive conservationist" is used to describe members and groups whose instrumental concerns are confined to actions directly related to the primary recreation goals of the organization. Thus, for example, a group of kyackers may become involved in a controversy over a dam proposed along one of their favorite rivers, but resist involvement in an effort to block construction of a highway. "Instrumental conservationists," on the other hand, may also participate in outdoor recreation but they concentrate primarily on the "protection of areas and environments that members themselves may not have visited" (Hendee et al., 1969: 213). Instrumental conservation organizations are generally involved in a wide variety of environmental issues, and often considerable authority is delegated to executive committees to formulate positions on these issues and to represent the organization publicly.

The instrumental-expressive distinction as applied to these groups includes four related variables. Most obvious is the way in which the membership views the organization, reflected in the reasons why persons initially join the organization and the factors which sustain their active support. Expressive organizations would attract members primarily seeking outdoor recreation activities and companionship, while more instrumental organizations would draw members sympathetic with the organization's external action program. The second variable is the amount of member participation in organizational activities, and in the formal governance of the organization. In expressive conservation organizations, one would expect to find a high level of participation, and a broadly diffused administrative structure, while more instrumental groups would reflect a low level of direct participation and a highly concentrated leadership network. The emphasis on outdoor recreation in organizational programs is the third variable. More expressive organizations would maintain an extensive outing program, and the membership would be recruited from individuals who are active outdoor recreationists. In instrumentally oriented groups, on the other hand, such outing programs would concentrate on visits to disputed areas, and members may not be outdoor recreation enthusiasts, in spite of their strong support of recreation-related environmental issues. Finally, the fourth variable concerns the total involvement of the members in various instrumental and expressive organizations related to outdoor recreation and the environment. We would not expect members of one expressive organization to belong to many other similar groups because of the high level of participation within these recreation-oriented clubs. On the other hand, members of a more instrumental organization, lending their support to the group's position on issues, and not necessarily participating directly in the operation of the group, may well extend their commitment to a variety of instrumental organizations concerned with environmental protection.

The distinction between instrumental and expressive conservation, and the four variables which further elaborate this distinction, form the basis for the analysis which follows. We suggest that some of the leisure-based outdoor recreation organizations which were initially dedicated to expressive, membership-oriented goals, will increasingly become instrumentally involved in the environmental movement. Where organizations undergo this transformation, we would expect to find similar changes in the expectations of the membership, the level of participation in the organization, and in the involvement of the members in outdoor recreation as a leisure-time activity. Ideally, a test of this general hypothesis would rely on a diachronic analysis of an expressive outdoor recreation organization. Unfortunately, this type of systematic data is not available, in part because of the very rapid growth of the environmental movement in the past two years. Instead, we draw on data from a sample survey of the membership of a large national organization which has, in the past several years, become involved in a variety of environmental issues, even though the organization was for many years very similar to the "expressive conservation" model, and still maintains an extensive outing program. To obtain some indication of change in membership, we will compare members in terms of the amount of time they have been members of the organization. Although this approach to an analysis of change involves some readily challengeable·assumptions, we believe the data are suitable for a preliminary examination of the distinctions discussed previously.

THE PUGET SOUND GROUP OF THE SIERRA CLUB

The data to be reported in this paper were drawn from an internal survey conducted by a regional section of a large national outdoor recreation and environmental organization. The Sierra Club began before the turn of the century, as an expressive conservationist organization with a membership concentrated in California, particularly within the San Franciso Bay Area (Jones, 1965). The club had a long history of involvement in issues which were of direct concern to the wilderness recreation enthusiasts who constituted most of the membership. The extensive outing program reinforced member commitment to basic preservationist goals. About 1955, the club began to acquire a national membership, and to extend its instrumental activity into issues not necessarily related to wilderness recreation. In 1971, the club had over 100,000 members throughout the United States and had been "declared" an (excessively) instrumental conservationist organization by the Internal Revenue Service, which revoked the tax-deductible status of the club.

There are two component units in the club—the chapter and the group. Initially, Sierra Club members in California communities joined together to form local chapters of the club. When the club began to acquire a membership outside the state of California; new chapters were formed, usually on a regional basis. As chapters grew, members who were concentrated in large population centers within a region sought to form locally based units. Then the group became the local unit and regional chapters are now frequently composed of a number of widely dispersed local groups.

As of 1971, the Pacific Northwest Chapter of the Sierra Club had nearly 2,500 members in the state of Oregon and the western part of Washington. Of the six local groups within the chapter, the largest is the Puget Sound Group, with nearly 700 members living in the Seattle-Tacoma metropolitan area. Though only one of numerous environmental organizations in the area, the Puget Sound Group is one of the best known groups of this type because of its extensive outing program and frequent pronouncements on environmental issues. Though no group or chapter can be said to be "typical" of the Sierra Club, it is possible, however, that members of the Puget Sound Group may be somewhat more instrumentally oriented than their fellow members in other areas. In the Los Angeles area, for example, the club is a major outing organization but less well known for its political activities. The involvement of the Puget Sound Group is further reinforced by the fact that the club's Northwest Conservation Representative is headquartered in Seattle. Rather than viewing our respondents as representative either of members of the entire Sierra Club or of other outdoor recreation organizations, in general, they should be seen as reflecting a perspective which, we would argue, will increasingly pervade those individuals who seek to implement their hopes for a better environment through membership in an instrumental voluntary organization.

Although the response rate to the mail questionnaire was far from optimal (45%), and the survey was designed to obtain data on membership interests in environmental issues and club activities, the data are of sufficient quality to permit an exploration of questions emerging from previous research. After briefly examining the demographic characteristics of the membership, we will discuss data which bear on each of the four variables outlined above.

THE RESPONDENTS

As found in previous studies of the Sierra Club (Hendee et al., 1968) and other outing-conservation groups (Devall, 1970a, 1970b), the members of the Puget Sound Group are noteworthy for their high levels of educational attainment and occupational status. Professional positions are held by fully 73.8% of our respondents, an additional 9.8% are administrators and 9.2% students; only 2.8% are clerical workers and another 2.8% are unemployed. A mere 3% of the members have never attended college, while 25% have doctorates, 45.5% have master's degrees, and 17.4% the baccalaureate. Though data on income levels were not obtained, the education and occupation distributions reveal rather clearly that members of the Puget Sound Group come predominantly from the upper-middle and upper socioeconomic strata.

Two-thirds of the respondents are male, and a similar proportion of the sample is married. Nearly half, 48.3%, are childless, and 46% have three or fewer children, mostly under age 18. One-half of our respondents are 30-44, with the modal group, 25% being 30-34. The members are rather evenly split between those who do and those who do not claim any church affiliation, with 38% citing membership in a Protestant denomination. And, finally, 42% of the respondents are independents, politically, one-third are Democrats and 24% identify themselves as Republicans. In summary, the profile of a typical Puget Sound Group member which emerges is that of a highly educated, married male in his early thirties, having no children or a small young family, in a high-status occupational position, and who is likely to be independent on both politcal and religious matters.

REASONS FOR AFFILIATION

Leisure-oriented expressive voluntary organizations attract individuals who seek to both enjoy leisure activities in a group setting and to become more proficient at them. Some outdoor recreation organizations require a demonstrated commitment to the activity which forms the central interest of the group. Thus, the Mazamas, a major outdoor recreation club in Oregon studied by Harry (1967), defines membership eligibility as follows: "any person who has climbed to the summit of a snowpeak on which there is at least one living glacier, the top of which can not be reached by any other means than on foot." According to Harry, membership in the club provides an opportunity for the appreciation of nature, a chance to gain honors and awards for participating in club activities (summit certificates were awarded for climbing mountains), and occasions to get together with other people. In a more instrumentally oriented organization, we would expect such interests to be secondary, and that both the initial attraction to the organization, and the factors which sustain interest in the organization would relate more to the organization's externally directed actions. Our questionnaire included two open-ended questions allowing us to examine this distinction: one dealing with the reasons for initial attraction to the club, and the other inquiring about the reasons for retaining membership in it.

Our data show a definite shift in the reasons for affiliating with the Sierra Club. Puget Sound Group members who joined seven to nine years ago were nearly equally divided between those who affiliated because of opportunities for outdoor experiences and fellowship (43%), and those who saw their membership as a vehicle for increasing their knowledge on conservation issues and for having the club represent them on these issues (45%). In more recent years, however, opportunities for recreation and fellowship have steadily declined as the main reasons for joining the organization: 20.3% of the members of four to six years' standing cited these reasons, as did 9.3% of those joining two to three years ago, and similarly for only 4.5% of the newest members surveyed, those affiliating within a year of the time of the survey. Likewise, consistently larger proportions of the members have joined in recent years because they see the club as a source of information and a vehicle to represent their views on conservation issues: 64.4% of those who joined four to six years ago cited these reasons, as did 70.6% affiliating two to three years ago, and similarly for 72.7% of those joining most recently. Thus, in terms of the reasons for initial membership, the Puget Sound Group is increasingly viewed by its members as an instrumental organization. Rather than expecting their membership to yield the camaraderie and skills growing out of group outdoor experiences, the expressive services so frequently supplied by the Sierra Club in years past, new members tend to be attracted to the club as a source of more comprehensive information on conservation issues and as their voice in instrumental action on these issues.

The shift of Puget Sound Group members to a more instrumental orientation is increasingly apparent when we examine the reasons which members cite for remaining in the club. Depending on how long they have been in the club, between 76.7% and 81.7% reported that they continue their affiliation because of the club's involvement in environmental issues. Not more than 5.2% in any category of member seniority indicated that they renew their membership because of the club's extensive outdoor recreation program, its major expressive function. This finding is particularly striking in view of the fact that 43.3% of those who have been members at least seven years cited expressive factors as their reason for affiliation. The unknown factor, of course, and one which is of substantial import in changing organizations, is whether the increasingly instrumental orientation led other expressively oriented members to withdraw from the club. The orientation of newer members suggests even greater support for instrumental action, and perhaps an increasing strain on those older members who initially joined for more expressive reasons. At the present time, the instrumental orientation held by long-term members, coupled with this same perspective predominating among those joining more recently, suggests that the Puget Sound Group has indeed become a more instrumentally involved environmental organization.

PARTICIPATION IN ORGANIZATIONAL ACTIVITIES AND OUTDOOR RECREATION

Among the many aspects of membership participation, two are of special importance to an analysis of the environmental involvement of outdoor recreation organizations. First is the actual participation of members in the formal structure and activities of the organization. As indicated previously, expressive organizations are characterized by a high level of participation and involvement in organizational decision-making, while instrumental organizations usually exhibit a low degree of direct membership participation. The second aspect relates to actual participation in organized outdoor recreation activities. To the extent that current members of the Puget Sound Group of the Sierra Club still consider themselves "companions on the trail," we would expect a high level of individual participation in a variety of forms of outdoor recreation. However, to the extent that outdoor recreation becomes less linked to the club's instrumental activities, members would not be expected to reflect such a level of participation.

Although the Puget Sound Group has an elaborate committee structure and an executive committee, only 12.6% of the members reported that they have ever served as an officer or committee member, and more than half of those who have served are no longer incumbents. More striking is the members' lack of participation in other club activities, ranging from committee meetings to the annual banquet. Nearly three out of five members (57.2%) indicated that they do not attend club functions, while 31.4% reported that they do so at least once a year, but not monthly. Intensive involvement, at least once a month, was reported by 11.4% of the members. Thus, only a small fraction of the membership appears to be regularly involved in either the administrative structure or the activity program of the group, clearly characteristic of instrumentally rather than of expressively oriented organizations.

When the members' reports of their outdoor recreation activity over the past year are examined, it appears that they do *not* regularly participate in a wide variety of outdoor activities. Though it is not surprising, given the Sierra Club's emphasis on nonconsumptive uses of wilderness, that 92.6% of the members did not hunt during the previous twelve months, they also reported quite infrequent participation in the forms of outdoor recreation one might expect of wilderness-oriented conservationists—e.g., snowshoeing, fishing, wild-river boating, cross-country skiing. Less than a third reported any mountain-climbing trips, and backpacking was mentioned by slightly over half (51.3%) of the respondents. The activity which the greatest portion of the members pursued was hiking, with 76.5% indicating that they had gone on at least one trip during the past year; only half the hikers, however, had done so four or more times during the previous year. Thus, with the exception of hiking, and possibly of backpacking, the members of the Puget Sound Group do not regularly participate in outdoor recreation activities. One would expect both more frequent participation and a wider range of activities on the part of conservation activists whose primary motivation is to derive the expressive rewards found in group-based recreation. In terms of outdoor recreation activity, then, members of the Puget Sound Group exhibit a relatively low level of interest in the expressive enjoyment of the environment.

MEMBERSHIP IN OTHER OUTDOOR RECREATION AND ENVIRONMENTAL ORGANIZATIONS

Additional evidence which suggests that Puget Sound Group members are primarily instrumentally oriented is seen in the types of other groups to which they belong (two-thirds of the respondents reported at least one other group membership). Relatively few (17.1%) are also members of one or more outing clubs, while 24.1% are affiliated with at least one other mixed outing-environmental issue organization. Nearly half, however, belong to one or more exclusively issue-oriented organizations. Thus, of those with other environmental group affiliations, most belong to primarily instrumental environmental organizations, rather than to more expressively oriented outing or mixed outing-environmental issue groups. Moreover, those who are active in the Puget Sound Group tend also to be those who are affiliated with other environmental-issue groups. For example, a third of those who report weekly or monthly activity in the Sierra Club are also members of at least one other local outing-environmental issue group, as compared with 24.5% of those participating in the Sierra Club on an annual basis, and 19.7% of those who report that they never attend Sierra Club activities. Similarly, one-third of the weekly or monthly participants report membership in three or more exclusively instrumental environmental organizations, as compared to less than 10% of all other respondents. Thus, not only are other instrumental organizations generally favored by Puget Sound Group members who have other affiliations, but this relationship is accentuated for those who are regular participants in the Sierra Club group.

SUMMARY AND SUGGESTIONS FOR FUTURE RESEARCH

A preliminary analysis of our data indicates that members of the Puget Sound Group of the Sierra Club are more instrumentally concerned with the quality of the environment than expressively motivated to enjoy the environment through outdoor recreation. Drawn mainly from upper-middle and upper socioeconomic strata, almost all new members are initially attracted to the club out of their instrumental concern for the environment, and long-term members, up to one-half of whom may have originally joined the club for its outdoor program, have now largely shifted their primary concern to the quality and protection of the environment. Relatively few members participate in the governance of the organization or in its other activities, and, with the exception of hiking, and possibly backpacking, most members are not avid outdoor recreation enthusiasts. Finally, for those who also belong to other environmental organizations, most are affiliated with primarily issue-oriented groups, rather than with recreation clubs, with the more active participants in the Sierra Club group more likely to have these additional instrumental affiliations. We surmise, on the basis of these admittedly weak data, that the priorities of the Puget Sound Group members have shifted in recent years from outdoor recreation, mixed with an occasional concern for protecting certain wilderness areas, to an almost exclusive emphasis today on general environmental quality issues, ranging from wilderness protection and outdoor recreation, to urban pollution and population control. The members, in short, are no longer the outdoor recreationists of yesteryear, but rather today's environmental politicos, in the vanguard of society's newest social movement.

But the significance of our findings and conclusions lies neither in their substantive accuracy nor in their methodological adequacy, as much as in the directions they suggest for future research. Rather than examining only outdoor recreationists as persons highly concerned with the environment, as in previous studies, our data indicate that future research must range more widely to include persons who register their commitment to the environment via formal affiliation with appropriate voluntary organizations, rather than necessarily through their own recreation activities. Though the actual expenditure of leisure time in organizational programs, whether instrumental or expressive, may be generally low, as our data suggest, the environmentalists' allocations of time and energy are undoubtedly sporadic, peaking instrumentally, for example, when important issues are being considered in various public forums. Perhaps, like members of volunteer fire departments, the environmentalists stand ready to combat, when necessary, the major threats to environmental quality, but under ordinary circumstances they allow their organizational leaders—the regulars—to man the watchtowers.

But who are the environmentalists, those who care enough to join an environmental organization, if not to regularly participate in its activities? As already mentioned, our respondents may not be typical of Sierra Club members in other parts of the country, as indeed they may not be representative of the entire Puget Sound Group membership, and we strongly doubt that they are typical of environmentalists in general. Our data are consistent with past research in revealing that the environmental movement draws its strength mainly from high socioeconomic strata, but the base of support may now be broadening with the recent rapid growth of the movement. Also, the rather concentrated socioeconomic stations of the environmentalists may only be apparent, stemming from the fact that previous investigations of environmental organizations have focused primarily on major national groups or their more local subunits, and an examination of groups which are not national in scope may indeed reveal a broader socioeconomic base. Whatever the organizations examined, however, and regardless of their members' socioeconomic positions, a more systematic analysis of the questions we have addressed in this paper seems warranted. In addition, future research should extend far beyond an examination of the reasons for the members' original and continuing affiliation, their outdoor recreation preferences and frequency of activity, and the extent of their participation in other organizational functions. Of particular importance, it seems, would be a study of those who belong to a variety of environmental groups. Our data indicate, for example, that approximately two-thirds of the Puget Sound Group members also belong to at least one other environmental organization, and obviously much can be learned about the environmental movement in general from an examination of those with multiple memberships in a variety of related groups. Is there, as our data might suggest, a leadership elite, a relatively small core of highly committed people who devote perhaps almost all of their leisure time to the activities of several organizations? More generally, what is the sequence and etiology of affiliating with numerous environmental groups? Is it a "stepping-stone" process, as speculated by Hendee et al. (1968: 21), where individuals initially join local recreation-related groups and eventually extend their involvement by affiliating with national environmental issue organizations? And finally, to what extent do environmental activists also belong to other nonenvironmental voluntary organizations, such as civil rights groups and fraternal orders? Are they "specialists," confining their concern to largely environmental issues and outdoor recreation, or "generalists," who express a wide range of interests—avoca-tional, political, and vocational—through membership in a variety of voluntary organizations with diverse priorities and goals (Harry et al., 1969)? In short, we are suggesting that future research on individual environmentalists turn away from recreationists in the field, and focus instead on environmen-talists in the specific context of their voluntary organizational memberships and in the larger context of their general ideologies and perspectives on life.

But it would be remiss to encourage future research directed only at the members of a variety of environmental groups without emphasizing as well the importance of examining the differences among the organizations themselves. Indeed, the evolution of social movements may be viewed largely in terms of the complex web of voluntary organizations which advocate and oppose the goals of the movement. In the environmental movement, one notes considerable diversity, even among organizations which agree on the desired course of action on a specific environmental issue. Thus far, research has focused on those large national organizations which are in the forefront of the movement. But research must also include local groups, and issue-specific "Save the . . . " organizations. Further, relatively few outdoor recreation organizations approach the instrumen-tality of the Sierra Club. An important area of future research is the "triggering event," which impels the expressive organiza-tion into political action, and the impact of success or failure on the future instrumental involvement by the organization. Inability to satisfactorily resolve environmental issues which relate to recreational interests may "radicalize" the organiza-tion, along the lines of the residents of Santa Barbara who were continually frustrated in their attempts to "Get Oil Out" (Molotch, 1970).

Analysis of new organizations is especially critical for the understanding of the future of a social movement. Several new organizational forms have already appeared in the environ-mental movement, such as the statewide or regional environ-mental council and the national issue-specific coalition (Coal-ition Against the SST). New forms of outdoor recreation may also be expected to result in voluntary organizations, especially where the activity stimulates the development of a new industry to supply recreational equipment, as in the case of snow-mobiling, or requires a special natural setting, as in skin-diving. Some of the organizations, like the National Rifle Association and various ski associations, may include both citizens interested in the enjoyment of outdoor recreation, and those whose livelihood depends on the manufacture of equipment or operation of facilities for recreationists. Finally, there is another type of organization which should be of special interest to those who wish to understand the dynamics of the movement on the level of strategy or tactics. What might be called the "pseudo-citizen" organization may be formed to directly combat environmentalist groups. Externally, pseudo-citizen organizations appear to be spontaneously organized, noneconomic citizens' groups. In fact, however, they may be the result of deliberate action by industries. In Oregon, the timber industry and government officials formed the now-defunct Public Resources Council of Oregon. And in San Francisco, advertising agency employees organized "Artists For The Pyramid" to help their client, the Transamerica Corporation, win approval of a much-criticized office tower (Krizek, 1970).

Another area of needed research relates to the internal dynamics of organizational change. Data which suggest changes among members of groups must be matched by analysis of the behavior of the organization, as reflected in publications and resolutions about environmental issues, committee structure, organizational budgets, and political action. Further, we would expect to find evidence of intraorganizational stress and conflict in many outdoor recreation groups. Stable organizations may have a high degree of congruence between organizational goals, leadership implementation of these goals, and membership support and involvement. But we would expect few of the organizations which are pulled into the environmental movement to reflect such an optimal mix. Rather, analysis of the points of incongruity may yield especially incisive examples of the dynamics of organizational change. Some members may object to "making things all political," while others may forge a strong link between the group's conservation committee and a statewide environmental council. Meetings dedicated to a discussion of the group's strategy for environmental action may disappoint those who came seeking companionship and conversation. And the organization's "politicos" may feel that marching on the Forest Supervisor's office is more important than walking on a back-country trail.

Our future research will focus on these important changes, both on the level of individual members and in terms of organizational behavior. We encourage others to join us in examining what may be the major social movement of the seventies.

NOTES

1. In part, the environmental movement is a direct descendant of the earlier concern with the preservation of the natural environment. The "conservation-preservation" emphasis which led to the formation of the Redwoods and North Cascades National Parks is still seen in attempts to prohibit ocean-dumping of industrial wastes and other practices which have a negative impact on environments which may be far removed from back-country wilderness areas. Roderick Nash (1967) has written one of the best histories of the conservation-preservation movement. For a discussion of the role of one organization in that movement, see Holway Jones' (1965) history of the Sierra Club.

2. Instrumental voluntary associations are those which are designed to maintain or change some normative condition, while expressive associations focus on activities which have no external goal and are primarily for the benefit of members. In instrumental organizations, "members are committed to goals which do not(necessarily contribute to their own personal and immediate gratification" (Jacoby and Babchuk, 1963: 462).

3. In this paper, we treat "environmentalist" and "conservationist" as equivalent in meaning. Thus, the "conservation organizations" described in the previous research are referred to as "environmental organizations," since the older label does not adequately describe the new role of these organizations.

REFERENCES

Babchuk, Nicholas and John N. Edwards
    1965 "Voluntary associations and the integration hypothesis." Soc. Inquiry 35 (Spring): 149-167.
Burch, William R., Jr.
    1965 "The play world of camping: research into the social meaning of outdoor recreation." Amer. J. of Sociology 70 (March): 604-612.
    1969 "The social circles of leisure: competing explanations." J. of Leisure Research 1 (Spring): 125-148.

Devall, W. B.
  1970a "The governing of a voluntary organization: oligarchy and democracy in the Sierra Club." Ph.D. dissertation. University of Oregon.
  1970b "Conservation: an upper-middle class social movement: a replication." J. of Leisure Research 2 (Spring): 123-126.
Harry, Joseph
  1967 "Mazamas: who are we? why do we belong?" Mazama: 71-74.
  ––– Richard P. Gale, and John C. Hendee
  1969 "Conservation: an upper-middle class social movement." J. of Leisure Research 1 (Summer): 246-254.
Hendee, John C., Richard P. Gale, and Joseph Harry
  1969 "Conservation, politics, and democracy." J. of Soil and Water Conservation 24 (November/December): 212-215.
Hendee, John C., William R. Catton, Larry D. Marlow, and C. Frank Brockman
  1968 "Wilderness users in the Pacific Northwest–their characteristics, values, and management preferences." USDA Forest Service Research Paper PNW-61. Portland, Ore.: Forest and Range Experiment Station.
Jacoby, Arthur P. and Nicholas Babchuk
  1963 "Instrumental and expressive voluntary associations." Sociology and the Social Research 47 (July): 461-471.
Jones, Holway R.
  1965 John Muir and the Sierra Club: The Battle for Yosemite. San Francisco: Sierra Club.
King, David
  1966 "Activity patterns of campers." U.S. Forest Service Research Note NC-18. St. Paul, Minn.: North Central Forest Experimental Station.
Krizek, John
  1970 "How to build a pyramid: a kit of PR tools helps win San Francisco's approval for a new high-rise office building." Public Relations J. 26 (December): 17-21.
LaPage, Wilbur F.
  1967 "Camper characteristics differ at public and commercial campgrounds in New England." U.S. Forest Service Research Note NE-59. Upper Darby, Pa.: Northeast Forest Experiment Station.
Molotch, Harvey
  1970 "Oil in Santa Barbara and power in America." Soc. Inquiry 40 (Winter): 131-144.
Nash, Roderick
  1967 Wilderness and the American Mind. New Haven: Yale Univ. Press.
ORRRC–Outdoor Recreation Resources Review Commission
  1962 "Wilderness and recreation–a report on resources, values, and problems." ORRRC Study Report 3. Washington, D.C.: Government Printing Office.

APPENDIX

ENVIRONMENTAL PSYCHOLOGY

Scientific study of the interplay between human behavior and its environmental settings has gathered considerable momentum during the last decade, certainly enough to warrant its present initial treatment in this review series. The current intellectual vitality of this research area derives in part from its lively and thoroughgoing multidisciplinary character. In addition to psychologists, researchers in geography, environmental design and planning (architecture, urban design, landscape architecture, regional planning), natural resources management, political science, sociology, anthropology, and engineering have contributed scientific findings and have developed its scholarly apparatus of research conferences, associations, newsletters, journals, reviews and collected readings. The proceedings of two conferences held at the University of Utah (16, 247) and three conferences sponsored in part by the Environmental Design Research Association (EDRA) (13, 175, 220) form an important series in this country, while two significant conferences were held in Great Britain in 1969 and 1970 (45, 118). As a supplement to existing journals in the various disciplines, two recent publications, *Environment and Behavior* (268) and *Human Ecology* (254), serve an archival function for research reports in this field. The newsletters, *Man-Environment Systems*, issued by the Association for the Study of Man-Environment Relations (ASMER) in this country, and *Architectural Psychology*, issued in Great Britain, also facilitate communication of multidisciplinary endeavors (14, 120).

In an inherently and demonstratively multidisciplinary field, the matter of intellectual boundaries and labels offers recurrent, tantalizing, but only marginally important issues. In the present case, a general term, e.g. the study of man-environment relations, seems likely to be adopted for the field as a whole, while distinctive local terms may be employed within each discipline. For example, behavioral geography and psychogeography have been used by geographers in designating this area to colleagues within their discipline. Within psychology, the term architectural psychology has been employed, especially in Great Britain, by psychologists and research architects studying behavioral phenomena related to the built environment, while ecological psychology is associated with the pioneering theoretical perspective of Roger G. Barker and his associates (19). Environmental psychology seems to be useful as an inclusive, theoretically neutral term.

[1] Preparation of this survey was supported in part by Grant No. GS-30984X from the National Science Foundation.

In 1970, a comprehensive review of environmental psychology and a major collection of readings appeared (68, 202). The present review will provide a context of earlier contributions but will focus upon work appearing in the period from 1969 through early 1972. The selection of topics is illustrative but probably not inclusive.

Environmental assessment.—The novel value of man-environment studies for such professionals as architects, environmental planners, and natural resources managers lies in its systematic analysis of the human behavior that occurs in and responds to the environmental settings they plan, design, and manage. For psychologists, its distinctive attraction is just the opposite, namely, its serious attention to the environmental contexts of human behavior. Indeed, a taxonomic interest in the descriptive properties of places is a prerequisite to substantive research on man-environment relations (10, 88, 191, 225, 226). A recent review (69) identified five levels of environmental assessment. First, the physical-spatial properties of places can be assessed. For example, Shafer & Thompson (230) related 40 descriptive dimensions of Adirondack campsites (e.g. distance to lakeshore, number of white birches) to their frequency of use. Second, the organization of material artifacts in places can be assessed. Using the Living Room Check List, Laumann & House (143) assessed the contents of over 800 living rooms and, by smallest space analysis, identified a social class dimension and a traditional-versus-modern stylistic dimension. Third, the traits of places can be assessed by human observers. Adjective check lists, bipolar rating scales, and Q-sort decks are being developed to permit observers to record their impressions of places in quick, comparable and comprehensive ways (47, 69, 119, 236, 248, 275). Factor analysis of environmental rating scales (115, 129, 180, 224, 269) have yielded several competing arrays of fundamental environmental dimensions. The application of multidimensional scaling techniques is also being explored (34, 195). Fourth, the enduring behavioral attributes of places can be assessed. The analysis of activity patterns can yield a comparison of places on the basis of the relative frequency with which types of activities occur in them (19, 129). Fifth, the institutional attributes of places can be assessed. Following the model of Stern's studies (241) of educational institutions, Moos and his associates (178, 181) have developed the Ward Atmosphere Scales, which assess twelve dimensions, including spontaneity, order, practicality, and affiliation.

Environmental perception.—Just as environmental assessment has its parallel in personality assessment, the study of environmental perception is analogous to research on person perception, particularly in its focus upon the psychological and environmental factors which affect the impressions observers form of places and in its broad use of the term perception (2, 69, 98, 116, 216). The effect of cultural influences upon environmental perception has received considerable attention in recent geographical writings (98, 216). One well-sustained research program has examined the relationship of observer characteristics (e.g. previous experience, personality) and environmental variations (e.g. frequency of floods

326

per site) to perceptions of natural hazards (41, 95, 130). Employing the technique of standard walks in several cities in this country, Lowenthal (155, 156) has related observer characteristics to descriptive impressions of the urban environment. Some research has tested the widespread assumption that environmental designers differ from laymen (and clients) in their perception of the built environment (44, 114, 141) but apparently no study has explored the consequences, if any, that such differences may entail. Environmental settings can be presented to observers either directly (e.g. via a standard tour, a long-term residence) or indirectly by means of simulation techniques (e.g. films, photographs, models, videotapes, computer graphics). The complex task of appraising the degree to which each mode of simulation approximates response to direct presentations is currently under way (51, 80, 123, 142, 224, 274). The effects of relative complexity upon environmental perception and evaluation continues to interest psychologists and designers (128, 172, 203, 204, 271).

Cognitive representation of the large-scale environment.—In his *Image of the City*, Lynch (157) sought techniques for examining the relationship between the physical form of urban areas and inhabitants' images of them. His work also brought to life the general psychological question of how persons conceptualize the large-scale physical environment that cannot be seen all at once, from a single vantage point (35, 240). Although the map-sketch has become a popular technique, it must be supplemented by other indices (e.g. model arrangements, distance estimates, verbal descriptions, way-finding tasks) in converging upon the nature of cognitive representations (62, 99, 138, 147, 148, 240). The theories of cognitive development formulated by Piaget and Werner are useful in understanding the ontogenesis of topographic representations (109, 144, 159). In this regard, the finding that children as young as 5 years can interpret aerial photographs, and thus perform the mapping transformations of scale reduction and projective rotation, is provocative (35). By examining the map-sketches and verbal descriptions rendered by individuals at intervals along a walking tour through an unfamiliar city, Gittens (94) has initiated study of the microgenesis of topographic representations. The role of cognitive styles is suggested by the observed types of map-sketches (e.g. route or sequential maps; survey or spatial maps) (11, 109); however, this lead has not yet been pursued. Social class and sex-role differences, perhaps mediated by variations in the physical and social orbits of activity routines, are being examined as antecedent factors in the attainment of comprehensive cognitive representations of the urban environment (188, 189).

Personality and the environment.—Environmental psychology seems destined to extend the scope of personality research in at least two ways. First, it is contributing new techniques for assessing environmental dispositions, a heretofore neglected array of personality attributes (63, 67). The preliminary form of the Environmental Response Inventory (165) attempts to assess such dispositions as pastoralism, urbanism, sensation-seeking, abstract conservationism, and environmental adaptation. The Environmental Personality Inventory (237) seeks to measure sensitivity to the environment, control over the environment, mobility, and environmental risk-taking. Several scales have been developed to assess stimulus-seeking and similar dispositions (1, 162, 196, 280). Other recently introduced devices include the Wildernism-Urbanism Scale (112), the Privacy Preference Scales (160, 161), the Mechanization Scale (97), and the Attitudes about Wildlife Q-Sort Deck (82). An attempt has been made to modify the Rosenzweig Picture-Frustration Test as a means of assessing reactions to natural and social hazards (18). Analysis of TAT and sentence completion protocols have suggested styles of coping with two kinds of hazards: tornadoes (231) and sudden storms in drought regions (232).

Second, the basic paradigm of personality assessment research is being applied to the task of understanding and forecasting significant environmental behaviors and outcomes such as outdoor recreational activities, spatial behavior, adjustment to natural hazards, and status as various kinds of environmental decision-maker. Schiff (222) is relating locus of control and sensation-seeking to adoption of adjustments to natural hazards. The Environmental Response Inventory has been used in comparing national forest managers and users and in identifying subtypes of users (199). The Wildernism-Urbanism Scale has been related to preferences for management policies in national forests (112). Personality correlates of personal space measures have been sought (79, 209).

Environmental decision-making.—Human behavior plays an important role as an antecedent factor in transformations of the physical environment. The behavior of every individual has some impact upon the environment, but in comtemporary society, environmental decision-making is also structured along professional and institutional lines. An important impetus of current research is the oft-voiced assertion that the social and behavioral patterns which currently constitute planning, designing, and managing the environment must be examined, appraised, and probably altered (70, 121, 234). One direction of research is testing the subsidiary hypothesis that professional environmentalists differ from laymen in their attitudes, beliefs, and perceptions of the environment (9, 44, 113, 114), while other research is delineating the distinctive personality and social characteristics of various kinds of environmental decision-makers (24, 43, 64, 107, 243). Considering the intricate network of participants and modes of participation in environmental-decision-making throughout modern technological societies, the empirical analysis of differences between decision-makers and their clients and among types of decision-makers represents a formidable task. Thus far the effort has been rather scattered and fragmentary. Furthermore, the possible functional consequences of such differences for the decision-making process and for human behavior in the environment have not been examined. One mechanism for organizing research is to survey all types of decision-makers within a given environmental setting. Costantini & Hanf (60) have undertaken a study of this scope within the Lake Tahoe Basin in California. Another approach focuses upon behavioral factors in the design and planning process, including the implicit and explicit assumptions made about man-environment relations and the influence of personality and cognitive factors in the generation of design solutions (59, 90, 152, 174, 176, 228). Finally, the ways in which laymen become involved in decision-making and the means and consequences of expanding their level of participation are receiving attention (17, 36, 51).

Public attitudes toward the environment.—Environmental attitudes in this country and perhaps in others seem to have entered into a dynamic phase, highlighted by Earth Day in 1970 (91, 229). In recent years, a split within the conservation movement between the utilitarian-'wise use' orientation and the appreciative-preservationist orientation was followed by the broader environmental movement, with its expanded concern encompassing air and water pollution and overpopulation (108, 183). Use of wilderness areas and membership in conservation organizations appear related to upper middle class status, although it is not evident that the latter finding holds for local conservation groups as well as national organizations (108, 112). General environmental concern is positively related to educational level, and rather than bridging political cleavages, may be related to liberal views (60, 76, 247, 251). The rapidly proliferating programs in environmental education offer promising contexts for studying the nature and antecedents of environmental beliefs and attitudes (117, 246). Several studies of public attitudes and perceptions of air, water, and noise pollution have been reported (15, 187, 217). In a period of rapidly shifting public opinion and the formation of new environmental interest groups, attitude surveys may enlighten policy makers about the state of their constituency and the likely reaction to large-scale regional schemes such as water development plans and transportation projects (259). However, the limits to their usefulness have also been noted: declared attitudes may not predict other significant behaviors; decision networks actually involve the interaction of functional interest groups rather than an undifferentiated public opinion (187, 259). Furthermore, as White wisely observes (259), because the actual consequences and side-effects of major environmental projects are rarely studied, public judgments (but also expert appraisals) of proposed projects must necessarily be speculative. Until large-scale environmental transformations are treated as experiments, this situation will not change

The quality of the sensory environment.—Engen (81) has reviewed issues in the use of the sense of smell in appraising environmental quality. Using a mobile odor laboratory for field experiments on the effluents of sulfate pulp factories, Lindvall (151) has measured olfactory intensity at the source and monitored the effects of various counter-measures. The report of an international symposium held in Stockholm in 1970 (249) provides an excellent handbook on methods for measuring and evaluating odorous air pollutants at the source and in the ambient air. Psychological research on aircraft and traffic noise has focused upon subjective annoyance, qualitative descriptions, and behavioral disruptions (92, 100, 136, 166). The predictability of noise and the individual's control over its termination appear to affect the degree of annoyance and behavioral disruption (211). Auditory studies of positive aspects of the sonic environment (238) include the qualitative evaluation of architectural acoustics in classrooms (194) and concert auditoria (110). Research on the quality of drinking water may be shifting from the use of expert panels to consumer assessments (39). Studies of the thermal properties of the environment typically deal with comfort ratings (124, 213), but Griffitt (101) reports a negative relationship between ambient effective room temperatures (i.e. 67.5 vs 90.6 degrees Fahrenheit) and interpersonal attraction. Multivariate analysis of weather conditions and police calls in Ft. Worth, Texas (227), suggests a tendency for police work to increase in warm, fair weather; however, physiological and psychological effects of temperature pressure have not yet been disentangled from seasonal activity patterns, amount of daylight, and similar variables. Appraising the quality of interior lighting is complicated by a positive sentiment for natural daylight (257). Thus far studies of windowless classrooms and offices do not point to any enlightening trends (215, 250). As a factor in person perception, the angle of light may influence such evaluative attributions as "threatening," "hostile," "friendly," and "determined" (22).

Ecological psychology and the analysis of behavior settings.—Since Barker's presentation of the state of ecological psychology in 1968 (19), expansions and empirical tests of the theory of behavior settings have been reported, and the technique of behavior setting surveys has been extended from small towns and schools to urban areas and an array of institutional settings. Several studies add further support for the hypothesis that the degree to which behavior settings are relatively under- or overmanned has significant consequences for setting occupants, at the levels of both overt behavior and subjective experiences (260, 262). For example, Wicker (261, 263) has shown that small churches tend to be undermanned, members of small churches display greater support and participation, and new members report greater assimilation than new members of larger churches. In an effort to move research on behavior settings beyond static description, Wicker (262) also examined several theoretical viewpoints on processes which may mediate behavior-environment congruence. Bechtel and his associates conducted behavior setting surveys of two poor urban neighborhoods and a public housing project (27–29), which were compared to a small town (i.e. Barker's Midwest). Bechtel (27) also reviewed the methodological problems entailed in extending this technique to large cities. Wright (277) summarized a series of comparative studies within the framework of ecological psychology dealing with children in small towns (less than 2000 persons) and a large town (32,858 persons). The technique of behavior setting surveys found continued application in studies of school environments and also in studies of treatment environments and residential contexts (103, 105, 146, 265). Gump (104) has addressed himself directly to the implications of ecological psychology for environmental design and planning, while Willems (266) related it to the wider range of research on man-environment relations and to the ecological movement. Particularly in its emphasis upon naturally occurring human behavior (20), it would be difficult to overestimate the pervasive influence of ecological psychology upon current research.

Human spatial behavior.—Significant recent publications include the papers of an international symposium on the use of space by animals and men (84), a collection of reports on the spatial behavior of older persons (190), and a book by Sommer on personal space (233). Studies of home range in human behavior have dealt with everyday out-of-the-house activities and extended travels (8, 49, 54, 133, 139). Some evidence points to the influence in children and adults of sex-role differences and access to modes of transportation (8, 50, 185, 189). For example, bike ownership appears to be positively related to home range among second and fourth graders (8). Social and personal factors influencing extent of home area and neighborhood schemes have been studied (42, 148). Altman (4) contributed an excellent conceptual analysis of territoriality, and Roos (214) introduced the concept of jurisdiction in an analysis of institutionally sanctioned temporary territories. Several reports have related dominance to territoriality, suggesting that highly dominant persons tend to move more freely among areas and use highly desirable areas (75, 83), but the findings of Sundstrom & Altman (245) point to a more complex relationship. Studies of men living in confinement (i.e. limited home range) indicate that incompatibility on personality traits increases territoriality and that temporal patterns of territoriality differ between dyads who complete the mission and those who abort (7). Although Hall (106) has suggested broad as well as narrow definitions, the term proxemics is increasingly used to refer at least to the study of interpersonal spatial behavior (56, 78, 255). The measurement of personal space has received methodological attention (31, 85, 208). Correlates of sex, race, status, and personality variables with interpersonal distance are being explored (23, 25, 122, 149, 168). Violations of personal space continue to be used in studying compensatory reactions to spatial intrusions (163, 192). Patterson & Sechrest (193) examined the effects of interpersonal distance on impression formation, finding ratings of social activity (i.e. friendliness, extraversion, dominance, aggressiveness) to decrease with distance. Lett, Clark & Altman (150) issued a useful propositional inventory of research on interpersonal distance. Altman & Lett (5) offered a broad ecological model of interpersonal relations, encompassing antecedent factors, stiuational definitions, environmental props, and the use of self-markers. In the same spirit, Mehrabian & Diamond (167) studied the effects of furniture arrangement, environmental props, interpersonal distance, and personality variables upon affiliative behavior and memory for the experimental room.

Behavioral effects of density.—Recent reviews (52, 278) document the striking paucity of scientific knowledge about the effects of density upon human behavior, but there is an abundance of speculation in the popular press and generalizations from animal research. However, experimental studies have finally begun to appear. In a series of experiments employing spatial densities as high as 4 square feet per person, Freedman, Klevansky & Ehrlich (89) found no evidence for any effect of density upon the performance of a range of simple and complex tasks. In a study employing a comparable range of spatial densities, Griffitt & Veitch (102) found density to be positively related to dysphoric mood ratings, negative evaluations of the experimental room and the experiment, and low interpersonal attraction. On the basis of studies with preschool children, McGrew (164) suggested that social density (i.e. the number of persons available for interaction) may have more important behavioral consequences than the spatial density of settings. Under conditions other than high spatial density, interpersonal distance (i.e. the physical distance between persons) can vary independently of social and spatial density. For example, Baxter & Deanovich (26) report that inappropriate crowding (i.e. experimenter's right shoulder less than 6 inches from subject's left shoulder) results in a higher degree of anxiety attributed to dolls in the Make-A-Picture-Story Test. Experimental studies will inevitably be limited in the durations and range of activities that can be analyzed. However, studies in natural settings (e.g. 223, 235) also present problems, particularly in disentangling extraneous correlates of density which may account for the observed behavioral outcomes. A somewhat distinct and noteworthy approach to the study of density has focused upon pedestrian behavior in notably crowded spaces such as lower Manhattan and the ticket halls of the London Underground (30, 242).

Behavioral factors in residential environments.—Except for a notable study by Fanning (87), research on housing and neighborhoods has shifted from experimental and quasi-experimental studies of behavioral impact to the analysis of attitudes, conceptions, and preferences and to the monitoring of behavior patterns that actually occur within them (74, 218). Altman, Nelson & Lett (6) and Perin (197) conducted detailed ecological studies of the daily patterns of behavioral use of home environments; Cooper (58) contributed an insightful analysis of the house as symbol of self; and Rapoport (207) and Canter & Thorne (46) surveyed sociocultural variations in house form and house preference. Patterns of residential preference, choice, and satisfaction have been related to a wide range of inhabitant characteristics (132, 140, 221). This research strategy has also been extended from the house itself to attributes of neighborhoods (141, 171, 198). The willingness to trade off house qualities in exchange for attractive natural surroundings (169), the perception of environmental threats in the residential setting (53), and judgments of residential livability under varying levels of street traffic (12) illustrate the new, broader approach. There is a promising trend toward research relating behavioral outcomes to behavioral assumptions and goals embedded in residential planning and design (42, 57, 59, 141, 173). The requirements of special user groups such as the elderly (48, 145), children (33, 206, 219), college students (93, 201, 258), and members of long-duration missions in space and undersea (186, 276) have received attention. Studies of the behavioral impact of migration and relocation continue to appear (137, 264, 276).

Behavioral factors in institutional environments.—Behavioral mappings of a wide variety of psychiatric wards (21, 105, 125, 126, 212, 239) represent considerable descriptive accomplishments, including the monitoring of behavioral patterns subsequent to design alterations on one ward (126) and the evolution of spatial behavior patterns in a new facility (273). These studies, and similar reports on rehabilitation treatment environments (146, 265), suggest an array of variables that may influence observed behavioral patterns, most notably, the interaction of administrative policies with physical attributes of settings. Fortunately, techniques for systematically assessing the physical properties, descriptive traits, and social atmospheres of treatment wards are becoming available for use in conjunction with behavioral mapping in multivariate research designs (178–181). Efforts to analyze these factors, plus patient and staff characteristics of ward users, face formidable problems and will entail large samples of treatment units. In other research on the hospital environment, the influence of nursing unit layouts upon nurses' travel, subjective states, and interaction with patients has been studied (153, 253), while factors influencing the distances patients travel to hospitals also received attention (182). In the school environment, comparisons of traditional and open plan schools (38, 77, 252) reveal differences in activity patterns, but whether they reflect the structure of daily programs (32) or innovative spatial arrangements is not yet clear, nor have the interdependencies among these factors been delineated. The effects of interior landscaping substituted for more typical barriers (e.g. walls) constitutes a somewhat analogous topic of research on office environments (37, 73, 256). Remarkably little empirical research has been reported on behavioral reactions to transit vehicles and facilities (66, 96, 131, 158, 177, 184), but current developments of rapid transit facilities may serve as an impetus to research in this area.

Outdoor recreation and response to landscape.—With few exceptions, research on the diverse forms of outdoor recreation has focused upon demographic and sociological variables; a psychological understanding of them remains quite a way down the trail. Characteristics of wilderness users have received some study and consideration in management policies (112, 170). With the remarkable increase in the popularity of hiking, camping, and similar activities, the environmental consequencies of user impacts are a source of concern, and efforts to control depreciative behaviors are under way (55, 111). Burgess, Clark & Hendee (40), evaluating six antilitter procedures, found the incentive technique most effective. In an ingenious study, Adams (3) related the decision to travel to a New England coastal beach to: (a) evaluation of the accuracy of weather information (e.g. on the prior evening newscast); (b) predicted and on-site weather conditions; and (c) factors affecting beach users' tolerance of suboptimal weather conditions (e.g. length of planning for the trip, group size). Appreciation of scenery is a component of many forms of outdoor recreation. A role theoretical analysis of the scenic observer has been advanced but remains untested (65). Research on descriptive and evaluative assessments of landscape may provide an empirical, behavioral basis for landscape aesthetics (61, 71, 72, 86, 205). Objective assessments of landscape quality are likely to find application in decision-making concerning preservation, forest management, and site-selection for outdoor recreational facilities (154, 200, 267, 279). The proceedings of two recent symposia provide a useful overview of research on outdoor recreation and response to landscape (135, 210).

Overview.—A broad, thin, but rapidly expanding layer of empirical research underlies current knowledge in environmental psychology. An intriguing question is whether environmental psychology will function narrowly and usefully as a chapter title for disparate but related topics, or will instead come to signify a coherent theoretical framework for understanding man-environment relations from a psychological perspective. Certainly there are conceptual resources at hand for encouraging aspirations to the latter goal, including the approach of ecological psychology (19), multivariate analysis of the interplay among personalitys, social and environmental systems (70, 225, 226), study of the dynamics of behavior-contingent physical systems (134, 244), and general models of behavioral adaptation and adjustment (127, 130, 270, 271, 272).

In light of the number of fronts currently under investigation along the behavior-environment interface, it is evident that the field could tolerate a significant increase in research manpower yet still retain its status as an undermanned behavior setting, with all its consequent benefits for individual participants (e.g. heightened responsibility and assimilation, diversity of activities, and experiences of obligation, involvement, and self-worth). Research in environmental psychology also offers investigators the attractions of multidisciplinary enterprise, cross-field efforts within psychology, and potential societal contributions in the form of more enlightened environmental decision-making.

LITERATURE CITED

1. Acker, M., McReynolds, P. 1967. The "need of novelty"; A comparison of six instruments. *Psychol. Rec.* 17:177–82
2. Acking, C., Kuller, R. 1971. Perception of the human environment. See Ref. 118, 46–53
3. Adams, R. L. A. 1971. *Weather, weather information, and outdoor recreation decisions: A case study of the New England beach trip.* PhD thesis. Clark Univ., Worcester, Mass.
4. Altman, I. 1970. Territorial behavior in humans: an analysis of the concept. See Ref. 190, 1–24
5. Altman, I., Lett, E. E. 1970. The ecology of interpersonal relationships: A classification system and conceptual model. In *Social and Psychological Factors in Stress*, ed. J. E. McGrath, 177–201. New York: Holt, Rinehart & Winston
6. Altman, I., Nelson, P. A., Lett, E. E. 1972. *The Ecology of Home Environments.* Salt Lake City: Univ. Utah. 201 pp.
7. Altman, I., Taylor, D. A., Wheeler, L. 1971. Ecological aspects of group behavior in social isolation. *J. Appl. Soc. Psychol.* 1:76–100
8. Anderson, J., Tindall, M. 1972. The concept of home range: New data for the study of territorial behavior. See Ref. 175, 1-1-1 to 1-1-7
9. Appleyard, D. 1969. City designers and the pluralistic city. In *Planning Urban Growth and Development*, ed. L. Rodwin, 422–52. Cambridge: MIT Press
10. Appleyard, D. 1969. Why buildings are known: A predictive tool for architects and planners. *Environ. Behav.* 1:131–56
11. Ibid 1970. Styles and methods of structuring a city. 2:100–18
12. Appleyard, D., Lintell, M. 1972. The environmental quality of city streets: The residents' viewpoint. *J. Am. Inst. Planners* 38:84–101
13. Archea, J., Eastman, C., Eds. 1970. *EDRA Two: Proc. 2nd Ann. Environ. Design Res. Assoc. Conf.* Pittsburgh: Carnegie-Mellon Univ.
14. Archea, J., Esser, A. H., Eds. 1969–present. *Man-Environment Systems.* University Park: Penn. State Univ.
15. Auliciems, A., Burton, I. 1970. Perception and awareness of air pollution in Toronto. *Univ. Toronto Dep. Geogr. Natural Hazard Res. Work. Pap. 13*
16. Bailey, R., Branch, C. H. H., Taylor, C. W., Eds. 1961. *Architectural Psychology and Psychiatry: An exploratory national research conference.* Salt Lake City: Univ. Utah
17. Baird, J. C., Degerman, R., Paris, R., Noma, E. 1972. Student planning of town configuration. *Environ. Behav.* 4:159–88
18. Barker, M. L., Burton, I. 1969. Differential response to stress in natural and social environments: An application of a modified Rosenzweig Picture-Frustration Test. *Univ. Toronto Dep. Geogr., Natural Hazard Res. Work. Pap. 5*
19. Barker, R. G. 1968. *Ecological Psychology: Concepts and Methods for Studying the Environment of Human Behavior.* Stanford Univ. Press. 242 pp.
20. Baker, R. G. 1968. Wanted: An ecobehavioral science. In *Naturalistic Viewpoints in Psychological Research*, ed. E. P. Willems, H. L. Raush, 31–43. New York: Holt, Rinehart & Winston
21. Barton, M., Mishkin, D., Spivack, M. 1971. Behavior patterns related to spatially differentiated areas of psychiatric ward dayroom. *Lab. Community Psychiatry, Harvard Med. Sch. Environ. Anal. Design Res. Rep. Ser. 5*
22. Barton, M., Spivack, M., Powell, P. The effect of angle of light on the recognition and evaluation of faces. *J. Illum. Eng. Soc. London.* In press
23. Batchelor, J. P., Goethals, G. R. Spatial arrangements in freely formed groups. *Sociometry.* In press
24. Baumann, D. D. 1969. The recreational use of domestic water supply reservoirs: Perception and choice. *Univ. Chicago Dep. Geogr. Res. Pap. 121*
25. Baxter, J. C. 1970. Interpersonal spacing in natural settings. *Sociometry* 33:444–56
26. Baxter, J. C., Deanovich, B. F. 1970. Anxiety arousing effects of inap-

propriate crowding. *J. Consult. Clin. Psychol.* 35:174–78

27. Bechtel, R. B. 1970. A behavioral comparison of urban and small town environment. See Ref. 13, 347–53

28. Bechtel, R. B. 1972. The public housing environment: A few surprises. See Ref. 175, 13-1-1 to 13-1-9

29. Bechtel, R. B., Achelpohl, C., Binding, F. R. S. 1971. East side, west side and midwest: A behavioral comparison of three environments. *Greater Kansas City Mental Health Found. Epidemiological Field Station Rep.*

30. Beck, R., Okamoto, R. Y. 1971. *Human Response to Patterns of Urban Density.* New York: Reg. Planning Assoc.

31. Becker, F. D., Mayo, C. 1971. Delineating personal distance and territoriality. *Environ. Behav.* 3:375–81

32. Berk, L. E. 1971. Effects of variations in the nursery school setting on environmental constraints and children's modes of adaptation. *Child Develop.* 42:839–69

33. Bishop, R. L., Peterson, G. L., Michaels, R. M. 1972. Measurement of children's preference for the play environment. See Ref. 175, 6-2-1 to 6-2-9

34. Blasdel, H. C. 1972. Multidimensional scaling for architectural environments. See Ref. 175, 25-1-1 to 25-1-12

35. Blaut, J. M., McCleary, G. F. Jr., Blaut, A. S. 1970. Environmental mapping in young children. *Environ. Behav.* 2:335–49

36. Borton, T. E., Warner, K. P. 1971. Involving citizens in water resources planning: The communication-participation experiment in the Susquehanna River Basin. *Environ. Behav.* 3:284–307

37. Brookes, M. J. 1972. Changes in employee attitudes and work practices in an office landscape. See Ref. 175, 14-1-1 to 14-1-9

38. Brunetti, F. A. 1972. Noise, distraction and privacy in conventional and open school environments. See Ref. 175, 12-2-1 to 12-2-6

39. Bruvold, W. H., Ongerth, H. J., Dillehay, R. C. 1969. Consumer assessment of mineral taste in domestic water. *J. Am. Water Works Assoc.* 61:575–80

40. Burgess, R. L., Clark, R. N., Hendee, J. C. 1971. An experimental analysis of anti-litter procedures. *J. Appl. Behav. Anal.* 4:71–75

41. Burton, I., Kates, R. W., Snead, R. E. 1969. The human ecology of coastal flood hazard in megalopolis. *Univ. Chicago Dep. Geogr. Res. Pap. 115*

42. Buttimer, A. 1972. Social space and the planning of residential areas. *Environ. Behav.* 4:267–78

43. Campbell, S. 1972. Architectural values as a measure of design decision-making: An empirical study using the conceptual framework of political science. See Ref. 175, 17-2-1 to 17-2-8

44. Canter, D. 1969. An intergroup comparison of connotative dimensions in architecture. *Environ. Behav.* 1:37–48

45. Canter, D., Ed. 1970. *Architectural Psychology. Proc. Conf. at Dalandhui, Univ. Strathclyde, 1969.* London: RIBA Publ. 92 pp.

46. Canter, D., Thorne, R. 1972. Attitudes to housing: A cross-cultural comparison. *Environ. Behav.* 4:3–32

47. Canter, D., Wools, R. 1970. A technique for the subjective appraisal of buildings. *Build. Sci.* 5:187–98

48. Carp, F. M. 1970. Correlates of mobility among retired persons. See Ref. 13, 171–82

49. Carp, F. M. Retirement travel. *Gerontologist.* In press

50. Carr, S., Herr, P., Cavellini, W., Dowds, P. 1972. *Status report on the Ecologue/Cambridgeport project.* Cambridge, Mass.: MIT Dep. Urban Studies and Planning

51. Carr, S., Schissler, D. 1969. The city as a trip: Perceptual selection and memory in the view from the road. *Environ. Behav.* 1:7–36

52. Carson, D. H. 1969. Population concentration and human stress. In *Explorations in the Psychology of Stress and Anxiety,* ed. B. P. Rourke, 24–42. Ontario: Longmans

53. Carson, D. H. 1972. Residential descriptions and urban threats. In *Environment and the Social Sciences: Perspectives and Applications,* ed. J. F. Wohlwill, D. H. Carson, 154–68. Washington, D.C.: Am. Psychol. Assoc.

54. Chapin, F. S. Jr., Logan, T. H. 1969. Patterns of time and space use. In *The Quality of Urban Environment: Essays on "New Resources" in an*

Urban Age, ed. H. S. Perloff, 305–32. Washington, D. C.: Resources for the Future

55. Clark, R. N., Hendee, J. C., Campbell, F. L. 1971. Depreciative behavior in forest campgrounds: An exploratory study. *USDA Forest Serv. Res. Note PNW-161*

56. Cook, M. 1970. Experiments on orientation and proxemics. *Hum. Relat.* 23:61–76

57. Cooper, C. 1971. St. Francis Square: Attitudes of its residents. *Am. Inst. Architects J.* 53:22–27

58. Cooper, C. 1971. The house as symbol of self. *Univ. California Berkeley Inst. Urban Reg. Develop. Work. Pap. 120*

59. Cooper, C., Hackett, P. 1968. Analysis of the design process at two moderate-income housing developments. *Univ. California Berkeley Cent. Planning Develop. Res. Work. Pap. 126*

60. Costantini, E., Hanf, K. 1972. Environmental concern and Lake Tahoe: A study of elite perceptions, backgrounds, and attitudes. *Environ. Behav.* 4:209–42

61. Coughlin, R. E., Goldstein, K. A. 1970. The extent of agreement among observers on environmental attractiveness. *Reg. Sci. Res. Inst. Discuss. Pap. Ser. 37*

62. Cox, K. R., Golledge, R. G., Eds. 1969. Behavioral problems in geography: A symposium. *Northwestern Univ. Stud. Geogr. 17*

63. Craik, K. H. 1966. The prospects for an environmental psychology. *IPAR Res. Bull.* Berkeley: Univ. California. 18 pp.

64. Craik, K. H. 1969. The architectural student in architectural society. *J. Am. Inst. Architects* 51:84–89

65. Craik, K. H. 1969. Human responsiveness to landscape: An environmental psychological perspective. *Sch. Design, N. C. State Univ., Stud. Publ.* 18:169–93

66. Craik, K. H. 1969. Transportation and the person. *High Speed Ground Transp. J.* 3:86–91

67. Craik, K. H. 1970. The environmental dispositions of environmental decision-makers. In *Society and Its Physical Environment*, ed. S. Klausner. *Ann. Am. Acad. Polit. Soc. Sci.* 389:87–94

68. Craik, K. H. 1970. Environmental psychology. In *New Directions in Psychology*, ed. K. H. Craik et al,

4:1–121. New York: Holt, Rinehart & Winston

69. Craik, K. H. 1971. The assessment of places. In *Advances in Psychological Assessment*, ed. P. McReynolds, 2:40–62. Palo Alto: Science and Behavior Books. 395 pp.

70. Craik, K. H. 1972. An ecological perspective on environmental decision-making. *Human Ecology* 1:69–80

71. Craik, K. H. Appraising the objectivity of landscape dimensions. See Ref. 135

72. Craik, K. H. 1972. Psychological factors in landscape appraisal. *Environ. Behav.* 4:255–66

73. Davis, G. 1972. Using interviews of present office workers in planning new offices. See Ref. 175, 14-2-1 to 14-2-9

74. De Groot, I., Loring, W. C. 1968. Housing and health; A review of epidemiological assessments. *Proc. 5th Int. Congr. Hyg. Prev. Med.* 5:1–9

75. De Long, A. J. 1970. Dominance-territorial relations in a small group. *Environ. Behav.* 2:170–91

76. Dunlap, R., Gale, R. P. 1971. *Student recruitment into the environmental movement: A test of a reformulation of "mass society" theory.* Presented at Ann. Meet. Rural Sociol. Soc., Denver

77. Durlak, J. T., Beardsley, B. E., Murray, J. S. 1972. Observation of user activity patterns in open and traditional plan school environments. See Ref. 175, 12-4-1 to 12-4-8

78. Eastman, C. M., Harper, J. 1971. A study of proxemic behavior: Toward a predictive model. *Environ. Behav.* 3:418–38

79. Eberts, E. H. 1972. Social and personality correlates of personal space. See Ref. 175, 2-1-1 to 2-1-9

80. Edney, J. J. 1972. Place and space: The effects of experience with a physical locale. *J. Exp. Soc. Psychol.* 8:124–35

81. Engen, T. 1971. *Use of the sense of smell in determining environmental quality.* Presented at AAAS Symp.: Indicators of Environmental Quality, Philadelphia, Pa. 26 pp.

82. Erickson, D. L. 1971. Attitudes and communications about wildlife. *J. Environ. Educ.* 2:17–20

83. Esser, A. H. 1968. Dominance hierarchy and clinical course of psychiatrically hospitalized boys. *Child Develop.* 39:147–57

84. Esser, A. H., Ed. 1971. *Behavior and*

Environment: Use of Space by Animals and Men. New York: Plenum

85. Evans, G., Howard, R. B. 1972. A methodological investigation of personal space. See Ref. 175, 2-2-1 to 2-2-8

86. Fabos, J. 1971. An analysis of environmental quality ranking systems. In *Recreation Symp. Proc.* Upper Darby, Pa.: Northeast. Forest Exp. Sta. 211 pp.

87. Fanning, D. M. 1967. Families in flats. *Brit. Med. J.* 4:382–86

88. Frederiksen, M. 1972. Toward a taxonomy of situations. *Am. Psychol.* 27:114–23

89. Freedman, J. L., Klevansky, S., Ehrlich, P. R. 1971. The effect of crowding on human task performance. *J. Appl. Soc. Psychol.* 1:7–25

90. Friedman, S. M. 1969. *Relationship between cognitive complexity, interpersonal dimensions, and spatial preferences and propensities.* PhD thesis. Univ. California, Berkeley. 91 pp.

91. Gale, R. P. 1972. From sit-in to hike-in: A comparison of the civil rights and environmental movements. In *Social Behavior, Natural Resources, and the Environment,* ed. W. R. Burch Jr., N. H. Cheek Jr., L. Taylor, 280–305. New York: Harper and Row

92. Galloway, W. J., Clark, W. E., Kerrick, J. S. 1969. Highway noise; measurement, simulation, and mixed reactions. *Nat. Coop. Highway Res. Program Rep. 78*

93. Gerst, M. M., Moos, R. H. 1972. The psychological environment of university student residences. See Ref. 175, 13-3-1 to 13-3-9

94. Gittens, J. S. 1969. *Forming impressions of an unfamiliar city: A comparative study of aesthetic and scientific knowing.* MA thesis. Clark Univ., Worcester, Mass.

95. Golant, S. M., Burton, I. 1970. A semantic differential experiment in the interpretation and grouping of environmental hazards. *Geogr. Anal.* 2:120–34

96. Goldberg, T. 1969. The automobile: A social institution for adolescents. *Environ. Behav.* 1:157–86

97. Goldman, R., Platt, B., Kaplan, R. Dimensions of attitudes toward technology. *J. Appl. Psychol.* In press

98. Goodey, B. 1971. Perception of the

environment. *Univ. Birmingham Cent. Urban Reg. Stud. Occas. Pap. 17*

99. Goodey, B., Duffett, A. W., Gold, J. R., Spencer, D. 1971. Cityscene: An exploration into the image of central Birmingham as seen by area residents. *Univ. Birmingham Cent. Urban Reg. Stud. Res. Memo. 10*

100. Griffiths, I. D., Langdon, F. J. 1968. Subjective response to road traffic noise. *J. Sound Vib.* 8:1–16

101. Griffitt, W. 1970. Environmental effects on interpersonal affective behavior: Ambient effective temperature and attraction. *J. Pers. Soc. Psychol.* 15:240–44

102. Griffitt, W., Veitch, R. 1971. Hot and crowded: Influences of population density and temperature on interpersonal affective behavior. *J. Pers. Soc. Psychol.* 17:92–98

103. Gump, P. V. 1969. Intra-setting analysis: The third grade classroom as a special but illustrative case. See Ref. 20, 200–20

104. Gump, P. V. 1971. Milieu, environment and behavior. *Design Environ.* 2:48–50

105. Gump, P. V., James, E. V. 1970. *Patient Behavior in Wards of Traditional and of Modern Design.* Topeka: Environ. Res. Found. 115 pp.

106. Hall, E. T. 1968. Proxemics. *Curr. Anthropol.* 9:83–108

107. Hall, W. B., MacKinnon, D. W. 1969. Personality inventory correlates of creativity among architects. *J. Appl. Psychol.* 53:322–26

108. Harry, J., Gale, R., Hendee, J. 1969. Conservation: An upper-middle class social movement. *J. Leisure Res.* 1:246–54

109. Hart, R. A., Moore, G. T. The development of spatial cognition: a review. In *Images of Man's Spatial Environment,* ed. D. Stea, R. Downs. Chicago: Aldine-Atherton. In press

110. Hawkes, R. J., Douglas, H. 1971. Subjective acoustic experience in concern auditoria. *Acustica* 24:235–50

111. Heberlein, T. A. 1971. *Moral norms, threatened sanctions, and littering behavior.* PhD thesis. Univ. Wisconsin, Madison

112. Hendee, J. C., Catton, W. R. Jr., Marlow, L. D., Brockman, C. G. 1968. Wilderness users in the

Pacific Northwest—their characteristics, values, and management preferences. *USDA Forest Ser. Res. Pap. PNW-61*

113. Hendee, J. C., Harris, R. W. 1970. Foresters' perception of wilderness-user attitudes and preferences. *J. Forestry* 68:759–62

114. Hershberger, R. G. 1969. *A study of meaning and architecture.* PhD thesis. Univ. Pennsylvania, Philadelphia

115. Hershberger, R. G. 1972. Toward a set of semantic scales to measure the meaning of architectural environments. See Ref. 175, 6-4-1 to 6-4-10

116. Hesselgren, S. 1971. *Experimental Studies on Architectural Perception.* Stockholm: Nat. Swed. Inst. Build. Res. 104 pp.

117. Hill, W., White, R. C. 1969. New horizons for environmental education. *J. Environ. Educ.* 1:43–46

118. Honikman, B., Ed. 1971. *AP 70: Proc. Architect. Psychol. Conf. at Kingston Polytechnic 1970.* London: RIBA Publ. 98 pp.

119. Honikman, B. 1972. An investigation of the relationship between construing of the environment and its physical form. See Ref. 175, 6-5-1 to 6-5-11

120. Honikman, B., Bridge, A., Lee, S., Eds. 1969–present. *Architectural Psychology Newsletter.* Surrey, Engl.: Kingston Polytechnic

121. Horowitz, H. 1966. The architect's programme and the behavioural sciences. *Architect. Sci. Rev.* 9:71–79

122. Horowitz, M. J. 1968. Spatial behavior and psychopathology. *J. Nerv. Ment. Dis.* 146:24–35

123. Howard, R. B., Mlynarski, F. G., Sauer, G. C. Jr. 1972. A comparative analysis of affective responses to real and represented environments. See Ref. 175, 6-6-1 to 6-6-8

124. Humphreys, M. A., Nicol, J. F. 1970. An investigation into thermal comfort of office workers. *J. Inst. Heat Vent. Eng.* 38:181–89

125. Ittelson, W. H., Proshansky, H. M., Rivlin, L. G. 1970. Bedroom size and social interaction of the psychiatric ward. *Environ. Behav.* 2: 255–70

126. Ittelson, W. H., Proshansky, H. M., Rivlin, L. G. 1970. The environmental psychology of the psychiatric ward. See Ref. 202, 419–38

127. Kaplan, S. 1972. The challenge of environmental psychology: A proposal for a new functionalism. *Am. Psychol.* 27:140–43

128. Kaplan, S., Wendt, J. S. 1972. Preference and the visual environment: Complexity and some alternatives. See Ref. 175, 6-8-1 to 6-8-5

129. Kasmar, J. V. 1970. The development of a usable lexicon of environmental descriptors. *Environ. Behav.* 2:153–69

130. Kates, R. W. 1971. Natural hazard in human ecological perspective: Hypotheses and models. *Econ. Geogr.* 47:438–51

131. Ketola, H. N. et al 1970. *Bus Design: Concepts and Evaluation.* Troy, N. Y.: Rensselaer Res. Corp. 211 pp.

132. Knight, R. L. 1971. *Mobile home and conventional home owners: a comparative examination of socioeconomic characteristics and housing-related preferences of young families in Chicago.* PhD thesis. Northwestern Univ., Evanston, Ill. 236 pp.

133. Kranz, P. 1970. What do people do all day? *Behav. Sci.* 15:286–91

134. Krasner, L. 1971. Behavior therapy. *Ann. Rev. Psychol.* 22:483–532

135. Krutilla, J., Ed. *Natural Environments: Studies in Theoretical and Applied Analysis.* Baltimore: Johns Hopkins Univ. Press. In press

136. Kryter, K. D. 1970. *The Effects of Noise on Man.* New York: Academic

137. Kuhl, P. H., Koch-Nielsen, I. 1971. Slum clearance areas in Copenhagen. *Danish Nat. Inst. Soc. Res. Publ. 51*

138. Ladd, F. C. 1970. Black youths view their environment: Neighborhood maps. *Environ. Behav.* 2:74–99

139. Ladd, F. C. 1970. *Travels and travels in fantasy of black youths.* Presented at N. Engl. Psychol. Assoc. Meet., Boston

140. Ladd, F. C. Black youths view their environments: Some views of housing. *J. Am. Inst. Planners* 38: 108–15

141. Lansing, J. B., Marans, R. W. 1969. Evaluation of neighborhood quality. *J. Am. Inst. Planners* 35:195–99

142. Lau, J. 1970. Differences between full-size and scale-model rooms in the assessment of lighting quality. See Ref. 45, 43–48

143. Laumann, E. O., House, J. S. 1970.

339

Living room styles and social attributes: The patterning of material artifacts in a modern urban community. *Sociol. Soc. Res.* 54: 321–42

144. Laurendeau, M., Pinard, A. 1971. *The Development of the concept of space in the Child.* New York: Int. Univ. Press

145. Lawton, M. P. 1970. Public behavior of older people in congregate housing. See Ref. 13, 372–80

146. LeCompte, W. F., Willems, E. P. Ecological analysis of a hospital: Location dependencies in the behavior of staff and patients. See Ref. 13, 236–45

147. Lee, T. 1968. Urban neighborhood as a socio-spatial schema. *Hum. Relat.* 21:241–68

148. Lee, T. R. 1970. Perceived distance as a function of direction in the city. *Environ. Behav.* 2:40–51

149. Leibman, M. 1970. The effects of sex and race norms on personal space. *Environ. Behav.* 2:208–46

150. Lett, E. E., Clark, W., Altman, I. 1969. A propositional inventory of research on interpersonal distance. *Naval Med. Res. Inst. Res. Rep. 1*

151. Lindvall, T. 1970. On sensory evaluation of odorous air pollutant intensities. *Nord. Hyg. Tidskr.*, Suppl. 2

152. Lipman, A. 1969. The architectural belief system and social behaviour. *Brit. J. Sociol.* 20:190–204

153. Lippert, S. 1971. Travel in nursing units. *Hum. Factors* 13:269–82

154. Litton, R. B. Jr. Aesthetic dimensions of the landscape. See Ref. 135

155. Lowenthal, D. 1968. Environmental perception project. *Man Environ.* 1:3–6

156. Lowenthal, D. 1970. *The nature of perceived and imagined environments.* Presented at N. Engl. Psychol. Assoc. Meet. Boston

157. Lynch, K. 1960. *The Image of the City.* Cambridge: MIT Press

158. Marek, J., Sten, T. 1971. *Driver behavior and traffic environment: A critical examination and a point of view.* Trondheim, Norway: Norw. Inst. Technol., Univ. Trondheim

159. Mark, L. S. 1972. Modeling through toy play: A methodology for eliciting topographical representations in children. See Ref. 175, 1-3-1 to 1-3-9

160. Marshall, N. 1970. Environmental components of orientations toward privacy. See Ref. 13, 246–51

161. Ibid. Personality correlates of orientations toward privacy, 316–19

162. McCarroll, J. E., Mitchell, K. M., Carpenter, R. J., Anderson, J. P. 1967. Analysis of three stimulation-seeking scales. *Psychol. Rep.* 21: 853–56

163. McDowell, K. V. 1972. Violations of personal space. *Can. J. Behav. Sci.* 4:210–17

164. McGrew, W. C. 1972. Interpersonal spacing of preschool children. In *The Development of Competence in Early Childhood*, ed. J. S. Bruner, K. J. Connolly. London: Academic

165. McKechnie, G. E. 1970. Measuring environmental dispositions with the Environmental Response Inventory. See Ref. 13, 320–26

166. McKennel, A. C. 1969. Methodological problems in a survey of aircraft noise annoyance. *Statistician* 19:1–29

167. Mehrabian, A., Diamond, S. G. 1971. Effects of furniture arrangement, props, and personality on social interaction. *J. Pers. Soc. Psychol.* 20:18–30

168. Mehrabian, A., Diamond, S. G. 1971. Seating arrangement and conversation. *Sociometry* 34:281–89

169. Menchik, M. D. 1971. Residential environmental preferences and choice: Some preliminary empirical results relevant to urban form. *Reg. Sci. Res. Inst. Discuss. Pap. Ser. 46*

170. Merriam, L. C. Jr., Ammons, R. B. 1968. Wilderness users and management in three Montana areas. *J. Forestry* 66:390–95

171. Michelson, W. H. 1970. *Man and his Urban Environment: A Sociological Approach.* Reading, Mass.: Addison-Wesley

172. Milgram, S. 1970. The experience of living in cities. *Science* 167: 1461–68

173. Miller, A., Cook, J. A. 1967. Radburn Estates revisited: Report of a user study. *Architects J.* 146: 1075–82

174. Mitchell, B. 1971. Behavioral aspects of water management: A paradigm and a case study. *Environ. Behav.* 3:135–54

175. Mitchell, W. J., Ed. 1972. *Environmental design: Research and practice.* Proc. *EDRA Three/AR 8*

340

Conf. Jan. 1972. Los Angeles: Univ. California Press
176. Moore, G. T. 1970. *Emerging Methods in Environmental Design and Planning.* Cambridge: MIT Press
177. Moorhead, R., Lepper, R. 1970. Transit vehicle design and rider satisfaction. *Urban Soc. Change Rev.* 4:6–10
178. Moos, R. H. 1971. *Revision of the ward atmosphere scales (WAS): Technical report.* Soc. Ecol. Lab., Stanford Univ.
179. Ibid 1972. *British psychiatric ward treatment environments*
180. Moos, R. H., Harris, R., Schonborn, K. 1969. Psychiatric patients and staff reaction to their physical environments. *J. Clin. Psychol.* 25:322–24
181. Moos, R. H., Houts, P. S. 1970. Differential effects of the social atmospheres of psychiatric wards. *Hum. Relat.* 23:47–60
182. Morrill, R. L., Earickson, R. J., Rees, P. 1970. Factors influencing distances traveled to hospitals. *Econ. Geogr.* 46:161–71
183. Morrison, D. E., Hornback, K. E., Werner, W. K. 1972. The environmental movement: Some preliminary observations and predictions. See Ref. 91
184. Murray, J. J., Ed. *Urban and Regional Surveys and Readings in Ground Transportation.* New York: Wiley. In press
185. Nahemow, L., Kogan, L. S. 1971. *Reduced Fare for the Elderly.* New York: Environ. Psychol. Program, City Univ. New York
186. Nowlis, D. P., Wortz, E. C., Watters, H. 1972. *Tektite II: Habitability research program.* Marshall Space Flight Center, Ala.: NASA
187. O'Riordan, T. 1971. Public opinion and environmental quality: A reappraisal. *Environ. Behav.* 3:191–214
188. Orleans, P. A. Differential cognition of urban residents: Effects of social scale on mapping. See Ref. 109
189. Orleans, P. A., Schmidt, S. 1972. Mapping the city: Environmental cognition of urban residents. See Ref. 175, 1-4- to 1-4-9
190. Pastalan, L., Carson, D. H., Eds. 1970. *Spatial Behavior of Older People.* Ann Arbor: Univ. Michigan-Wayne State Univ. Press
191. Patterson, G. R., Bechtel, G. G. 1971. Formulating the situational environment in relation to states and traits. Ore. Res. Inst. Bull. 11:1–40
192. Patterson, M. L., Mullens, S., Romano, J. 1971. Compensatory reactions to spatial intrusion. *Sociometry* 34:114–21
193. Patterson, M. L., Sechrest, L. B. 1970. Interpersonal distance and impression formation. *J. Pers.* 38:161–66
194. Payne, I. 1972. New methods and research in qualitative evaluation of architectural acoustics. See Ref. 175, 25-3-1 to 25-3-18
195. Payne, I. Multidimensional scaling in environmental research. *Architectural Science Review.* In press
196. Pearson, P. H. 1970. Relationships tween global and specified measures of novelty seeking. *J. Consult. Clin. Psychol.* 34:199–204
197. Perin, C. 1972. Concepts and methods for studying environments in use. See Ref. 175, 13-6-1 to 13-6-10
198. Peterson, G. L. 1967. Measuring visual preferences of residential neighborhoods. *Ekistics* 23:169–73
199. Peterson, G. L. 1971. *Motivations, perceptions, satisfactions, and environmental dispositions of Boundary Waters Canoe Area users and managers.* Northwestern Univ. Technol. Inst.
200. Peterson, G. L., Neumann, E. S. 1969. Modeling and predicting human response to the visual recreation environment. *J. Leisure Res.* 1:219–37
201. Preiser, W. F. E. 1970. Behavioral design criteria in student housing. See Ref. 220, 243–69
202. Proshansky, H. M., Ittelson, W. H., Rivlin, L. G., Eds. 1970. *Environmental Psychology: Man and his Physical Setting.* New York: Holt, Rinehart & Winston. 690 pp.
203. Pyron, B. 1971. Form and space diversity in human habitats: Perceptual responses. *Environ. Behav.* 3:382–411
204. Ibid 1972. Form and diversity in human habitats: judgmental and attitude responses. 4:87–120
205. Rabinowitz, C. G., Coughlin, R. E. 1971. *Some experiments in quantitative measurement of landscape quality.* Philadelphia: Reg. Sci. Res. Inst.
206. Rand, G. 1972. Children's images of houses: A prolegomena to the study of why people still want

pitched roofs. See Ref. 175, 6-9-1 to 6-9-10

207. Rapoport, A. 1969. *House Form and Culture*. New York: Prentice-Hall

208. Rawls, J. R., Trego, R. E., Mc-Gaffrey, C. H. 1968. A comparison of personal space measures. *Texas Christian Univ. Inst. Behav. Res. Tech. Rep. 6*

209. Ibid 1968. Correlates of personal space. *Tech. Rep. 7*

210. *Recreation Symp. Proc.* 1971. Upper Darby, Pa.: Northeast. Forest Exp. Sta.

211. Reim, B., Glass, D. C., Singer, J. E. 1972. Behavioral consequences of exposure to uncontrollable and unpredictable noise. *J. Appl. Soc. Psychol.* 1:44–56

212. Rivlin, L. G., Wolfe, M. 1972. The early history of a psychiatric hospital for children: Expectations and reality. *Environ. Behav.* 4: 33–72

213. Rohles, F. H. Jr. 1970. The modal comfort envelope: A new approach toward defining the thermal environment in which sedentary man is comfortable. *ASHRAE Trans.* 76:308–17

214. Roos, P. D. 1968. Jurisdiction: an ecological concept. *Hum. Relat.* 21:75–84

215. Ruys, T. 1970. *Windowless offices*. MA thesis. Univ. Washington, Seattle. 63 pp.

216. Saarinen, T. F. 1969. Perception of environment. *Comm. Coll. Geogr. Resource Pap. 5*

217. Saarinen, T. F., Cooke, R. U. 1971. Public perception of environmental quality in Tucson, Arizona. *J. Ariz. Acad. Sci.* 6:260–74

218. Sanoff, H. 1971. The social implications of residential environments. *Int. J. Environ. Stud.* 2:13–19

219. Sanoff, ·H., Coates, G. 1970. Behavorial mapping: An ecological analysis of activities in a residential setting. *Int. J. Environ. Stud.* 1:1–9

220. Sanoff, H., Cohn, S., Eds. 1970. *EDRA One: Proc. 1st Ann. Environ. Design Res. Assoc. Conf.* Raleigh: North Carolina State Univ.

221. Sanoff, H., Sawhney, M. 1972. Residential livability: A study of user attitudes towards their residential environment. See Ref. 175, 13-8-1 to 13-8-10

222. Schiff, M. 1971. *Psychological factors related to human adjustment to natural hazards in London, Ontario.* Presented at Assoc. Am. Geogr. Meet., Boston

223. Schmitt, R. C. 1963. Implications of density in Hong Kong. *J. Am. Inst. Planners* 29:21–26

224. Seaton, R. W., Collins, J. B. 1972. Validity and reliability of ratings of simulated buildings. See Ref. 175, 6-10-1 to 6-10-12

225. Sells, S. B. 1969. Ecology and the science of psychology. See Ref. 20, 15–30

226. Sells, S. B. 1971. *Environmental assessment: A context for the study of human behavior.* Presented at APA Meet., Washington, D. C.

227. Sells, S. B., Will, D. P. Jr. 1971. *Accidents, police incidents and weather: A further study of the city of Fort Worth, Texas, 1968.* Fort Worth: Inst. Behav. Res., Texas Christian Univ.

228. Sewell, W. R. D. 1971. Environmental perceptions and attitudes of engineers and public health officials. *Environ. Behav.* 3:23–59

229. Sewell, W. R. D., Foster, H. D. 1971. Environmental revival: Promise and performance. *Environ. Behav.* 3:123–34

230. Shafer, E. L. Jr., Thompson, R. C. 1968. Models that describe use of Adirondack campgrounds. *Forest Sci.* 14:383–91

231. Sims, J., Baumann, D. D. 1971. *The tornado threat: Coping styles of the North and South.* Presented at Ann. Meet. Assoc. Am. Geogr., Boston

232. Sims, J., Saarinen, T. F. 1969. Coping with environmental threat: Great Plains farmers and the sudden storm. *Ann. Assoc. Am. Geogr.* 59: 677–86

233. Sommer, R. 1969. *Personal Space: The Behavioral Basis of Design.* Englewood Cliffs, N. J.: Prentice-Hall

234. Sommer, R. 1972. *Design Awareness.* San Francisco: Rinehart

235. Sommer, R., Becker, F. D. 1971. Room density and user satisfaction. *Environ. Behav.* 3:412–17

236. Sonnenfeld, J. 1969. Equivalence and distortion of the·perceptual environment. *Environ. Behav.* 1: 83–100

237. Sonnenfeld, J. 1969. Personality and behavior in environment. *Proc. Assoc. Am. Geogr.* 1:136–40

238. Southworth, M. 1969. The sonic en-

vironment of cities. *Environ. Behav.* 1:49–70

239. Srivastava, R. K., Good, L. R. 1968. Human movement as a function of color stimulation. *Environ. Res. Found. Rep.*

240. Stea, D. 1969. On the measurement of mental maps: An experimental model for studying conceptual spaces. *Northwestern Univ. Stud. Geogr. 17*

241. Stern, G. G. 1970. *People in Context: The Measurement of Environmental Interaction in School and Society.* New York: Wiley

242. Stilitz, I. B. 1969. The role of static pedestrian groups in crowded spaces. *Ergonomics* 12:821–39

243. Stringer, P. 1971. Spatial ability in relation to design problem solving. See Ref. 118, 21–23

244. Studer, R. G. 1970. The dynamics of behavior-contingent physical systems. See Ref. 202, 56–75

245. Sundstrom, E., Altman, I. 1972. *Relationships between dominance and territorial behavior: A field study in a youth rehabilitation setting.* Salt Lake City: Univ. Utah

246. Swan, J. 1970. Response to air pollution: A study of attitudes and coping strategies of high school youths. *Environ. Behav.* 2: 127–53

247. Taylor, C. W., Bailey, R., Branch, C. H. H., Eds. 1967. *Nat. Conf. Architect. Psychol., 2nd.* Salt Lake City: Univ. Utah

248. Thiel, P. 1970. Notes on the description, scaling, notation, and scoring of some perceptual and cognitive attributes of the physical environment. See Ref. 202, 593–618

249. Third Karolinska Inst. Symp. Environ. Health 1970. Methods for measuring and evaluating odorous air pollutants at the source and in the ambient air. *Nord. Hyg. Tidskr.* 51:1–77

250. Tikkanen, K. T. 1970. *Significance of windows in classrooms.* MA thesis. Univ. Calif., Berkeley. 58 pp.

251. Tognacci, L. N., Weigel, R. H., Wideen, M. F., Vernon, D. T. A. 1972. Environmental quality: How universal is public concern? *Environ. Behav.* 4:73–86

252. Trieschmann, G. V. 1970. *Open plan schools, a comparative study.* PhD thesis. Univ. Utah, Salt Lake City 182 pp.

253. Trites, D. K., Galbraith, F. D. Jr., Sturdavant, M., Leckwart, J. F. 1970. Influence of nursing—unit design on the activities and subjective feelings of nursing personnel. *Environ. Behav.* 2:303–34

254. Vayda, A. P., Ed. 1972–present. *Human Ecology.* New York: Plenum

255. Watson, O. M. 1972. *Symbolic and Expressive Uses of Space: An Introduction to Proxemic Behavior.* Reading, Mass.: Addison-Wesley

256. Wells, B. W. P. 1965. The psychosocial influence of building environment: Sociometric findings in large and small office spaces. *Build. Sci.* 1:153–65

257. Ibid. Subjective responses to the lighting installation in a modern office building and their design implications, 57–68

258. Wheeler, L. 1972. Student reactions to campus planning options: A regional comparison. See Ref. 175, 12-8-1 to 12-8-9

259. White, G. F. 1971. The role of public opinion. In *Environmental Quality and Water Development.* Nat. Water Comm., Washington, D. C.

260. Wicker, A. W. 1968. Undermanning, performances, and students' subjective experiences in behavior settings of large and small high schools. *J. Pers. Soc. Psychol.* 10: 255–61

261. Ibid 1969. Size of church membership and members' support of church behavior settings. 13: 278–88

262. Wicker, A. W. 1972. Processes which mediate behavior-environment congruence. *Behav. Sci.* 17:265–77

263. Wicker, A. W., Mehler, A. 1971. Assimilation of new members in a large and a small church. *J. Appl. Psychol.* 55:151–56

264. Wilkie, R. W. 1971. Toward a behavioral model of peasant migration: An Argentine case of spatial behavior by social class level. Washington, D. C.: Panam. Inst. Geogr. Hist.

265. Willems, E. P. 1972. Place and motivation: Independence and complexity in patient behavior. See Ref. 175, 4-3-1 to 4-3-8

266. Willems, E. P. Behavioral ecology and experimental analysis: Courtship is not enough. In *Methodological Issues in Life-Span Developmental Psychology*, ed. H.

Reese, T. Nesselroade. New York: Academic. In press
267. Wilson, S. O., Beavers, D. J., Fullen, B., Pierson, N. 1970. Potential recreation and open space areas in New York State. *Tech. Pap. 6, NY State Off. Parks & Recreation*
268. Winkel, G. H., Ed. 1969–present. *Environment and Behavior.* Beverly Hills, Calif.: Sage
269. Winkel, G. H., Malek, R., Thiel, P. 1969. The role of personality differences in judgments of roadside quality. *Environ. Behav.* 1:199–224
270. Wohlwill, J. F. 1970. The emerging discipline of environmental psychology. *Am. Psychol.* 25:303–12
271. Wohlwill, J. F. Behavioral response and adaptation to environmental stimulation. In *Physiological Anthropology,* ed. A. Damon. Cambridge: Harvard Univ. Press. In press
272. Wohlwill, J. F., Kohn, I. 1971. *Migrants' response to their new environment: An adaptation-level Approach.* Presented at AAAS Symp. Human Response to Environ. Stimulation, Philadelphia
273. Wolfe, M., Rivlin, L. 1972. Evolution of space utilization patterns in a children's psychiatric hospital. See Ref. 175, 5-2-1 to 5-2-10
274. Wood, W. 1971. Simulation: A comparison of color film, black & white film, and video tape to reality in the simulation of architectural models. Vancouver: Univ. British Columbia
275. Wools, R., Canter, D. 1970. The effect of the meaning of buildings on behavior. *Appl. Ergonomics* 1: 144–50
276. Wortis, E. C., Ed. 1970. *1st Nat. Symp. Habitability.* Los Angeles: Airsearch Mfg. Co. 4 vols.
277. Wright, H. F. 1970. *Children in smalltown and largetown USA: A summary of studies in the ecological psychology of community size.* Lawrence: Univ. Kansas
278. Zlutnick, S., Altman, I. 1972. Crowding and human behavior. See Ref. 53, 44–60
279. Zube, E. H. 1970. Evaluating the visual and cultural landscape. *J. Soil Water Conserv.* 25:137–41
280. Zuckerman, M. 1971. Dimensions of sensation seeking. *J. Consult. Clin. Psychol.* 36:45–52

THE POLLS:

POLLUTION AND ITS COSTS

BY HAZEL ERSKINE

A miracle of public opinion has been the unprecedented speed and urgency with which ecological issues have burst into American consciousness. Alarm about the environment sprang from nowhere to major proportions in a few short years. When the first polls on pollution appeared in 1965, only about one in ten considered the problem very serious. Today most people have come to that realization. Easterners are the most concerned about both water and air pollution, Southerners the least. In the Midwest unclean water is a primary issue; in the West air pollution ranks comparatively higher. Suburban dwellers seem to be more aroused over the environment than big city residents, perhaps because of higher average education, and because many of the suburbanites are commuters or refugees from smog.

By 1970 conservation had even crept into the volunteered list of the most important national problems facing the nation today—though usually behind the perennially massive worries about war, the economy, and social unrest, which regularly dominate the list.

The environment does approach top priority today for expanded governmental spending in the opinion of the citizenry. This is not to say that individuals are personally anxious to foot the bill for correcting pollution damage, although willingness to pay for pollution control is growing. According to the Harris Survey in 1965, only three or four out of ten were personally willing to spend any money at all for correction of air or water pollution. From 1967 to 1971 they reported the numbers "willing to pay $15 a year more in taxes to finance a federal program to control air pollution" had moved from 44 to 59 percent. Most other surveys show the number who would commit small amounts to battle pollution has risen well above the midpoint. But the amounts are very small. For example, in 1969 Harris reported few would add as much as a dollar a month to their electric bills to combat the pollution caused by the generating plants, but 61 percent would invest 25 cents a month for this purpose. In late 1971 Roper found six or seven out of ten would pay ten percent higher prices for a number of products if it were essential to pay for eliminating pollutants produced by their manufacture.

Professionals should be disconcerted at the wide array of scattered questions on this new topic, of which the public's willingness to pay the bill for pollution is an example. Base questions which could be repeated indefinitely without changes in wording should be established. The body of knowledge about public opinion since 1935 is sadly lacking in continuity, and the demonstrated gaps in information on old social problems should be leading to sophistication and precision in planning for meaningful trends on a new issue such as this one.

The amount of data already collected on pollution has outrun the space

PUBLIC OPINION QUARTERLY, Spring, 1972, Vol. 36, pp. 120-135.

limitations of any one issue of the *Quarterly*. Questions which follow are confined to degree of concern over the problem, opinion on government spending for pollution control, and willingness to spend money personally to reach a solution. Opinion by size of community and geographic region are shown whenever available. All other cross-tabulations have been omitted for lack of space. Further information about other facets of the environmental problem will follow in a later issue.

Research organizations to which credit is due for permitting these data to be republished are:

CALIF   California Poll, San Francisco, California
GALLUP   Gallup Poll, Princeton, New Jersey, and its clients *Newsweek* Magazine and the National Wildlife Federation
HARRIS   Louis Harris and Associates, New York, New York, and their clients *Life* Magazine and the National Wildlife Federation
MINN   Minnesota Poll, Minneapolis, Minnesota
ORC   Opinion Research Coproration, Princeton, New Jersey
ROPER   The Roper Organization, New York, New York, and its former client *Fortune* Magazine

All figures are based on U.S. national samples unless otherwise indicated. Dates ordinarily reflect time of publication, but in recent years may represent interviewing dates. Questions about these data should be directed either to the originators of the studies or to the Polls Editor of the *Public Opinion Quarterly*, Mrs. Hazel Erskine, 4300 Swanson Lane, Reno, NV 89502.

CONCERN OVER POLLUTION

ORC
Compared to other parts of the country, how serious, in your opinion, do you think the problem of air/water pollution is in this area—very serious, somewhat serious, or not very serious?

		Very, Somewhat Serious	
		Air	Water
1965:	May	28%	35%
1966:	November	48	49
1967:	November	53	52
1968:	November	55	58
1970:	June	69	74
Big city residents:			
1965		52	45
1966		70	59
1967		76	62
1968		84	73
1970		93	89

	Very Serious	
	Air	Water
By geographic region:		
Northeast:		
1965	20%	21%
1967	29	30
1968	34	35
1970	51	53

| | Very Serious | |
	Air	Water
Midwest:		
1965	8	14
1967	29	28
1968	26	35
1970	33	41
South:		
1965	3	9
1967	14	18
1968	12	18
1970	20	27
West:		
1965	13	6
1967	42	17
1968	37	22
1970	42	28

HARRIS

As an American, have you often, sometimes, or hardly ever felt bad because of the pollution of rivers and streams?
1965: August 9

Often or sometimes feel concern	43%
Hardly ever feel concern	57

HARRIS

As far as the rivers, lakes, and streams around here go, do you feel that a lot of them, some but not a lot, only a few, or almost none are polluted?
1966:   November 28

	Lot	Some	Few	None
National total	56%	23%	11%	10%
By size of community:				
Cities	63	21	10	6
Suburbs	72	16	6	6
Towns	52	26	11	11
Rural	35	28	17	20
By geographic region:				
East	72	19	6	3
Midwest	59	22	10	9
South	41	25	18	16
West	36	30	14	20

MINN

Do you think pollution of Minnesota's rivers and lakes is or is not a serious problem?
1967:   January

Minnesota opinion:	
Is a serious problem	76%
Is not	15
No opinion	9

HARRIS

Compared with a few years ago, do you feel that air pollution has become worse around here, that the situation has improved, or that it has remained about the same?

1967:   July 24

	Worse	Improved	Same	Not Sure
National total	38%	5%	52%	5%
By size of community:				
Cities	53	3	40	4
Suburbs	49	8	38	5
Towns	23	3	64	10
Rural	22	2	68	8

HARRIS

From what you know or have heard, do you think there is a lot of air pollution around here, some but not a lot, only a little, or hardly any?

	A Lot, Some	Little, Hardly Any	Not Sure
1967: July 24	56%	40%	4%
1970: April 20	70	28	2
1967 opinion, by size of community:			
Cities	72	21	7
Suburbs	75	22	3
Towns	36	61	3
Rural	33	63	4

GALLUP for WILDLIFE

You may have heard or read claims that our natural surroundings are being spoiled by air pollution, water pollution, soil erosion, destruction of wildlife, and so forth. How concerned are you about this—deeply concerned, somewhat concerned, or not very concerned?

1969:   February

	Deeply Concerned	Somewhat Concerned	Not Very Concerned	No Opinion
National total	51%	35%	12%	2%
By size of community:				
1,000,000 and over	51	36	8	5
250,000–999,999	52	35	11	2
50,000–249,999	55	35	9	1
2,500–49,999	52	31	16	1
Under 2,500	46	37	14	3
By geographic region:				
East	46	38	12	4
Midwest	56	34	9	1
South	44	36	16	4
West	59	31	10	*

* Less than half of one per cent.

CALIF

In the last year or so do you think smog is worse than it used to be, about the same, or not as bad?

1969:   March 14

California opinion:

Worse	50%

About the same	34
Not as bad	6
Don't know	10

MINN
Conservation refers to saving our natural resources. How much interest do you have in conservation, a great deal, some interest, or very little?

Minnesota opinion:	Great Deal	Some	Very Little	None
1969: July 6	52%	34%	12%	2%
December 7	48	34	13	5

MINN
Some people say life itself is in danger unless something is done about pollution. Others say pollution is not that serious. Do you think life as we know it today will or will not be in serious trouble if nothing is done about pollution?
1970: March 12

Minnesota opinion:	
Will be in serious trouble	87%
Will not	10
No opinion	3

HARRIS
Compared with a few years ago, do you feel that air and water pollution have become worse around here, that the situation has improved, or that it has remained about the same?
1970: April 20

	Worse	Improved	Same	Not Sure
National total	53%	3%	39%	5%
By size of community:				
Cities	61	3	30	6
Suburbs	74	3	20	3
Towns	45	4	43	8
Rural	34	2	58	6

HARRIS
How serious a problem do you feel water pollution—the pollution of the rivers, streams, lakes, and water supply—is around here: very serious, somewhat serious, or not very serious at all?
.1970: April 20

	Very Serious	Somewhat Serious	Not Serious	Not Sure
National total	47%	22%	26%	5%
By size of community:				
Cities	55	23	17	5
Suburbs	66	20	11	3
Towns	38	23	33	6
Rural	30	23	42	5

GALLUP

When people around here go to vote on November 3rd for a candidate for Congress, how important will pollution be in their thinking? Do you think it is extremely important, fairly important, or not so important?

1970: October 9–13	Extremely Important	Fairly Important	Not So Important	Don't Know
National total	58%	30%	9%	3%
By size of community:				
1,000,000 and over	72	24	4	—
500,000–999,999	54	40	4	2
50,000–499,999	62	27	20	1
2,500–49,999	60	27	10	3
Under 2,500, rural	47	34	13	6
By geographic region:				
East	61	31	6	2
Midwest	59	29	10	2
South	51	30	12	7
West	64	30	5	1

MINN

Do you think pollution will or will not be an important issue in the campaign?

1970: October 26

Minnesota opinion:

Will be important	76%
Will not	21
No opinion	3

HARRIS

What are the two or three top problems facing people such as yourself that you would like to see the new Congress do something about? Anything else?

1971: January 4

State of the economy	63%
Control of air and water pollution	41
War in Vietnam	31
Taxes and spending	31
Crime	28
Drugs	18
Student unrest	15
Education	11
Increase Social Security	9
Racial problems	8
National health insurance	7
Housing	6
Farm problems	5
Labor problems	4
Cut foreign aid	4
Abolish the draft	4

GOVERNMENT SPENDING

ROPER for FORTUNE

Which three of the seventeen individual things we have just been talking about do you think are, or might be, the ones justifying the expenditure of the most money and effort?

1940:   April

The navy	11%
The air force	11
The army	6
Airports	3
Providing work relief	10
Providing old-age pensions	9
Slum clearance and better housing	8
Training skilled labor	7
Reforestation and soil conservation	7
Flood control	7
Subsidizing farmers	5
Controlling farm crop pests	3
Removing poor farmland from cultivation	3
Controlling farm production	2
Big national highways	3
Training civilian pilots	3
Federal power plants	2

MINN

On this card are some major parts of the proposed federal budget. Do you think any of those items should be cut by Congress for the year ahead?

1965:   March

Minnesota opinion:	Should Be Cut	Did Not Suggest a Cut
Natural resources	2%	98%
Education	3	97
Atomic energy	6	94
Health, labor, and welfare	7	93
Agriculture	10	90
Military defense	10	90
Foreign military aid	28	72
Space research	31	69
Foreign economic aid	39	61

HARRIS

Besides providing for the military security of the country, the federal government conducts a number of programs in many different areas. I want to run down some of these programs. For each, tell me if you think it should be expanded, kept as is, or cut back?

1967:   April 3

	Expand	Keep As Is	Cut Back	Not Sure
Program to curb air pollution	50%	31%	9%	10%
Program to curb water pollution	50	35	5	10
Aid to set up mental health clinics	47	39	5	9

	Expand	Keep As Is	Cut Back	Not Sure
Federal scholarships for needy college students	47	38	9	6
Federal aid to education	45	42	10	3
Medicare for the aged	35	51	8	6
Federal housing for low-income families	25	48	19	8
The Head Start program	23	33	21	23
Federal aid in highway building	22	51	19	8
The war on poverty	23	37	31	9
Aid for welfare and relief payments	16	46	31	7
Aid to cities	15	43	26	16
Aid to provide for adequate commuter trains	14	24	29	33
The space program	13	38	42	7
Subsidy payments for farmers	12	34	37	17

HARRIS

I want to give you this list of government programs. If one program had to be reduced, which one would you cut first? Which one of these government programs would you most like to see kept or even increased, if you had to choose one?

	January 29, 1968		February 18, 1969	
	Keep, Increase	Cut First	Keep, Increase	Cut First
Anti-crime law enforcement programs	15%	1%	22%	1%
Aid to education	20	1	19	1
Anti-poverty program	15	1	17	6
Medicaid	7	2	9	2
Air and water pollution programs	4	2	8	2
Welfare and relief	6	10	8	10
Aid to cities	3	6	5	5
Subsidies to farmers	5	6	4	7
Financing Vietnam war	23	5	4	18
Building more highways	1	13	2	9
Space program	3	32	2	39

ORC

Would you be for or against spending federal government funds on research to find new ways to control pollution?

		For	Against	No Opinion
1968:	February 15	72%	18%	10%
1970:	June	74	19	7

HARRIS for WILDLIFE

Considering priorities, would you like to see more or less of the federal money go into each of these purposes?
1969: July 10

	More	Less	Not Sure
Education	76%	9%	15%
Veterans benefits	64	10	26
Natural resources	62	12	26

	More	Less	Not Sure
Housing, community development	52	24	24
Health, labor, and welfare	50	30	20
Agriculture	47	28	25
Commerce, transportation	27	39	34
National defense	18	55	27
Space program	12	69	19
International affairs	7	74	19
Opinion on natural resources, by size of community:			
Cities	58	6	36
Suburbs	81	5	14
Towns	58	16	26
Rural	57	21	22
Opinion on natural resources, by geographic region:			
East	76	4	20
Midwest	65	15	20
South	44	18	38
West	63	13	24

HARRIS for WILDLIFE

This card shows the percentage of the federal budget now being spent for various purposes. Considering priorities, would you like to see more or less of the federal money go into each of these purposes?

1969: July 10

	More	Less	Not Sure
Education (2%)	78%	8%	14%
Natural resources (1%)	68	9	23
Veterans benefits (4%)	62	11	27
Housing, community development (1%)	58	18	24
Health, labor, and welfare (28%)	48	32	20
Agriculture (2%)	45	25	30
Commerce, transportation (4%)	29	34	37
Space program (3%)	16	61	23
National defense (44%)	13	61	26
International affairs (2%)	12	64	24
Opinion on natural resources, by size of community:			
Cities	68	8	24
Suburbs	73	6	21
Towns	67	9	24
Rural	62	14	24
Opinion on natural resources by geographic region:			
East	66	10	24
Midwest	77	7	16
South	57	11	32
West	71	8	21

HARRIS for WILDLIFE

Thinking about air and water pollution, improvement of land and water, forests, fish and wildlife, recreation and park areas—do you think programs for improvement of the natural environment now receive too little attention and support from the government, now receive too much attention and financial support, or just about the right amount?

1969:   July 10

	Too Little	Too Much	About Right	Not Sure
National total	52%	5%	22%	21%
By size of community:				
Cities	58	4	16	22
Suburbs	66	2	21	11
Towns	42	7	24	27
Rural	42	6	27	25
By geographic region:				
East	58	3	18	21
Midwest	53	6	27	14
South	44	4	21	31
West	54	7	21	18

HARRIS

Here is a card which lists areas of federal government[a] spending. Which three or four on this list[a] would you like to see cut first in federal government spending? Now which three or four would you least like to see cut?

	August 15, 1969[b] Cut Least	August 15, 1969[b] Cut First	March 26, 1970 Cut Least	March 26, 1970 Cut First
Federal aid to education	60%		56%	3%
Pollution control	38		55	3
Federal poverty program	34		35	15
Federal aid to cities	26		24	13
Federal highway financing	24		25	12
Farm subsidies		24	16	23
Non-Vietnam defense spending		26	15	27
Federal welfare spending		37	26	28
Space program		51	14	56
Vietnam spending		64	12	59
Foreign aid		69	3	66

[a] The words "government" and "on this list" were omitted from the 1970 wording.

[b] Survey conducted for *Life* Magazine.

CALIF

Here is a list of some government programs which require large expenditures of money. Which of these would you like to see increased or kept at the same level of spending? Which would you like to see reduced in spending?

1969:   August 26

	Increased, Kept Same	Cut Back
California opinion:		
Air and water pollution	91%	5%
Anti-crime, law enforcement	88	6
Federal aid to cities	71	22

	Increased, Kept Same	Cut Back
Welfare, relief, poverty	60	35
Defense other than Vietnam	59	32
Space program	56	40
Vietnam war	25	69
None, don't know	1	10

GALLUP for NEWSWEEK

On which problems do you think the government should be spending more money—and on which should it be spending less money?

1969:   October 6

Whites only:	Spend More	Spend Less
Air and water pollution	56%	3%
Job training for the unemployed	56	7
Fighting organized crime	55	3
Medical care for the old and needy	47	5
Fighting crime in the streets	44	4
Improving schools	44	7
Better housing, especially ghettos	39	13
Building highways	23	14
Defense expenditures	16	26
Space exploration	10	56
Foreign economic aid	6	57
Foreign military aid	1	66

CALIF

I am going to read some government programs or efforts which require large expenditures of money. As I read each one I would like you to tell me which of the statements on this card comes closest to your opinion of where this program should fit in our government spending.

1. More money should be put into this effort, should have top priority in our government spending programs.

2. While this effort should not have priority, it is an important program which should be given adequate government funds so that it can make as much progress as possible.

3. This program should not be given a top priority position and should be given funds only after more important programs have been taken care of.

4. This effort should have very low priority. The whole idea should be reviewed and eliminated entirely if possible.

1970:   August 29

California opinion:	(1)	(2)	(3)	(4)	No Opinion
Air and water pollution	72%	18%	4%	3%	3%
Anti-crime, law enforcement	70	21	4	2	3
Federal aid to cities	32	33	19	11	5
Welfare, relief, poverty	26	38	18	15	3
Defense programs other than Vietnam	25	37	21	11	6
Vietnam war	21	26	12	36	5
Space program	11	39	29	19	2
Supersonic transport development (SST)	5	12	31	42	10

HARRIS

Now let me read you some stands that some men in public life have taken. Spending more money on air and water pollution control. Do you tend to agree or disagree with that stand?

1971:   January 21

Agree	83%
Disagree	7
Not sure	10

ORC

How do you think government should raise the money it needs to help clean up pollution?

1971:   January 27–February 20

Charge people and industries a fee based on the amount of pollution each one is causing	44%
Add a special tax on the prices of products that can cause pollution, such as autos, detergents, and nonreturnable bottles	28
Increase general taxes, such as sales and income taxes	8
Increase taxes on property, such as homes and businesses	2
Other answers	12
No opinion	12

HARRIS

Here is a list of various areas in which the federal government now is spending money. If you had to choose, on which two or three would you like to see spending cut first? From the same list, which two or three areas of government spending would you like to see cut least?

1971:   August 5

	Cut Least	Cut First
Pollution control	57%	3%
Aid to education	66	4
Aid to cities	30	9
Poverty programs	34	13
Highway financing	19	14
Farm subsidies	17	20
Other defense spending	16	30
Welfare spending	21	37
Space program	13	50
Foreign aid	3	61
Vietnam spending	8	64

356

ORC

If it would cost each family an extra $100 a year in taxes to have water/air pollution greatly reduced, would you be willing to accept this expense? IF NO: How much would you be willing to pay?

1965:   September

| | Willing to Pay: | | |
	$100	Less than $100	Not Willing
Water pollution:			
National total	29%	8%	63%
By size of community:			
1,000,000 and over	30	10	60
100,000–999,999	27	9	64
2,500–99,999	31	6	63
Small towns, rural	29	19	61
By geographic region:			
Northeast	29	9	62
Midwest	29	9	62
South	32	8	60
West	21	9	70
Air pollution:			
National total	21	9	70
By size of community:			
1,000,000 and over	19	14	67
100,000–999,999	27	3·	70
2,500–99,999	23	8	69
Small towns, rural	16	9	75
By geographic region:			
Northeast	23	11	66
Midwest	17	6	77
South	21	8	71
West	21	15	64

HARRIS

Would you be willing[c] to pay $15 a year more in taxes to finance a federal program to control air pollution?

	Willing	Unwilling	Not Sure
1967: July 24	44%	46%	10%
1970: April 23	54	34	12
1971: ·June 9–15	59	34	7
By size of community:			
Cities			
1967	44	47	9
1970	53		
Suburbs:			
1967	54	38	8
1970	63		
Towns:			
1967	43	46	11
1970	55		
Rural:			
1967	32	53	15
1970	48		

[c] The words "or unwilling" were added in the 1971 question.

GALLUP for WILDLIFE

How much would you be willing to pay each year in additional taxes earmarked to improve our natural surroundings—a small amount such as $10 or less, a moderate amount such as $50, or a large amount such as $100 or more?

1969: February

	Large	Moderate	Small	None	Don't Know
National total	4%	18%	51%	9%	18%
By size of community:					
1,000,000 and over	5	19	52	4	20
250,000–999,999	6	28	43	8	15
50,000–249,999	2	16	53	12	17
2,500–49,999	4	18	49	12	17
Under 2,500	2	13	56	9	20
By geographic area:					
East	6	17	49	9	19
Midwest	3	19	56	11	11
South	3	15	51	6	25
West	3	24	47	9	17

HARRIS for WILDLIFE

You are already sharing in the costs brought to us all by air and water pollution. In order to solve our national problems of air and water pollution, the public may have to pay higher taxes and higher prices for some products. To get real clean-up in your natural environment, would you be willing to accept a per-year increase in your family's total expenses of $200/$100/$50/$20?

1969: July 10

	Willing	Unwilling	Not Sure
$200 increase	22%	65%	13%
$100 increase	32	56	12
$50 increase	42	47	11
$20 increase	55	35	10
By size of community:			
Cities:			
$200 increase	24	62	14
$20 increase	54	34	12
Suburbs:			
$200 increase	28	64	8
$20 increase	66	26	8
Towns:			
$200 increase	18	66	16
$20 increase	47	39	14
Rural:			
$200 increase	16	70	14
$20 increase	50	41	9
By geographic region:			
East:			
$200 increase	22	68	10
$20 increase	57	33	10
Midwest:			
$200 increase	26	64	10
$20 increase	65	30	5

	Willing	Unwilling	Not Sure
South:			
$200 increase	12	68	20
$20 increase	39	45	16
West:			
$200 increase	30	57	13
$20 increase	63	32	5

HARRIS for WILDLIFE

Currently many electric generating plants are increasing air and water pollution. The electric companies say it will be expensive to eliminate this pollution. To stop the pollution destroying our plantlife and wildlife, would you be willing to pay an increase in your monthly electric bill of $2/$1/$25¢?

1969:   July 10

	Willing	Unwilling	Not Sure
$2 a month	14%	77%	9%
$1 a month	28	62	10
25¢ a month	61	30	9
By size of community:			
Cities:			
$2 a month	14	78	8
$1 a month	29	62	9
25¢ a month	60	30	10
Suburbs:			
$2 a month	20	73	7
$1 a month	35	58	7
25¢ a month	68	27	5
Towns:			
$2 a month	10	77	13
$1 a month	26	62	12
25¢ a month	59	29	12
Rural:			
$2 a month	10	80	10
$1 a month	23	66	11
25¢ a month	56	34	10
By geographic region:			
East:			
$2 a month	14	79	7
$1 a month	28	64	8
25¢ a month	61	32	7
Midwest:			
$2 a month	14	81	5
$1 a month	33	63	4
25¢ a month	70	23	7
South:			
$2 a month	9	75	16
$1 a month	17	67	16
25¢ a month	46	39	15
West:			
$2 a month	20	67	13
$1 a month	35	52	13
25¢ a month	63	27	10

MINN

It has been suggested that a 65¢/$5 surcharge be added to the cost of Minnesota license plates each year to finance the additional cost of recycling junked cars into reusable steel. Would you be for or against that?

Minnesota auto owners:

1971: January 18:

65¢ surcharge	58	40	2

1971: March 10:

$5 surtax	41	55	4

ORC

As you may know, America faces serious pollution problems which will be very expensive to solve. One recent estimate said it might cost more than $1,000 for each family in this country, in order to clean up existing pollution. Do you think that the American people can afford whatever it takes to clean up pollution, or can't they?

1971: January 27–February 20

Yes	48%
No	41
Don't know	11

ORC

How much would you personally be willing to pay this year in extra taxes or higher prices to help clean up pollution?

1971: January 27–February 20

Something	22%
Nothing	40
Don't know	38

ROPER

A good many products in one way or another are contributing to the pollution of our air and water—and it will probably cost quite a lot to develop methods to prevent the pollution effects. Would you be willing to pay 10% more for (each proposition below) or do you think the problem is not that serious?

1971: October

	Willing	Not Serious	Undecided
Detergents if it turns out to be the only way to eliminate their pollution of water supplies?	69%	17%	13%
Gasoline if it turns out to be the only way to eliminate the pollution caused by automobile exhausts?	68	16	15
An automobile if it turns out to be the only way to eliminate the pollution caused by the exhausts?	67	17	17
Electricity if it turns out to be the only way to eliminate the pollution caused by power plants?	64	22	14
Magazines and newspapers if it turns out to be the only way to eliminate pollution caused by paper mills?	60	20	20
Airplane tickets if it turns out to be the only way to eliminate pollution caused by their exhausts?	59	18	22

THE POLLS:
POLLUTION AND INDUSTRY

BY HAZEL ERSKINE

This is the second successive presentation of opinion on the environment. The first section, "Pollution and Its Costs," appeared in the Spring 1972 issue of the *Quarterly*. Topics covered below are: what people consider to be the main sources of pollution in general, which industries in particular are blamed for air and for water pollution, how people rate private and public antipollution efforts to date, and what incentives and penalties are thought to be in order to prevent further desecration of the environment by industry.

American industry is the prime culprit on the ecological scene, as the public sees it. Industrial wastes are considered the major pollutants of both air and water. Vehicle exhaust fumes are a close second in fouling the air (but both the vehicles and the gasoline are also products of industry). Sewage is the second most sinister contaminant of water. People see much less harm from all domestic and farm byproducts, though all such sources have experienced growing censure during the years since pollution problems have been mounting in public awareness. Natural pollutants such as pollens, dust, and mud washing into rivers and streams are the only substances which now loom less large in the public eye than formerly.

The bigger the city, the more people worry about exhaust fumes. The farm population tends to mention insecticides and fertilizers as well as pollens and dust more than city folk, but is least plagued by pollution altogether. Thirty percent of the rural as compared with two percent of New York metropolitan area residents say there is no air pollution where they live.

People are bothered most by exhaust in the Northeast and in the West. Westerners also consider insecticides and fertilizers greater dangers to water supplies than anywhere else in the country. The Midwest is worried predominantly by industry, the South by dust.

In 1970 the Opinion Research Corporation found the same seven industries bearing the brunt of the blame for all types of environmental destruction. The same seven head the list for both air and water problems in somewhat different order, and to varying degrees, as follows:

To blame for air pollution:		*To blame for water pollution:*	
Chemical industry	50%	Chemical industry	62%
Oil industry	41	Oil industry	49
Steel industry	39	Electric power industry	27
Electric power industry	31	Steel industry	25
Auto manufacturers	30	Pulp and paper industry	19
Rubber industry	27	Auto manufacturers	17
Pulp and paper industry	19	Rubber industry	15

PUBLIC OPINION QUARTERLY, Summer, 1972, Vol. 36, pp. 263-280.

Businesses dealing in chemicals get by far the lion's share of the blame, followed closely by the oil industry. This is true for both air and water pollution, although numerically more people decry their effects on water than on the atmosphere. Blame for air pollution is much more evenly distributed among these seven types of manufacturing than is blame for water pollution. The chemical and oil industries stand out head and shoulders above all others as the greatest foulers of water supplies.

Hardly an industry has escaped rising public criticism, but censure has grown most rapidly for the electric power and auto manufacturers. They both ranked low on the list of polluters when studies began in 1965, but now occupy much higher positions of infamy than a few years ago. Steel is mentioned among the top offenders everywhere but the South, and is also particularly on the rise.

Public censure of different manufacturing processes varies considerably in the different regions of the country. Naturally each industry comes in for the greatest unfavorable attention in the areas where it operates in greatest volume. For example, steel and automobiles get the most blame in the Midwest; pulp and paper plants are more berated in the South and in the West. Oil leaps to first place regionally only for its water pollution in the West, obviously because of the widely publicized oil slick disasters on the Pacific coast.

The vast majority of the U.S. public feels that improvement in the environment can come only through government action, that voluntary means are ineffective. Four in ten think companies in general do very little toward reclaiming the environment, as compared with one out of ten who credit business with doing a great deal. But outstanding is the fact that seven in ten persons do not know anything at all about antipollution efforts in any specific industries.

A majority would favor tax incentives for private industry to acquire pollution control equipment. Surprisingly a large block of people would actually shut down offending plants quite ruthlessly, regardless of the number of jobs such closure might involve.

Research organizations to which thanks are due for permitting their data to be republished in the *Quarterly* are:

CALIF California Poll, San Francisco, California
GALLUP Gallup Poll, Princeton, New Jersey, and its client, the National Wildlife Federation
GE General Electric, Public Relations Planning and Research Operation, New York, New York
HARRIS Louis Harris and Associates, New York, New York
IOWA Iowa Poll, Des Moines, Iowa
MINN Minnesota Poll, Minneapolis, Minnesota
ORC Opinion Research Corporation, Princeton, New Jersey
SRC Survey Research Center, University of Michigan, Ann Arbor, Michigan

Credit is especially due the Opinion Research Corporation for its detailed and continuing studies of the responsibilities of industry in the ecological field.

Findings represent national U.S. cross-sections of respondents unless otherwise indicated. For reasons of space, many available cross-tabulations were omitted, except for those by size of community and geographic region. Dates given usually indicate the period during which interviewing took place, but may sometimes represent the time of publication. Questions on these data should be directed either to the authors of the surveys, or to the Polls Editor of the *Public Opinion Quarterly*, Hazel Erskine, 4300 Swanson Lane, Reno, NV 89502.

SOURCES OF POLLUTION

AIR

ORC

There are many possible sources of air pollution as listed on this card. Please look through the list and pick out those things that you think are the most important causes of air pollution here in this part of the country.

	May 1965	November 1967	November 1968	May 1970
National total:				
Factories and plants	34%	53%	54%	64%
Exhaust from trucks and buses	32	51	48	
Exhaust from automobiles	27	51	47	62
Garbage and trash dumps	16	22	24	34
General dust from streets, fields, etc.	33	21	24	
Public incinerators	8	14	16	
Insecticides, plant sprays, etc.	11	12	14	
Pollen from such plants as ragweed	16	11	12	
Heating of public buildings	4	9	8	
Heating of private houses	4	4	5	
None	17	7	7	
No opinion	7	8	8	
Residents of cities 1,000,000 and over:				
Factories and plants	54		71	
Exhaust from trucks and buses	54		68	
Exhaust from automobiles	51		64	
Garbage and trash dumps	13		24	
General dust from streets, fields, etc.	28		23	
Public incinerators	17		26	
Insecticides, plant sprays, etc.	9		11	
Pollen from such plants as ragweed	10		10	
Heating of large buildings	10		15	
Heating of private houses	5		8	
None	3		*	
No opinion	5		5	

* Less than half of one percent.

1965 opinion, by size of community:	NY Metropolitan Area	1,000,000– and Over	100,000– 999,999	2,500– 99,999	Small Towns, Rural
Factories and plants	44%	54%	42%	28%	18%
Exhaust from trucks and buses	50	54	35	27	16
Exhaust from automobiles	55	51	28	23	11

363

1965 opinion, by size of community:	NY Metropolitan Area	1,000,000 and Over	100,000-999,999	2,500-99,999	Small Towns, Rural
Garbage and trash dumps	15	13	23	15	14
General dust from streets, fields, etc.	28	28	37	39	31
Public incinerators	28	17	10	4	2
Insecticides, plant sprays, etc.	12	9	6	10	17
Pollen from such plants as ragweed	12	10	12	15	23
Heating of public buildings	8	10	6	2	2
Heating of private houses	5	5	5	6	3
None	2	3	9	22	30
No opinion	7	5	5	6	11

1965 opinion, by geographic region:	East	Midwest	South	West
Factories and plants	45%	37%	22%	35%
Exhaust from trucks and buses	48	25	22	36
Exhaust from automobiles	40	24	16	35
Garbage and trash dumps	16	16	17	8
General dust from streets, fields, etc.	30	30	38	31
Public incinerators	14	5	5	6
Insecticides, plant sprays, etc.	10	12	12	6
Pollen from such plants as ragweed	15	16	16	16
Heating of public buildings	5	3	5	3
Heating of private houses	5	3	5	3
None	6	20	22	21
No opinion	6	5	11	5

HARRIS
Who or what do you think causes most of the air pollution around here?
1967:   July 24

Motor vehicle exhaust	45%
Industry smoke, fumes	40
Burning garbage, waste	9
Airplanes, trains	3
Dust and dirt	2
Insecticides	1

CALIF
What do you personally think are the main causes of smog?
1969:   March 14
California opinion:

Automobile exhausts	70%
Industry (not specified)	29
Factories (not specified)	24
Bus or truck exhausts	18

Oil refineries			9	
Aircraft, jets, airports			6	
Diesel truck fumes			5	

(No other cause mentioned by more than 4%)

WATER

ORC

There are many possible sources of water pollution as listed on this card. Please look through the list and pick out those things that you think are the most important causes of water pollution here in this part of the country.

National total:	May 1965	November 1967	November 1968	May 1970
Factories and plants dumping wastes	42%	57%	56%	69%
Sewage from town and city sewer systems	33	43	47	58
Insecticides, plant sprays, etc.	19	30	33	46
Septic tanks of private homes	18	19	17	
Mud washing into rivers and streams	15	16	15	
Wastes from power boats	10	13	14	
None	14	8	6	
No opinion	17	10	10	
Residents of cities 1,000,000 and over:				
Factories and plants dumping wastes	58		74	
Sewage from town and city sewer systems	41		56	
Insecticides, plant sprays, etc.	26		36	
Septic tanks of private homes	14		14	
Mud washing into rivers and streams	19		13	
Wastes from power boats	17		19	
None	6		2	
No opinion	14		8	

1965 opinion, by size of community:	NY Metropolitan Area	1,000,000 and Over	100,000–999,999	2,500–99,999	Small Towns, Rural
Factories and plants dumping wastes	56%	58%	50%	32%	29%
Sewage from town and city sewer systems	44	41	36	30	26
Insecticides, plant sprays, etc.	27	26	16	14	20
Septic tanks of private homes	21	14	18	13	24
Mud washing into rivers and streams	17	19	15	11	15
Wastes from power boats	19	17	10	1	10
None	7	6	6	20	24
No opinion	12	14	17	27	14

1965 opinion, by geographic region:	East	Midwest	South	West
Factories and plants dumping wastes	55%	46%	34%	30%
Sewage from town and city sewer systems	38	36	29	30
Insecticides, plant sprays, etc.	18	20	20	22
Septic tanks of private homes	25	16	17	14
Mud washing into rivers and and streams	15	13	16	19
Wastes from power boats	13	7	11	8
None	8	13	17	24
No opinion	16	14	21	15

HARRIS
Who or what do you think causes most of the pollution of rivers and streams around here?
1966:   November 28

Local industry	50%
People in general	23
Local government	9
Federal government	5
Sewage system	7
Lack of regulations	3
Insecticides	1
Boats	1
No one to blame	1

MINN
Who or what do you think is mainly responsible for water pollution?
1967:   January
Minnesota opinion:

Manufacturers, factories, industries	53%
The public, tourists, sportsmen	23
Cities, towns	16
Sewage, drainage from ditches	14
Farmers, fertilizers, insecticides	4
Motorboats, ships	4
Detergents, soaps	3
Other causes	6
No opinion	16
SOME PERSONS GAVE MORE THAN ONE ANSWER	139%

GALLUP for WILDLIFE
In this country, which one of these (show respondent card) *do you think is the most pressing problem connected with our natural surroundings?*
1969:   February

	Total	East	Midwest	South	West
Air pollution	36%	43%	34%	26%	47%
Water pollution	32	31	38	30	24
Pesticides	7	5	6	10	6
Preservation of open green spaces	6	6	5	6	6

	Total	East	Midwest	South	West
Wildlife preservation	5	3	5	7	6
Soil erosion	4	2	4	6	5
Don't know	10	10	8	15	6

By size of community:	1,000,000 and Over	250,000– 999,999	50,000– 249,999	2,500– 49,999	Under 2,500
Air pollution	55%	41%	41%	29%	23%
Water pollution	22	33	32	34	34
Pesticides	6	5	5	8	10
Preservation of open green spaces	6	5	5	8	6
Wildlife preservation	1	3	3	6	10
Soil erosion	2	4	4	4	5
Don't know	8	9	10	11	12

IF THE ANSWER TO THE PRECEDING QUESTION WAS AIR POLLUTION:

In your opinion what can be done to correct this problem?

Find way to control auto exhaust	24%
Control of chemical and industrial wastes	17
Provide filters, smoke control devices	16
Enforce present laws or pass new legislation	10
Careful study, research	7
Do away with gasoline engine	6
Control burning of rubbish or garbage	3
Move industry to the suburbs	2
Educate the public	1
Other answers	3
Don't know	31
SOME PERSONS GAVE MORE THAN ONE ANSWER	120%

IF THE ANSWER TO THE FIRST QUESTION WAS WATER POLLUTION:

In your opinion what can be done to correct this problem?

Stop industrial pollution	26%
Enforce present laws, pass new legislation	23
Keep sewage out of water	12
Individuals should be more careful	8
Careful study, research	5
Sewage conversion plants	5
Educate the public	3
Chemically purify the water	3
Use filters	2
Other answers	2
Don't know	27
SOME PERSONS GAVE MORE THAN ONE ANSWER	116%

IOWA

Each of the following contributes some form of pollution to our environment. Please indicate how serious you think each of the following is in polluting your local community or area. Is it very serious, fairly serious, or not too serious?

1971:   January

Iowa opinion:	Very Serious	Fairly Serious	Not Too Serious	Don't Know
Industrial wastes	47%	19%	29%	5%
Farm chemicals	40	31	19	10
Cans, bottles	31	36	29	4
Automobiles, trucks	29	32	36	3
Detergents, enzymes	27	34	29	10
Home pesticides, etc.	20	29	44	7
Airplanes	12	16	65	7
Residential burning	11	22	64	3
Billboards, signs	7	12	71	10

WHICH INDUSTRIES POLLUTE?

AIR

ORC

There are certainly many causes of air pollution and they vary from place to place. I'd like you now to think about just one of the possible sources—factories and plants. This card lists a number of different industries. Please look over the list and pick out the ones you think are most responsible for the air pollution here in this part of the country.

Industry:	1965 National Total	1967 National Total	1967 Think Pollution Very Serious	1970 Big City Residents
Chemical	23%	32%	53%	50%
Oil	14	24	41	41
Steel	12	22	33	39
Electric power	5	14	23	31
Automobile manufacturers	3	10	15	30
Rubber	10	16	24	27
Pulp and paper	10	15	17	19
Railroads	10	12	12	19
Textile	4	9	11	16
Coal mining	6	9	12	16
Nonferrous metals	5	9	12	15
Drug	3	3	6	11
Food	6	3	5	9
None	29	15	2	
No opinion	17	15	9	

Industries arranged in the order of 1970 opinion of big city residents.

1965 opinion, by size of community: Industry:	NY Metropolitan Area	1,000,000 and Over	100,000–999,999	2,500–99,999	Rural, Small Towns
Chemical	40%	36%	24%	25%	13%

1965 opinion, by size of community:	NY Metropolitan Area	1,000,000 and Over	100,000–999,999	2,500–99,999	Rural, Small Towns
Oil	27	28	9	15	5
Steel	12	23	10	11	6
Electric power	13	9	8	2	3
Automobile manufacturers	8	8	3	2	1
Rubber	17	15	18	6	4
Pulp and paper	15	13	7	15	6
Railroads	16	14	10	9	8
Textile	11	10	5	2	1
Coal mining	16	14	6	6	1
Nonferrous metals	11	8	7	6	2
Drug	12	6	2	1	2
Food	12	8	10	3	3
None	10	11	24	29	48
No opinion	26	21	14	12	17

1965 opinion, by geographic area: Industry:	East	Midwest	South	West
Chemical	35%	20%	15%	30%
Oil	21	11	10	15
Steel	16	20	3	12
Electric power	11	3	3	8
Automobile manufacturers	4	4	2	5
Rubber	20	5	7	8
Pulp and paper	13	7	10	11
Railroads	16	8	9	6
Textile	7	2	3	8
Coal mining	11	5	5	5
Nonferrous metals	7	7	3	8
Drug	5	3	1	3
Food	6	5	6	8
None	16	35	35	33
No opinion	16	12	21	16

1967 opinion, by geographic area: Industry:	East	Midwest	South	West
Chemical	40	36	21	30
Oil	30	21	14	35
Steel	23	36	10	16
Electric power	25	14	8	9
Automobile manufacturers	10	15	5	13
Rubber	19	17	13	14
Pulp and paper	12	13	17	22
Railroads	12	16	8	9
Textile	13	5	13	3
Coal mining	11	9	7	9
Nonferrous metals	11	11	5	13
Drug	5	4	1	1

	East	Midwest	South	West
Food	5	5	1	1
None	5	13	30	6
No opinion	15	12	15	18

1968 opinion, by geographic area:
Industry:

	East	Midwest	South	West
Chemical	38	36	25	35
Oil	27	19	14	29
Steel	21	33	9	18
Electric power	19	12	6	8
Automobile manufacturers	8	12	4	11
Rubber	19	19	10	13
Pulp and paper	12	12	18	27
Railroads	13	15	10	12
Textile	8	5	10	6
Coal mining	12	14	6	10
Nonferrous metals	7	12	4	9
Drug	7	5	2	2
Food	4	6	3	8
None	8	9	22	9
No opinion	16	14	17	8

1970 opinion, by geographic area:
Industry:

	East	Midwest	South	West
Chemical	44	39	26	35
Oil	31	23	15	30
Steel	30	37	11	22
Electric power	30	22	12	11
Automobile manufacturers	17	25	12	15
Rubber	25	22	13	18
Pulp and paper	17	19	27	35
Nonferrous metals	14	12	8	12

WATER

ORC

There are certainly many causes of water pollution and they vary from place to place. I'd like you now to think about just one of the possible sources—factories and plants. This card lists a number of different industries. Please look over the list and pick out the ones you think are most responsible for the water pollution here in this part of the country.

Industry:	1965 National Total	1967 National Total	1967 Think Pollution Very Serious	1970 Big City Residents
Chemical	28%	41%	60%	62%
Oil	17	24	34	49
Electric power	3	9	11	27
Steel	9	16	31	25
Pulp and paper	16	20	27	19
Automobile manufacturers	2	5	9	17
Textile	5	10	14	15
Rubber	4	10	15	15
Drug	3	4	5	14
Coal mining	6	8	9	13

	1965 National Total	1957 National Total	1967 Think Pollytion Very Serious	1970 Big City Residents
Food	6	6	8	11
Nonferrous metals	4	6	13	10
Railroads	2	4	7	5
None	19	12	3	
No opinion	25	15	5	

1965 opinion, by community size: Industry:	NY Metropolitan Area	1,000,000 and Over	100,000– 999,999	2,500– 99,999	Small Towns, Rural
Chemical	47%	44%	34%	18%	17%
Oil	35	29	7	18	17
Electric power	5	4	3	3	5
Steel	6	17	9	6	6
Pulp and paper	7	7	20	19	18
Automobile manufacturers	4	5	2	0	1
Textile	16	8	6	9	3
Rubber	13	8	6	2	2
Drug	13	7	4	1	2
Coal mining	6	11	9	4	3
Food	14	10	7	6	4
Nonferrous metals	4	5	5	2	5
Railroads	3	3	2	1	3
None	7	7	11	21	32
No opinion	22	25	25	30	23

1965 opinion, by geographic area: Industry:	East	Midwest	South	West
Chemical	40%	28%	24%	16%
Oil	31	11	16	7
Electric power	5	2	4	3
Steel	17	10	6	3
Pulp and paper	9	12	23	19
Automobile manufacturers	2	2	2	3
Textile	8	0	9	2
Rubber	8	5	2	1
Drug	6	3	3	2
Coal mining	13	7	2	2
Food	6	6	7	6
Nonferrous metals	8	6	1	3
Railroads	2	2	3	1
None	8	21	17	40
No opinion	21	25	29	22

1967 opinion, by geographic area: Industry:				
Chemical	51	45	30	34
Oil	29	22	18	26

	East	Midwest	South	West
Electric power	14	8	7	2
Steel	18	29	6	7
Pulp and paper	20	20	18	24
Automobile manufacturers	6	9	3	2
Textile	16	5	10	5
Rubber	17	8	10	4
Drug	8	3	2	1
Coal mining	11	8	7	5
Food	7	6	2	11
Nonferrous metals	5	9	5	5
Railroads	3	6	4	2
None	5	8	27	7
No opinion	14	12	16	25

1968 opinion, by geographic area:
Industry:

	East	Midwest	South	West
Chemical	49	42	27	35
Oil	30	23	19	26
Electric power	10	10	5	6
Steel	14	26	7	9
Pulp and paper	15	19	21	26
Automobile manufacturers	5	10	1	3
Textile	9	6	11	4
Rubber	10	11	4	5
Drug	7	5	2	3
Coal mining	12	13	7	7
Food	6	9	3	19
Nonferrous metals	6	10	2	9
Railroads	5	6	4	4
None	8	7	23	12
No opinion	17	15	17	13

1970 opinion, by geographic area:
Industry:

	East	Midwest	South	West
Chemical	54	53	31	34
Oil	39	30	26	36
Electric power	27	23	15	10
Steel	23	30	5	7
Pulp and paper	21	22	29	35
Rubber	14	13	7	7

EFFORTS AT POLLUTION CONTROL

ORC
Which of these industries (listed on a card), *as far as you know, are doing the best job of trying to cut down on air pollution here in this part of the country?*
1965: May

Industry:	Total	East	Midwest	South	West
Steel	9%	12%	14%	5%	2%
Chemical	8	6	10	10	5
Electric power	8	10	6	10	7

	Total	East	Midwest	South	West
Oil	5	4	4	7	4
Railroads	5	4	4	9	3
Food	4	4	4	6	5
Nonferrous metals	4	3	5	7	2
Pulp and paper	4	3	3	6	6
Automobile manufacturers	3	2	4	5	3
Coal mining	3	4	2	5	1
Drug	3	3	3	6	1
Rubber	3	3	3	5	1
Textile	3	2	2	5	1
None	17	11	16	19	30
No opinion	51	53	49	53	43

1965 opinion, by size of community: Industry:	NY Metropolitan Area	1,000,000 and Over	100,000–999,999	2,500–99,999	Rural, Small Towns
Steel	2%	11%	11%	11%	6%
Chemical	4	7	8	13	7
Electric power	13	11	10	5	8
Oil	3	6	8	4	4
Railroads	2	4	7	4	8
Food	4	4	7	4	5
Nonferrous metals	2	2	8	6	4
Pulp and paper	0	1	6	6	5
Auto manufacturing	2	5	5	4	3
Coal mining	0	1	6	5	3
Drug	4	3	5	3	4
Rubber	1	2	6	2	4
Textile	2	2	5	3	3
None	14	9	18	17	23
No opinion	59	55	47	48	52

ORC

Which of these industries (show respondent card), *as far as you know, are doing the best job of trying to cut down on water pollution here in this part of the country?*
1965: May

Industry:	Total	East	Midwest	South	West
Electric power	12%	14%	12%	11%	11%
Chemical	9	9	12	6	6
Oil	9	11	8	8	6
Pulp and paper	8	6	9	8	8
Food	7	8	9	3	7
Steel	6	10	7	2	5
Drug	6	7	8	4	6
Nonferrous metals	5	6	7	1	5
Textile	5	4	5	4	5
Coal mining	4	5	7	0	6
Automobile manufacturers	4	4	6	0	5
Railroads	4	4	5	1	5

	Total	East	Midwest	South	West
Rubber	3	3	6	0	5
None	14	13	14	11	26
No opinion	52	48	53	53	55

1965 opinion, by size of community:	NY Metropolitan Area	1,000,000 and Over	100,000–999,999	2,500–99,999	Small Towns, Rural
Industry:					
Electric power	14%	13%	17%	5%	11%
Chemical	7	10	13	10	4
Oil	4	6	9	10	9
Pulp and paper	4	6	11	6	7
Food	6	7	10	5	5
Steel	2	8	9	1	5
Drug	9	9	8	3	4
Nonferrous metals	3	4	9	1	3
Textile	4	5	6	5	2
Coal mining	2	5	8	2	2
Automobile manufacturers	4	4	6	1	2
Railroads	2	4	8	1	1
Rubber	2	4	6	1	2
None	19	12	10	18	18
No opinion	52	53	51	52	52

ORC

On which of these aspects does your company put forth what you consider to be a satisfactory effort? Which of these aspects, if any, do you think your company should be giving more attention to?

1965: May

Corporate executives:	Satisfactory Effort	Should Have More Attention
Working jointly with state or local government officials on pollution problems	79%	9%
Developing better pollution control techniques	74	19
Fully implementing present pollution control techniques	72	4
Maintaining regular liaison with pollution control authorities on techniques and public information	70	11
Participating with trade associations in their efforts directed at the pollution problem	64	6
Working jointly with other companies in the communities where you operate to control pollution	53	13
Informing the public of pollution control efforts	35	50
Educating all levels of employees about the need for pollution control	31	31
None	6	20

HARRIS

How would you rate the job the following have done in helping to control water pollution—excellent, pretty good, only fair, or poor?
1966:   November 28

	Positive	Negative
Local government	35%	65%
State government	34	66
Federal government	33	67
Local industry	32	68
Fellow citizens	18	82

HARRIS

How would you rate the job the following have done in helping to control air pollution—excellent, pretty good, only fair, or poor?

	Positive	Negative	Not Sure
Local industry:			
1967: July 24	29%	44%	27%
1970: February	19	62	19
1971: June 9–15	33	60	7
Federal government:			
1967	24	45	31
1970	21	61	18
1971	31	58	11
State government:			
1967	23	45	32
1970	18	63	19
1971	30	60	10
Local government:			
1967	24	45	31
1970	18	63	19
1971	30	61	9
Auto manufacturers:			
1967	21	47	32
1970	17	68	15
1971	24	61	15
Average citizen:			
1967	21	47	32
1970	18	66	16
1971	24	61	15

ORC

Based on what you have read or heard, how much effort would you say companies in general are devoting to controlling air and water pollution—a great deal, a fair amount, or very little?
1970:   May

	Very Little	Fair Amount	Great Deal	No Opinion
National total	41%	41%	11%	7%
By city size:				
1,000,000 and over	48	36	10	6
100,000–999,999	42	37	14	7
2,500–99,999	38	47	9	6
Rural	36	44	12	8

375

By geographic region:	East	Midwest	South	West
1967: November	40%	40%	34%	35%
1968: November	37	33	31	39
1970: May	48	38	40	38

GE

This is a survey of attitudes towards business. We'd like to ask whether you agree or disagree with various criticisms that have been made. For example, it has been said that. . . . Do you think this is true of all large companies, most large companies, some, or not true of any?

	All	Most	Some	None	Don't Know
Industry will not willingly spend money to clean up the environment and will have to be forced to.					
National total (telephone survey):					
1970: May	10%	26%	42%	19%	2%
Student opinion:					
1970: May	12	36	41	11	1
1971: September	9	39	44	8	1
Business will not do anything in the public interest if it reduces their profits.					
National total (telephone survey):					
1970: May	7	19	46	24	4
Student opinion:					
1970: May	6	30	51	13	1
1971: September	5	33	51	10	1
The technical progress made by large companies does more to worsen the quality of life than to improve it.					
National total (telephone survey):					
1970: May	3	8	23	59	7
Student opinion:					
1970: May	2	9	26	60	3
1971: September	3	8	33	54	3

SRC

There are many sources of air and water pollution; one of them is private industry. Some say the government should force private industry to stop its polluting. Others believe industries should be left alone to handle these matters in their own way. Given these two approaches, where would you place yourself on this scale (from 1 to 7), or haven't you thought much about this?

1970: November–December; 1971: January

1 Government should force industry to stop	45%
2	12
3	8
4	11
5	3
6	3

7 Industries should handle in own way   6
Don't know, no answer   2
Haven't thought about it much   10

HARRIS

Now as far as these things go—controlling air and water pollution—do you feel business has been a help or not?

	Helped	Not helped	Not Sure
1966	35%	42%	23%
1971: November 22	28	57	15

INCENTIVES TO ANTI-POLLUTION EFFORTS

ORC

Would you be for or against companies being given tax reductions to help them cover the cost of installing pollution control equipment?

	For	Against	No Opinion
1967: November	63%	25%	12%
1968: November	57	29	14
1970: May	58	34	8

MINN

Do you favor or oppose providing federal income tax incentives to companies to help meet the cost of installing anti-pollution control devices in their plants?

1970: August 9			
Minnesota opinion	53	41	6
By size of community:			
Cities	55	39	6
Towns	59	36	5
Rural	44	51	5

JOBS vs. POLLUTION

HARRIS

It has been argued that if industry is to provide jobs in an area it is likely to cause some air pollution; (therefore some air pollution has to be put up with[b]). Do you agree with this point of view?

	Agree	Disagree	Not Sure
1967: July 24	63%	25%	12%
1970: February	64	23	13
1971: June 9–15	64	27	9
By geographic region:			
East	65	22	13
Midwest	67	23	10
South	65	18	17
West	59	32	9
By size of community:			
Cities	61	24	15
Suburbs	60	31	9
Towns	68	22	10
Rural	70	16	14

Clause in parentheses was asked in 1967 only.

ORC
If a factory or plant continually violates laws regulating pollution, would you be for or against forcing it to close down until the problem can be solved?

		For	Against	No Opinion
1967:	November	71%	15%	14%
1968:	November	67	17	16
1970:	May	77	15	8

MINN
Should old and absolete plants be shut down if they can't comply with antipollution standards, or should standards be lower for them?

1970: August 9	Shut Down	Lower Standards	Other, No Opinion
Minnesota opinion	65%	23%	12%
By size of community:			
Cities	57	30	13
Towns	73	16	11
Rural	60	27	13

ORC
Suppose that a plant in your neighborhood was causing severe pollution and it could not be fixed. Also, suppose that many of your neighbors worked in that plant. Would you be in favor of closing down the plant to stop the pollution, or not?

1971: February	Close Down	Put Up with Pollution	Should Not Have to Choose*	No Opinion
National total	45%	22%	21%	12%
By geographic region:				
East	36	26	24	14
Midwest	41	28	19	12
South	44	18	23	15
West	66	14	16	4

Volunteered.

MISCELLANEOUS

HARRIS
What are the two or three biggest problems you feel science has created as far as you personally are concerned? Any others?

1972:   February 17

Air, water, environmental pollution	45%
Space can create health problems	9
Threat of atomic bombs	7
Man's loss of inspiration, values	4
Too much automation	4
Food quality poor	3
Drugs, control of life and death by medicine	3
Cars go too fast	2
Overpopulation	2
Birth control pills unsafe	1
Insecticides used wrong way	1
None	34